MATTHEW COLLIN is a British journalist and the author of *Altered State*, the story of the origins of acid house and rave culture in Britain. He has worked as a foreign correspondent for the BBC, Al Jazeera and Agence France-Presse, and as editor for *i-D* magazine, the *Time Out* website, the *Big Issue* and the Balkan Investigative Reporting Network. He has also written for many newspapers and magazines, including the *Guardian*, the *Observer*, *Mixmag*, the *Wire* and *Mojo*. His other books are *This is Serbia Calling*, *The Time of the Rebels* and *Pop Grenade*.

Also by Matthew Collin

Altered State
This is Serbia Calling
The Time of the Rebels
Pop Grenade

MATTHEW COLLIN

RAVE ON

Global Adventures in
Electronic Dance Music

First published in Great Britain in 2018 by
Profile Books Ltd
3 Holford Yard
Bevin Way
London
WC1X 9HD

www.profilebooks.com

1 3 5 7 9 10 8 6 4 2

Typeset in Dante by MacGuru Ltd
Printed and bound in Great Britain by Clays, St Ives plc

A CIP catalogue record for this book is available from the British Library.

ISBN 978 1 78125 425 7
eISBN 978 1 78283 145 7

FSC
www.fsc.org
MIX
Paper from
responsible sources
FSC® C018072

Contents

For Audrey Collin

1935–2015

A lifetime inspiration

Introduction

Let the Music Use You

THEY CAME IN THEIR HUNDREDS that night to the Progressive Baptist Church on South Wentworth Avenue in Chicago. They drove there from all across the city and they flew in from as far away as New York and London – not to sing or to celebrate, although they did that too, in the end, but because it was the right thing to do. They queued down the block, lining up to fill the pews and pay their last respects to a man whose music had helped to define a generation and, in its own way, made our world a more beautiful place.

There were speeches and there were tears as they remembered the life of Francis Nicholls – Frankie Knuckles – who had died after suffering complications from diabetes in March 2014, at the age of 59. Frankie Knuckles, the DJ whose sessions at Chicago's Warehouse club had given house music its name, whose innovative approach to playing that music had shaped its form, and whose recordings had revealed some of its richness and depth. 'House music was a particular type of spiritual music,' the Reverend Roderick Norton told the mourners as he reached for a phrase that would illuminate what had been achieved by this black, gay DJ who had managed to unite celestial yearnings and secular desires.[1]

Others recalled how Frankie Knuckles had conjured a sense of unity and togetherness from nightlife's perennial darkness. 'From midnight to 6am, he was our therapist,' one said.[2] Robert Owens sang 'Tears', the bittersweet lament that the two men had fashioned together, and as Ann Nesby of Sounds of Blackness led a gospel choir into the swelling chords of the song that Knuckles had turned into one of his most emotionally cathartic remixes, 'The Pressure', people started to rise to their feet, clapping, singing and weeping with joy and grief as they commemorated not only the man he was and the music he had given us but the freedom it had made us feel.

The memorial service that night in Chicago was held just a few minutes' walk away from where dance music was once declared to be dead, more than three decades earlier. During a baseball game at Comiskey Park in 1979, a white radio DJ called Steve Dahl symbolically blew up a funeral pyre of disco records in what has since looked more and more like a homophobic, racist attempt to destroy the iconography of a culture of liberation – an attempt that failed, of course, as history has since decided.

The church was also about 20 minutes' drive from the old Power Plant club where Frankie Knuckles, who had already started to re-edit disco classics for a new generation at The Warehouse, began to run a Roland TR-909 drum machine under some of the records he was playing in the early eighties to give them more percussive power and electronic energy, pointing a way forward to what would become house music, the sound that he described as 'disco's revenge'.

I first heard him play several years after that, at the Delirium club in London in early 1988, when house was still little more than an obscure cult in Britain and the rave explosion was months away. He played one of his greatest productions that night, 'Let the Music Use You' by The Nightwriters, a song that still encapsulates some of the fragile wonder of all that is best about house music, with its brightly optimistic chords that surge towards the heavens as the singer beseeches us to join hands with him and allow this sonic spirit to gather us up and take us higher, ever higher.

It would have been impossible to imagine, that night in London, that one day, reverential obituaries to Frankie Knuckles would be broadcast on the BBC and CNN, and that even the president of the United States would be offering up his respect to this wise and decent gentleman who brought such happiness. But so it was: 'Frankie's work helped open minds and bring people together, blending genres to capture our attention and ignite our imaginations,' wrote Barack and Michelle Obama in an unexpectedly heartfelt letter from the White House after Knuckles' death. 'While he will be dearly missed, we trust Frankie's spirit will remain a guiding force.'

The passing of Frankie Knuckles caused an outpouring of collective anguish that, for the first time in years, brought dance music's disparate clans together in mourning and remembrance. It showed how much passion and belief had endured in a pop culture that was already more than three decades old, but also how far we had come since he had helped to transform disco into house in the black and gay clubs of the United States.

At the high end, the culture had turned into a feeding frenzy of gargantuan proportions, an orgy of capitalistic exploitation. By the end of 2015, a market analyst at research company Danceonomics estimated, electronic dance music was taking in revenues of $7.1 billion a year worldwide – and as is customary in a global capitalist market, the biggest purses went to the few at the top. According to a report entitled 'Electronic Cash Kings' that was published by business magazine *Forbes*, the highest-earning DJ that year, a man called Adam Richard Wiles from Dumfries in Scotland, made an estimated total of $63 million from live shows, recordings, merchandise sales, endorsements and other commercial activities conducted under his stage name, Calvin Harris.

Electronic cash kings… back in the mid-nineties, there was a lot of talk about 'superstar DJs' with their top-of-the-range sports cars and costly drug habits, but they were Lilliputian figures compared to the hulking leviathans who followed them. All the top showmen – these 'cash kings' were almost always men, of course – had become perennial globetrotters, jetting from gig to gig and cutting new tracks on their laptops in VIP departure lounges and five-star hotel rooms as they sipped the complimentary champagne and racked up the air miles.

Even those who specialised in less populist forms of electronic music were constantly on the road or in the air, shuttling back and forth between the disparate nodes of their international cult followings. Just to take one example, during the course of a single month – May 2016 – Berlin techno DJ Ellen Allien was billed to play at parties in 11 different countries: Germany, France, Italy, Spain, Austria, Turkey, Israel, India, Colombia, Ecuador and the US. These were punishing schedules that showed little forgiveness to the weak-hearted or mentally unfit.

The same year, Swedish trance DJ Avicii announced that he was retiring from touring at the age of just 26 after reportedly suffering from alcoholism and exhaustion exacerbated by the pressures of his itinerant lifestyle. For the winners, the spoils were lavish indeed, but there were toxic perils along the wayside too.

The unexpected longevity and commercial advancement of the scene meant that DJing had become a lifetime career for some of those who started out as little more than ardent enthusiasts. It wasn't unusual to see DJs in their fifties playing records to adulatory clubbers who were young enough to be their children (indeed, the children of veterans like Pete Tong and Kevin Saunderson also became DJs). And the DJs weren't just the vinyl junkies anymore – at a festival, you might see a septuagenarian disco producer like Giorgio Moroder playing a set, or a rap star like Snoop Dogg, an alternative rock hero like Radiohead singer Thom Yorke or New Order/Joy Division bassist Peter Hook, or even a wealthy socialite like Paris Hilton. 'You can book *anyone* now – if the price is right,' suggested Detroit techno icon Derrick May.

There was now, as Hunter S. Thompson once wrote about California in the sixties, madness in any direction, at any hour. As electronic dance music culture became increasingly globalised from the nineties onwards, it became possible to find DJs playing almost any style in any major city – dubstep in Istanbul, psytrance in Shanghai, footwork in Belgrade. It would have been virtually impossible to set out a comprehensive guide to these global scenes and their many musical variations, unless it had come in a series of constantly updated encyclopaedic volumes, or was perhaps auto-generated by some astutely programmed online aggregator.

The global expansion of internet access helped to propagate trends that might previously have remained localised for much longer, and allowed new borderless networks to coalesce around any kind of sound that one might hope to invent. Electronic dance music culture grew up at the same time as the internet and took advantage of its possibilities instinctively; this was a digital culture for digital times.

The bounteous attractions of dance music festivals and the

extravagant audio-visual spectaculars of the American 'EDM' circuit also changed perceptions about what the culture could be. What, exactly, made a good club? Was all you needed, as the veteran British house DJ Terry Farley once suggested, 'a basement, a flashing light… and some good pills'?[3] Or was it a lavish bespoke video-mapping display and an arsenal of pyrotechnics synched up to fire when the bass dropped? Did you need bottle service and VIP tables by the DJ booth? Scantily clad showgirls or depilated muscle boys? A pristine Funktion One sound system and a line-up full of the most exalted techno specialists from Berlin? Or just a field or a forest or a far-flung beach or some dirty old warehouse that you could occupy for one night of madness and then do a runner before the law moved in?

Back in the early nineties, when I first started work on *Altered State*, a book that explored the origins of the acid house and rave scene in Britain, there was already a lot of talk about how the culture had become too big, too commercial, too fractured, how it had started to lose its renegade spirit. But with hindsight, those were still times of innocence.

The 'house nation' or the 'techno community', whatever you might want to call it, was still relatively small and insular back then, and its essence was still Terry Farley's ideal of a dark room with some banging tunes, pulsing strobes and mind-altering chemicals. Even the promoters who we thought were high-rollers were really just small-time operators compared to the corporate giants that sought to turn a profit from the culture in later years.

These new party moguls were the serious players who spoke of something they called the 'dance music industry', of professionalism and production values, of branding and sponsorship deals and digital reach and media synergies. In the US in particular, the rise of the raucous Americanised version of dance music known as EDM attracted entertainment corporations which had little invested in terms of personal experience in all of this; for them, it was just another form of show business. They even rebranded raves as 'festivals' in a bid to obscure the role played by of one of the scene's most powerful motivational forces: drugs.

They weren't really fooling anyone though, except perhaps the most naïve of licensing authorities. While the culture itself was no longer defined by Ecstasy, as it had been during the early years of the rave scene, and the music had a vivid life of its own outside the nightclub environment, getting loved-up on illicit narcotics remained a crucial part of the experience for many people. In the mid-eighties, only small circles of adepts and psychedelic explorers knew anything about Ecstasy, but by 2013, there might have been as many as 28 million users worldwide, according to a United Nations estimate, as canny manufacturers and distributors responded to nocturnal market forces. MDMA plus electronic dance music equals rapture was the formula that had worked back in 1988, and sometimes it seemed that nothing better had come along since.

Looking back again through some of the old press clippings, flyers and fanzines that I drew on while writing *Altered State*, what strikes me is their charming utopian naïvety – a sense of pure belief that this was the best of all possible worlds, a culture of racial, sexual and social tolerance with a hazily ill-defined but essentially liberal and progressive politics. Old-school American ravers even had an acronym for it, PLUR – 'peace, love, unity and respect'. Obviously a lot of this was inspired by Ecstasy, but it was none the less genuinely felt.

In a photocopied zine produced for the inner circle at Danny and Jenni Rampling's Shoom club in the early months of 1988, when London's acid house devotees could probably have been numbered in the hundreds, the affectionate tributes are touchingly innocent: 'The greatest thing that Shoom creates is the freedom in which we can be ourselves,' says one. 'Shoom has never been a club, it's just like one happy family, who care about each other,' offers another.[4] The same kind of blissed-out rhetoric can be seen in bulletin-board messages from the early days of the US rave scene, in German zines published around the same time, and probably in many other places too.

The initial mass media coverage of the British rave scene, although mostly critical, was similarly naïve. There was sheer amazement at the emergence of this 'sinister "hug drug" craze', as Britain's *Daily Express* newspaper called it in 1989.[5] 'Acid house is the most bizarre phenomenon of the decade,' the tabloid *Daily Mirror* declared.[6] A frenzied moral panic took hold as reporters tried to find what *The Sun* newspaper called the 'Acid House Mr Big', the kingpin who was responsible for staging the latest 'evil night of Ecstasy' where 'sweating bodies gyrate to the mind-bending beat'.[7]

When British Prime Minister Margaret Thatcher was personally informed about the rave menace in a letter from one of her MPs in 1989, she demanded to know what powers the police had to stamp it out. 'If this is a new "fashion" we must be prepared for it and preferably prevent such things from starting,' Thatcher scribbled in response to the letter, which was among a batch of classified British government documents on acid house that was released to the public almost three decades later.[8]

It all sounds rather quaint now, and most of these reactions were ludicrously ill-informed; this was something created out of desires for communal transcendence and elation, not some nefarious scheme dreamed up by a criminal mastermind – and very few of the many attempts to 'prevent' it over the years that followed would succeed.

The early rave scene was also widely seen as an ephemeral novelty, a fleeting moment of youthful eccentricity that would pass with the changing of the seasons. When I approached various British publishers with the proposal for *Altered State* in the early nineties, several of them insisted that rave was already dead, supplanted in people's affections by Nirvana and grunge. That seems preposterous now, when all eras and styles of music are simultaneously alive, churning in an endless loop on the internet – and when electronic dance music has long since gone beyond its subterranean origins to become a genuinely global movement, as influential as rock 'n' roll and hip-hop have been in shaping the sound and form of popular music. Much of the music made in the early twenty-first century, from alternative rock to glossy pop, from Radiohead to Rihanna, was touched in some way by the techniques that Frankie Knuckles and people like him were investigating in the eighties.

At the same time, several decades on, it had amassed this vast back catalogue – a rich musicological hinterland to be revered, revived, reinterpreted or rejected at will. Ancient house and techno records from obscure labels became almost cultic artefacts, sometimes worth many times what they originally cost in their hastily pressed editions of 500 or so that were never released with any thought to their potential historical significance (not that they ever should have been). Vintage acid house club flyers and posters also became collector's items to be cherished or traded for cash, while middle-aged veterans wistfully recounted their wild clubbing years in comments on old-school dance tracks on internet video sites – annotations that were exquisitely poignant because the emotions expressed were so raw. As one man wrote on a comment thread below an all-but-forgotten rave tune from 1989: 'We had it all… I'm still struggling to understand where it all went…'

Rave nostalgia became a lucrative concern – and not only the 'back to '88', 'back to '91' or 'back to '95' revival parties that started in Britain not so long after the years themselves had passed. Producers like Jeff Mills and Derrick May began to perform their vintage classics with symphony orchestras in concert halls – about as far from a filthy warehouse as an entertainment venue can get – while British clubs like the Haçienda and Cream followed suit by staging events featuring orchestrated rearrangements of eighties and nineties dancefloor hits. That acid house peak experience – so powerfully felt, but like our youth, so ephemeral – was clearly something that many people were unwilling or unable to let go, because it was so full of meaning and wonder.

But the most significant development was the transformation from a series of localised scenes to a genuinely global culture. When I first heard a DJ called Graeme Park playing those early house, techno and garage tracks from Chicago, Detroit and New York at a black-walled little sweatbox of a nightclub called The Garage in my hometown, Nottingham, in the mid-eighties, it would have seemed highly improbable that similar records could have been played at exactly the same time in similar clubs in Moscow, Johannesburg, Dubai or Rio de Janeiro. Thirty years later, it was just the way things were.

As the culture began to spread across the world in the years before internet access became commonplace, it was – in its initial stages at least – very much a DIY movement. This was something that was nurtured by enthusiastic independents, maverick impresarios and musical obsessives simply because they adored it, although this endearingly anarchic approach was destined to change as the years passed and the music's popularity continued to grow.

In an attempt to understand how all this happened, three decades after the first house and techno records emerged, I decided to go on a journey across continents and time zones to take a look at how the culture had mutated and thrived in the environments in which it had developed outside my home country – how it had taken on its own idiosyncratic character, created its own heroes, enjoyed its own peak moments and suffered its own tribulations.

I wanted to find out how the culture's values changed when its location shifted, how its sound developed differently in new circumstances, and whether something as fragile and nebulous as its 'spirit' – whatever that was – could be preserved in an unforgivingly materialist world, under constant siege from the predatory robber-barons of the digital age, as well as from officialdom and increasingly, in the West at least, from the forces of gentrification. I wanted to talk to some of the iconoclasts, misfits, fanatics and hustlers who inhabited these scenes, to ask them how they saw their own history and to find out why they had chosen to dedicate their lives to this peculiar hedonistic world.

The road took me to some of the world's established party capitals (Berlin, New York, Ibiza, Las Vegas) as well as to the frontier outposts of the culture, where everything still seemed to be up for grabs – places like China, which at the time was seen as the last great unexploited market for electronic dance music, and the United Arab Emirates, where techno hedonism had somehow managed to find a place amid the repressive regimes and political turmoil of the Middle East. It also took me to parts of Europe where piratical rave tribes still roamed the byways in search of an outlaw paradise. I sought out curious localised subcults like Israeli psytrance and South African gqom – phenomena shaped by very specific social and political environments, and which could not have developed in the same way anywhere else.

Nightlife has long been a vital cultural motivator, an incubator for new sonic art forms which can inspire creative innovations, foster alternative cultures and help to regenerate urban environments. But what struck me on my journeys was how so many people in so many different places explained their stories as a search for free space. For some, this was space to create temporary havens for musical, cultural, sexual or even spiritual expression; for others, it was space in which to build empires or exploit business opportunities; for a few, it was space in which to celebrate social resistance. But for the majority perhaps, it was simply space for a bit of weekend lunacy and a release from the strictures of everyday 'normality', to let loose until the dawn broke, the music stopped or the drugs ran out.

What had endured since the acid house era of the late eighties was the perpetual ideological struggle between art and commerce, between romantic visions and mercantile impulses. Even in the early days of rave, it was as much an entrepreneurial culture as it was utopian; in *Altered State*, I suggested that acid house expressed deeply felt desires for communal experiences, but it was also an open-access scene that offered people the chance to get involved in whatever way they chose, to participate rather than to simply observe or consume – 'to *do something*, whether it was recording a techno track in a bedroom studio, organising a warehouse party or selling a bag of pills'.[9] There also seemed to be an essential difference between those who sought to create and sustain small but committed communities of like minds, and those who sought perpetual growth, to make it all as big as it could be – not just one nation under a groove, but the entire free-market world dancing to the same beat.

Everywhere I went, I found dreamers and pragmatists, believers and cynics, locked in this perennial conflict about what electronic dance music should be and why. The fact that people *cared* about all this stuff so deeply – and argued about it so passionately – was a constant remind-er of how many people saw it not just as a branch of the entertainment business that could offer them material benefits, but as a culture in which they had invested huge amounts of commitment, emotion and belief, something that they felt must be cherished and defended.

'When you create something out of nothing it's the most thrilling thing,' Frankie Knuckles once said.[10] The music and the culture that he helped to create had reshaped the soundtrack to our world and influenced so many lives in so many places in so many ways, mine included. This book is an attempt to find out if it was still worth believing in, so many years down the line – and if it still had the power, as Barack Obama put it, to ignite our imaginations and open our minds.

Techno Cities #1

Detroit

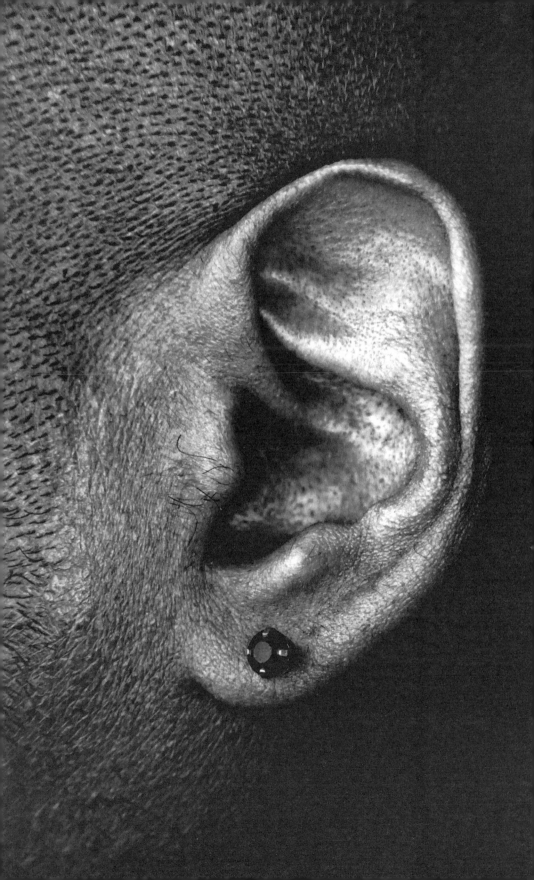

WE PILE INTO THE VAN and pull out into the frostbitten afternoon, the raddled cityscape leering back at us like the crooked teeth of a voodoo skull. As we accelerate past the snowdrifts that line the pavements, a powerfully built young man in combat fatigues announces that today, he is to be our guide. 'I'm going to show you the *real* Detroit, the one that the tourists never see,' he booms in a stern preacher's voice.

Gesturing at various psychogeographical landmarks along the route, he delivers a parable about institutional racism, structural poverty, police violence and urban decay – a tale of curdled dreams that passes through the riots that set Detroit ablaze in 1967 and his own childhood experiences of the decline of this great city that gave the world automotive capitalism. The environment that shaped his music: techno.

His name is Mike Banks. 'Mad' Mike, he calls himself, but he's not at all crazy, just charged up with righteous anger and trying to strike back using whatever tools he can get his hands on. As well as being a compulsive speaker of uncomfortable truths, Mad Mike Banks considers himself a techno militant and a champion of economic self-reliance. Underground Resistance is the name of his crew and his record label, a collective of young black men from Detroit bound together on a mission into the sonic unknown, wherever it may take them. His ideology, he explains, is complete independence from the music business, creating his own networks and systems to ensure UR's long-term survival and creative integrity – in other words, an attempt to ensure they never get screwed like so many other creative young black people have been before them.

This was back in January 1992, deep into another callous midwinter in Detroit, and even though the sun had been shining, the temperature had reached 19 degrees below freezing point. As we cruised onwards, we entered the realm of the truly surreal, a dystopian landscape where entire blocks had simply been torn away, like a petulant child had ripped out buildings from a Lego cityscape, and where nature was creeping back in to reclaim the land. It was turning into some kind of urban prairie; a scene that's often been compared to the mysterious 'Zone' in Andrei Tarkovsky's Soviet-era sci-fi film *Stalker*, a place where normal physical laws seem to have ceased to exist. Nothing, no photographs, could really prepare you for seeing the ruins of Detroit up close, unless perhaps you grew up in post-war Bosnia and Herzegovina; it was simply outside a western European's everyday experience – offensively, heart-breakingly monstrous, and at the same time, compulsively fascinating.

The only establishments that seemed to be doing much business around here were the churches offering heavenly salvation and the liquor stores promising a more rapid respite from life's woes. As the city's social anatomy ulcerated and necrotised, even some of its supposed guardians had become complicit in its demise; the police chief was being prosecuted for stealing from a fund to combat drug abuse, I was told, while part of his force had been made redundant because there wasn't enough money left to pay them. 'Crack ate a hole in the city,' Banks said several years later. 'They dumped that crack and those weapons in here, and it was pretty much an apocalypse – right-wing undercover genocide, if you ask me.'

Passing near the site of the now-demolished illegal soul-music bar where the 1967 riots erupted after police busted up a party that was being held to celebrate two black GIs' homecoming from Vietnam, we end up on West Grand Boulevard, where Motown's old headquarters was now a museum celebrating the production-line genius of Berry Gordy and his glorious roster of stars – 'Hitsville USA', as the sign outside said. In the preserved basement studio, Banks excitedly points out a miniature toy piano that was used for sound effects on some of Motown's sixties hits: 'Just like techno, they picked up any old shit that was laying around and used it,' he enthuses.

Underground Resistance were part of Detroit techno's second wave, building on what had been created in the eighties by the genre's instigators, Juan Atkins, Derrick May and Kevin Saunderson. By the early nineties, UR constituted the heaviest package to come out of the Motor City since Iggy and the Stooges. When they appeared live, they looked like a platoon of shock troops, swathed in black with their faces masked to disguise their identities. Played loud in a club, tracks like 'Sonic Destroyer' and 'The Punisher' felt as if they might shatter your ribcage. Even Kevin Saunderson, a man renowned for his jackhammer drum sound and surging bass noise, told me that he was stunned when he first heard them: 'They're so heavy, they kinda shocked me,' he said. 'I never knew anyone would get that hard in Detroit, especially two black guys. It catches you off guard.'[1]

I had met up with Banks and Mills earlier that day at the UR office, a spartan set-up which consisted of little more than a desk with a phone and a world map tacked to the wall. On the map, South Africa, which at that time in 1992 was still ruled by F.W. de Klerk's white minority regime, had been blanked out with a marker pen, and on the country's black mass was pasted one photocopied word: 'RIOT.'

'A riot is the language of the unheard,' Martin Luther King once said. UR's former MC and 'minister of information', Robert Hood, describes the crew as children of the 1967 unrest in Detroit, driven by an urgent calling to *take action*, inspired by their mutual hatred of injustice and collective fury about a city that was disintegrating in front of their eyes. 'That was a time when crack cocaine was rampant. You had a lot of layoffs from the automotive industry, families were falling apart, succumbing to the drug epidemic, single mothers were strug-gling to support their children. You had drug gangs who started to take over and there were drive-by shootings and carjackings. Schools were being closed and more jails were opening,' Hood explains.

'We were observing all of what's going on; we could feel the pres-sure. The city was imploding. You could feel the grip tightening and how the politicians didn't want to deal with Detroit and how the city was being written off. So when you hear tracks like [UR's 1991 release] 'Riot', that's Detroit screaming from the pressures of a racist society surrounding the city and bleeding it to death from the inside out.'

Their incendiary sound was shaped by these blighted surroundings, as Mike Banks had illustrated on our journey through the city that afternoon in the winter of 1992. But like Sun Ra, George Clinton and so many other Afro-futurist musicians, including Detroit techno originators like Juan Atkins, they also dreamed of loosening the bounds of earthly restraint and escaping into interstellar otherworlds free from oppression and prejudice – visions explored in Mike Banks' releases as The Martian for his other record label, Red Planet, on tracks like 'Cosmic Movement' and 'Star Dancer'.

UR's reaction to the economic hardship they saw around them was to declare independence. They developed a philosophy of self-reliance that might have felt familiar to someone like Berry Gordy, and which would serve them and others who emulated them well in the decades to come. 'We understood how black musicians from the forties, fifties and sixties had been exploited and left high and dry by music industry executives who were savvy enough to take advantage of these artists and their lack of knowledge of the music industry,' explains Hood.

'We could cut our own records, do the artwork, the distribution; we didn't have to concede to any higher power. We could do it ourselves and be self-sufficient. It was a guerrilla way of thinking – nobody's going to tell us how to make it, distribute it or market it. Nobody's going to control our music. We're going to say how it's going to be.'

Their music was also a reaction to the commodification of black American culture, Banks told me in 1992. He was repelled by the glossy aspirational fantasies of contemporary R&B – despicable lies, he said, sold by rapacious corporations to ease the unpalatable realities of African-American lives. He insisted that UR were the alternative, the antidote: 'hard music from a hard city'.

'Black folks don't live like groups like New Edition in $900 suits. Real life is more like Public Enemy portrays it,' he asserted.

'So what we stand for is resistance,' added Jeff Mills. 'We'll always be fighting against that shit. Revolution for change.'[2]

'Our music is a phoenix rising from the ashes of the crumbling industrial state.'

Juan Atkins, 1988

More than two decades later, I'm standing in downtown Hart Plaza as electric snares crackle and fizz like fireworks across the Detroit River shore, the rhythms reverberating around the septet of glass-fronted skyscrapers on the waterfront while Mike Banks and his shadowy crew of techno seditionaries bring the first night of the 2014 Movement festival to a crescendo in front of a reverent hometown crowd.

By this point, Underground Resistance were veterans of a musical genre that had helped to change the sound of popular music right across the world over the course of the previous 30 years. From blues and jazz to Motown, from Parliament-Funkadelic, the MC5 and the Stooges to Eminem, Detroit had nurtured some remarkable sonic pioneers who had redefined what music could be and what it could mean. Now techno's influence could be heard in everything from the most banal of pop hits to the most challenging avant-garde electronica. As Kevin Saunderson jokingly put it: 'We *are* history now!'

He was correct, literally – at the Detroit Historical Museum, there was a display about techno's pioneers amidst the Hard Rock Café-style memorabilia depicting the city's magnificent musical past, with Derrick May's picture hanging rather incongruously next to a photo of a young Madonna – although perhaps May, Atkins and Saunderson, the genre's founding fathers, should have been in the museum's 'gallery of innovation' instead, alongside Henry Ford and Berry Gordy.

Techno's history was better told by a self-funded and lovingly curated little installation called Exhibit: 3000 on the ground floor of a former laundry workers' union building which now served as the Underground Resistance and Submerge Records HQ, just a few minutes' walk from the Motown museum. Mike Banks, still lean and muscled in his late forties, wearing a khaki T-shirt and workman's jeans with tools dangling from his belt and a paintbrush in his back pocket, opened the front door when I rang the bell. 'Come with me, you got to see this shit,' he urged in that same implacable voice.

John Collins, a senior Detroit DJ who once played house and disco at Detroit's Cheeks club in the pre-techno eighties and later became part of the UR crew, gave me the guided tour. 'The museum was needed. It's important,' Collins explained. 'It's just as important as it ever was because the battle isn't won yet. We still have a way to go – some people don't even know that techno was created by black people.'

In the gallery, there were pictures of techno's originators, but other heroes too – Bruce Lee, Geronimo, Sun Tzu, the Tuskegee Airmen of World War Two, Public Enemy and Nichelle Nichols, the actor who played the USS Enterprise's chief communications officer, Nyota Uhura, in the original *Star Trek* series – setting UR firmly in the historical continuum of progressive black cultural politics. One photo had a caption declaring Detroit to be 'a city of freaks and fighters'.

But central to the narrative laid out in the old photographs, record sleeves, paintings, magazine clippings and vintage Roland drum computers carefully mounted in glass cases along the walls were Atkins, May and Saunderson, the three young black men who met in the eighties at high school in Belleville, a small and decorously suburban white-majority town on the Huron River some 30 miles west of Detroit.

Detroit's first proto-techno records had come out as early as 1981 – 'Sharevari' by A Number of Names and 'Alleys of Your Mind' by Cybotron, an electronic duo made up of the young, Kraftwerk-obsessed Atkins and a Vietnam War veteran and synthesizer enthusiast called Rik Davis, who named himself 3070. Cybotron were feeling their way towards a new kind of post-electro dance music: 'This stuff was punk: you play it first and then learn what you were doing afterwards,' Davis once said.[3]

Atkins and May also established their own Deep Space DJ crew, with its 'secret weapon', a Roland TR-909 that they used to jack up their mixes. After Cybotron's biggest hit in 1985, the gliding cold-wave electro track 'Clear', Atkins quit the band and started recording alone as Model 500, and all three men launched their own record labels – Atkins'

Metroplex, May's Transmat and Saunderson's KMS – to release their music independently. Along with their friend Eddie 'Flashin' Fowlkes, the so-called 'Belleville Three' became the originators of techno as a distinct genre of its own, in parallel to the emergence of house in Chicago. And while they had a clear plan for the kind of sound they wanted to make, they had no idea what kind of impact it would ultimately have.

May adopted the aliases Rhythim is Rhythim and Mayday, while Saunderson took a whole variety of pseudonyms, including Reese, Kreem, Tronik House and E-Dancer, as well as becoming the musical force behind the internationally successful duo Inner City. The Belleville Three drew inspiration from Kraftwerk, Yellow Magic Orchestra, European electro-pop and Italo-disco, but also from Parliament-Funkadelic and the post-disco, synth-spangled club tracks being issued by labels like Prelude. The wild-card factor was the pervasive otherworldliness of Detroit, where they all set up studios on the same block on Gratiot Street in the Eastern Market district, a stretch that came to be nicknamed 'Techno Boulevard'. 'I just react to my environment,' May told me when I first met him there in 1988. 'The people, the intensity, the paranoia, all the things that make Detroit what it is.'[4]

Another crucial influence was Detroit radio – specifically, the idiosyncratic broadcasts of Charles Johnson, alias The Electrifying Mojo, who fulfilled an inspirational role in the city similar to BBC presenter John Peel in Britain. From 1977 onwards, The Electrifying Mojo's shows defied all the racially defined conventions of US radio formatting; what he once called 'apartheid on the dial'.[5] His links were often lyrical sociopolitical soliloquies or homilies preaching decency and tolerance, and his musical favourites were mavericks like Prince, Parliament, the B52s and Kraftwerk, whose *Computer World* album he played again and again when it came out in 1981. One of his quotes was prominently displayed in the Underground Resistance museum: 'The price you pay for freedom is very costly. If you are passionate about it, it compensates what you have to sacrifice.'

The young men who would create Detroit techno were all listening, and when they became DJs and producers, Mojo started to play their early mixes. May says that there might not even have been what is now known as Detroit techno without the broadcaster: 'He was a teacher, an inspiration, a visionary. He showed there could be another way.'

Around the same time in the eighties, a young Jeff Mills was developing his discombobulatory fast-cutting DJ style on local radio under the pseudonym The Wizard. From 1987, Detroit listeners could also hear the *Fast Forward* radio show, which promoted techno as well as 'electronic body music' bands like Front 242 and Skinny Puppy, acid house, Belgian New Beat and British indie dance. It was presented by Alan Oldham, who did the iconic graphic novel-style artwork for many of the city's techno labels and would go on to become an Underground Resistance DJ under the name T-1000.

Like The Electrifying Mojo, the Detroit techno originators had little respect for any of the traditional racial boundaries in American pop culture. 'I remember one interviewer asking me what inspired this, and I was talking about Ultravox and Visage and groups like that, and he was amazed that I knew who Midge Ure and Steve Strange and Gary Numan were, and I said how important Depeche Mode was for the black community here – he was shocked! But to us, it was normal,' May recalls.

'We didn't know we weren't supposed to be digging that shit. Nobody told us that we couldn't get down to George Clinton and then flip the switch and listen to some Visage. Nobody told us, 'You're not *allowed* to listen to "Fade to Grey", motherfucker!' We didn't know we weren't supposed to listen to the Cocteau Twins or Echo and the Bunnymen or "Bela Lugosi's Dead" by Bauhaus.'

Kraftwerk were also showcased in the UR museum, their *Man-Machine* album displayed next to a Funkadelic record. The rise of techno and the constant homages paid by Atkins, May and Saunderson burnished the Germans' reputation as innovators, as they have acknowledged. 'Ralf Hütter sat right here in this very spot where we are sitting now, more than ten years ago, and he said to me: "Thank you",' May recalled as we chatted at his studio.

Hütter has also spoken emotionally of his meetings in Detroit with May and Atkins, and of the Düsseldorf band's admiration for the musical aesthetics of the American city. 'The industrial sound of Motor City and Kraftwerk on the autobahn, there's a spiritual connection. Automatic rhythms, robotic work, robotic music – all kinds of fantasies are going on,' he said.[6]

But the idea that Kraftwerk were the undisputed godfathers of techno is hardly the whole story. The sonic Afro-futurism of musicians like Herbie Hancock, George Clinton, Stevie Wonder and all the others who pioneered the use of electronic textures, synthesized basslines and rhythmic technologies in the seventies and eighties was equally vital in terms of laying out a palette of possibilities for the electronic dance music that followed.

The other key factors were house and disco – synthetic Italo-disco and European electro-pop grooves as well as the American classics. Because of the elegiac chord sequences and wistful melodies of some early Detroit techno, it has sometimes been interpreted as pure head music, but many of the original tracks were actually hard-pumping machine funk purpose-built for the dancefloor, which is why tunes like May's 'Nude Photo' and Saunderson's 'The Sound' became anthems at British clubs like the Haçienda. Detroit also had a thriving disco and house scene in the eighties with DJs like the late Ken Collier at the gay club Heaven, a pivotal figure who helped remix some of the early Was (Not Was) records and has been described as Detroit's equivalent of icons like Frankie Knuckles or Larry Levan. 'If you were into dance music in Detroit, the only place you could hear it was in the gay clubs, so that's where I went,' May recalls. When I heard Ken Collier play once in the late eighties in Detroit, he was jamming down New York garage cuts by Adeva and Paul Simpson into the sounds of his young compatriots from the emerging techno scene; they were all part of the same story, back then.

The Detroit DJ Carlos Souffront remembers how his world was reshaped when he went to Collier's club for the first time as a trepidatious gay teenager: 'When I found Heaven, it was almost too much for me,' Souffront says. 'It was scary because I wasn't ready to be out, but I was compelled by the music and the energy of the audience and the total commitment to the experience – it was inspiring. It looked to me like a collective of all sorts of misfits, all kinds of marginalised people were coming together there. I always felt like an outsider, but right away it felt like something I needed to be involved in.'

Club culture had an emancipatory impact on the young techno producers. Saunderson was thrilled by hearing Larry Levan at the Paradise Garage in New York, while May was entranced by Ron Hardy at the Music Box and Frankie Knuckles at the Power Plant in Chicago. 'This vision of making a moment this euphoric… it changed me,' May once marvelled at Knuckles' command of his congregation.[7]

The experienced Chicago DJ Knuckles adopted the hyperactive young Detroiter May as a kind of musical protégé. Cementing the creative links between the two cities, May sold a Roland drum machine to Knuckles, which he used to make the emotive anthem 'Your Love' with Jamie Principle, and to augment the grooves at the Power Plant club, where he relocated after The Warehouse. 'I would program different patterns into it throughout the week, and then use it throughout the course of a night, running it live, depending on the song, and playing it underneath, or using it to segue between some things,' Knuckles later recalled.[8] It's sometimes been reported that Knuckles also loaned out the second-hand Roland box to some of Chicago's early house producers to cut their rowdy DIY jack-tracks.

The Detroit trio's decision to name their music 'techno' – to define the Belleville Three's sound as different from all the other forms of electronic dance music on the scene at the time – was partly inspired by futurologist Alvin Toffler's 1980 book *The Third Wave*. In the book, Toffler set out his vision of a technological revolution led by a new generation of 'techno rebels' who would catalyse humanity's progress towards 'a new stage of civilisation'. He also inadvertently predicted how the musicians of the electronic dance era would operate, deploying cheap equipment creatively. 'The techno-rebels contend that technology need not be big, costly or complex in order to be "sophisticated",' he wrote.[9]

Giving their own name to their sound was a smart move, one that ensured that the Belleville Three were seen as historic creators of a new form rather than just another bunch of American house music guys who were into Kraftwerk, although the German DJ Talla 2XLC (Andreas Tomalla) had used the word 'techno' before them in the early eighties to categorise electronic bands like New Order, Kraftwerk, Depeche Mode and Front 242 when he worked in a record shop in Frankfurt. Indeed, Talla 2XLC started his Technoclub night in the German city as far back as 1984, and documentary footage from the time shows clubbers using the term 'techno' to describe hard-stomping industrial electro and 'electronic body music' tracks.

The Detroit trio only decided what their music would be called not long before the 1988 release of *Techno! The New Dance Sound of Detroit*, a landmark British compilation album showcasing early material from Atkins, May, Saunderson, Eddie Fowlkes, Blake Baxter and Anthony Shakir. May says that it might not even have ever been called techno if he had got his own way: 'I wanted to call it "high-tech soul",' he recalls. 'But Juan said, "No, this ain't no high-tech soul, man. This is *techno*."' The album, released as Britain's acid house 'summer of love' began to escalate towards its frenzied peak, sealed their image as the intellectual vanguard of electronic dance music and ensured their place in pop-culture history.

Even this might never have happened, says May. Techno went on to become a global phenomenon, but back then in the late eighties, it was often seen as little more than a novelty sound destined for inevitable oblivion like so many other pop fads. 'When I went to England on my first trip, we spent a day visiting record companies in London, and nobody gave a shit,' he remembers. 'Everybody just thought this music was a joke. We played [May's classic track] "Strings of Life" to one A&R guy and he was just on the phone. He didn't even look at me. So we just left.'

'You know money is one thing, but soul is another.'

Prince, speaking in a radio interview with The Electrifying Mojo, 1986

From the outset, the Belleville Three envisioned themselves as voyagers on a mission to map out a new landscape. Like those other era-defining black musicians who emerged around the same time – Public Enemy and their production team, the Bomb Squad – they found some of their inspiration in sci-fi, a literature of a parallel world in which the brutal racist history of the United States might never have happened. 'The original essence was black futurism and black science fiction,' says Alan Oldham. 'I was a comic book fan. You had guys like Juan Atkins who were sci-fi fans. A lot of my friends were *Star Trek* fans, and when *Star Wars* came out when I was in eighth grade, everybody went crazy for that.'

The US state of Michigan has a tradition of imagining the future, from Oldsmobile's introduction of assembly-line mass-production to General Motors' pioneering of consumer credit to Berry Gordy's Motown hit factory. But techno also reflected the era which the Belleville Three inhabited. 'Visions of the future are really about the present, and the idea of the future shifts depending on the era,' says the Underground Resistance crew's manager and occasional vocalist, Cornelius Harris. 'It speaks to where people are right now, and it's all based on our hopes and expectations.'

For young black people growing up in Detroit in the eighties, the future was not the optimistic fifties vision of liberating domestic technology, day trips to Mars and jetpacks for all. It had become threatening and malevolent, a promise of a world like the one shown in the dystopian sci-fi film *Robocop*, which was shot in Detroit around that time.

'If you look at the eighties, when techno started, that was the time of AIDS, when crack was introduced into the neighbourhoods, when there was economic recession and crime was at an all-time high. I even remember this news report about Detroit that said in the future, the average black male in the city would be dead by the age of 24,' Harris recalls.

Techno, he suggests, was an attempt to *dream* another potential destiny into existence. 'What these guys did was, instead of accepting that, they envisioned a very different future for themselves, where instead of being shot or getting addicted to drugs or going to jail, they got to make this great music and travel the world. They basically invented their own future in the midst of all this negativity. Sometimes it's conscious, sometimes it's subconscious, but you had these guys doing the complete opposite of what they were expected to be, and *they made their own future* – in what was supposed to be the worst city in the country.'

Dreaming a way out… I flashed back to what Juan Atkins had said to me when I first interviewed him in 1988: 'In order to build the new Detroit, we have to destroy the old Detroit,' he asserted. 'It's so easy to go wrong in this city. It's so easy for a young black man to be tempted to do drugs, to be seduced into crime. There's nothing to do here. There's nowhere to go; the scene is dead. That's why our stuff sounds like it does.'[10]

Atkins has often spoken of techno as a kind of alternate reality, a portal to an imagined realm of freedom. But in 1988 he also said that he believed it was necessary to tear down history in order to create the future. 'We want to repudiate everything that reminds us of the past,' he insisted. 'We don't sit down and say, "Let's make the weirdest music we can"; it's just a result of our environment. Detroit is a post-industrial city; industry is closing down and technology is coming to the forefront. The city has dried up and our music is a phoenix rising from the ashes of the crumbling industrial state.'[11]

It's hard to recall now, when techno is ubiquitous across the globe and the rattle and boom of Roland's 808 and 909 machines has become as familiar as a power chord from a Gibson Les Paul, how militant-ly alien, how shockingly *radical* it sounded when it first emerged on labels like May's Transmat, Atkins' Metroplex and Saunderson's KMS. Like the house and acid tracks coming out of Chicago at around the same time, it had this compulsive simplicity and transcendent intensity that was simply thrilling. As the second-wave Detroit producer Stacey Pullen has suggested, these early recordings had the peculiar ability to open up spaces in the mind and plunge listeners into the esoteric: 'They made me think about things differently. How we are as people, and what path should we take.'[12]

Inspired or directly nurtured by the Belleville Three and Fowlkes, a second generation rapidly emerged – people like May's prodigiously talented protégé Carl Craig; Mike Banks, Jeff Mills and Robert Hood of Underground Resistance; brothers Lenny and Lawrence Burden and their band Octave One, and just across the river in Canada, Richie Hawtin and John Acquaviva, who ran Plus 8 Records and also released records by Detroit newcomer Kenny Larkin.

It was a remarkable outpouring of talent in such a short space of time, with an artistic élan that was often reflected in the design of their 12-inch vinyl releases. The cumulative effect was enthralling, as if we were hearing transmissions from some parallel universe, as I once marvelled after picking up a stack of records in the city: 'They often have messages from the artists in the run-out grooves ("Take a trip to a higher state of mind"; "The needs of the many outweigh the needs of the few"; "Do you believe in witches?"). Some, confusingly, play from the inside out. Others are covered with home drawings of deep sea divers, astronauts, crazed graphics. Yet others carry no information whatsoever, just a black label in a black bag, or electric blue vinyl in a white shrinkwrap.'[13]

But by the turn of the nineties, techno's originators had already lost their jurisdiction over the genre they created, as musicians across the Atlantic picked up their inspiration and took it in their own directions. This caused some discontent in Detroit, a feeling that black music was again being exploited by white Europeans. Fuelled by the seemingly insatiable demand for new recordings from the rapidly rising rave scene of the time, the Brits, Germans, Belgians and Dutch quickly became prodigious producers of techno. Some of them, like 808 State, A Guy Called Gerald, Baby Ford and LFO, won respect from their Detroit peers. But others were seen as venal cash-in merchants – and worse, they had no soul, no *groove*. 'It's just bastardised music,' Derrick May once complained. 'It's just not *funky*.'

The fact that the European rave scene was fuelled by Ecstasy also disturbed some of the Detroit musicians. Most of them didn't do chemicals, and they didn't understand people who did, even though these early-adopting E-heads would become their faithful supporters for decades to come. For the Detroiters, drugs meant crack, the genocidal poison which had helped to bring down Armageddon on their city. 'It was hauntingly strange to see all those people on drugs,' Lawrence Burden of Octave One said about his experience of playing a massive rave in Germany in the early nineties. 'I really couldn't relate to or understand that part of what was going on. It freaked me out. Night of the living dead. I just thought, "Look at all these zombies!"'[14]

They were also uneasy about some of the cultural interpretations of techno in Europe, where some white neo-hippies had decided that the rave scene signified the dawn of a new psychedelic revolution. Back in 1993, a panel discussion about techno at London's Institute of Contemporary Arts became the forum for an ideological showdown between Derrick May and Fraser Clark, the editor of *Evolution* magazine and promoter of London's Megatripolis hippie-rave club. May completely rejected any connection between techno and narcotics: 'I never took Ecstasy, never smoked a joint – *never*. I don't need drugs to take me out there.' Clark was a psychedelic evangelist who believed that techno was the soundtrack for neo-pagan rituals reconnecting humans to the earth's primal energies; dancing to electronic music on Ecstasy was a shamanic rite with its roots in ancient African ceremonies, he argued. When Clark offered up this opinion at the ICA, May snapped back in disgust: 'If that's African dancing, my ancestors should have had their asses kicked.' May got the last laugh that day, but it was clear that techno's founding fathers could no longer dictate how the music was to be understood.

May eventually gave up releasing his own recordings for two decades, citing disillusionment with the business of music; he denied suggestions that his early tracks like 'Strings of Life' and 'Nude Photo' were so good that he feared he could never surpass them. He says that his decision stemmed from 1991, when he, Atkins and Saunderson hatched a plan to record together as a trio under the name Intelex. They saw Intelex as their own take on Kraftwerk, but Trevor Horn, the boss of ZTT, the label they were planning to sign to – the man whose widescreen electronic productions made stars of Frankie Goes to Hollywood – wanted something too commercial for them to accept, May claims.

May went on to record some valedictory material with Steve Hillage's System 7 project, but the failure of the Intelex initiative helped to sour his outlook so much that he did not release anything more until 2016, when he worked on an album with pianist Francesco Tristano. 'I was used to making music on my own, in my own way. I was used to finishing it in my own time, however long it took,' he explains. 'I wasn't used to being told what to make, who to work with or that I should change something because someone else thought it would sound better that way.' May would continue to work as a DJ, but others would push the music forward, taking inspiration from their own interpretations of what Detroit could mean.

From the Underground Resistance headquarters, Cornelius Harris and I drove across to the nearby Packard Automotive Plant, an enormous derelict car factory which had shut down in the fifties and had since become a ravaged symbol of this busted boomtown. We stepped delicately through the rubble and climbed the shattered concrete stairs, picking our way past spray-painted ghoul faces and fading Smileys on our way up to the roof, where we looked down over 330,000 square metres of dead industry, stripped by scrappers and left to rot, an early warning of what would happen to a lot of the rest of the city.

The Packard building has been used as a suitably apocalyptic setting for various Hollywood movies and even featured in a wistful doomsday verse written by former US poet laureate Philip Levine, 'The Last Shift'. British street artist Banksy once did a mural somewhere in the building – a stencil painting showing a sad-looking boy and the words: 'I remember when all this was trees.' It was later removed, and sold off for $137,500.

It was here in this graffiti-spattered skeleton of a building that Richie Hawtin and John Acquaviva used to hold raves in the nineties. The two white technoheads were born in Britain and Italy respectively but grew up in the Canadian cities of Windsor and London, not far across the border from Detroit. They used to travel down to the city to hear Derrick May play from midnight until dawn at the Music Institute club from 1988 to 1990, when his manic artistry was at its youthful peak, as Alan Oldham wrote in a testimonial to the short-lived club: 'Many times, he'd play tracks right off a Fostex two-track recorder that he'd just cut hours before at his studio, something I never got over. He'd beat mix between the reel to reel and [Technics] 1200s and back, using the pitch control on the reel. He'd cut, edit and destroy other people's tracks, too, as he did with his fucked-up psycho re-edit of the MI theme "We Call It Aciiiieeed" by D-Mob.'[15]

After the Music Institute shut down, Hawtin and Acquaviva started looking for places to throw their own parties. Like Britain in the late eighties, when disused warehouses and industrial buildings left empty by economic recession provided perfect spaces in which the illegal rave scene could thrive, Detroit had no shortage of options. 'The advantage of Detroit was finding abandoned buildings and parts of the city where the police didn't really go and we were able to do whatever we wanted,' Hawtin recalls.

At the Packard building, they covered the walls in black PVC and then let rip with the deranged psychotronic sounds that made the early tracks released by their Plus 8 label so exciting. 'People would go on this crazy trip in this dark room covered in black plastic and you always felt that they had all come together, united by this intensity of sound,' says Hawtin.

One of the Packard parties celebrated the release in 1993 of Hawtin's first album as Plastikman, *Sheet One*, a remarkable collection of acid house tracks with a CD cover designed to resemble a perforated sheet of trips (it was so realistic that someone in Texas was even arrested for possessing it; the police couldn't believe they weren't real LSD blotters). The vibe of the times was definitely utopian, Hawtin says: 'I think the ethos of techno was looking towards a brighter future. I also think that's why it came up in Detroit – it was a way to escape the future that was laid out before you, for many people. Electronic music enabled us to dream of a brighter future, and actually did create a brighter future for many of us.'

There were also raves in disused factories, abandoned warehouses and even a car workshop where the DJ would play in a booth made out of cast-off auto parts. In the late nineties, however, the police began cracking down on the illegal parties, and by 2000, the city's rave scene had been eviscerated. Detroit had given techno to the world, fuelling the European rave explosion, but back at home, its pioneers were still virtually unknown and there were very few places left for them to play.

'Detroit has been a mass social experiment. The future of America hit here first.'

DJ Seoul, Detroit Techno Militia

'This postindustrial sarcophagus' – that's how Detroit writer Charlie LeDuff has described his hometown.[16] Derrick May has his own take: 'Detroit is like the wreck of the Titanic – but *above water*,' he suggests as we sit on the roof deck at his Transmat studio on Gratiot Street while dusk draws gently down over the city. The evening air is soft and warm, and the playful chirrup of birdsong can still be heard over the screaming of the police sirens in the streets below.

Across the road, the windows of the building opposite May's studio are bricked up. On the ground floor is a shop called Cheap Charlies, offering second-hand work clothes and 'dollar items', while at the traffic lights are a couple of billboards, one advertising cut-price deals on McDonald's cheeseburgers – 'Single. Double. Triple. Every day' – and another touting easy loans: 'Get a good car. Even with bad credit'. The target demographic seemed clear – although the Eastern Market neighbourhood was becoming one of the most fashionable in the city, with new boutiques and hipster restaurants springing up along the Techno Boulevard block, these slogans were not aimed at the affluent. We weren't far from the downtown area, where tens of thousands of people had gathered for the biggest techno party of the year, but there were few signs of life outside and the only people passing by this Friday evening were vagrants.

When I first interviewed May in 1988, Detroit had already been drifting downwards in a spiral of economic decline for several decades, but it was still America's seventh-largest city, with a population of around a million. 'Seventh City Techno' was actually the headline of the first major feature on techno, a genre-defining piece of reportage by Stuart Cosgrove in the British youth culture magazine *The Face*. 'Ten years after Motown left for sunnier climes, the Motor City moves to a beat more inspired by Henry Ford's factories than Berry Gordy's dream,' its introduction promised. 'Techno is the sound of young Detroit: built with machines, and driven by despair.' In the article, May gave Cosgrove his all-time classic quote, describing techno as a sound that was 'like Kraftwerk and George Clinton stuck in an elevator with only a sequencer to keep them company'.[17]

Some 25 years on, Detroit was no longer America's seventh city, and had not been for a long time. It had dropped below 20th place in the US rankings, and its population was down to under 700,000 – back to what it had been around the beginning of the automobile boom in the early twentieth century. Numbers had fallen by an incredible 25 per cent between 2000 and 2010 – nothing less than a mass exodus – leaving more than 80,000 buildings abandoned. Little wonder that the effects of this desertion could be seen on the streets, with their eerie feeling of absence, as if some plague or conflict had decimated the human stock. Urban blight had created a bizarre landscape in which prosperous enclaves of bourgeois tranquillity nestled up against derelict blocks where forlorn stumps of burnt-out homes poked out from abandoned land and rotting hulks of shuttered factories loomed over deserted lots. 'Detroit feels like Ground Zero for… what, exactly?' asked author Mark Binelli in his book about his hometown. 'The end of the American way of life? Or the beginning of something else?'[18]

Detroit was eventually declared bankrupt in 2013 – the largest ever municipal bankruptcy in US history. As the title of an Underground Resistance track released around the same time asked: 'Has God Left This City?'

The talk at Transmat that evening was about the latest population figures, and about how Detroit's chief of police, James Craig – Carl Craig's cousin – had just been featured in the National Rifle Association magazine, urging the city's crime-haunted residents to arm themselves. 'People find it hard to believe that I'm still living here. They ask, "Why are you still in Detroit?"' May remarked. 'But I'm happy. I have everything I want and I can get on a plane and go wherever I want. So why do I need to leave?'

And a strange thing had happened after the turn of the millennium. After being immortalised in all its decaying splendour by photographers like Camilo José Vergara and websites like The Fabulous Ruins of Detroit, the haggard cityscape had become something of a tourist attraction for aficionados of what had become known as 'ruin porn'. 'Visitors are coming to see a city that looks like a disaster movie set,' May said. 'They're coming here to tour the ruins that we are still living in.'

Detroit was where the tidal wave of twentieth-century automotive capitalism washed up onto the shore and then receded, leaving the detritus of an urban settlement that could sometimes look as if it had been ravaged by a tsunami. Inevitably this contributed to techno's mystique; to the kind of twisted romanticism that entranced its European devotees. 'There's this European Blade Runner fantasy about Detroit – this beautiful music rising from the concrete ruins,' says Alan Oldham. A music full of reveries of escape into the cosmos or under the sea, of apocalyptic visions of a world in which eternal darkness has fallen, of angry blasts of noise to soundtrack riots and rebellions against a brutal oppressor.

But there was something else now in Detroit that captured the eye: urban farmlands and community gardens established on vacant plots where houses once stood. New settlers had been moving in: homesteading bohemians and intrepid artists recolonising the landscape as if the Motor City was the new American frontier; young creatives attracted by cheap rents, free spaces to experiment and the progressive aura that techno helped to create. 'Detroit is a prime example of what the propaganda about the United States is all about – you have the freedom to do what you want, and to do it on your own terms,' Carl Craig insisted. A glossy promotional magazine that I picked up at the airport even boosted the place as 'America's greatest comeback city'. 'We've had thousands of these settlers moving here. Maybe, just maybe, some will stay and help to form a creative class which will help rebuild the city,' suggested May.

One of the symbols of this hoped-for creative revitalisation was the Heidelberg Project, two blocks of land which Detroit artist Tyree Guyton had reimagined as a surreal piece of urban bricolage – houses, trees and old cars decorated with wild jumbles of home-made wooden clocks, abandoned children's toys, odd shoes and various cast-off domestic items that Guyton had collected and repurposed. It turned out that he was an old friend of Derrick May and saw his artwork in some of the same terms, as an act of alchemy, transmuting degradation into beauty. 'It's magic, like what Derrick does. It's being able to take what life has brought your way and do something greater with it. Art is a medicine, like music; it helps you to see,' Guyton explains. 'Derrick took music to another level. I'm taking art to another level – another level of consciousness. I am using art to transform environments – and people.'

Independent arts projects, urban farming initiatives on abandoned plots and hip eateries like the knowingly named Craft Work restaurant generated a lot of media interest, although some locals were understandably dubious about how much of a salvage operation could be implemented by enthusiastic white bohemians when majority-black Detroit remained the poorest big city in the US and needed total financial resuscitation. 'People talk about art and culture, how this can save the city, but I got a real sceptical view,' said Mike Banks, looking out beyond the back porch of the Underground Resistance building, where there was a vacant lot being farmed by some post-industrial pilgrims. 'This is the inner-city perspective: you got three choices if you want to get out – you got sport and athletics, you got the plant if they're selling some cars, and then you got the army. We are so fucked here – capitalism is eating democracy's ass off, man…'

And yet the question was still being asked: could the city – maybe, just maybe – *rise again*? 'Who knows? Crazier things have happened in Detroit,' mused Mark Binelli in 2013. 'It's a place so unspooled, one's wildest experiments, ideas that would never be seriously considered in a functioning city, might actually have a shot here.'[19]

Anyone who was hanging around Hart Plaza during the Movement festival in May 2014 might have been able to convince themselves that this kind of optimism was not misplaced (*maybe, just maybe*). For one weekend at least, downtown Detroit had come alive as the children of Transmat and Metroplex and KMS and UR and Submerge and Carl Craig's Planet E and all the others had come home to say hello. The central streets were full of technoheads – electronic music obsessives in cult record-label T-shirts, teenage 'candy ravers' in gaudy cyberwear, childish backpacks and fluffy moonboots, intricately bearded hipsters, pumped-up jocks in shorts and lithe disco queens in hotpants, as well as ordinary men and women of disparate ethnicities and origins who had always loved and would always love techno.

Some of the freakier heads had even arrived in costume – there was a Captain America, and a man dressed as the American flag, and a peculiar little person totally encased from head to toe in a purple body stocking, making him look like a cartoon imp. There was also a girl wearing just her knickers and bra, but with full surgical bandages covering her face.

And there was techno everywhere this weekend, right across the downtown area, not just at the festival – after-parties, symposiums, presentations, pop-up raves on sound systems set up on the pavements, hangouts at record stores, internet DJ broadcasts and random encounters of like-minded souls from across the United States and beyond. An ageing religious evangelist had even put speakers on the sidewalk and was jamming out some hard trance while improvising bizarre atonal riffs over the top, his keyboard set up next to a placard urging: 'Give your heart to Jesus.'

On sale at a row of stalls at the festival was an array of T-shirts with slogans declaring loyalty to the city, the tribe, the drugs: 'Detroit

Hustles Harder', a screenprint of Frankie Knuckles with the slogan 'Frankie Forever', a cartoon of an alien gobbling multicoloured pills.

By the waterfront, Berlin DJ Dixon (Steffen Berkhahn) was entrancing the crowd with drones and tones that weaved and glided, interconnecting and harmonising with each other like the low registers of a cathedral organ while cavernous dub bass throbbed beneath. Clouds of dope smoke rose from the nearby jungle stage as young dancers threw down hyperkinetic footwork steps, crusties hopped around in their combat boots and a middle-aged man jived and jittered around an intricately carved wooden staff.

But the 'Made in Detroit' stage was where the hardcore techno aficionados had gathered and the urban boho dancers arranged themselves in circles to show off their balletic moves as local legends like Mike Huckaby, Delano Smith, Terrence Dixon, Kenny Larkin and Stacey Pullen laid the grooves down. The sheer energy and verve of the younger generation of local DJs playing on the stage over the weekend – including one of Kevin Saunderson's sons, Dantiez – also suggested that Detroit techno had not yet become a heritage genre atrophied in past glories.

Yet it was a man from the early days of 'hi-tech soul', a producer who had appeared on that first techno compilation back in 1988, who turned it right out. Anthony 'Shake' Shakir, who suffered from multiple sclerosis and was DJing in a wheelchair, mixed old-school techno into 'Wheel Me Out' by Detroit's Was (Not Was), and then dropped Derrick May's 'Strings of Life', sending Detroiters of all races, teenaged and middle-aged, boys with Afros and men with greying temples, leaping skyward in a transcendent moment of communal bliss, united in their city by their song. Shakir finished up with an astonishing virtuoso mix, cutting back and forth for ten minutes, the beats churning and clashing before resolving back into the groove, the rhythm transforming from avant-garde percussion storm to throbbing Eurobeat to disco frenzy. As he played on, a tall redhead in cowgirl jeans whirled a hula-hoop around her body, twisting and turning, lost in celestial oblivion.

On Sunday night after the festival, Derrick May played at the White

House club on nearby Shelby Street. As relentlessly energetic in his early fifties as he had ever been, May worked the system hard from his booth high up above the floor as hi-hats tinkled like glass raindrops falling from the ceiling and synth waves soared like rushes of the purest MDMA.

The first-ever Detroit Electronic Music Festival, the precursor to Movement, had been held in 2000, in the wake of the police crackdown on outlaw raves. Initiated by May and programmed by Carl Craig, the festival was intended as techno's grand homecoming. 'The music has taken over the world. Now we're taking over Detroit,' Craig declared in an unreleased film about the event, *The Drive Home*.

It was clear at that point that the city needed a major showcase for its greatest musical export since Motown, Craig told me: 'The festival was intended to make a statement to the community because techno was underestimated and underappreciated here. Our attitude was, how come this kind of thing can happen somewhere else, but it can't happen here?'

Because techno had always been more popular abroad than it was in the US. Even with the rise of EDM, America's own bleached-out, pumped-up, hetero-friendly take on electronic dance music in the second decade of the twenty-first century, people like May, Atkins, Saunderson, Craig and all the others might have been viewed as genuine cultural originators by many Europeans but they remained marginal figures in their home country. France decorated Jeff Mills with its prestigious Order of Arts and Letters medal in 2017 in honour of his contribution to the enrichment of French culture – but when asked once whether he would be touring his latest project in the United States, Mills responded sadly: 'America just isn't interested in what I'm doing and never really has been.'[20]

I asked Robert Hood what he thought, and he offered a similarly downbeat response: 'North America has no idea of where the music began. They all think it came from Europe,' he said. 'Race plays a factor. People have had over time and history a natural propensity to discount black art and what black folks have created, and that's the same thing with electronic music. Over history, anything that a black inventor has produced has been downplayed and belittled.

'But the question is, what are we going to do about it? Are we going to fight the power and continue the struggle, or are we going to sit down and take it? I think we have to stand up and speak, not just sit in the back of the bus.'

Even ghettotech – a foul-mouthed local relative of Miami bass and Chicago juke which took influences from Cybotron and early electro, and was exemplified by DJ Assault's 1996 track 'Ass N Titties' (sample lyric: 'Ass. Titties. Ass and titties. Ass ass ass ass ass and titties') – seemed to be as popular in the city as classic old-school techno. In a taxi heading downtown to the Movement festival, the bodywork juddered and groaned to a series of lowdown ghettotech booty basslines and a stream of sleazy invective from testosterone-deranged MCs on the car radio. 'Do you want to fuck?' one of them demanded brusquely, as if he had an urgent appointment to attend and had to get it over immediately to avoid being late. *'Dirty fucker,'* growled another. 'Jump on this dick!'

Outside the US however, Detroit techno DJs ranging from old-school veterans like the fifty-something Delano Smith to new talents like the twenty-something Kyle Hall were still rapturously received when they played around the world. And despite his 'retirement' from studio recording, Derrick May's back catalogue had also continued to be a rich source of kudos and employment; in 2014, he began touring a show featuring the Macedonian Symphony Orchestra playing orchestrated interpretations of his Transmat classics. Jeff Mills did a similar project with the Montpellier Philharmonic Orchestra. But although taking the music away from the clubs and into the concert halls might have suggested that Detroit techno had traded its dancefloor mojo for highbrow approval, the city kept turning out iconoclastic auteurs who continued to redefine what the music could be.

Freighted with Detroit mythology, the funky minimalism and twisted disco cut-ups of Chicago-raised Theo Parrish, the late-night red-light grooviness of Moodymann, the raucous sleaze and whacked-out psychedelia of Omar S and the off-kilter epics of Stacey Pullen all managed to twist the genre into fascinating new shapes as the decades progressed. This was also a bunch of wayward nonconformists in the city's tradition of independence who usually preferred to release their music on their own labels to avoid outside interference, and gave few interviews to explain themselves – but when they did speak, they were often as forthright as Mad Mike Banks. Most of them were also resolute champions of their hometown. 'Detroit is a dying city. Well, I'm going to die with that motherfucker,' Moodymann (Kenny Dixon Jr) insisted. 'If it wasn't for Detroit, I wouldn't be the motherfucker I am today. So I am not leaving my baby, I'm going to stick with it.'[21]

One of the youngest amongst them, Kyle Hall, was born in 1991, the year that UR's 'Riot' came out. From his teenage years onwards, Hall had picked up and reshaped elements of house and techno into novel forms. But he had never been to a rave; by the time he was old enough to get in, the Detroit scene was already on its knees. 'We had the whole War on Drugs, and that kind of killed the club culture, so that's why my generation wasn't really able to partake in that experience,' he explains. 'There was such a backlash from government that by the time I was of age, it was pretty much illegal.'

His first album in 2013, *The Boat Party*, came wrapped in an incisively sardonic cover that pictured Hall sitting on an abandoned motorboat in the middle of a desolate, snow-covered urban wasteland. The photograph seemed to be an intentional inversion of the Duran Duran-style playboy image projected by DJs who played records on daytime disco cruises in the Mediterranean or the Adriatic, a sideswipe at what he saw as a decadent mainstream from the faraway vantage point of the anguished city which had helped to create its soundtrack.

'At the time, I remember there were all these boat parties in Europe, DJs playing on boats in places like Croatia,' Hall says. 'It was like dance music was starting to turn into this luxury, elitist activity, but bringing in DJs from places that are maybe underprivileged and have issues with racism, cities that are disenfranchised – but these people are being hired to serve a certain clientele of people that do not have to engage with a lot of these hardships; they're in a position of privilege. So it was kind of an ironic statement – *here's* your boat party.'

While still a teenager, Hall found a mentor in Omar S, who put out some of his early tracks on his FXHE label; he also went on to collaborate with one of techno's pioneers, Anthony Shakir, a man from a generation twice his age. But he says he didn't want to be constrained by the aesthetic parameters of the Detroit legacy: 'Anyone who has a sense of ancestry has a pride in what they are, a sense of direction. But that can be a limiting thing as well as a positive motivation, you know.'

One of the ideas that he did fully embrace was Detroit techno's tradition of self-reliance. Like many other producers from the city, dating back to Atkins' Metroplex, May's Transmat and Saunderson's KMS in the late eighties, he set up his own label, Wild Oats, to release his music in the way he thought it should be released. 'In Detroit, there's always been a black entrepreneurial spirit,' he explains. 'Also not having people there to do things for you makes a different mentality – if you want something done, you've got to do it yourself.'

'There is a Detroit that you don't see on the news.'

John Collins, Underground Resistance

The inaugural Detroit Electronic Music Festival in 2000 was intended to be an opportunity to raise a standard for the music in its hometown, recalls Rita Sayegh, one of the filmmakers who worked on the unreleased documentary about the event, *The Drive Home*. 'As the festival started coming together, we realised what a big moment this was for Detroit and for techno,' says Sayegh, a designer who has also done artwork for Craig, Hawtin and Mills.

'After the city cracked down on the warehouse parties, busted everyone and essentially put an end to it completely, for a while no one had any place to go,' adds another of the filmmakers, Timothy Aten. 'So the festival gave them the chance to finally come together and celebrate the music again, out in the open.'

'It was overwhelming,' says Sayegh. 'There was such a feeling of family and closeness when it happened, a feeling of something so big and positive that came from this really grassroots idea and this small, tight-knit group of creative people. And Derrick May, there was this certain look in his eye – I'm sure he's played everywhere there is to play around the world, but he looks up while he's playing and he is in disbelief – *total* disbelief – that this is happening in Detroit.'

But the annual free event, whose programming was later taken over by May and then by Saunderson, was always on the verge of financial collapse. One year, May had to put in tens of thousands of dollars of his own money to make up a shortfall caused by the city's withdrawal of municipal funding for the festival, which led to some creditors going unpaid for months and angrily threatening law suits. He even resorted to begging in the crowd for extra cash to keep the party going.

'The city didn't give me any money and I wasn't allowed to charge,' May recalls. 'So in the middle of the festival, I realised that I didn't have enough money to pay the bills, so I got in this golf cart with another guy and we had a big garbage can and we were shouting, "Please give us money! The festival is going to close down if you don't give us money!" We got about $20,000. It wasn't enough, but at least people gave.'

Ultimately the three-day event, renamed Movement, was taken over in 2006 by a group of local promoters called Paxahau who had been involved with staging raves at the Packard Plant in the nineties. Paxahau professionalised the operation and started to charge an entrance fee, ensuring its survival as a major US festival, but as techno believers, they also tried to ensure that the line-up retained its 'underground' credibility.

'We honestly feel that we are historical torchbearers of this music in the place where it was created,' Sam Fotias, Paxahau's operational director, told me before the festival in 2014. 'It's imperative that this city continues to be a beacon for this music. Having been a part of the true underground and being able to identify with what that means – a counterculture – those ideas and principles have remained with us to this day. It's more important to us than any amount of money.'

When Kraftwerk headlined Movement in 2016, it felt like a kind of homecoming, reported Detroit-raised journalist Tamara Warren, a veteran of the first festival in Hart Plaza 16 years earlier: 'When they dropped the beat on "Trans-Europe Express", I shivered,' Warren wrote. 'On the screen, a projection of a flying saucer landed on our Techno Boulevard. For Detroit – and anyone who is a student of legit electronic music history – this was a full-circle moment.'[22]

But as she also noted, Movement's largely white crowd inevitably reflected the continuing racial and economic divisions in the city, where 40 per cent of its overwhelmingly black population lived below the poverty line. For those who felt that the festival had lost some of its inclusive spirit when it became a paid-for event, meaning that curious locals of all ages and economic backgrounds could no longer just wander in, check out the tunes and find out what this techno thing was all about, there were still cheaper alternatives, like the low-cost Charivari festival, or the completely free, community-oriented Tec-Troit, which ran for five years before encountering financial difficulties.

There was also the Backpack Festival, a dance-music charity event co-organised by John Collins of Underground Resistance. People supported the festival by donating backpacks filled with school supplies, which were then distributed to deprived children. 'It goes with the Underground Resistance philosophy,' Collins explains. 'It was started by Judy Shelton, who is part of the scene here; she saw kids walking down the street to school, carrying their books in *paper bags*... in the wintertime... *they didn't even have backpacks*... The underground techno scene supported us and Derrick May was our first sponsor. Everyone has played there – Juan, Kevin, Eddie Fowlkes – and they all did it for free.

'If you come from the inner city and you went on to be successful, it is your *duty* to give back to your city and your people to help inspire them and let them know: "This is where I came from. I had nothing, and here I am today, and you can do the same."'

Grassroots activism is a little-known but significant aspect of the Detroit techno scene. Because a genuine sense of community seemed to have developed among this little clan of producers and DJs who had chosen to stay and live in the city; even though there were all the bitter-ly divisive personal disputes that a small scene inevitably suffers, there was still a deeply felt empathy for those who were suffering amid this very American urban meltdown. A feeling that inspired them to do what they thought they could to make their city better, or at least to sustain its cultural life, as well as a fierce sense of pride in saying: *I'm from Detroit*... So the city is bankrupt, so what? We will not only survive – *we will overcome*. 'Things had to change, and that's what's happening: you can feel it, you can see it,' argues Collins. 'After Detroit hit rock bottom, the only way was up.'

And he was not alone, that weekend in Detroit. At a downtown coffee bar that they had occupied for an evening to record their weekly internet radio show, Tom Linder (alias T.Linder) and Bill Stacy (DJ Seoul) of the Detroit Techno Militia collective told me that their city had become a kind of social experiment in post-industrial survival, but that they too believed that a revival was possible. And that music (techno, even) could play its part in bringing it back from the brink – *maybe, just maybe*...

'There's this spirit of people making the best that they can with the shit that they've got. We're hoping that as Berlin has rebuilt after the Wall came down, we can rebuild too,' explained Linder, as Land Cruis-ers eased by noiselessly on the half-deserted street outside the café.

'We're told that it's over. We're told that Detroit doesn't have a future – so we're going to create that future,' declared Stacy, his face framed by the shadows of the tower blocks built by the corporate barons of a thriving metropolis that had ceased to exist.

'No matter what, this is my city, and I'm going to stay here. I'm not going anywhere and I'm going to help contribute to the growth of this city,' he insisted. 'There's a soul here that's never going to die.' And then he recalled Detroit's motto – *Speramus meliora; resurget cineribus*.

'We hope for better things,' the motto says. 'It will rise from the ashes.'

2

Techno Cities #2
Berlin

THE HUGE TURBINE HALL starts to rumble and hum as if an electrical storm is gathering, streaks of noise flashing back and forth across the lighting gantries high above us, swelling steadily until they finally resolve into an imperious motorik bassline and the mighty speaker stacks start to pick out the individual chatterings of the 808 snares, splashing them around the room like a shower of hailstones in the wind. The sound system breathes sub-bass frequencies through our stomachs and fusillades of percussion detonate like mortar shells as the treble notes soar and swoop around our heads while the next sonic surge begins to gather force before crashing down hard yet again.

We are many hours deep into it now, and the music has grown wilder and looser, careening maniacally like the whirling of a dervish troupe as night becomes day in the perpetual darkness of a place where time has lost all meaning and reality slipped away into the shadows long ago. Angular, sculpted girls and boys are spinning out right at the centre, right in that sweet spot where the sound is at its most exquisite, top-knots sprouting at outlandish angles from shaven heads as their hands slice abstract patterns into the low-rolling cloud of dry ice, smiling just for each other and yet consumed in the mass by the magic of this collective ritual that has somehow – in this moment at least – connected us all.

And as the dawn evaporates into light outside, the dancers around us seem to have become purposeful in their dedication, more *hardcore*... Among us now, as if they came from nowhere, are the bear-like men in leather harnesses who have filtered in from the darkrooms downstairs, stripped down to jockstraps to display muscled hairiness and sturdy masculinity, and the slender young lads in Adidas shorts and football socks like wayward strikers gone astray after a cup-winning bender, and the headstrong divas disrobed to reveal their diaphanous lingerie, and those characters with such androgynous features and peculiar garments who in this dim light could be of any or every gender. *All freaks, all beautiful…* A lanky transvestite cools the DJ with his fan as churning loops of rhythm coalesce out of the mix and then begin to rise and rise again, steadily at first and then racing harder towards another crescendo, until the DJ reins the beat in, tempting and teasing, before going back in again for the next gradual ascent towards release.

It seems like days ago now that we were in that cavernous entrance hall and marvelled at all those so-serious dancers getting changed into aerobic disco gear in preparation for the most punishing of workouts, then headed for the stairs towards the turbine room, anticipation gathering as the muffled pounding of the drums emerged into focus. In front of us at the top of the stairs, two elegant silhouettes appeared to be cut out against the white light – male or female or maybe something else, and anyway who really cares in here? – and then we gazed down in awe at the rippling mass of adrenalised flesh on the dancefloor below, reverberating with the irrepressible force of human vitality.

With the walls stretching 18 metres from the concrete floor to the ceiling of the old power plant, Berghain seemed more like a set from Fritz Lang's *Metropolis* than a nightclub, its monumental brutalist architecture seemingly designed to make the individual feel so small as to be almost invisible in the face of an all-powerful, inscrutable force. The dancers below looked as if they could be fabulous extras in this grand drama of sound and chemistry and lust, perfectly costume-designed in austere black or brilliant white, arms inked with cryptic hieroglyphs and runic phrases, hair slashed with flawless barbarity.

Up another metal staircase to Panoramabar on the next floor, where a little filtered light seeped in through a colour-gelled window, red, green, blue and yellow like some kind of secular stained glass in this basilica of emancipated desires, casting a soft warmth over the people sprawled underneath, caressing each other's bare skin while they take brief respite from their exertions and recharge themselves with all manner of pills and powders and potions.

As the hours pass, it feels like some kind of psychological barrier has been breached and all the repressed fantasies are pouring out and everyone has somehow dissolved into the mass, into the music itself… and in the darkened alcoves and secluded cloisters, the boys are snorting and sucking greedily, babbling and philosophising and declaring their love and vowing eternal friendship and saying all those other things that need to be said before the long night's journey into day is finally over.

'Berlin was always hardcore.'

Tanith

Berghain was the pre-eminent symbol of Berlin nightlife in the second decade of the twenty-first century. Imposing and mysterious, mythologised and feared and adored as any nightclub ever had been, this grey hulk of a former East German heat-and-electricity-generating plant was the grandest landmark of the techno capital of Europe. It could rekindle all those cloudy half-remembered sensations of lost immaculate nights in warehouses and aircraft hangars and old factories – those huge spaces in which we had lost ourselves deliciously and utterly in transcendent oblivion – but it was not those places, hijacked for a one-night stand in the darkness. Standing stern and seemingly invulnerable in the nondescript streets near the Ostbahnhof, Berghain was an institution; one that could only have come into being through the collective will for it to exist, the efforts of an able and committed few to make that happen, and the historical serendipity that had allowed all of it to be possible.

It was a club that existed because of the political and cultural forces which had converged over the previous decades, coming together in a specific time and place at the epicentre of a historic upheaval – in Berlin, at the end of the Cold War and the beginning of the reunification of Germany.

As the muted throb of techno pulses through the walls of a cluttered office up another metal staircase in another hulk of a former heat-and-electricity-generating plant on the opposite side of the River Spree, Dimitri Hegemann, the founder of the Tresor club, tries to explain how we got here, and how he arrived at the right time to be part of it all.

'I came from this small village and I moved to West Berlin in 1978 because of the things I wanted to do – I wanted to change the world but I couldn't do it in the village. My parents were from the war generation; it was very Catholic, nobody wanted to talk about sexuality,' Hegemann recalls, abstractedly sweeping back his floppy white hair. 'I was inspired by Woodstock, by seeing Pink Floyd, by this hippie idea of community. So I moved to Berlin looking for a community, and I found a lot of people like me who wanted to change things too.'

At that point, Berlin had been divided between communist East and capitalist West since the Wall – the 'anti-fascist protection barrier', as the East German authorities called it – went up in 1961, and the city was split into four zones overseen by the United States, France, Britain and the Soviet Union. In the middle was no man's land, with its barbed wire and armed sentries and military observation posts – a constant reminder that the city remained on the frontline of a frozen conflict.

Berlin had been a bohemian metropolis in the pre-World War Two years of the Weimar Republic, but in the post-war period, it had become something altogether darker and more forbidding. It's hard to imagine now that the German capital is a thriving European cultural powerhouse, but in the seventies and eighties it was regarded as one of the grimmest places in the Western world.

But because young West German males could avoid military service if they lived in West Berlin, and because rents were cheap and benefits more generous in this parcel of land that was marooned deep in Eastern Bloc territory, it naturally attracted nonconformists and free-thinkers who found creative nourishment in its sombre gloom and bizarre isolation – squatters, anarchists, left-wing activists, punks, gays, artists, musicians like David Bowie and Iggy Pop, and refugees from conservative small-town Germany like Dimitri Hegemann.

'Berlin was like an island, it collected many people who thought differently and had different ideas about how things could work. Open-minded people. In German we use the word *querdenker* – mavericks,' says Hegemann.

Some of these mavericks came together at the Geniale Dilletanten festival, Berlin's seminal postpunk gathering of the clans in 1981. Hegemann then started the annual Atonal festival, which showcased industrial music heroes like Psychic TV and Test Department as well as their local comrades Einstürzende Neubauten. West Germany already had a history of musical innovation going back to Kraftwerk and Tangerine Dream, Can, Faust and Amon Düül II and the *kosmische* sound known in Britain as Krautrock. The Neue Deutsche Welle movement – Germany's postpunk movement – threw up new variations, spiky electro-punk outfits like Düsseldorf's DAF and the Berlin-based Malaria!, while in the mid-eighties, a young man who would become Berlin's first DJ pop star was also making his first electronic tracks.

Westbam, whose real name is Maximilian Lenz, had originally styled himself Westfalia Bambaataa in tribute to South Bronx hip-hop pioneer Afrika Bambaataa and the West German region of Westphalia from which he himself came. Westbam had played at the Geniale Dilletanten festival under the alias Frank Zerox, released his novelty hit '17 (This is Not a Boris Becker Song)' in 1983, and moved to Berlin and started playing Hi-NRG, hip-hop and electro-pop at the Metropol club the year afterwards. In 1984, he also wrote a seminal article entitled 'What is Record Art?', in which he made the case for hip-hop cutting and scratching as a new sonic departure – 'not only a new way of presenting music, but actually a completely new production method for a new kind of music,' he insisted.[1]

After hip-hop came the sounds of Chicago, Detroit and New York – sounds that would change everything for Berlin. Matthias Roeingh, an idealistic young dreamer who had played in a punk band called DPA that also appeared at the Geniale Dilletanten festival, and went on to become a DJ in the late eighties under the name Dr. Motte, describes the early house and techno imports that managed to reach the city in those days as almost talismanic objects.

'Suddenly there came this new music – house music! – and it was totally different than what was before,' Motte recalls. 'And it was not just new music, it was a new life, a new atmosphere, and suddenly everyone was dancing. It was the beginning of the beginning.'

For Motte, acid house was the key to unlock a new psychic realm. 'It was like discovering a new territory. There was a wall in Berlin and then suddenly there is a door in that wall, and you can look *behind*... it was incredible. It opened up our minds and we discovered ourselves.'[2]

Motte claims credit for staging the first ever acid house party in West Berlin at the Turbine Rosenheim club in September 1988, along with another DJ called Jonzon (Jürgen Stöckemann). By the end of that year, Hegemann and his colleague Achim Kohlberger had also set up the first permanent acid house venue, UFO, in the cellar of the Fischbüro, a Dadaist bar they were running in an old shoe shop. Motte and Jonzon would become two of its resident DJs, alongside others who would form the nucleus of the early Berlin scene, people like Tanith and Kid Paul.

While the city was still divided, teenagers living on the other side of the Wall in East Berlin could listen to radio broadcasts from the west side – Barry Graves' influential disco-mix shows on the US-run RIAS station, or John Peel on the British Forces Broadcasting Service, or Monika Dietl propagandising the early house scene on Berlin broadcaster SFB's youth channel. 'We taped all of it. We lived off those tape mixes,' said Wolle XDP (Wolfram Neugebauer), an East Berliner who would become an influential DJ and rave promoter. There had been small hip-hop and postpunk scenes on the eastern side of the Wall, but discovering techno and house for the first time was exhilarating, even though it wasn't yet possible to hear it in a club, recalled Frank Blümel, another East Berliner: 'It gave you energy,' Blümel said. 'East Germany was collapsing so it was the music that we drew our energy from.'[3]

On 9 November 1989, after months of demonstrations and as increasing numbers of people fled the country, the East German authorities unexpectedly decided to open up the border crossings and let people pass through freely. The barrier which had divided the city for almost three decades was breached and Berlin erupted in celebration. 'This has to be the biggest rave this century, only there's no house music,' techno producer Stephan Fischer told visiting British journalist Jack Barron that evening while they watched people on Potsdamer Platz hammering away in unison as they began to demolish the despised concrete structure and bring the city together.[4]

'It came totally by surprise. Nobody believed it at first. It was like, "No, it can't be happening!" We knew there would probably be some changes in the East but you never thought the Wall would come down. It was the last thing that anybody was expecting,' says Thomas Andrezak, another charismatic ex-punk, who had taken the name Tanith. This gaunt and imposing figure with an impeccable flair for rave theatrics became perhaps the hardest and most uncompromising of Berlin's original techno DJs, first at UFO and then at Dimitri Hegemann's next club, Tresor – but also at the city's first raves, the Tekknozid parties run by Wolle XDP, which started in April 1990 and were held in venues like the Haus der Jüngen Talente, an East German state youth centre.

Techno was the common musical language that brought young people together in those first months after the Wall was breached, believes Tanith. It appeared in the right place and at the right time to become the soundtrack and inspiration for the first major German youth culture of the post-Wall era, on both sides of the former barrier. It was too new to be defined by past divisions or to be 'owned' by either side; it belonged to everyone who wanted to be part of it. 'East and West, we started at zero together,' Tanith says. 'Techno was the first youth culture that started at zero on both sides. All of us came together at this zero point and there was no difference where you were from.'[5]

What Westbam describes as Germany's 'liberation dance' had begun. 'When the Wall came down, imagine all these kids coming out of this oppressed state, and the police not knowing how to act anymore because they didn't have any more authority,' Westbam explains. 'All these things you have been fantasising about, they are now all possible. I remember at the early raves in the days after the Wall came down, they had never been full but now they were packed and there were all these East German cars outside the club. You could feel the energy – it was like a vacuum going pop.'

Techno was to become the soundtrack of reunification and Berlin was to be its new European home. 'It was like everything has been set to zero now, everything else from the past doesn't matter, we're starting something new,' says journalist Tobias Rapp, who moved to Berlin in 1990 at the age of 19 and became caught up in the early scene. 'It's somehow a very German idea in pop culture, to start from scratch – it has to do with the Nazis; pop culture is always saying, "We can't be linked to the past, we have to start anew."'

And Berlin was ready for the new. It already had its creative counterculture, its Geniale Dilletanten and its anarchist squatters who had become adept at occupying vacant properties. Now it had fresh innocent energy from the inquisitive young explorers from the East and scores of enticing old factories and warehouses left abandoned by the collapse of the East German regime. Free spaces had opened up around where the Wall had slashed through the centre of the city. It was time to recolonise them.

'Lots of industrial buildings in East Berlin became empty because the companies were owned by the state and the state didn't exist anymore, so nobody gave a fuck,' says Robert Henke, who also moved to Berlin in 1990 and would go on to record hypnotic electronic soundscapes under the name Monolake. 'So you could go into former workspaces where everything had just been left because they had closed down – a coffee mug with coffee in it was still there, the newspaper from two days before the Wall came down was still there – it was like after a nuclear explosion. And you just walked in and turned it into a club.'

Berlin also had some of the most liberal licensing laws in Europe. Its clubs and bars had been able to open around the clock since the post-World War Two curfew was abolished in 1949, when a hotelier called Heinz Zellermayer convinced the commanders of the occupied sectors to relax the licensing regulations.

The Wall-era counterculture of West Berlin had been a sort of training camp for the techno scene, suggests Hegemann. 'When the Wall came down, hundreds of small cells started to do things, but the seeds came from this subcultural movement in West Berlin,' he explains. 'We were prepared to experiment. We knew how to do a bar, a gallery, a club. We could fill the empty spaces that opened up. For three years, there were no authorities and we could do anything we wanted.'

'There are a lot of senses in which the Second World War didn't end in Berlin until the Wall came down,' says Dave Rimmer, the author of *Once Upon a Time in the East*, one of the great Berlin books of the period. 'Once it did come down, everything started changing *really fast*, and you had no idea where the changes were going to stop. It was absolutely the right time for a new kind of music – a genuine *Stunde Null* [hour zero] feeling – and techno also had that sense of ripping up the past, kicking out the old, accelerating into the future.'[6]

After UFO closed, Hegemann and his partners started looking for a new venue. They found it close to the no man's land of Potsdamer Platz, a site of immense psychogeographical significance. Potsdamer Platz had been the heart of Berlin nightlife in the Weimar years, and then home to various Nazi administration buildings during Hitler's reign, but had been bombed into rubble by the Allies during World War Two before the Wall went up across it. Now it existed as a kind of urban wasteland, waiting for new life.

Hegemann says that the first time he descended into the crepuscular underground room on Leipziger Strasse that would become the Tresor club in 1991, it was like opening up the tomb of an ancient pyramid. It was the abandoned vault of the former Wertheim department store which decades earlier had been expropriated from its Jewish owners by the Nazis.

'When I first saw it, I knew something special would happen there, but we had no idea that techno and electronic music would take off as it did,' he says. 'It was a perfect location, right near the Wall, perfect for kids from east and west to come together. It was symbolic of a new beginning and a new generation of music.'

Going down into the Tresor basement, with its low ceiling, cage-like steel partitions and old bank fittings on the walls, was like descending into an infernal netherworld, with a sound system so powerful it made your internal organs vibrate in time with the heaviest and most metallic of techno.

'My first night at Tresor I can only describe as a shock,' recalls Robert Henke. 'It was overwhelming in almost every way. It was louder than I ever experienced music before, it had more bass, it was darker, it was more intense, it was more people in less space... just complete craziness. The light show was basically a red strobe, a blue strobe, a white strobe and tons of fog. I was there for half an hour and I had to leave, it was just too much – and the next weekend I was back, of course. It was deeply confusing and at the same time fascinating.'

As was Berlin, as the city began to reinvent itself in those chaotic and lawless years that followed the fall of the Wall and the end of the Communist East German Deutsche Demokratische Republik the year afterwards with the reunification of the country in October 1990. Tanith remembers it as a time of psychic liberation made possible by the absence of any kind of certainty. 'At that time you could do anything. You could just open doors and move in and do something because nobody knew what is the law and what is not,' he says. 'We thought: we have a new playground, we can do what we want now.'

All manner of wild schemes now seemed feasible, many of them inspired by altered states of consciousness. Hegemann even convinced an official at East Germany's prestigious Humboldt University on the grand thoroughfare of Under den Linden to allow psychedelic evangelist Timothy Leary to give a keynote lecture in 1990, just before the East German state ceased to exist: 'I said, "I have a professor coming over from Harvard, is it possible to have the main auditorium?" He said, "Hmmmm... OK, yes!" He wanted to show he was "open to the West" now. So Timothy Leary came and he made a great speech – "From Psychedelics to Cybernetics", it was called. Things like that were possible in those days.'

Leary, who really had been a Harvard University professor until he was fired in 1963 amid controversy about his advocacy of LSD, was trying at the turn of the nineties to rebrand himself as a father figure to the E generation. Those who came to hear him speak were fascinated by his outspoken promotion of psychedelic experimentation, says Mark Reeder, the founder of the first Berlin trance label, MfS, who was in the audience.

'We listened intensely and hung onto his every word. He was a bit like a mystic, confirming everything we already believed. Remember, almost all the kids of East Germany had never experienced hard drugs of any kind, maybe only prescription drugs, or alcohol and cigarettes, nothing up until the fall of the Berlin Wall, and so they were very inquisitive, especially when it came to psychedelic drugs… and here was the guru himself, talking about it,' Reeder recalls. 'As Timothy said, "My job is to corrupt young people."' The lecture was sampled for an album by System 01, which Hegemann released. 'Any Reality is an Opinion', one track was called – a title that summed up the moment as well as anything could.

The city also began to attract new mavericks who were seeking spaces free from control and social orthodoxy, including a couple of Britain's most notorious free-party crews, who set up camp on Potsdamer Platz. Salvage-sculpture art-travellers the Mutoid Waste Company built a dayglo-painted Stonehenge out of decommissioned Eastern Bloc tanks and sowed the ground with Soviet MiG fighter jets which had apparently been discarded by the Red Army when they pulled out of East Germany. The Mutoids were joined by Spiral Tribe, the techno sound system militants who fled Britain after four of their leaders were indicted on conspiracy charges for their role in staging Britain's biggest-ever free illegal rave at Castlemorton Common in May 1992.

Even for Berlin, Spiral Tribe were hardcore. Many people on the city scene at the time found their uncompromising attitude, apocalyptic music and seemingly insatiable appetite for drugs too extreme to comprehend – 'a real attack against the social norm', according to DJ Alec Empire, who helped to organise some parties with them while they were in town.[7]

But for the Spirals, Berlin was just a temporary stopover where they managed to amass a decommissioned arsenal of cast-off Soviet military hardware before setting off eastwards to stage outlaw parties that inspired a whole new illegal rave movement. 'Going out into Eastern Europe was really like a feeling of pushing it beyond the frontiers of what we know,' Spiral Tribe's Mark Harrison told me later. 'We had a huge convoy, two MiG fighter planes on tank transporters, huge circus trailers and massive six-wheel-drive amphibious vehicles... It was like being musclebound.'[8]

With Tresor ensconced in its subterranean strobe-lit vault, other clubs opened in similarly unconventional spaces, repurposing what the past had left behind to create an alternative vision of the future of the city. The Bunker – which described itself as 'the world's hardest club' because of its brutal gabba and acid soundtrack – occupied a huge Nazi-era air-raid shelter which had also been used as a Red Army detention centre for prisoners of war. Planet opened in an old soap factory in 1991; three years later, its promoters would also launch the monumental E-Werk club in a former power plant near Checkpoint Charlie.

After the Wall came down, people could explore ideas and spaces that were off limits during the years of division. Some German ravers even took to wearing camouflage fatigues, gas masks and radiation suits, as if they had formed a survivalist cult ready to traverse the harshest frontiers of this strange new world of chaotic political uncertainty. Tanith and his camouflage-clad techno crew meanwhile looked like a renegade gang of *Mad Max* marauders on a psychotropic mission beyond the frontiers of civilisation. 'We had hooligans and students and ex-punks and ex-disco people and we all got into this big melting pot and realised we are all together, we are all humans,' Tanith says, before adding with a conspiratorial smile: 'I think the Ecstasy helped...'

Like the early acid house scene in Britain, there was a feeling that they were all part of a secret society; adepts who were scaling the peaks of human experience, bound together by sound and chemistry on their great adventure into the unknown. 'It was certainly not normal,' remembers Robert Henke. 'You clearly felt you belonged to a small community of people who had different ideas; that was very strong.

Part of the beauty for me was that I felt I had suddenly found people who think on the same wavelength. This was incredibly beautiful.'

In his office at Tresor, Dimitri Hegemann leaps up out of his chair and pulls down a couple of old vinyl albums from the top of a filing cabinet, records that he released on his Interfisch label before the Tresor club got started in 1991: *Buried Dreams* by British industrial band Clock DVA, and Final Cut's *Deep into the Cut*. Final Cut were an electronic body music duo from Detroit, inspired by Front 242, Nitzer Ebb and Ministry: 'Heavy beats, handmade edits, very modern at the time, pointing to the way things were going,' Hegemann says. Crucially, one member of Final Cut was the young Jeff Mills, before he quit the band to set up Underground Resistance with Mike Banks. Hegemann brought Final Cut over to play at his Atonal festival, and it turned out to be the beginning of a passionate cultural relationship between Berlin and Detroit that would endure for decades to come.

The first release on Hegemann's new Tresor label was 'Sonic Destroyer' by X-101, an Underground Resistance alias. With its slasher riff and sinister, surging drones, it was the perfect soundtrack for the Tresor basement. Hegemann then flew in UR's Mike Banks, Jeff Mills, Blake Baxter and Robert Hood to play at the club in 1991 – another pivotal moment. Down in the Tresor sweatbox, the black-masked marauders from Detroit unleashed a fearsome sonic assault that laid waste to the past and illuminated a pathway to the future. 'A bomb of sound and smoke went off and blew everything away,' Hegemann recalled. 'It was something special. An incredible intensity. For me, the way forward was totally clear after that.'[9]

Berlin was to become so much of a home from home for the Detroiters that Mills and Baxter even relocated to the city for several years in the nineties. Here was a place that could support them economically as well as creatively, at a time when most people in their own country had no idea that their music even existed. Robert Hood says that a common bond developed because they were all using the alchemical energies of techno to liberate themselves from a shattered environment bequeathed to them by a brutal past. The Detroit native hadn't travelled much at that point, but he felt an immediate emotional connection when he arrived in Berlin: 'The impression I had was of a city that was still in the process of coming out of darkness through underground progressive art. Like Detroit, you had this progressive scene that was emerging from the basements, from the cellars, from the bunkers,' Hood recalls. 'The music that we were making was "hard music from a hard city" – that was our battle cry – and I think Berlin connected with that because it was also trying to get past its own past. You had these two cities trying to express themselves to get through adversity.'

Tresor's second major compilation album was subtitled 'Berlin Detroit: A Techno Alliance' and featured tracks by UR and Mills, and a collaboration between Juan Atkins and two Berlin-based producers, Thomas Felhmann and Moritz von Oswald, under the name 3MB ('Three Men in Berlin'). On the shelves of Fehlmann's studio in the genteel Charlottenberg district of the city, among the mementoes of his long and illustrious career in electronic music, are old master tapes labelled with the first names of some of Detroit's originators: 'Juan', 'Eddie', 'Blake'. Swiss-born Felhmann, who many years later went on to join The Orb, was another veteran of the eighties Neue Deutsche Welle movement, when he played with postpunk band Palais Schaumburg alongside Moritz von Oswald. Both Fehlmann and von Oswald would become pivotal figures in the new Berlin techno scene, giving it yet more countercultural depth and history.

'I fell madly in love with this music from Detroit. It changed my perception,' Fehlmann recalls. After his new heroes began to visit Berlin, he started to record with them: 'When they first came here, the Detroit guys opened themselves up as humans because they felt comfortable in these surroundings. They had the space to express themselves, to play their music for people on a regular basis and to hear their music played in clubs on a regular basis, and they saw how it connected with people.'

As well as the fiery rave tracks coming out of Britain, Holland and Belgium, the Detroit musicians' Afro-futurist visions became a kind of psychic catalyst for the movement that would redefine the cultural landscape of Berlin, transform its eighties image as a lugubrious Cold

War enclave and rebrand it as one of Europe's most vital and creative cities. In the wealthier, more socially conventional German city of Frankfurt around the same time, DJs and producers like Sven Väth, Marc Spoon (Markus Löffel), Jam El Mar (Rolf Ellmer) and DJ Dag (Dag Lerner) were developing the sumptuously melodic textures of trance at clubs like Dorian Gray and the Omen, but Detroit techno was Berlin's guiding spirit.

The Detroiters' admiration for German electronic music also gave the Berliners confidence to explore their own interpretations of what techno could mean, at a time when dance culture was dominated by the US and Britain. This was still a period when European electronic music – Kraftwerk, DAF and Yello aside – was often disdained, Fehlmann says: 'When we met them, German electronic dance music, in fact electronic dance music from mainland Europe in general, was not considered to be particularly hip. So our self-image at that time was rather low. But when I connected with the Detroit guys and they told us about their big influence that came from Germany, that started to change.'

Felhmann's friend Mark Ernestus had already opened the Hard Wax record shop in Kreuzberg, which established itself as a daytime social hub for Berlin's techno DJs. Around the shop and around clubs like Tresor grew a nexus of creative talent that would give the world some of the most beautiful electronic music ever recorded – the sublime, mesmeric dub-techno of Ernestus and Moritz von Oswald's Basic Channel label and its successor, Chain Reaction, which would both remain hugely influential for many years to come. German electronic dance music would never again be seen as inferior.

'Friends of mine told me about underground parties they went to in London, Manchester and Sheffield, where police came and stopped the parties and took the sound system but people were still dancing outside in the streets with ghetto blasters, having a street party. Ah, *street party*! It was immediately in my mind, how can we do that here? A spontaneous street party – *how*?'

Dr. Motte

A few months before the Wall was breached in 1989, Dr. Motte was standing outside a club in the early hours of the morning when he had a vision. It was a vision of himself and his friends, the frontiersmen of acid house, coming out of the darkness and into the light in a glorious burst of colour and sound which would illuminate the city centre – a protest march, not *against* anything, but *for* the raver's values of good vibrations and ecstatic unity: 'I said, let's declare a demonstration, and do it with our music. And call it Love Parade.'[10]

But unlike most 3am visionaries, Motte hadn't forgotten about it the next day. He applied for the event to be registered as a political demonstration, which meant that he wouldn't have to pay for the policing or the post-party clean-up. He chose a slogan – 'Friede, Freude, Eierkuchen' – 'Peace, Joy and Pancakes'. And the same year as the British police were doing their best to bust any open-air rave they could find, the Berlin authorities issued him a permit and told him to go ahead.

The first Love Parade in July 1989 brought together around 150 people, the nucleus of Berlin's emerging acid house scene. 'There was a fine rain, like British weather, raining but not exactly raining,' Motte recalls. 'We stood there and didn't know when to start. Then the police came and asked us: "Do you want to start now?"' He laughs at the absurdity: 'We had no clue! Nobody had done it before...'[11]

They played mixtapes of club anthems pre-recorded by DJs Westbam, Jonzon and Kid Paul from speakers mounted on three little vans as this raggedy tribe of mavericks – some of them wearing Smiley T-shirts for the occasion – danced down the Kurfürstendamm, West Berlin's main shopping drag, flashing peace signs and freaking out the Saturday shoppers. 'Even though it was just this handful of people, in a crazy way we felt that we were writing history,' says Westbam. 'But would anybody on that day have said that in a few years there would be a million people [at the Love Parade]? I don't think so. If you had told me the Wall would come down a few months later? No, no!'[12]

As the Berlin techno scene gathered strength, the Love Parade became its most prominent public symbol. By 1992, there were a couple of dozen sound-system floats from clubs like Tresor and Planet on the parade and numbers had grown to 15,000 people, coming from Frankfurt, Cologne, Munich, Dresden and Leipzig as well as Berlin. An incredible mass, it seemed to me at the time as I gazed out over the churning crowd of ravers from a float run by *i-D*, the magazine I was editing at the time, and NovaMute, a new techno label set up by Mute Records, the home of Depeche Mode. As I marvelled at the sheer energy of the parade, the screeching strings and clattering rhythm of that year's anthem, 'Der Klang der Familie' by 3Phase and Dr. Motte, erupted from the speakers over and over again.

Tanith's truck that year was like a military assault vehicle draped in camouflage and netting, with his wild-eyed acolytes in camouflage fatigues setting off orange flares as they surged past; the following year he would arrive at the parade on a decommissioned Soviet tank, waving a voodoo skull from its gun turret like a techno shaman conjuring ritualistic mayhem from the crowds.

As the parade ended and the sound-system trucks pulled into Wittenbergplatz, the skies opened and rain came scything down, with lightning flashing like a strobe and thunder booming out an awesome counterpoint to the hammering of techno beats while smoke machines blurted white foggy clouds into the evening air and rain-drenched ravers lifted their arms skywards to embrace the downpour as they capered and pranced along the glistening pavements. In an era of great techno parties, the Love Parade seemed to have taken it to the next level.

'The Love Parade symbolised this new optimism and this anarchic energy,' says Sven von Thülen, co-author of the essential history of Berlin techno, also entitled *Der Klang der Familie*. 'For the first years, I think it was an annual meeting point for the culture so you could see how powerful it was.' It was also a symbolic reclaiming of public space, showing that the city streets could be places for communal celebration as well as commerce and traffic.

But what I thought in 1992 was an enormous gathering of Germany's techno clans was actually tiny in comparison to what would follow. The Love Parade grew exponentially each summer, and by 1995, numbers had reached 280,000 – far too many for the Ku'damm. The next year, it moved to the Strasse des 17. Juni, which runs from the Brandenburg Gate through the lush expanse of the Tiergarten park, past the Siegessäule, the Prussian victory column topped by a golden winged statue. This was the street that the Nazis had once used for their parades; now it had become a place for mass festivities. 'The Love Parade made it possible to have a million people on a street like that and not think of Hitler. It really changed the perception of Germany and of Germans,' says von Thülen.[13]

In 1997, the organisers estimated that a million people had joined the festivities. The world's media became entranced by the annual extravaganza and its exuberant images of photogenic girls in fluorescent bra-tops going wild with water pistols, bare-chested boys waving and screaming in delight as they hung from lamp posts high above the dancing crowds and lasers flashing back and forth across the Siegessäule as epic trance tracks soared through the evening air.

But at the same time, some of the original Love Parade ravers, the ones who had graduated from the postpunk underground of the eighties, were becoming disillusioned with the mass-market music, the ubiquitous sponsorship, the bland Love Parade 'anthems' that were released each year by Westbam's Low Spirit label, and the sense that a subcultural happening had turned into a tourist attraction with about as much dissident spirit as the Munich beer festival. 'The Love Parade has sold its soul in the truest sense of the phrase,' Frankfurt DJ Sven Väth, who had once been one of the event's most enthusiastically flamboyant participants, said in 2001.[14]

From 1996 onwards, Motte's annual demonstration was also targeted by its own counterdemonstration, a rival protest staged by techno anarchists who believed that the Love Parade had become a bloated charade. Initially called the Hate Parade but renamed the Fuck Parade the year afterwards, it became an annual march against gentrification and commercialisation and for spiky, disruptive techno.

'The Love Parade claimed to be political, but "peace, joy and pancakes" is not really a political statement,' says Thomas Rupp, one of the Fuck Parade's organisers. 'The idea of the Love Parade was only about sponsors and only about money. The Love Parade organisers were always claiming that they were supporting the subculture but they were not, so we were fighting against that. This was underground against mainstream.'[15]

The Love Parade peaked around the turn of the millennium and then slowly started to decline in size. When the Berlin authorities finally decided that they would no longer issue the parade a permit to operate as a political demonstration, the organisers couldn't afford to pay for the policing and the clean-up, so it was cancelled in 2004 and 2005.

Eventually they decided to sell the Love Parade name to a German tycoon called Rainer Schaller, president of the low-cost exercise-club chain McFit, who supplied the money so that it could return to the Strasse des 17. Juni in 2006. Dr. Motte was furious and decided to quit the event that he had dreamed up one ecstatic night so many years earlier in the old divided city.

'This is the question I have: if you have a culture and a happening that goes with it, does this happening belong to the culture, or in private hands?' Motte asks. 'I thought it should be not-for-profit forever because this culture belongs to everybody. You can sell a brand, but not a spirit.'

The 2006 Love Parade would be the last to be held in Berlin. The following year, Schaller made the decision to move it to the industrial Ruhr Valley. Motte was in despair: 'Politicians wanted the image of a young creative city and we gave them this picture,' he says. 'But then they killed an event that was such a worldwide advertisement for Berlin and brought so much money to the city every year.'[16]

After successful events in Essen in 2007 and Dortmund in 2008, the following year's parade, which was scheduled to take place in Bochum, was cancelled because the local authorities believed that they could not host so many ravers safely. In July 2010, the parade was set to take place in Duisburg, a dour coal-mining and steel-making city. Even beforehand, the event looked like it had become a dismal parody of its former self – there would be no parade through the city, no symbolic reclaiming of public space, and the sound-system floats would only trundle around the arena, a former railway freight station, before the rave began.

The city's mayor was excited by the anticipated revenue and eagerly announced that he expected around 1.4 million ravers to join the dance, even though the arena only had a capacity of around 250,000. But advance planning by the organisers and local authorities was wretched, and as the floats started to roll, a massive crush of ravers started to build up at the entrance tunnel to the arena. Panic took hold as ravers stampeded in fear, crushing each other to death in their desperate attempts to flee. Twenty-one people were killed and more than 500 injured.

German current-affairs magazine *Der Spiegel* reported that the tragedy was the result of 'a series of failures made by the city, the police and the event organisers' who had ignored safety warnings, failed to provide escape routes and were prepared to admit almost twice as many people as their permit allowed.[17]

A police union leader claimed that the victims had been 'sacrificed for material interests', while Motte accused the organisers of dangerous negligence: 'When we did Love Parade in Berlin, our first point was safety, safety, safety, and then music. Their first point was profit,' he alleged.

Immediately afterwards, McFit boss Schaller announced that the party was over, forever: 'Out of respect for the victims, the Love Parade will never take place again.'[18]

'Record Art is minimal music, it is unpopular and uncommercial.'
Westbam, 'What is Record Art?', 1984

After the millennium, the landscape of Berlin club culture was transformed yet again as its focus shifted eastwards when many of the original techno venues were displaced from the central Mitte district by redevelopment projects. The Bunker was shut down by a police raid in 1996 and E-Werk closed its doors the year afterwards. Tresor would hang on in Mitte until 2005, but it too would eventually move east to a huge former heating plant close to the Spree. Dimitri Hegemann had hoped to develop its original Leipziger Strasse home into a multifunctional Tresor Tower, but instead an insurance company moved in. He took some of the rusty old Wertheim bank deposit boxes with him and installed them in the new venue to give it some of the feel of the old.

The clubs of the nineties had always felt like temporary boltholes which were never intended to become established entertainment institutions – and that was part of their charm, of course. So now it was time for change again. 'It was necessary after this whole hysteria and this massive energy rush,' suggests Sven von Thülen. 'Then the scene continued and got even stronger.'

It was also time for new sounds and new vibes, for new clubs to take the scene forward. A time for new DJ stars playing a new form of techno – repetitive, softly insistent, endlessly looping and evolving in almost unperceivable graduations, the sound of a scene turning back in on itself: *minimal*, as it became known. The name probably came from Robert Hood's classic album *Minimal Nation*, in which he tried to strip out all extraneous influences to intensify the focus on the unadorned essentials. Hood never expected his work to have such an impact: 'I did not realise that it would affect people to the point where it took on its own life,' he says. 'It's like you've programmed a robot, but then that robot starts to think on its own and feel and move and create.'

The minimal techno tracks released by labels like Perlon, Kompakt and Richie Hawtin's Minus became the soundtrack of the mid-2000s after-party era, when club nights seemed to be just the warm-up for the Sunday that followed, for the hours when time stretched out of shape and reality warped into all kinds of unpredictable forms, when the flamboyantly chic and the elegantly wasted partied right into Monday morning at infamously licentious dives like Bar 25 on the banks of the Spree.

But the mid-2000s would also see the emergence of another new phenomenon that would have a growing impact on the Berlin scene – a huge influx of techno tourists using low-cost airlines for weekend raving missions to the city. At Tegel Airport, the arrivals hall would be full of young clubbers in skinny jeans and T-shirts decorated with the oblique logos of techno labels, wheeling their suitcases towards the bus queue while dreaming of the nights to come. Tourism boomed in Berlin in the 2000s, with the number of visitors to Berlin rising dramatically from 13 million overnight stays in 2004 to 27 million in 2013. Music was key to this because it reshaped Berlin's image and acted as an 'essential business driver for the city', according to Tobias Maul, a publicity officer at the city tourism authority, visitBerlin. 'The techno scene in particular is very important. One could say that it is some kind of hallmark for the German capital,' Maul told me, confirming how seriously nightlife was taken by the municipal authorities as a revenue-generator.

Tobias Rapp, a veteran raver who had become culture editor for *Der Spiegel*, published a book called *Lost and Sound* about the round-the-clock clubbing scene in the minimal era, which identified the techno tourists as the 'Easyjet set'. After hearing increasing amounts of foreign accents while queueing to get into clubs like Berghain, Rapp realised that low-cost airlines were changing the cultural landscape of the city. As Europe became increasingly integrated, Berlin's 'club mile' had turned into a kind of nocturnal Schengen Zone. The rave scene had long championed communication across borders, but the impulse was boosted by the relaxation of air transport regulations, which led to a huge expansion in routes and a fall in the cost of fares. 'We're seeing the formation of new public networks which aren't bound by national frameworks,' he suggested in the book.[19]

But Rapp says that when he wrote *Lost and Sound* in the mid-2000s, he actually underestimated how far the whole thing might go. 'It looked very big back then, but it was in its early stages,' he explains. 'It was quite difficult to understand for a German, that a German city could be attractive for so many people from around the world. But this really exploded in a way that nobody could have predicted. What came out of it was this strange situation of a big city, Berlin, which turns into a world metropolis, not on an economic basis but on a cultural basis. Cities like Paris or New York became world cities because of trade or finance or industry. Berlin doesn't have that – it just has culture.'

EasyJet ravers could make clubs feel like transient destinations – not exactly airport lounge discos, but not cohesive and contiguous social scenes where people see each other week after week and create some collective sense of purpose. The EasyJet raver simply arrived, partied through the weekend and then left again on the Monday plane without necessarily taking any active involvement in building the culture.

'Sometimes you have all these tourists coming and they don't give a shit about anything, they just want to get fucked up – "Let's have it large in Berlin, let's get wasted,"' says von Thülen. 'Obviously you have a lot of people coming who really know what Berlin's about, but then you have all these others who don't give a shit and just want to *consume* the idea of what Berlin is and not give anything back. It is an economy, obviously, and a lot of people live off that, but in the long run it fucks a city up. It turns it into a theme park.'

But some people did stay and give something back, and make music that enhanced Berlin's urban mythos. After the Detroit pioneers came DJ-producers like Richie Hawtin, Ricardo Villalobos, Miss Kittin (Caroline Hervé), Alan Oldham, Daniel Wang and Ewan Pearson, among many others, and for them, Berlin was not only cheap and convenient for onward travel to their gigs around Europe; it was endlessly inspiring. 'There's only one city in the world like this – it's not New York, it's not London, it's not Paris; there's only Berlin that is so vibrant in so many different ways,' argues Hawtin. The Chilean-born DJ Villalobos even pictured the city in the mid-2000s as a kind of freeform techno salon, a creative hothouse in which ideas were swapped, experiences shared and beats traded. 'It is amazing because we have parties together with all the artists, all the artists go to the studios of other artists. It's a very fertile city in this way,' he said.[20]

Villalobos was born in Santiago but his family fled Chile for Germany when he was three years old to escape Augusto Pinochet's military dictatorship after the right-wing coup in 1973. In the 2000s, he became the lord of the after-hours, the dissolute magus of minimal; his epic sets at parties in the riverside bars along the Spree were instant city legends. Moving with a distinctive off-kilter sway and playing with an idiosyncratic feel for unconventional rhythms and textures, he was a charismatic figurehead for the technoheads who Rapp described as the '72-hour party people'. Villalobos was also a truly visionary producer, the creator of *Fizheuer Zieheuer*, a bewitching 37-minute minimal masterpiece built around samples of a Balkan brass band, and the enchanting *Enfants*, constructed out of a snippet of children singing a song from Magma's extraordinary progressive rock epic from 1973, *Mëkanïk Dëstruktïẁ Kömmandöh*.

People like Villalobos and Hawtin provided fresh influences and helped inspire others to come to Berlin and bring yet more vitality, reshaping its image so that the dour and ominous walled city of the Cold War era was now not only seen as a hedonist wonderland, but as a centre of creativity.

'The scene had a massive role in developing and reinventing cultural life in Berlin,' says Thomas Fehlmann – although he admits that he didn't fully understand that at the time. 'When you are in the middle of it, you don't actually realise that you are inventing something. You only find out what it all means later,' he smiles.

'It is not about delicate, rarefied beauty, or ironic wit, or sentimental nostalgia. It is about the human body, the present moment – stamina, bliss, perpetual motion.'

Daniel Wang on Berghain, 2004

When it opened in 2004, Berghain, with its upstairs Panoramabar dancefloor and downstairs Lab.Oratory men-only sex club, seemed to have somehow refined all the nocturnal obsessions that the city had been pursuing since the eighties: rigorous techno, reclaimed industrial spaces, edgy bohemianism, sexual permissiveness, hedonistic abandon. 'The best club in the world' is a highly subjective accolade – a description that's been attached to places like the Paradise Garage in New York, Amnesia in Ibiza, the Haçienda in Manchester and so many other places over the decades – but for technoheads of a certain generation, Berghain was the one.

'It's the best club in the world because of the variety of experiences going on at the same time,' says Marea Stamper, an American DJ better known as The Black Madonna. 'In Berghain itself you have this amazing, enormous, chilly, mechanical techno machine. Then you walk up the steps into Panoramabar and it's this bright, warm, engaging, human celebration. Then you have the Lab which is this sweaty hypersexual space. For me, those three kinds of worlds are what created dance music as we understand it, and to have them all happening at once and people crossing between them is just so unique and special.'

The club's roots ran deep into the Berlin subculture that developed after the fall of the Wall in 1989. Its owners, Michael Teufele and Norbert Thormann, organised first their Snax sex parties in the nineties at the Bunker club, an abandoned World War Two air-raid shelter occupied by ravers in 1992 and run as a hardcore outpost for acid techno, gabba and BDSM parties, amongst other niche predilections, until it was raided and shuttered in 1996.

Two years later, Teufele and Thormann founded Ostgut in an old railway depot in the Friedrichshein district, which at the time was a drab and desolate sector of what had been East Berlin. It was a point when the energies of the post-Wall nightlife uprising had cooled, says Thilo Schneider, the reviews editor of the German electronic music magazine *Groove*, who was an Ostgut regular. The Love Parade had become commercialised and culturally neutered, E-Werk and the Bunker had both closed, Tresor had become a kind of institution, and techno appeared to be finished as a creative phenomenon, or so people were saying. The revolution was over – or was it?

'It was the end of the nineties, techno was out of fashion, but Ostgut was a place where people were still doing Ecstasy and having a great time, with parties going on until the afternoon,' Schneider recalls. 'It was a well-kept secret, no magazine wrote about it; it was really a special place for the people who went there and no one else. We wanted to keep it a secret because when something becomes too public, it loses its spirit. Nowadays, because of the internet, you couldn't do that.'

Ostgut finally closed in 2003 and the building was demolished to make way for a car park serving the huge O2 World entertainment arena. But Teufele and Thormann managed to secure an ambitious replacement – a fifties-era East German *Heizkraftwerk* near the Ostbahnhof which had shut in the twilight years of the DDR. The disused power plant, with its neoclassical façade, stark interior and vast turbine room, was absolutely colossal. 'When they showed me the place before it opened, I remember people were saying, "This is great, but you are crazy, it's so big,"' says Schneider, who edited the texts for Berghain's elaborate monthly flyers. 'It was a big risk. It could have gone totally wrong.'

Instead, Berghain became a Mecca for techno aficionados and a haven for sexual dissidents. It was much more than just a disco; it was also a subcultural meeting point, a nexus of musical creativity and an alternative arts institution. On an unprecedented scale.

A sign at the door in English, French, Russian and German warned sternly that photography was not permitted inside. At the entrance, the staff placed little stickers over the camera lenses of people's mobile phones; any transgressors spotted trying to take a quick snap were brusquely ejected. Even a Twitter feed called Inside Berghain made it clear that it would not contravene the club's no-photography rule: 'No pictures from inside,' it declared. 'No leaks. No sellout. No selfies.'

The almost complete absence of visual documentation of what happened inside – in an era when everything and everyone was photographed, all the time, and in the most banal of detail – not only allowed clubbers to discard their inhibitions and experiment with fantasies that they would not necessarily want to be captured in pictures, but also contributed to the club's powerful mystique. A night at Berghain would not be digitally preserved for posterity. It existed in its moment and only endured as memory, gossip, rumour or wild speculation. This was a kind of reality-blocking mechanism that cultivated a liberating sense of total disconnection from the everyday panopticon. Berghain was one of the few remaining places in Western Europe where you could exit the matrix.

'People want to be uncontrolled, but in a normal club in London or New York you have people walking around with earpieces, video cameras everywhere, toilets under surveillance – it's a complete atmosphere of control,' says the artist Wolfgang Tillmans, whose huge photographic prints on the Panoramabar walls were one of the club's great visual delights.

Inside Berghain, external influences were effectively erased and nothing mattered but the here and now. 'It's just a grey building with a black hole inside, so you can just project your own ideas and make it into whatever you like,' says Boris Dolinski, a resident DJ at Panoramabar. 'The most special thing is that you can just close your eyes and dissolve yourself into the music. You feel like you are somewhere that has no connection to the outside world at all.'

This feeling was enhanced by the lack of mirrors inside the club and the total absence of commercial branding. No illuminated logos whispering their corporate imprecations from the gloom, even from the beer fridges at the bar. In a club culture that had become desensitised to the ubiquity of sponsorship, it was another thing that set Berghain apart.

'I think that's quite remarkable,' says Tillmans. 'Nowadays every large gathering of people is seen as a marketing opportunity. But in Berghain it's not used. It must seem crazy to a marketing person to go to the club and see 2,000 happy faces and no message is being broadcasted to them. I think that is an active statement nowadays, more than it was before.'

Teufele and Thormann added to the mystique by consistently refusing to be interviewed. It was a smart move; anything they said could only have detracted from the legend that built up around the club, or undermined its esoteric allure.

In one of the rare public insights into their thinking, the American DJ Daniel Wang reported a conversation he had with the two men in 2004, the year that Berghain opened. It was one of the only credibly sourced explanations of their motives: 'Norbert and Michael stated that they wanted to create a club as a work of art,' Wang said.[21]

But a work of art sometimes needs care and protection. On the sandy track that led up to the club, corralled between metal barriers, the queue shuffled forwards slowly from midnight on Saturday through the following day, as hopeful clubbers nervously awaited inspection and possible rejection by the bouncers at the great building's entrance. The club's highly selective door policy became notorious in the years after it opened, with angry tales from those turned away proliferating online alongside tip sheets on how to look and act if you wanted to get in (which also added to the club's cultish image as some kind of techno secret society). The fearsome-looking Berghain bouncers were not so much rude as utterly *severe*, as if demanding that each guest made some kind of self-flagellating gesture of submission to the club's punishing physical regime. Their role was to be the gatekeepers to the otherworld, the frontline guardians of the freedoms inside.

'I feel like I have a responsibility to make Berghain a safe place for people who come purely to enjoy the music and celebrate – to preserve it as a place where people can forget about space and time for a little while and enjoy themselves,' explained the head doorman, the stern Sven Marquardt, whose face was criss-crossed with tattoos and piercings. 'The club evolved from the gay scene in Berlin in the nineties. It's important to me we preserve some of that heritage, that it still feels like a welcoming place for the original sort of club-goers.'[22]

Because Berghain was intended to be a kind of sanctuary for the nocturnal freaks of all persuasions and proclivities who had made Berlin nightlife what it was, its door policy – once described by Tobias Rapp as exuding 'a faint sense of Jacobin Terror' – was intended to ensure that everyone inside was not going to fuck up the vibe.

And so they could have sex, if they so desired, perhaps in one of the club's darkrooms just off the dancefloor, or in the men-only Lab. Oratory club. Lab.Oratory laid out its attractions on its website – there was the weekly Naked Sex Party, where one could check one's clothes at the door and enjoy 'a lot of group action', as well as nights for rubber fetishists, fisting fans and piss lovers, and an occasional event called Filthy Farm, offering 'peasant barn action'. It was even recommended by the Lonely Planet travel guide as a suitable place for 'advanced sexual experimentation in what looks like the engine room of an aircraft carrier'; a tenebrous dive where Crisco was sold at the bar and making intimate new friends at short notice never seemed to pose too much of a problem.[23]

Outside the darkrooms, it was not unusual to see completely bollock-naked men wandering around, or semi-clothed women – and it also became something of a journalistic cliché to remark that no one seemed to take much notice of this kind of casual nudity. But without an uncompromising door policy aimed at excluding those with no commitment to the libertine cause, this would never have been possible, even in Berlin. 'This is a special place. It's a place where people go to lose themselves. It's a place where queer people go to have encounters. And all of that changes if you have a bunch of drunk, straight techno tourists there. It becomes a zoo, not a safe space,' says The Black Madonna. 'So if that means that some lovely straight people get turned away occasionally, I'm OK with that because it's one of the few places in the world where straight white guys with lots of money aren't necessarily at the top of the heap.'

At the irregular men-only Snax parties, areas of the club that were usually shuttered were opened up to accommodate around 2,500 gay revellers and redecorated with unorthodox one-off installations; one Easter, there was a coal-mining theme with colliery-style tunnels, rotating steel saws and an artificial lake filled with lube. 'You don't *have* to have sex but everybody is expected to be open to whatever may happen,' says one Snax regular. 'What makes it special is not that you're allowed to do it, because you're always allowed to do it, but what's different is some kind of shared excitement.'

For Boris Dolinski, the sheer vastness of the sexual possibilities on offer was what set Snax apart. 'I know other places are gay and have sex, but not on that scale, you know, not in that *magnitude*,' he says. 'It is a celebration. You can engulf yourself in it and lose yourself in it, but you know you are going to be taken care of if anything happens to you. You can cross your limits if you want – and a few people did that, of course. There are things that happen there that you could never imagine doing anywhere else, even at home.'

Club culture and the art world had always had close connections since Jean-Michel Basquiat and Keith Haring prowled the New York downtown scene of the eighties. Berghain actively cultivated such links; Wolfgang Tillmans provided a series of magnificent pictures – an exposed vulva, a puckered anus, his vast liquidic abstract *Freischwimmer* and a tapestry-like banner of static shot from a TV set in a Russian hotel room – while the club's monthly flyers also featured original works by important artists. 'It's because they did the Snax parties – all the gay artists who attended the parties gave their works because they were so thankful for that: "Thank you, Berghain, for all the fun I've had here with thousands of naked men from all over the world!"' laughs Thilo Schneider, before continuing, more seriously: 'This is very unique, the aesthetic they offer. Some clubs want to create an image that they are more underground, some want to be more glamorous and sexy, but this is unique and outstanding.'

The club celebrated its tenth anniversary with an art exhibition including gritty photographs taken by chief doorman Marquardt and a glowing aquarium-like installation by former Berghain bartender Sarah Schönfeld that was filled with 1,000 litres of clubbers' urine collected from the club toilets over a period of several months in biohazard containers. A coffee-table book was even published, *Berghain: Art in the Club*, featuring interviews with the artists.

The creativity that the club sought to nurture was musical as well as artistic and sexual: in the entrance hall, records from the club's own Ostgut Ton label were mounted on the walls in industrial studded frames as if in a museum (their covers, too, were created by artists associated with the club). Berghain's most globally renowned DJs, Marcel Dettmann and Ben Klock, both Berlin scene veterans from the nineties, became famous for their cold-as-concrete, aggressively unadorned marathon sets in the turbine hall that sometimes lasted longer than ten hours, way into Monday morning. If there was a 'Berghain sound', it was probably theirs.

Klock, who grew up in West Berlin, explained that he was aiming for 'a perfect balance between hypnotic deep tripping and strong energy'.[24]

His comrade Dettmann, who grew up on the eastern side of the Wall listening to Depeche Mode and electronic body music before graduating to clubs like Tresor and E-Werk, preferred an even more austere noise, bordering on the downright brutal. Techno, Dettmann once said approvingly, 'can make you lose your mind'. And to appreciate it properly, there must definitely be an element of *filth*, he insisted: 'Techno is dirty. When you come back from a techno party, you should be dirty. Your jeans are filthy, you smell like cigarettes, you are covered in sweat. This is very important for me.'[25]

Neukölln-raised Boris Dolinski had been with the club since its Ostgut days, and his personal history wove another strand into the fabric of its cultural significance. The dapper bearded DJ had lived in New York in the eighties and had been a regular at the Paradise Garage, an acolyte of Larry Levan, the man he calls his musical mentor.

After the Garage closed in 1987, Dolinski says he felt like a chapter in his life had ended. 'New York stopped for me,' he recalls. 'There was no reason for me to stay there anymore.' Then the Wall came down and he returned to Berlin to see how his hometown was changing, bringing his collection of classic Garage tunes with him – and met Mark Ernestus, who asked him to become the first employee at his Hard Wax record shop in Kreuzberg.

Dolinski was responsible for ordering all the original Chicago and Detroit 12-inches for the Hard Wax shop in the early nineties, making it one of the most important outlets in central Europe for this new music. He bought up everything he could find from the early Chicago and Detroit labels, and he and Ernestus would go to the airport to pick them up from Customs: 'That made it very special – you had this shop in Kreuzberg where you could get some stuff that you could not get anywhere else in Germany.' DJs like Tanith, Westbam, Jonzon and Dr. Motte made sure they were there each week when the new shipments arrived. 'It was very competitive. We were lucky to get just a few copies sometimes, and there were never enough records for everybody, so there were even fights sometimes over who would get the records,' Dolinski says.

But with his Paradise Garage background, he was not immediately seduced by the harder European techno sound. 'I really couldn't relate to it, coming from a club that is predominantly black and Hispanic, with people dancing half-naked to disco, house and funk. I had no connection to this European scene at all,' he explains. 'I was an alien in my own city, actually.'

For Dolinski, who went on to host the libidinous Cocktail d'Amore parties as well as becoming a Panoramabar resident, the influence of gay culture on Berlin nightlife was crucial to its creative vitality, just like its political history. 'Because Berlin was ruled by the Allied superpowers, it wasn't actually German until 1989. We never had a German identity card when we were living in Berlin, and there was no military draft like there was in the rest of Germany,' he recalls. 'That made it very attractive to people who didn't want to be drafted, especially homosexuals. So they left to move to Berlin, and that is why Berlin became a really big gay haven. There was the highest percentage of gay people in Germany.

'Of course that nurtured a certain subculture, and also Berlin was very politically committed. There were always demonstrations and people are still more militant politically than anywhere else in Germany. All of that condensed into the club culture; it made the club culture harder and stronger.'

Without its powerful gay influence, Berghain could never have sustained its liberating atmosphere, believes Thilo Schneider. 'The gay crowd in Berghain is very faithful. They go there every weekend. They have been going there for years and they are keeping the spirit of sharing and being nice to each other,' he says. 'It's a certain kind of body language; you can feel it when it's a straight club, people are different with their body language. I have seen a lot of girls dancing topless – you can't imagine that in a predominantly straight club, it's impossible. So gay culture is very important for that discovery of sexual freedom. If Berghain lost the gay crowd, then it would just be a big-room discotheque.'

In the words of people like Schneider and Tillmans, one can discern a feeling of deep commitment to Berghain – not in the sense of the ravers who got tattoos of the Cream or Gatecrasher logos during the British superclub era of the 1990s, but rather a feeling of personal investment in a project whose social and artistic vision they embraced as much as its sonic palette.

'There are people who would say that Berghain is a spiritual experience,' says Sven von Thülen. 'Of course you can find people who will say "It's not what it used to be" – but you will always find such people anywhere. For me, it still has its magic. Last time I was there, it was amazing, the intensity inside that club – there were naked men dancing, and naked women too. That's what it's about, total freedom.

'And if you go up the staircase and look down on the dancefloor, you can see everyone is *really dancing*, really moving in their own way, not just facing the DJ, everyone is doing their own thing, there is no conformity – it's an amazing thing.'

'The clubs of the new party district have made Berlin into a pop-cultural destination of choice; a city which successfully gives a great number of people the feeling that there are still places where people have not sacrificed freedom for security – that there is another way.'

Tobias Rapp, Lost and Sound

Berlin in the 2010s was no longer the city of the Wall, of Einstürzende Neubauten and anarchist squatters and May Day riots and postpunk derangement of the senses; nor was it the lawless playground of early-nineties techno. What it had become was a European centre for young creatives as well as the continent's party capital.

Part of the reason was economic: Berlin did not immediately transform itself into the financial powerhouse that it was expected to become after the fall of the Wall and the reunification of Germany. While there was massive redevelopment – the makeover of Potsdamer Platz and the embourgeoisement of the Mitte district forcing many clubs to move east to find affordable homes – top German companies did not relocate their headquarters to Berlin, and rents remained relatively cheap despite increasing gentrification, allowing a series of interlocking creative communities to thrive while remaining true to their visions.

'People don't just do *anything* to make as much money as possible. They have ideas and values that are central to what they actually do. They don't want to do things that they don't consider to be part of their culture,' says Jan-Michael Kühn, an academic who wrote his PhD on the economy of the city's techno scene (while also – because this was Berlin of course – having a parallel career as a DJ under the alias Fresh Meat).

Kühn's theory was that the Berlin nightlife economy had an intrinsic sense of its own ethics, prioritising freedom over profit, and made this work in practice by building self-sustaining micro-economies to support the people involved. 'They have their own cultural products and their own ways to disseminate them,' he explains. 'Money means the freedom to make their lives and their artistic activities possible.'

Even some of those who had profited from their involvement in the scene insisted that freedom remained more important than money – ideals that seemed to be drawn from the counterculture of the old West Berlin. Steffen Hack (better known by his nickname Stoffel) became one of the city's most prominent nocturnal entrepreneurs when he opened the Watergate club by the Oberbaumbrücke in Kreuzberg, with its huge windows offering its dancers immaculate views out onto the Spree, but he originally came to West Berlin in the eighties at the age of 17 to dodge the military draft. 'I was a punk squatter and left-wing political activist. I played drums in a punk band called Loose Nut – the name was from the title of a Black Flag song. We liked it because we were nutters,' he says.

Many of the strategies employed by the Berlin techno scene were based on the experience of living through the Wall years, Hack insists: 'We had this possibility then to live without having to do this stupid morning-to-evening job shit and buy these stupid fucking things you don't need. We learned through how we lived that we didn't need much money – what we needed was ideas and space.'

In 2005, the city's mayor, Klaus Wowereit, declared that 'Berlin will be the mecca for the creative class'. Wowereit was known for his phrase-making, his most renowned quote being the assertion that Berlin was 'poor but sexy'. But in some ways, his prediction came true, as the city became home to many of Europe's 'digital bohemians', even to the point where some began describing it as 'Silicon Allee', the place where world-renowned tech companies like Native Instruments and Ableton developed their game-changing music software for DJs and producers.

Native Instruments first came to life in the living room of an unemployed synthesizer player called Stephan Schmitt in the Kreuzberg district in the mid-nineties, when he developed the idea of turning computers into virtual instruments. Two decades later, the company was still in Kreuzberg but was now occupying 15 floors of a cluster of red-brick blocks set back in a courtyard off Schlesisches Strasse. Instead of a couple of enthusiasts, it employed over 300 people in Berlin by this time, hip young programmers staring studiously at their monitor screens in glass-fronted booths along its pristine white corridors. Its roots were still visible, however; on the wall of the conference room was a poster for a Carl Craig club night.

'The end of the eighties and the nineties, techno was my life,' recalls Native Instruments' chief technology officer, Mate Galić. 'The music had a progressive nature, especially back then, it was about redefining the sound every month or every week, and this is how I got excited about computers and how I ended up with Native Instruments.'

Galić had been a techno DJ on the early nineties scene; he played the massive Mayday rave in 1993 alongside the likes of Jeff Mills, Tanith and Westbam. The culture of that time 'helped to shape ideas of what does music mean and how can music sound,' he insists.

Being based in Berlin was crucial to Native Instruments' success with products like its Traktor DJ software and Reaktor modular studio, suggests the company's CEO, Daniel Haver. 'Berlin was the place where electronic music was happening and new sounds were being created, where people wanted to be innovative,' Haver explains. 'Because of its club culture, Berlin appealed to a lot of very talented people that wanted to be part of this new thing. We benefited tremendously from that movement – and we are both part of that movement because we were living on the dancefloors for years, Mate and I, which was great because we could hear at night what we were creating in the daytime.'

A short walk away from the Native Instruments offices, in an airy top-floor apartment near Görlitzer Park, lived Robert Henke, the computer artist and Monolake producer who helped to develop the highly successful Ableton Live software for composing and performing electronic music. Ableton, which was co-founded by Gerhard Behles, Henke's sometime partner in Monolake and a former Native Instruments employee, created the software as a practical solution to the problems faced by techno producers in the nineties who wanted to cut tracks spontaneously on a limited budget, rather than booking time in a recording studio.

'I remember an advert at that time – it was a photo of a studio with a big long console and expensive speakers, and on the edge of the desk was a Porsche car key. So the gist of the advertisement was, this is for the "super-pro". This was certainly not something that was interesting to someone who was using an 808 to make electronic punk in a squatted house,' Henke says.

'Our idea of software was that we need something we can rave with – we need to work fast on rhythmical stuff. So that's what we developed for ourselves. It was clear to us that sooner or later, every one of our techno friends would need something like this. What was not clear was that people from non-electronic dance music genres would also embrace it.'

But not everyone was immediately convinced. Henke remembers showing the software at a trade fair in Los Angeles in around 2000, and being paid a visit by someone from a major tech company who sneered at Ableton's graphic interface and mocked its potential: 'He said, "Boy, this looks ugly, what is it?" And I explained it was for making music on stage. He replied, "A laptop on stage? You guys are insane!" And he walked away. So it was a hilarious joke, back then.'

Henke was also struck by a peculiar phenomenon: because he

worked on the pre-set sounds for the software, when he went out to listen to music in the clubs, he could often hear himself in the mix even though he hadn't produced the tunes. Ableton Live had made Monolake ubiquitous and Henke the ghost in everyone's machine.

'It was strange, I have to admit – as a person who is constantly full of doubt about what I am doing, I had moments when I had really, really strange emotions about all this,' he says. 'I was always thinking, instead of making the tools for other people, I should make fantastic records that change the world. And I came to the conclusion that I should do both. I need to embrace the fact that what I did changed the world. Because without me – no Skrillex! I'm exaggerating, but in a way it's strangely true.'

'Tomorrow belongs to those who can hear it coming.'
Press advertisement for David Bowie's Heroes, *1977*

'Detroit techno arrived just after the Wall came down and gave us a new direction,' says Tresor's founder Dimitri Hegemann as he delivers the keynote speech at the Museum of Contemporary Art Detroit during Movement festival weekend in May 2014, using the opportunity to pay homage to his American heroes.

'This music has influenced Berlin in so many ways,' he continues. 'It was the right timing, the right moment, and it was the beginning of a change for the city of Berlin... Now I think it's time for us to give something back.'

Hegemann was speaking at an event staged by the Detroit-Berlin Connection, an organisation that was set up to cultivate creative links in the hope of using post-Wall cultural strategies to help revitalise the Motor City.

'Detroit has this magic,' he tells me a few months later when we are both back in Berlin. 'I went there because of the music but I fell in love with the city. It has these problems but it has this new energy now. I see the hope there, I see the opportunities. What was very important for Berlin was that it had space, and they have space in Detroit – and affordable space. And they have an incredible music history; they have Motown, they have MC5, they have Iggy Pop, they have Detroit techno.'

Hegemann, a man not noted for putting restrictions on his dreams, had the vision of turning one of Detroit's abandoned auto plants into a cultural hub for the city. He had attempted a similar venture in Beijing a few years beforehand and it hadn't worked out, but all the same he was still buzzing with optimism about the possibilities.

The conventional models of capitalist urban redevelopment – building ritzy shopping malls, business centres and luxury apartments – did not regenerate Berlin, Hegemann argues. It was pop culture – techno, and the creative talents that techno attracted – that transformed the city. 'Berlin changed because people changed the city. It's places like Tresor and now Berghain – this is why people come to Berlin. It's not about a shopping mall where you can buy a Rolex. That brings nobody. We had this magical ingredient of new thinking – subcultural thinking.'

Richie Hawtin, who did his early parties at the derelict Packard plant in Detroit and later relocated to Berlin, was also optimistic: 'What you've seen in Berlin in the last 20 or so years since the Wall came down is an incredible resurgence of creativity which has actually driven the economic growth of the city. And I think that will be one of the lifelines of the resurgence of Detroit,' he said.

But while Detroit had a surfeit of empty properties, the authorities were far less forgiving of nocturnal transgressions; the Motor City was no 24-hour metropolis, and it was blighted by poverty and de facto segregation and institutional failures. Licensing laws were far stricter, and there was no EasyJet flying in ravers for a weekend bender. Outside the Movement festival weekend, techno parties in Detroit often only managed to muster a few hundred people.

If Detroit really did help to create the new Berlin, it would be much harder to pull off the trick in reverse, because this was the United States of America, not Germany, cautions Alan Oldham: 'The similarities in my view are surface similarities only – desolate cities with difficult histories. The realities of both cities are very different,' Oldham says. 'Many people say that Detroit could be the next Berlin because a lot of young people are moving to Detroit to do their thing because of the low cost and low rents. But unfortunately Detroit has this mental force field – it's still in America, so there's only so much like Berlin it can be.'

As if to illustrate his point about the difference between the two social worlds, Oldham invited me to his gig at a club in the Revaler Strasse complex of disused industrial buildings sprawling out across a former railway wagon plant that had been repurposed as a kind of hipster playground. In the daytime sunlight, Revaler Strasse looked like the freaks had inherited the earth – for a while anyway, until redevelopment moved them on again. A New Orleans jazz trio wandered around blowing their horns and cadging cigarettes while grubby punks with dayglo Mohicans swilled lager and begged for change outside the Suicide Circus club. There were shabby-chic furniture stores, pop-up restaurants, an organic food market, a martial arts studio, and crusty tourists with dreadlocks and backpacks milling around, photographing the drug-addled rave-nation graffiti – grinning skulls, melting faces, technicolour aliens and bad-trip monsters, along with posters urging an uprising against the forces of surveillance and control.

By night, the labyrinthine complex throbbed with darker energies. A searchlight played out over the Spree above the dilapidated warehouses and dimly lit walkways, while drug dealers of many nations muttered their sales pitches from the shadows.

'Join in the music, the music of drums!' a voice intoned with familiar menace from the towering speaker stacks as arms reached out through the musty gloom towards the high concrete ceiling of the bunker-like den where Oldham was playing. As Nitzer Ebb's powerdrill beats juddered forward, a six-foot German blonde in an op-art dress twirled and pranced, her eyes tight shut in abandon, and two young Poles, their hair dyed matching violent pink, dragged their black-clad boyfriends into the sonic vortex of the dank chamber. Three young Turkish lads, looking on and smiling, took swift surreptitious dabs from a bag of white powder that they shared amongst themselves, briefly grimacing at the bitter taste before throwing themselves back into the rhythm as

Oldham hammered onwards into one of his own T-1000 tracks, 'Loop and Destroy'...

But there was always a feeling that places like the Revaler Strasse complex were temporary, that they could at any moment be displaced by redevelopment schemes, as the old Tresor and E-Werk had been before. As young hipsters flowed in to Berlin, landlords cashed in, driving up rents, while unemployment remained high. Questions were also asked about whether the influx of these lifestyle bohemians with their organic grocery stores, bikram yoga studios and artisanal bakeries did much to enrich the locals, unless they were renting out their flats to weekend ravers through some accommodation website. Because one of the major things that had changed since the early years of rave culture – in New York and London even more so than in Berlin – was that clubs were no longer just under threat from disapproving officials and the police, but from the sanitising forces of gentrification.

Several kilometres across town, swathed in scarves against the autumn chill, Billie Ray Martin is wheeling her bicycle through the fallen leaves on a fresh Schöneberg afternoon, stopping briefly at a non-descript Altbau apartment building on Hauptstrasse to point up at the first-floor window. Number 155. 'That's the place where David Bowie and Iggy Pop lived while they were in Berlin,' she tells me. She gestures at the café next door, an unremarkable little place called Neues Ufer, which has a photo of Bowie on one of the walls: 'They used to have breakfast in this café, which at the time was the only openly gay café in the city.' More history: when Bowie and Iggy made *Heroes* and *The Idiot* here in the seventies, they embellished Berlin's metropolitan mythos as a locus of renegade creativity, an image that continued to project its influence for years afterwards, long after the Wall was gone. After Bowie died in 2016, the pavement outside Hauptstrasse 155 became an improvised shrine.

Billie Ray Martin's powerful and idiosyncratic voice had ennobled many an electronic anthem since her days as the singer with the band Electribe 101 in the late eighties, not least my own favourite end-of-the-night blissed-out-into-the-void tune from Manchester's Haçienda,

'Talking with Myself'. The Hamburg-born vocalist was one of those cultural misfits who grew up on Cabaret Voltaire and Throbbing Gristle, was inspired by the liberating possibilities of electronic music, and somehow ended up in Berlin. She tells me however that she doesn't even really like the German capital much, but relocated from London because it was cheaper. 'I make no money. I don't make money from sales, I don't make much from gigs,' she explains. 'The advent of streaming sites has rammed the final nail in the coffin of getting paid, for me. It's horrible, it's ridiculous. And there's nothing you can do about it.'

Despite her ambivalence about the city in which she lived, Berlin did seem to have had some kind of influence on her work; the day before we met, she had recorded a protest song about gentrification called 'Soul Defender'. 'It's about being screwed by the whole process and how can you fight that,' she says. 'There's a touch of "We shall rise" about it. I'm very inspired by Occupy and peaceful protest. Gentrification is definitely something you can see in this neighbourhood – they just cut down these beautiful old trees to build a house that neither you or I could afford.'

Her single 'Off the Rails', with another Berlin-based misfit, Venezuela-born Aérea Negrot, was also intended as a call-to-arms for metropolitan outsiders: 'It's about Grace Jones, but it is a freak anthem – for all of those who are different, to show them that there is still space for being different,' Martin says. 'The people who are being pushed into obscurity by gentrification, like in New York, all the freaks who have been pushed out of Manhattan.' Or out of Schöneberg, maybe

At this point, there were still liberated spaces along the River Spree where bohos, ravers, hipster tourists and random crusties could lounge on summery Sunday afternoons in open-air bars as minimal techno and dub reggae floated gently across the waters, but it was by no means certain how long this state of affairs could continue. Back in 2012, I had stumbled across a scruffy settlement of refusenik squatters holed up in tents and teepees behind an advertising hoarding on a patch of waste ground by the river in Kreuzberg, under a building decorated with a huge mural of a businessman with his arms chained between the two gold Rolexes on his wrists. 'Occupy your dream!' a scrawl on the nearby pavement urged. A couple of years later, some of the graffiti was still there, but the renegade settlement had been cleared, leaving the land ready for redevelopment.

Police and bailiffs also shut down the huge Tacheles alternative arts centre in Kreuzberg, which had been squatted a few months after the Wall fell but was eventually bought by investors. Its closure in 2012 looked like another inevitable victory for capitalist realism over the remnants of Berlin's anarchic past, but Tacheles at least went out with a final dramatic statement, as black-clad artists played a funeral march outside the building before the police moved in. An intriguing exception to the trend was the ambitious Holzmarkt project, opened in 2017 by the former operators of the notoriously twisted Bar 25. They managed to convince a Swiss pension fund to buy the plot of land on the banks of the Spree where Bar 25 used to stand, and then lease it back to them to set up a 'creative village' with a club, restaurant and studio spaces that could be rented by musicians and artists, in an attempt to sustain an outpost of alternative culture on a piece of prime-value riverfront real estate.

This alternative culture, inspired by techno, had helped to raise a new Berlin, but in doing so had also attracted profiteers to the city – although it remained one of Europe's most tolerant capitals, a place where freaks could find some kind of acceptance, or at least more than they could elsewhere. In 2005, Mayor Wowereit was criticised for sending a letter welcoming people to a fetish party in the city. When asked to defend this shameless promotion of perversity, Wowereit responded: 'There's no question it is a flamboyant scene, but that is also Berlin... and as long as nothing illegal happens, I expect tolerance.'[26]

This tolerance also extended to chemically inspired hedonism. 'It is mainstream culture here,' Tobias Rapp says as we sit in a bar in Kreuzberg where minimal techno is pulsing gently beneath the hubbub of voices; another sign of how deeply entwined the music had become with the city's everyday life. 'You can pretend it's not, but it is. As a weekend practice, it's accepted to go out, pop some pills and dance. It's accepted social behaviour. The music itself is still underground, in that it's not mainstream or commercialised. But Berghain is as important to Berliners as the Berlin Philharmonic – these are the two main places for music in the city.'

Rapp recounts an anecdote to illustrate his point: 'The famous Berghain bouncer, Sven Marquardt, told me that he met the mayor of Berlin at an event, and the mayor comes up and talks to him. They had never spoken before, they didn't know each other, but it was the mayor who went up to the Berghain bouncer to say hello…'

It demonstrated how the Berlin authorities had accepted that techno was beneficial for the city. In Britain, Conservative governments passed laws intended to neuter the rave scene on three separate occasions in the nineties. In Berlin in those same years, the authorities provided free security for not only the Love Parade, but for its anti-establishment rival, the Fuck Parade. The notoriously hedonistic Berghain was even granted the same tax status as the capital's opera houses and concert halls in recognition of the importance of its cultural role in the city. 'What's interesting in Berlin is the sanguine reaction of government to the existence of this huge scene – they haven't been afraid of it or tried to legislate it out of existence,' says the British producer Ewan Pearson, who lived in the city for many years. 'You have to have licences and be above board, but it's not considered to be a sign that society's breaking down. There is no moral panic. There is no backlash.'

And as European cities became more homogenised, expensive and resistant to any kind of nocturnal disruption, Berlin seemed to have managed to retain some of its anarchic feel and its sense of possibility – but for how long, who could really know…

'On a beat with the freaks, where we belong…'
Billie Ray Martin and Aérea Negrot, 'Off the Rails'

Thousands of illuminated helium balloons mounted on a long line of poles trace out the course of what was once the Berlin Wall, as reminiscing crowds walk the route of the old Cold War barrier. In front of the Brandenburg Gate, Peter Gabriel sings David Bowie's 'Heroes' and the Staatskapelle Berlin orchestra plays 'Ode to Joy' from Beethoven's Ninth Symphony, the anthem of unified Europe. There are diplomats and acrobats and fireworks and lasers and choirs and Mikhail Gorbachev and Lech Wałęsa. As evening draws in, the pale globes are released from their moorings into the crisp night air and drift gracefully upwards into the darkness. It's 9 November 2014, the 25th anniversary of the day that the Berlin Wall was finally ruptured: a day that reconfigured global political realities and opened up a new direction for the culture of a city that had been divided and disfigured by the Cold War.

'The fall of the Berlin Wall showed us that dreams can come true,' German Chancellor Angela Merkel, who grew up on the eastern side of the divide, said in her keynote speech. 'Nothing and no one can stand in the way of freedom,' said Mayor Wowereit, who grew up on the western side.[27]

Over at Berghain that November day, they were trying to channel the moment. On the bill was Jonzon, who organised Berlin's first acid house party with Dr. Motte in 1988 while the Wall still stood. There were also some of Detroit's finest, Octave One and Kenny Larkin, men from the city whose music offered the promise of aesthetic renaissance to the post-Wall scene; there was Ostgut veteran Boris Dolinski, and the Scion duo who recorded for the Chain Reaction label, and Sven von Thülen, who had chronicled the Berlin techno movement's early years, and exciting new faces from Berghain's younger generation, DJs like Virginia and Steffi. It was a remarkable combination for a historic anniversary – *der Klang der Familie*, even... 'How could one better celebrate the opening up of the Berlin Wall,' the text on the Berghain flyer asked, 'than with a line-up that tries to represent the optimism of the temporary autonomous zone of Berlin in the years that followed?'

After the official anniversary commemorations wound down for the night, one Berlin DJ was still in the mood to celebrate her own reminiscences of 25 years gone by. 'I remember when it happened, I cried for happiness!' she wrote in an unchecked outpouring of joy that she posted on social media. 'TECHNO brought us together – EAST and WEST!'[28]

Born in the late sixties, she was a daughter of the divided city and all that came afterwards. Born into 'interesting times', she seized the opportunity in those liberating years to define herself as she wished. Born Ellen Fraatz – but Ellen Allien was the name she chose.

'I saw the fall of the Berlin Wall. My mother was born during the Second World War. In light of the city's political history, I see it as my task as a woman to create something that will stand the test of time,' she told me later. Ellen Allien had a quintessential Berlin CV – she had lived in a squat in the Schöneberg district, studied acrobatics, and spent some heady months in London during the peak rave year of 1989. Then she came back home and worked at Dimitri Hegemann's Fischlabor bar, which led to DJ residencies at Tresor and E-Werk – and eventually to founding her own BPitch Control record label, which further elevated her status: 'I took these steps to make myself independent, and this independence remains very important to me.'

And to Berlin itself, where independence was still one of the defining values that had sustained the techno scene for decades in the post-Wall era. Judging by the titles of some of her albums – *Stadtkind* (*City Child*) and *Berlinette* – one might have described Ellen Allien as a patriot, if someone can be patriotic about a city rather than a country. Even when the German capital was immured each year in its grey winter coma, it was home, a place where new things could be created from those that were destroyed, and where inspiration might be kindled from the debris that history left behind. 'That's what Berlin is for me,' she explained, 'spaces of freedom and the chance to contribute something significant myself.'

Twenty-five years after the fall of the Wall threw all possibilities wide open, I wanted to ask her if the city could continue to be a haven for nonconformists, whether people seeking the opportunity to remake themselves and the world around them – like the young Ellen Fraatz seeking her independence maybe, or Dr. Motte dreaming of a love parade, or Dimitri Hegemann trying to find a new creative community, or Ricardo Villalobos twisting electronic music into beguiling new forms, or any of the others who have drawn magic from beneath these leaden skies – whether people like them could still find room to thrive in this transfigured environment, where the forces of capital were advancing slowly but inexorably into the territories of possibility.

'As long as we're being creative and Berlin is attracting new creative people, as long as the government doesn't limit our chances to find our own spaces for creativity,' she responded defiantly.

'Rents are going up, small shops have been forced out, families have had to move to other districts. That's the crazy logic of capitalist politics. But despite all this, we still have space and freedom. Otherwise we'll be out on the streets to defend ourselves…'

3

Fantasy Island

Ibiza

IT'S LONG PAST MIDNIGHT at the bus station in San Antonio, and a couple of dozen enthusiastically wasted revellers are trying their hazy best to form what they think might be an orderly queue. When the doors of the Disco Bus judder open, they scramble aboard, jabbering and giggling and sprawling across the seats as distorted house rhythms blare unintelligibly from the loudspeakers and the driver hurtles off along the highway towards Ibiza Town.

This was how the island's party proletariat travelled, economy class on the Disco Bus, standing room only for the latecomers, everyone rocking their Balearic finery – bra-tops and boob tubes, short-shorts and vests, all sun-charged and ready for anything with the discount-entry wristbands they bought from some tout that afternoon at the beach. A young couple from Wales are already glossy-eyed with antici-pation, both dressed in white to offset their tanned and toned flesh, befriending anyone they can to tell them they're from Bridgend and they're going to Pacha and they just can't wait to get there. 'Where are you from? Where are you going? Where have you been?' the woman asks me as the bus barrels onwards through the darkness. She fires off a list of the DJs she wants to hear before her holiday comes to an end – although of course she never wants it to end. 'It's like living in a dream here, isn't it?' she bubbles joyfully.

Two English lads are sitting in the seats behind me, talking intently but barely holding the conversation together enough for it to make sense as they come up on the pills they've necked early in case they get searched by the bouncers on the door. 'We've been to nearly all the clubs, we've got to do something else here too, something *meaningful*,' one of them says as his friend slowly caresses the contours of his own cranium, deep in the rush. 'We should go to Es Vedrà, it's a really spiritual place…'

He starts trying to explain how Es Vedrà is this rocky outcrop off the southern shore of Ibiza, the supposed holy island of the Phoenician goddess Tanit and the place where a nineteenth-century Carmelite friar called Francisco Palau claimed to have experienced mystical revelations and encountered unearthly beings. But his friend's eyes are now rolling backwards in his head like a slot machine ticking over in slow-motion reverse, and he's lost in inner space, out of signal range Across the aisle, another conversation starts to heat up as an Italian boy tries to get a Mexican girl to join him for the night by offering to demonstrate what he insists is his unique kissing technique. She looks at him quizzically for a few seconds, then decides to give it a try – and why not? It's night-time in the Balearic Isles and normal rules have been suspended.

Anyone looking for a snapshot of the 'real Ibiza' could find it here on the Disco Bus, these keen questing youths with their irrepressible will to turn the night into magic, every night of the week until they had to go back home to Bridgend or Bologna or wherever they came from. Deep into the small hours, the jolly red-and-yellow buses hammered up and down the highways, disgorging their optimistic young passengers into Amnesia, Privilege and Pacha, Ushuaïa and Sankeys and Space, into the endless possibilities of the hours ahead.

It's like living in a dream here, isn't it? For a week or two, every one of them was a millionaire hippie, living the highest of lives in the best of all possible worlds, even if they were staying in a frowsy towerblock hotel and surviving on a diet of bocadillos, San Miguel and MDMA, as they blew a whole year's savings on one colossal, extravagant, you-only-live-once binge…

And down at the airport were some of the men whose reputations drew them in. As you stepped out from the arrivals hall into the sultry afternoon, theirs were the faces you saw, scaled up large, skin and teeth digitally airbrushed to preternatural perfection, the gilded princelings who lorded it over the island for a couple of months every year, the men who kept the beats dropping and the pills popping.

Their posters were like roadside effigies to the transitory idols of this place and time, the Ibiza of the 2010s. They might have been unrecognisable to many people outside their own nocturnal world, but here they were the special ones. A bearded playboy lounging against the side of an American muscle car, grinning beatifically at the heavens – it's David Guetta! A plasma-faced android-boy surrounded by carnival clowns and harlequin masqueraders – Hardwell! A clean-cut, sporty-looking chap raising his arms in a swooping V as if, in his imagination, he was beginning his own descent onto the island's airstrip – Armin van Buuren!

On the road from the airport to Ibiza Town, every single billboard was advertising this DJ or that party, a sign of how nightlife tourism had come to dominate the local economy. But it had not been this way forever. As recently as the early nineties, before the global domination of house and techno, before the advent of low-cost airlines and before the transnational expansion of illegal drug manufacturing helped bring clubbing to a global market, the island's discotheques were still mainly for the disco cognoscenti and the European elite. A few decades before that, Ibiza was little more than a largely impoverished agrarian settlement that could only be reached from the Spanish mainland by boat. As the travel writer Paul Richardson once put it: 'Outside Ibiza Town, the island in the 1950s was one of the most archaic communities in Europe.'[1]

'The hippie influence is really basic because the spirit really comes from them – that freedom and wild kind of life. That's the heritage and the real spirit of Ibiza – free parties, open air, the moon and the stars, good music, dancing.'

José Padilla

'I was in harmony with the world for the first time...' The words of a spaced-out traveller in Barbet Schroeder's 1967 film *More* – shot in Ibiza with a Pink Floyd soundtrack – will not sound unusual to those who have sought bliss here. But the contemporary vision of Ibiza as the island of freedom is a composite image that has been embellished and retouched over the years, taking in centuries of influences that have washed up upon its shores.

Ibiza is a place that attracts people with the power of its myths, a Mediterranean idyll of rich red soil, pine-covered hills and expansive salt flats which has captured the imagination of beatniks, hippies, musicians, artists, writers and hedonists for decades. The first settlers came to the island around the seventh century BC – the Phoenicians, who were looking for a staging post to service their maritime trading routes. They named it after Bes, their god of music and dance (amongst other things), who was also believed to ward off evil spirits. Over the centuries that followed, Carthaginians, Romans, Moors and Arabs also controlled the island, leaving behind their traces in its culture, until it finally came under Spanish rule in the thirteenth century.

Those seeking mystic precedents cite the naming of Ibiza after Bes as an indication that its spiritual magnetism meant that it was fated to become a place of revelries. But the modern Ibiza – or at least the club-bers' paradise with its extravagant pleasuredromes and wild terrace debauches under the airplane flight paths, its sunset bliss-outs and clan-destine beach parties – was also partly a product of the dictatorship of General Francisco Franco, who ruled Spain from his victory in the Civil War in 1939 until his death in 1975. Franco opened up seaside havens like Ibiza to mass tourism in an opportunistic hustle for foreign revenue to prop up his regime. In the late fifties, the island only received a few thousand visitors annually. It was only after the airport started operat-ing international flights in 1966 that the pace of development started to quicken, and by 2000, more than two million tourists were arriving each year.

In the decades before holiday developments threw down their con-crete foundations amid the bucolic agricultural landscape, visitors to the White Island were often bohemian adventurers and artistic liberty-seekers; people like the Berlin Dadaist Raoul Hausmann, who had fled Germany fearing repression in the thirties after his art was branded 'decadent' by the Nazis, as well as other writers and painters from around Europe spooked by the rise of fascism and Stalinism.

The idea of Ibiza as a tolerant haven had been already been established when the island gave refuge to Jews fleeing the Spanish Inquisition, and was compounded when another wave of people escaping from twentieth-century repression found safety here.

The fifties brought beatniks seeking alternatives to San Francisco, Paris and Tangier as well as sunshine, cheap digs and cut-price booze. Among them was a shady former US serviceman and jazz aficionado known as Bad Jack Hand, one of the many foreigners of dubious reputation and licentious appetites who have taken temporary asylum on the island over the years. Sources are vague, but Bad Jack Hand has been credited with helping to nurture an expatriate nightlife scene in Ibiza by booking American jazz players in the late fifties, although the reason for his nickname became clear when he ended up in a Barcelona prison serving time for murder.

Apart from visiting celebrities like Errol Flynn, Elizabeth Taylor and Ursula Andress, the expats living in Ibiza at this point were mainly 'artists, would-be artists, drifters, mystery men and ne'er-do-wells', according to Damien Enright, an Irishman who arrived in 1960. Enright joined the tiny beatnik circle in Ibiza Town, surviving by doing petty scams and small-time dope deals. 'None of us were more than 30 years old and there were rarely more than a dozen of us, a band of dropouts of various nationalities, united by our use of marijuana and LSD,' he wrote in his illuminating memoir of the time, *Dope in the Age of Innocence*. 'We were forerunners of a culture that was about to sweep the coffee shops and colleges of Europe but it was secretive then; if you smoked grass you didn't talk about it even amongst the expats of Ibiza, the island of hedonism and liberty.'[2]

As the sixties progressed, the beatniks were joined by Americans dodging the Vietnam draft, and by the hippies – or *peluts* ('hairies'), as the locals called them – whose nocturnal bongo parties enhanced this image of an 'island of hedonism and liberty'. Pepe Roselló, who started one of the first nightspots on the island in 1962, the Playboy Club in San Antonio, said that the music they carried with them offered a glimpse of freedom after years of dictatorship. 'It was amazing what they brought here – I remember they celebrated the full moon with a big party, dancing around the fire with guitars,' Roselló recalled.[3]

Although Franco ruled Spain, life was believed to be more relaxed on the Balearic Islands, attracting Spanish gays, who added another layer to the image – a playground for sexual nonconformists – as well as drawing in spiritual renegades seeking forms of enlightenment unavailable elsewhere. 'Ibiza may be one of those centres where the representatives of the avant-garde of a new civilisation are experimenting with a new way of life,' filmmaker Barbet Schroeder mused in 1969.[4] The hippies delighted in suggestions that the island could be the focus of some powerful magnetic field, or maybe that its abundance of quartz made it a natural 'tuning fork' for spiritual energies – ideas that continued to circulate for decades afterwards. The desire to believe that Ibiza was special made some of its more zealous admirers willing to accept the wildest theories as fact.

When Richard Neville, the editor of the counterculture magazine *Oz*, visited in 1970, he reported that it was still a 'hippie hide-away', full of good vibes, cheap drugs and 'beautiful people' – Velvet Underground singer Nico, actor Terence Stamp and American bluesman Taj Mahal were around at the same time, he wrote. Neville recalled being greeted by a couple of Californian hippies who immediately sparked up a spliff and hailed him with the salutation: 'Welcome to this jewel of decadent splendour.'[5]

But life wasn't quite so decadently splendiferous for the locals who didn't have a return ticket out of Franco's dictatorship. Pepe Roselló recounted how younger Ibicencos were deeply frustrated by the social and political restrictions of the general's regime: 'We want to play music, we want to amuse ourselves, we want to dance, we want to be like everybody is around the world... [but] it was impossible to import records – records you had to buy *contrabando*,' he explained.[6] Roselló made an illicit connection to get records bought for him through the US Air Force's Torrejón base in Madrid. Once he was raided and all his vinyl was seized; for years afterwards, he kept a copy of the official notice from September 1973 stating that 363 seven-inch singles and 31 LPs had been confiscated from his Playboy Club.

By the eighties, Ibiza had started to wrap itself in the gossamer of glamour as increasing numbers of wealthy jet-setters and showbiz icons began to frequent the island. International pop stars became regular holiday guests, affluent hedonists who liked to frolic by the pool at a hotel run by another Ibiza renegade, buccaneering Australian yachtsman Tony Pike, a moustachioed lothario who claimed to have had sex with more than 3,000 women, including Grace Jones. (In her memoirs, Jones described Pike as 'very Hugh Hefner' and his hotel 'notorious for hedonistic excess'.)[7]

If Pike's testimony is to be believed, his hotel, a converted *finca* up in the rufous hills above San Antonio, was a roiling smorgasbord of drugs and sex throughout the eighties. He liked to entertain journalists with tales of Freddie Mercury's orgiastic 41st birthday party at Pike's Hotel in 1987, when a flamenco troupe entertained revellers as they guzzled their way through thousands of bottles of champagne and countless grammes of cocaine, then screwed each other senseless in a narcotised frenzy. 'I want it to be remembered for years to come,' the Queen frontman apparently told the hotelier.[8] And it was.

Pike also starred as a louche barman in a promotional video that was shot poolside at the hotel in 1983 for Wham!'s chirpy cocktail-bar hit 'Club Tropicana', with its lyrics that unintentionally foreshadowed the entreaties of the Ecstasy era: 'Let me take you to the place where membership's a smiling face... Where strangers take you by the hand and welcome you to wonderland,' the song proposes, as if it's offering a free ticket to the best club ever with a wrap of top-quality MDMA thrown in.

By the mid-eighties, with strongman Franco several years dead and a new democratic Spain developing, most of the elements that would define Ibiza's image as a disco paradise were already in place. Pacha had opened in 1973, Amnesia in 1976, and then Ku, an enormous open-air fantasyland built around a swimming pool, started operating as a nightclub in 1978. All of them were lavish Arcadian pleasure palaces, channelling the jet-set glamour along with the post-hippie afterglow.

'The nice thing back then is that it was full of hippies, people who came from everywhere,' Pacha's owner Ricardo Urgell told journalist Bill Brewster. 'In the seventies, Ibiza was cheap and you could live with little money, completely the opposite to now. Because there was little money, the people were more particular, more authentic. Nothing to do with some of the rich people that come now; they are like plastic.'[9]

'It was a wild time, wilder than now, everyone would dress up, all in white, in African costume or whatever the theme of the party was, or sometimes they would be completely naked, and people would buy champagne just to throw around. It was very extravagant,' seventies Pacha regular Rosetta Montenegro added. 'And people took lots of drugs: marijuana and LSD. I remember one night Ricardo [Urgell] put a swimming pool in the middle of the dancefloor and we all jumped in and swam around like children.'[10]

For the club's resident DJ Pippi (Italian-born Giuseppe Nuzzo), the fact that Ibiza was purely a holiday island gave people license to shed their inhibitions. This, he insisted, was the real origin of the 'Ibiza magic'. 'It was natural and full of love and peace. The people that came there were liberated and they only came there to dance and enjoy themselves and go crazy about the music,' he said.[11]

Perhaps just as importantly, an expatriate colony of devotees of the millionaire guru Bhagwan Shree Rajneesh (later known as Osho) was also living on the island in the mid-eighties and bringing in supplies of MDMA to use in its rituals. The little-known 'love drug' would soon percolate through to Ibiza's clubs.

At Amnesia, half of the dancefloor was open to the pine-scented Ibizan air with pools surrounded by mirrored pyramids and balconies jutting out above the main road, the other half shaded with tented drapes and parasols. It was a perfect setting for the bewitching musical selections of Alfredo Fiorito, a former journalist from the Argentinean city of Rosario. Alfredo had been writing about music for a newspaper called *La Capital*, but fled his home country after the right-wing military coup in 1976. 'I had problems. I'd been promoting Argentinean rock 'n' roll, and they banned every rock 'n' roll group,' he recalls. 'They closed newspapers, psychology schools, everything – it was fascist, you know.'[12] In Ibiza, he found the peace and freedom he was missing in Argentina: 'It was like coming to paradise.'

After selling anything from cakes to candles to make a living in his new homeland, he learned to mix records while working as a barman. When his skills became recognised, he was recruited by Amnesia, where from 1984 onwards he started to play from around 3am until deep into the morning light – the first after-hours club on the island. His style was a mixture of summery classics, indie dance and electronic Eurobeat, songs by Prince, Talking Heads, The Cure and Bob Marley as well as good-time hip-hop and, as they started to emerge, the brand-new house sounds from Chicago labels like Trax and DJ International.

Alfredo was aware that his approach was unusual, but he had no idea that it would later be codified as 'Balearic Beat', or that it would bring him worldwide renown as one of DJ culture's genuine originators, alongside figures like Larry Levan, Ron Hardy and Frankie Knuckles; people who changed the way that music was played in nightclubs. 'My music was open-minded, and that brought open-minded people to the club,' he says. 'But I was only focused on the party, on the next night at Amnesia; I never thought I was creating some new thing. I never thought this would get so big. I never thought it would be a career.'

By 1987, Alfredo had reached some kind of aesthetic peak, according to another veteran Ibiza DJ, José Padilla: 'He had the space – Amnesia was still open-air. He had the Ibiza spirit, he had the sound, he had the people, the new generation – all that together. It doesn't last long, but that's life.'[13] Leo Mas, who played there alongside Alfredo that year, said that 1987 was 'the year of the revolution' at Amnesia: 'Those were unique moments, where you knew something new was about to start and you were its witness and protagonist.'[14]

By that time, a group of young, mainly working-class Brits had become intoxicated by Alfredo's music, and were going to Amnesia and taking Ecstasy as often as they could get it; they coalesced around the Project Bar in San Antonio, run by London DJ Trevor Fung and promoter Ian St Paul. They were soon joined by four relatively unknown British DJs who were destined to further enhance the contemporary Ibiza myth and help to instigate a global dance-drug movement, although they could hardly have sensed it at the time.

One night in September 1987, these four unlikely history-makers, Paul Oakenfold, Danny Rampling, Nicky Holloway and Johnny Walker, took Ecstasy for the first time and went off with Trevor Fung to hear Alfredo playing records at Amnesia. As they danced into the Mediterranean dawn alongside flash Spanish boys and glamorous Italian girls, wealthy dilettantes and flamboyant transvestites, designer-clad extroverts and tanned fifty-something libertines, they realised they had discovered something truly special, as Oakenfold recounted: 'We'd found the holy grail; we'd found this spirit, this music, this energy that changed our lives.'[15]

Alfredo suggests that, crucially, these were the first of the holidaymaking Brits he had met to embrace a *European* identity: 'They discovered the Ibiza that is Europe – that is the most important thing about how they started,' he says. 'They were looking for something – something new.'

But what was more significant was how they succeeded in reappropriating their seemingly ephemeral holiday experience, demonstrating again the British flair for repackaging pop-cultural ideas. Desperate to keep the Balearic vibe alive, they decided to take their holiday back with them to dreary London and started clubs like Shoom, Future, Spectrum and The Trip – clubs that would launch Britain's acid house movement in 1988, turn Ecstasy into a mass-market narcotic and Ibiza into Europe's nightlife mecca. 'It was a brand-new energy,' Rampling recalled. 'The way I was feeling at that point was the golden age was dawning, Aquarius was on us, and I wanted to share that with other people – let's get together, bring people together!'[16]

Ecstasy played a decisive role in creating this feeling that a euphoric wave of pure benevolence had swept them aloft and was lifting them ever higher. In an article for the cult *Boy's Own* zine in the spring of 1988, Oakenfold paid tribute to the delights of the drug that 'takes you up and gives you a feeling of freedom'.[17] But crucially for the events that would follow, it was also a drug that opened minds to new possibilities and inspired people to take action, Oakenfold recalled later: 'Ecstasy makes you think: "I could do this, I'm going to do it." And you do it.'[18]

The first major article about the Balearic scene was published in youth-culture magazine *i-D* in the late spring of 1988, at the point when all of this was still unknown to all but a few hundred metropolitan adepts. It featured photojournalist Dave Swindells' kinetic images of several of the Amnesia Brits, people like fledgling DJs Nancy Noise and Lisa Loud, along with a helpful guide to their Ibiza-influenced beach-bum fashions (Smiley T-shirts, dungarees, Converse baseball boots, 'anything two sizes too big').

I remember being shown the contact sheets for the photos at the *i-D* office one afternoon not long before they were published. The way these brightly clad flower children were dancing – arms thrown high, hands chopping out geometrical shapes in front of them, pupils dilated, peace signs flashing... it looked like nothing I'd ever seen in a club before. Although the article didn't mention drugs directly, writer John Godfrey liberally quoted the E-head slang of the nascent Balearic cult. He concluded by urging his readers: 'Peace and love mateys and get on one right now. Aciieed!!'[19]

The *i-D* feature laid out the creation myth of Britain's acid house Year Zero, a tale which has, as the journalist Dom Phillips has noted, been 'buffed up and polished and turned into legend' over the decades that followed.[20] All movements need their founding fables; this one had the effect of repackaging dance culture, lightly glossing over its roots in black and gay American nightlife and unintentionally but effectively rebranding it as a concept imported from Ibiza by four canny British chaps.

It could be argued that Oakenfold, Rampling, Holloway and Walker deserve some kind of public monument in Ibiza for their services to the island's economy – perhaps a statue by the roadside next to Amnesia depicting the four lads dancing on a podium in Smiley T-shirts and ban-danas, rapturous grins on their faces, proffering illicit delights in their outstretched palms.

But while it's clear that this was a crucial moment in nightlife history, it did not arise from a void. All the records already existed and house music had become a focus for subcultural scenes in several of Britain's major cities long before the four Londoners even got to Amnesia. Some have argued that the mythologisation of their 'Ibiza conversion' obscured the real grassroots of the British house movement in the racially mixed underground clubs of the mid-eighties – that the story is, literally, a whitewashing of history. And while it can't be denied that DJs like Graeme Park, Mike Pickering, Mark Moore, Colin Faver, Jazzy M, Colin Dale, Steve Jackson and many others across the country were already preaching the new gospel of electronic dance music, the four Londoners' Ibiza experience did make a genuine difference. By adding MDMA to the mix and sketching out an alluring Ibizan image for the subculture, they invoked vital energies that were to surge beyond anyone's control, let alone their own.

'For more than 2,000 years, Ibiza's been in a constant state of invasion… Yet the most successful invaders conquered the island without even drawing a sword.'

Danny Rampling, 'Tales from Ibiza', BBC Radio 1, 1999

Acid house effectively acted as a massive free advertisement for Ibiza, selling its charms to Europe's youth and encouraging successive waves of club promoters to try their luck on the island each summer. The enterprising Brits who came after Oakenfold and his friends decided that they wanted nothing less than a slice of Balearic paradise, and they had the determination and the entrepreneurial savvy to take it. By doing so, they also ended up transforming the island itself. As one long-term Ibiza resident told me: 'The British made things happen here that weren't happening before, and that changed everything. For better or for worse, the British made the island what it is today.'

The first attempts to run British acid-house nights on the island came at the end of the eighties, when promoter Tommy Mack organised a clubbing trip to the island. In 1990, Mack then teamed up with Charlie Chester, who ran a Balearic-inspired club and record shop in London called Flying, and sold a disco holiday package called Ibiza 90 to a couple of hundred eager clubbers who had been inspired by the tales of Mediterranean bliss and wanted to see how they matched up to reality.

Chester was well-connected on the scene of the time and his entourage included some important taste-makers – not only DJs like Terry Farley and Andrew Weatherall from the influential *Boy's Own* crew, the Slam duo from Glasgow, bands like 808 State and A Man Called Adam and a couple of random pop-culture journalists like myself, but also a film crew who would chronicle the holiday in a television documentary for Britain's Channel 4, which became another advertisement for the island, *A Short Film About Chilling*. Looking back on that little excursion now, it seems so naïve and freewheelingly chaotic, organised with a devil-may-care bravado and the youthful confidence that the splendid surroundings, some good tunes, a spot of sunshine and a couple of decent pills would make everything all right on the night.

After a series of such exploratory sorties by the advance guard of the Anglo-Saxon hordes, the nightlife 'brands' began to arrive on the island in the nineties, a full-on British invasion led by clubs like Cream and Clockwork Orange, Renaissance and the Ministry of Sound. The Ibizan club owners realised that the Brits could draw the crowds, and between them they went on to make the island the world's pre-eminent holiday clubbing destination. But the name that would give a lubricious sheen to this hedonistic image was little-known in Britain itself at that point.

Manumission was a club that had its origins in Manchester's 'gay village' quarter, and was launched at a time when armed criminal gangs were menacing the city's nightlife, causing the Haçienda to shut down and the 'Madchester' era to come to a bitter and violent end. Fleeing the turmoil at home, Manumission's instigators, two brothers called Andy and Mike McKay, pitched up on the Balearic island in 1994 with little money but a lot of grand intentions. Mike McKay once recalled living in one room with no windows with two drag queens and a crazy artist, hitchhiking around putting up posters for the first Manumission night himself. They managed to secure a residency at the biggest venue on the island, Ku (later to be renamed Privilege), which could have ended up being a spectacular failure, but instead attracted

8,000 people each week, setting new economic parameters for club-bing on the island.

They brought a new creative concept too. Manumission means 'emancipation from slavery', and the McKay brothers wanted to rein-vent raving as a kind of decadent vaudeville – to liberate repressed fantasies, to incite and provoke. They didn't want the kind of party where people just danced all night to underground house tracks; they wanted to put on a *show*. Full-on burlesque excess was what they were after, and nothing less would do.

For them, that meant dancing dwarves and drag queens, clowns and jugglers, bare-breasted chorus girls and an onstage sex show star-ring Mike McKay and his girlfriend Claire Davies. Their weekly erotic routine rapidly became another of the island's legends, as much a part of its dissolute history as Freddie Mercury's birthday party at Pike's Hotel. 'The reaction was so intense,' Davies recalls. 'The acceptance from the gay scene was amazing; the gay scene in Ibiza was really vibrant back then and they really embraced me. But the reactions from some other people were harsh, and it just brought up all these questions of freedom.' Some of course thought it was just a tawdry sideshow for drugged-out gawpers: 'They perform acts of sexual depravity in front of thousands of strangers,' British tabloid the *Daily Mail* reported with prudish glee.[21]

But Davies and McKay argued that the sex show was intended to be genuinely liberating. 'For us it was like two fingers up to the estab-lishment, saying you are free to do anything you want to do,' insists McKay. 'Ibiza was a very liberating place to be at that time.'

Incredibly, they were never prosecuted. 'The funny thing is that people are so embarrassed, they can't even talk about sex,' explains Davies. 'The club owner spoke to Mike's brother and said, "They have to stop it, it's illegal." We said, "We'll stop when somebody tells us to." But nobody dared, even the police.'

Invigorated by their success, they went on to take over an old brothel in Ibiza Town called the Pink Pussy and turned it into the Manumis-sion Motel. With its sex-themed rooms and pole-dancing strippers, it became a licentious vortex that sucked in people like the celebrity dope smuggler Howard Marks, hard-partying DJ Derek Dahlarge and the radio presenter Lisa I'Anson, who was sacked by BBC Radio 1 after missing a broadcast slot because she was on a bender at the motel. Andrew Innes of Primal Scream, who was no stranger to excess, once described it as 'the most decadent place I've ever been in'.[22]

At one point in the late nineties, when British clubbing started to enter its early corporate phase, the Manumission crew seemed to some observers to be the last of the desperados holding out against the advance of commercialisation: 'As the rest of clubland has slowly embraced a kind of reluctant respectability – sponsorship deals, dress codes, "brand identities" – Manumission alone seemed untouchable,' Dom Phillips suggested.[23] But by 1999, the weekly naked performance had also become just another routine. Video footage from the time shows glassy-eyed punters standing and staring in a circle around the squirming bodies – not shocked, not titillated, and certainly not liberated from moral slavery. The limits of possibility seemed to have been reached, and McKay and Davies decided to call a halt. The sex show was replaced by a dance troupe, although Manumission continued to run until 2009, when the McKay brothers fell out.

When the end came, it was swift and brutal: 'The club owner at Privilege locked the doors on us. He just didn't open the club at all. Thousands of people had bought tickets and were outside,' Mike McKay recalls. 'It wasn't a happy ending – we were heartbroken.' Andy McKay and his partner Dawn Hindle went on to establish their Ibiza Rocks promotions company, seeking a sustainable sequel to the Manumission epic by focusing on live music rather than DJ culture, but his estranged brother Mike and Claire Davies ended up skint and jobless.

'We always ploughed all the money we made from Manumission straight back into it, so as well as being heartbroken and exhausted, we were also financially ruined, which is something that people just wouldn't expect,' says Davies. 'We went from being on billboards all over the island to being told to go and queue up in the dole office. It was humbling.'

But while they lasted, these were some of the wildest of times for those who enjoyed them to their decadent fullest. This was the era of 'havin' it' excess, of 'superstar DJs' with monstrous egos hoovering up endless grammes of coke then forgetting where they left the keys to the Ferrari. It was the era that made stars of British DJs like Brandon Block and Alex P, the impish pranksters who ruled the terrace at Space each Sunday for several summers in the mid-nineties. Such laddish characters were celebrated by the British dance-music media not for their craft, but as heroic 'caners' – partying so hard that some of them eventually had to retreat into rehab or had their lifestyles crippled by massive tax bills accrued over years of spendthrift excess.

Brandon Block's misfortune was perhaps the most distressing – even when he was hospitalised back in Britain with tuberculosis, he continued to snort as much cocaine as he could get, although his doctor warned him that he was facing imminent death if he didn't stop. The perennial party boy who once described himself as 'the Keith Richards of DJing' had become desperately ill, pleading with his friends to supply him with drugs in his hospital bed. 'I was so addicted I forced them to bring cocaine in for me. You have to remember I was Brandon Block – "superstar DJ" – and I would blackmail them, saying I would never speak to them ever again if they didn't do what I asked,' he recalled.[24] Block managed to survive and continue his career, but he certainly wasn't the only DJ to lose his bearings in those intemperate years.

'What has happened these past two or three years is not because of me or Paul Oakenfold or Danny Rampling or anyone else who came to the club originally. It's because of these kids, what's inside them. It was, and always will be *them* – they make the atmosphere special.'
Alfredo Fiorito, 1990

From the far side of the cavernous room, high up near the ceiling above the seething swell of outstretched hands, a celestial glow radiates outwards like dawn breaking through cathedral windows. The music surges suddenly, and a flash of white light illuminates the master of ceremonies at his tribune, grinning mischievously behind his wire-rimmed spectacles and beckoning suggestively to the masses below.

The ringmaster at Amnesia tonight is Sven Väth, the puckish quinquagenarian with his shaven scalp, tight black vest and beaded necklace, a techno showman with decades of experience in orchestrating the emotions of his people. He's laying down a soundtrack that is suitably dramatic for this enormous room, trancelike and melodic but never too coercively sentimental, with enough blasts of raging drug noise for the hardcore. That year, 2015, had seen a significant rise in the purity of Ecstasy – not for nothing were DJ Koze's 'XTC' and Paul Woolford's 'MDMA' among the summer season's biggest anthems – and Väth knew more than most how to fine-tune the mental chemistry and bring the euphoria on.

The German DJ was another of those drawn by the Ibiza myth. Väth came to the island for the first time in the early eighties as a teenage backpacker, hitchhiking down from his hometown of Obertshausen near Frankfurt and spending three months sleeping on a sun-lounger in the woods. 'I experienced something which was so unbelievable and full of love and good music and hippieness… This was my big inspiration,' he recalled in an interview at the International Music Summit in Ibiza many years later. Hearing DJs like Pippi at Pacha and Cesar at Ku mixing up Italo-disco, African percussion tracks, reggae and psychedelic rock was an experience that made him want to play and produce music, he explained: 'I started as a DJ when I was 16 in my parents' club, and from then on, every year I came here to Ibiza for the opening parties and the closing parties, and my biggest goal, my biggest motivation was that one of the DJs would play one of my records.'[25]

The young Väth secured a prestigious residency at the influential Dorian Gray club at Frankfurt Airport, where Talla 2XLC's pioneering Technoclub night was also housed at one point. In 1985, Väth made his first electro-pop record, *Bad News*, under the name OFF. He then returned to Ibiza in the hope of persuading Pippi, Cesar and Alfredo to play it, and ended up in the middle of the dancefloor at Amnesia, flying on mescaline punch, surrounded by impossibly glamorous luminaries like Grace Jones, Duran Duran and Jean-Paul Gaultier. The next year, he rose yet further, becoming a European pop star himself with OFF's million-selling hit 'Electrica Salsa'.

When his chart success faded in the late eighties, he opened the Omen club in Frankfurt and became a pioneer of German trance with his Eye Q and Harthouse labels, as well as one of the most colourful icons of the Berlin Love Parade. But he kept on returning to Ibiza, season after season, even as he gradually started to find the soundtrack disappointingly mainstream.

'In the nineties, when all the big English club promoters came on the island and changed the music and kicked out the Spanish DJs, and trance music and real commercial house music became so popular here, I didn't feel the vibe any more from "my" Ibiza,' Väth explained. 'I felt so sorry and I said, "I have to change something here"… I wanted to bring back the feeling I had when I went to Ibiza.' In 1999, he brought his travelling Cocoon revue to the island and scored a summer residency at Amnesia, offering an alternative to the British superclubs which had succeeded in dominating Ibiza – a Mediterranean outpost for real techno. He had finally become a resident at the club where he had once raved as a teenager: 'For me, my dream came true,' he said.[26]

Cocoon booked more inventive DJs like Richie Hawtin and Ricardo Villalobos, and helped to rejuvenate Ibiza's reputation for underground dance music in the 2000s, restoring an element of subcultural credibility which had almost been obliterated by the pilled-up populism of the Brits. Väth also began a series of free after-club parties and would play for hours on end, long into the day after Amnesia had closed, in what he said was a conscious effort to uphold the island's bohemian traditions. 'Cocoon somehow reinvented the after-hours culture here, doing illegal parties on the beach, in the countryside. We always risked to get in trouble with the police, but we didn't care,' he said.[27]

Väth – or 'Papa Sven', as he became known around the time of his fiftieth birthday – was renowned for his irrepressible exuberance, his indomitable stamina behind the decks and his free-spirited charisma in the rather earnest world of techno. Even in his early fifties, he still looked fresh and vital – there were improbable rumours that he would spend each winter at some upscale clinic getting his entire blood supply replaced with purer corpuscles like some kind of techno Dracula, although actually his annual off-season detox involved taking Ayurvedic cures that he first discovered in Goa.

His Cocoon dancers at Amnesia remained eternally youthful of course – wearing their Louise Brooks wigs and sleek costumes cut to show off their supple haunches, they writhe tonight on their podium as Väth theatrically sets off an ice cannon and a massive body-freezing rush of cold steam spurts across the dancefloor with a cacophonous explosion of white noise. Such pageants of female flesh are almost ubiquitous in the carnivalesque world of Ibiza nightlife, although of course they are little more than titillation, the sort of display that might be mocked from the stage if it was attempted in some more politically progressive environment. When Väth did an all-day Cocoon show in a park in Leeds one year, his dancers looked underdressed and faintly ludicrous in the dour northern English daylight.

As the night draws on, Väth swigs from a wine glass and sneaks a kiss from a woman who rubs herself against him as she dances, cooling him with the rhythmic fluttering of her fan. On a huge screen above him, what looks like a huge kinetic sensor trace of his silhouette mimics his every move, a monstrous doppelganger jerking to its puppetmaster's beat, along with all the rest of us. Tonight his guest in the rustic-looking stone-sided booth is the Bosnia and Herzegovina-born, German-raised DJ Mladen Solomun, whose bearish frame dwarfs the dapper little man from Frankfurt. The sun is already up as they close the show with a piece of dreamy, post-coital trance; a calibrated moment of rapture. One clubber who posted an online review later that day could not manage to contain his excitement, recounting how Amnesia had been driven into a 'state of nirvana' by these two 'gods among men', Solomun and Väth. 'As the sun reached well overhead I felt more alive than I ever have before,' he wrote.[28]

This was wide-eyed hyperbole without any doubt, but no more exaggerated than the kind of impassioned reminiscences you might have heard any afternoon on the beach after long nights out in Ibiza. And it seemed somehow fitting that Väth, who first came to the island in the early eighties because of its myth of unrestrained liberty, had ended up adding his own layer to that same myth for the generations that came after him.

Ibiza is magical because people wish it to be so; it is a fantasy made reality by the collective force of desire. It's a magic that is enhanced by the tales of the exploits of its heroic characters but escapes cold definition because it is so nebulous, perennially slipping out of the grasp of rationality and logic. As Nick Mason of Pink Floyd, who owned a house in Ibiza, once observed: 'The best thing about this island is that it can be whatever you want it to be.'[29]

Ibiza has been mythologised in films as a decadent idyll, although not always in a positive way. Barbet Schroeder's *More*, with its 'beautiful people' losing their minds to heroin, feels like an elegy for the death of the hippie dream, while Michael Dowse's 2005 film *It's All Gone Pete Tong*, which chronicles the decline of a cocaine-addled celebrity DJ, could be seen as an obituary for the money-crazed 'superclub' era of the late nineties that saw the beatific visions of acid house torn apart in a savage frenzy of drug-fucked materialism. Even the ravers'-favourite documentary, *A Short Film About Chilling*, failed to fully define the island's magic, signing off with a mere sun-blessed whimsy: 'It's just a really wonderful feeling...'[30]

Ill-defined or not, magic there must be in a place that manages to attract generation after generation of artistic innovators, argues journalist Johnny Lee, who spent several summers working as the Ibiza correspondent for dance-music magazine *Mixmag*. 'There's absolutely no doubt in my mind that Ibiza is a spiritual hub of some kind,' Lee insists. 'Interestingly, when we look at the history of the place, the island has always been a magnet for countercultural creatives, many of whom came here by chance or accident.'

One of them was Mark Broadbent, an enterprising Yorkshire-man who saved up enough money to jack in his career in the nineties and journey to India, before landing a job with the Ibiza franchise of

Liverpool's Cream club, spending each summer working on the island then heading back to Asia to resume his travels for the rest of the year.

'At that time, Ibiza was full of people who had been in Goa or Koh Phangan, Rajasthan or Kathmandu. People were going and buying things in India and fetching them back here to Ibiza and selling them. We sold bindis and sarongs and things like that – you could spend a couple of hundred pounds in India and make a couple of thousand here,' Broadbent says.

He eventually became the musical director of the We Love nights at Space, winning praise for bringing some of the more imaginative line-ups to the island at the time. For Broadbent and his wife Sarah, Ibiza looked like the promised land, and they made it their home.

'Ibiza symbolises the ability to escape and recreate yourself. You can come here for a weekend and have a Balearic experience or you can come here and fall in love with it and stay here forever,' he explains.

'Growing up under Thatcher, especially in the north of England where I'm from, we didn't think that a laidback libertarian lifestyle was possible. Then we came here and found out that it was. Certainly when we arrived, it was still possible to live here relatively cheaply but feel like a millionaire. And that was certainly something you couldn't do in Huddersfield.'

But while the 'hippie market' at Las Dalias continued to trade to the tourists and the sunset drum ritual each Sunday on Benirrás beach upheld the island's nonconformist traditions, many of the bohemian freaks were gone by the mid-nineties as the island became increasingly developed, suggested José Padilla: 'Hippies had two choices: either leave Ibiza and find somewhere else they could still live the same way, or stay there and change,' Padilla said at the time. 'The hippie thing is finished, but they've been used in a way to give an image of Ibiza to the rest of Europe – the free island, the island of love.'[31]

This carefree image was comprehensively commodified as the years progressed. The Hippie Market trinket chain sold beads and buddhas at various outlets around the island, and even had a concession in the airport's departures area, while Pacha staged a hippie theme night called Flower Power, which featured a CND logo and yellow submarines in its marketing material and the club's original seventies DJ, Piti Urgell, on the decks. 'The clubbers of Flower Power get really into the hippie spirit, encouraged by the props splayed around the venue, and have been known to all chant together John Lennon's "Give Peace a Chance",' burbled an advertisement for the club. A 'standard' VIP table for four at Flower Power was a peace-loving giveaway at €1,120.

'Ibiza is a kind of dance music Hollywood, a place where dreams can be made as easily as minds can be lost.'

Clive Martin, Vice

Under the broad reach of the Matutes family – the pre-eminent players in the Ibiza nightlife and hospitality industry, who were once reported to own around ten per cent of the island – Playa d'en Bossa beach on the southern coast became a new focus of development in the 2010s, as what had been a family-orientated resort area with dowdy hotels and downmarket eateries aimed at the package-tour crowd gradually became transformed into an upscale leisure strip.

Paterfamilias Abel Matutes Juan was an influential businessman and politician, at various times serving as the mayor of Ibiza, as an MP in the European Parliament and as Spain's foreign minister. His son, Abel Matutes Prats, headed the Palladium Hotel Group, which was owned by the family firm Grupo Empresas Matutes and operated a series of hotels in Spain, Italy, Brazil, Mexico, Jamaica and the Dominican Republic – more than ten of them in Ibiza itself. Among them was a series of five-star establishments along Playa d'en Bossa, where they also had ambitions to build an upscale complex with a shopping mall and a golf course. The younger Matutes spoke of establishing Ibiza in the 'luxury league'.

From the Matutes' Ushuaïa Tower to the Bora Bora rave bar, a kilometre or so of sunblock-greased, gym-pumped and tattooed flesh down the bay, Playa d'en Bossa had become a symbol of shifting perspectives on the island. As I wandered down the beach one afternoon, I decided not to sample a cocktail at the Matutes' Hard Rock Hotel (mission statement: 'to spread the rock 'n' roll spirit by creating authentic trend-setting experiences'). Neither did I dine at the hotel's Sublimotion restaurant, which was proclaimed by some media at the time to be the most expensive eatery in the world, offering a 'gastro-sensory spectacle' for around €1,500 a head.

I did drop in to the No Name beach bar where German DJ tINI (Tini Günter) was hosting a free afternoon party, with bare-chested ravers pumping their biceps to rolling tech-house under the shade of military scrim-nets casually suspended from wooden poles in the sand. But an hour or so later, the police moved in to shut it down, causing tINI to lament that the island's liberties were slowly being curtailed. 'It's sad to see Ibiza changing so much, and not for the better… what once brought all likeminded people together gets slowly destroyed,' she said.[32]

The raid was part of a wider crackdown on free beach parties in the summer of 2015 as part of an apparent attempt to tighten up entertainment regulations and sanitise the island's image in order to attract a wealthier class of tourist – a gambit aimed at the 'luxury league', perhaps. Free events run by Carl Craig and Israeli DJ Guy Gerber were also cancelled.

Despite its gradual gentrification, Playa d'en Bossa at that point still had some rougher edges left to savour, while they lasted. On the nearby main road where the souvenir shops catered to the package tourists, you could buy a chrome-plated coke spoon and T-shirts depicting a wasted Mickey Mouse dancing in Smiley-faced attire – as well as perhaps a paella fridge magnet to remind you of your gastronomical adventures in Spain. Billboards promoting EDM DJs like Hardwell competed for eyeball time with hoardings advertising KFC and Burger King, while propped up next to a stall selling David Guetta merchandise was a fuzzily laser-copied menu offering cut-price kebabs and pizzas. All the while, drug dealers in baseball caps lobbied the holidaymakers who were cutting through the side-streets to the beach, calling out hopefully: 'Good stuff? You want good stuff?'

The other hustlers on daytime patrol at Playa d'en Bossa were the nightclub touts, relentlessly pestering people to buy wristbands ensuring them cheaper entry into a club that night. These keen young promo people – in Ibiza they were usually referred to simply as 'workers' – trawled the resorts all day for potential customers. They were willing to endure the privations of poverty and malnourishment in order to live the Balearic dream, just like the bright young doleites and itinerant chancers who formed the core of the original British Amnesia crowd back in 1987 when Paul Oakenfold and his friends flew in.

Some of these 'workers' return again and again, summer after summer, hoping to graft their way up into careers as DJs or promoters – but not all of them manage to last out their first season. Some spend too much time partying, lose their jobs and turn to selling pills and powders to prolong their holiday. Not all of them go home friends; sometimes the money runs out, drug deals go wrong and relationships splinter as chemical derangement and too many sleepless nights wrench the consciousness out of shape. Ibiza could be like a hall of mirrors; to become bewitched by its distortions could be dangerous.

For the DJs meanwhile, the summer season in Ibiza had become the couture catwalk of the global electronic music scene, the sparkling vitrine in which the latest confections were put on display. 'Everybody who plays a role in the global dance music industry plays, played or will play in Ibiza,' says Mladen Solomun. 'And a tune which is massive in Ibiza has a good chance to become massive in the rest of the world, so in a way yes, it is the shop window for the dance world.'

In his book about nineties nightclub excess, *Superstar DJs Here We Go!*, Dom Phillips recounted a tale about DJ Sasha entrancing the crowd on the terrace at Space, glugging from a bottle of Jägermeister that he 'brandished like a sword' with one hand while mixing with the other.[33] Sasha then went missing after a post-set partying session and was eventually found unconscious in a ditch near the DC10 club with a wad of cash in his pocket and another bottle of Jägermeister lying nearby, according to Phillips.

A couple of decades on, this kind of public debauchery seemed almost archaic; the etiquette of a bygone era, according to Johnny Lee:

'The age of the drunken, drugged-up DJ is over and the truth is that it's been like that for a very long time,' Lee argues. 'Dance music is now a serious business. In peak season, the top EDM DJs here are earning salaries that would make a top-level footballer salivate. Do you really think these guys are going to turn up unprepared or fucked up when the stakes are so high?'

That meant the kind of intoxicated high-jinks beloved of the party-boy DJs of the nineties *havin' it* generation had become much less prominent, while any public misbehaviour was likely to be captured by smartphones and lead to instant online ridicule. Ricardo Villalobos once complained bitterly about a snapshot someone took of him looking sweaty and wasted after seven hours behind the decks: 'I am just closing my eyes and he takes the photo in this moment. Then he puts the photo on the internet, "Look how fucked up Ricardo is!" Then people call me two weeks later, "Ricardo, I am really worried about you. I saw a photo on the internet." Fuck off,' Villalobos grumbled.[34]

A video of David Guetta looking a bit spaced out on stage at a festival in Belgium also went viral in 2014, even though there was no evidence that the French DJ was off his face and the brief clip was utterly tame compared to the exploits of roguish 'caners' like Brandon Block two decades earlier. 'There's no hiding place anymore,' says Lee. 'These days, everyone has a camera and any mad or erratic behaviour would go viral within the hour.' Not for the first time, Berghain's sternly enforced no-photos rule seemed to make a lot of sense, guaranteeing a temporary privacy from the all-seeing eye of the smartphone. In most venues by the 2010s, clubbers and DJs had to assume that they were potentially under some kind of surveillance – either official or amateur – pretty much all the time.

For some of Ibiza's wannabe heroes, the Balearic dream could still come true, if they had the talent, the commitment and the sheer will to succeed. 'The world of the dance industry always has an eye on Ibiza,' says Solomun, paraphrasing the classic Frank Sinatra song: 'It's a little bit like: if you make it there, you make it anywhere.'

But you had to hustle hard. I once heard the German DJ Loco Dice

(Yassine Ben Achour) explaining how, when he was still a 'nobody', he flew to Ibiza for the summer with an open return ticket and slept on another DJ's couch while he canvassed for work. He took whatever gigs came his way until he managed to penetrate the island's consciousness, then used his achievements in Ibiza as stepping stones to global renown.

'I know Ibiza is over-hyped, overrated, you have all that bullshit talk about Ibiza, but *Ibiza is the mecca of electronic music*. Each summer the whole world comes together there,' Ben Achour advised up-and-coming DJs: 'Invest your money, go there – it's expensive but there's always ways to live easy, normal, and go to all these after-hours, all these free parties. Don't even go to the clubs and spend €60, that's bullshit. Go. Learn. Observe. See how the people are DJing, see how the scene is. And sooner or later you'll get your job.'[35]

This is how it worked for Clara da Costa, a straight-talking house music head from Surrey in southern England who moved to the island at the age of 17, scored a job as promoter and resident DJ at the Es Paradis club, and never looked back.

'I just felt so at home here, I immersed myself in the language and the culture,' she recalls. 'It's a very non-judgmental place, everything goes and everyone's kind of accepted. I never felt like I fitted in at school, but I felt like I fitted in here – it just felt right.'

I met da Costa at the Golden Buddha, which at the time was the last bar on the strip that runs along the San Antonio shoreline. It was a tranquil afternoon; yachts rocked back and forth in the bay and the Mediterranean sun prepared to embark on its long slow dip below the horizon as the Balearic classic 'Don't Dream It's Over' played gently on the sound system.

'There have been immense changes over the past couple of decades,' she told me as the shadows lengthened. 'I remember I was on this TV show about clubbing about 20 years ago and I was asked how Ibiza was changing and I said, "It's becoming a bit of a money pit." Which is incredible – it couldn't have been further from the truth compared to what's happening now.'

But Ibiza had become her home and she believed that the dream wasn't over – not yet, anyway. 'I believe it's still possible to come out here and have that life-changing experience,' she insisted. 'But you've got to be completely in love with it, and you've got to be dedicated. You've got to work hard to make the right connections and make them work for you. Some people get lucky, but it's mostly hard graft.

'You've got to have imagination and not give up, because the highs are so high and the lows are so very low.'

'For me, "Balearic" is not a musical style but a way of putting music together.'

Alfredo Fiorito

The original *i-D* article about the beginnings of the British acid house scene in 1988 described the resort of San Antonio as 'the toilet of the Englishman abroad, where every cliché of Lads-at-Play is enacted with the zest of newly freed convicts'.[36] Sant Antoni de Portmany, as the Ibicencos call it, was once a sleepy fishing village until it began to be developed as a holiday destination for package tourists from the late fifties onwards, gaining an unsavoury (but not ill-deserved) reputation as a rowdy den of iniquity where you could dine on sausages, eggs, baked beans and chips while watching English football on huge screens at Irish- and Scottish-themed pubs and boozing yourself into oblivion before having a punch-up outside and then puking all over the pavement.

This was still the case to some extent in the 2010s, when reporter Clive Martin took a tour through the resort as he filmed a documentary about the island, picking his way through gurning, mooning beer boys in San Antonio's rambunctious West End pubbing zone. He then went on to a daytime party where he homed in on a group of female Brits and asked them if they thought Ibiza was a 'spiritual' place. 'Yeah, it's got such a spiritual vibe,' one of them responded, before another jostled forward to show off her rump, which had been tattooed with the words 'Balearic Badgirl'. Except Balearic was spelled wrong – 'Balleriac Badgirl', the tattoo actually read. 'But fuck it, I'm in Ibiza!' she giggled.[37]

Despite all this, even in San Antonio there were indications of the changing tastes of Brits abroad. Many of the young men sunning their bodies on the seafront looked like stylistic acolytes of David Beckham, with their intricate 'sleeve' tattoos, gym-sculpted torsos and expensive swimwear, sometimes augmented with diligently barbered facial hair. Some of them resembled pumped-up Muscle Marys from the dance-floors of New York's Sound Factory or London's Trade in the nineties, but the apparent influence of gay culture on their appearance was not necessarily an indicator of alternative thinking; the look had simply become a new orthodoxy.

Unfortunately, while I was in San Antonio I didn't run into anyone from 24–7 Ibiza, a group of evangelical Christians who had been trying to save the island's waifs and strays from intoxicated self-destruction. Sometimes they just ferried vulnerable drunks back to their hotels in their Vomit Van, but occasionally they managed to convince people to pray with them. Rather charmingly, they saw themselves as part of the Ibiza culture, in their own idiosyncratic way. And maybe this was fair enough: amidst all the 'spiritual' bric-a-brac cluttering up the ideological byways of the island, why shouldn't traditional Christianity get a shot at people's souls too?

Indeed, the group's leader, Charlie Clayton, argued that there was 'a lot of very spiritual imagery' in house music – although he wasn't prepared in any way to take seriously the idea that a blissed-out rave experience was some form of religious epiphany: 'I'm not linking someone taking five pills and dancing in a club to any kind of faith,' he said tersely.[38]

Despite its dismal reputation, San Antonio had played a crucial role in defining the Balearic sound through José Padilla's lengthy sets at the beachside Café del Mar in the late eighties and nineties, which climaxed at sunset with ethereal melodies like Art of Noise's 'Moments in Love'. After Alfredo Fiorito, José Padilla *was* Balearic, at least in those early days.

Fiorito defined the Balearic Beat for the dancefloor – the Alfredo-inspired playlist in the 1988 *i-D* article listed tunes by Mory Kanté, The Woodentops, Mr Fingers and Mandy Smith, which became early scene classics in London. But Padilla developed a more ambient beach-bar approach that went on to inspire hundreds of chill-out compilations; a sound once described by American writer Philip Sherburne as 'a hippie-dippie, candy-flipping fusion of synth pop, yacht rock, acid house, faux reggae, and ambient music'.[39] (It was also more irreverently described by British journalist Frank Tope as 'pop records that sound good on pills'.)[40]

There was no accepted definition of what Balearic music was; just a series of possibilities for what it could be. Indeed it was always more of a mood or a mental attitude than a genre, although delicate flutes, languidly strummed Spanish guitars and oceanic sound effects did seem to be recurring motifs. Nevertheless, Balearic aficionados were notoriously passionate about their anti-genre genre; the few salvaged recordings of mixes and videos from clubs like Amnesia and Ku in the eighties were lovingly curated online alongside whatever photographs and memorabilia had survived from that time. Producers meanwhile kept on seeking the sonic essence of Ibiza; a Japanese DJ called Marbo even claimed to have invented his own version – 'Tokyo Balearic' – by slowing down trance tracks, while two British devotees set up a record label called Is It Balearic? 'To me it will always be music that I would love to hear on the beach or under the stars, plenty of bongos and guitars, or just maybe a feeling,' said the label's co-founder, Timm Sure, when asked for his personal definition of the genre. 'My stock answer to this age-old question "What is Balearic?" is "Who feels it knows it."'

The Café del Mar became an international brand that sold several million Balearic compilation albums, their contents selected by José Padilla. But before all that, back in the late eighties, the Spanish DJ also had to serve coffee to customers from a machine next to the decks while he was playing his sets, so lowly and functional was his role considered in those less starry times. DJs in later years did not take kindly to being asked for audience requests, let alone for a *café con leche*.

Padilla had originally moved to Ibiza from the mainland in the mid-seventies, seeking freedom from Franco's fascist Spain on an island where the LSD and Nepalese hash was plentiful. 'When I came here, it was the end of the hippie era. Pacha was just a small room and Amnesia was a place where hippies played live around a bonfire – you could see people like Pink Floyd or Paco de Lucía there,' he recalls. 'The clubs were business but it was kind of love at the same time. The owners were more naïve; of course they wanted to make money, but it wasn't the first priority.'

He first found work as a DJ at the Es Paradis club, playing every night throughout the summer, and sold mixtapes by Alfredo and other Ibiza DJs to make a little extra cash on the side. In the winter, he would take any part-time job to make ends meet, until the Café del Mar made him its evening resident and his reputation soared as his talent for sound-tracking the sunset was embraced by holidaying clubbers.

His association with the Café del Mar ended badly though, in a court case over the proceeds of the lucrative chill-out albums. Padilla ended up losing the case, then went into a period of self-destructive depression. As he languished on the sidelines, he saw the wages of others less significant to the island's musical history escalate beyond what he could ever have imagined earning himself. He felt he had been carelessly discarded by a culture that he had helped to create.

'It does hurt when you see how everyone else got rich and you didn't,' he says. 'The money these guys make – well, it's out of my understanding, really. I can't think about that. I say to myself, "Be humble, José, don't think about the past."'

After what he describes as 'a really heavy period of bad experiences and no gigs', the Ibizan sun began to shine on Padilla again as his album *So Many Colours*, a delightful pot-pourri of contemporary Balearic themes, brought him back from the wilderness in 2015. Yes, he said, DJs had become brand names – 'like McDonald's or Walmart' – but there was still space for an unconventional character like him to survive on the fringes of the mainstream, playing the music that he loved.

By that time, the Café del Mar was showing off its elevated status with a glitzy new annexe which had been built next to the original bar, with its delightfully whimsical interior decor. The scruffy, poorly lit path which used to run along the rocky beachfront had also been developed into a modern pleasure promenade, with several bars clustering cheek to cheek, each blasting out its own take on the Balearic sound.

Sometimes though the old tunes still drifted across the shimmering waters – Donna Summer's 'Love to Love You Baby', Soul II Soul's 'Back to Life' – as wristband touts worked the walkway and a promotional team from Pacha's Flower Power theme night paraded up and down carrying heart-shaped placards and strumming their guitars along to some psychedelic sixties tune.

A song from Padilla's album was playing from one of the seafront bars as I lingered for a while on the promenade, its serene chords synchronising with the gentle glide of the yachts as they eased back towards their moorings in San Antonio bay for the evening. Everything might change in Ibiza, but the sunset remained the same for everyone, however wealthy or impecunious. You could still buy a bagful of cheap beers from the nearest supermarket, perch on the rocks outside the Café del Mar, skin up a spliff and wait for the sea to swallow down the vast orange tablet of the sun in preparation for the night ahead.

And a couple of kilometres out of San Antonio, that other Balearic survivor, Alfredo Fiorito, had also found a new haven that year amid the pinks and purples of the bougainvillea, oleander and hibiscus flowers, up in the hills where the cicadas saw out their relentless Penderecki symphony in the afternoon heat and the scent of the blooms grows sweeter and heavier as evening draws in.

Alfredo had secured a weekly residency at the poolside bar at Pike's, the enchantingly rambling hotel which had been taken over from the ageing Tony Pike by Andy McKay and Dawn Hindle of Manumission, who had made it part of their Ibiza Rocks mini-empire. His eyes twinkling benevolently behind the spectacles he now wore while playing his records, Alfredo fashioned a typically affirmational mix of eighties Eurobeat, indie oddities, sun-drenched Compass Point funk and mellifluous disco, his selection a testament to his enduring talent for enkindling the most positive of vibrations.

As he played on into the evening, club veterans in their thirties, forties and fifties lounged around the pool, gulping cocktails and splashing in the water. These were the kind of people who perhaps once came here to rave hard on E, but now preferred the more agreeable environment of a boutique hotel when they made their annual pilgrimage to the White Island. They were maybe a little plumper these days, and wearing more expensive sunglasses, but for them, the Balearic beat had never stopped. And although they no longer defined the essence of the scene, they remained part of it, because this was still their music. Spelled out on a white wall outside, the hotel's slogan offered the reminder: 'You can check in but you can never check out.'

Alfredo had been in Ibiza since 1976, long enough to see his fortunes ebb and flow several times over the seasons, from the eighties extravagances of Amnesia to this rather more modest gathering by the pool at Pike's. Amnesia had secured his reputation as an innovator, but like the other original Ibiza DJs from the eighties, the men who influenced Paul Oakenfold, Sven Väth and all those others who came afterwards, he never really achieved global superstar status. The people who appreciated Alfredo were the aficionados, the ones who valued their history. 'If you want to be a star, you've got to play the game and act like one, and he hasn't done it. He's not that person,' explains Mark Broadbent, who booked him for the weekly session at Pike's.

The island wouldn't be the same if Alfredo didn't have a residency somewhere, Broadbent insists with genuine feeling. 'I love Alfredo – to me, the guy is an absolute hero,' he says. 'I wouldn't be here now, living the life that I'm living, if it wasn't for Alfredo. I owe him a lot, and there's an awful lot of people who owe him a lot, and I think sometimes that goes unnoticed.'

Like José Padilla, Alfredo saw his bookings on the island take a downturn in the 2010s. As he approached the age of 60, he had become a legend who commanded deep respect but not necessarily someone who would be booked to headline a main room packed with thousands of twenty-something clubbers. 'I'm older now and the young people now don't really know me – they're the people who pay for the tickets, and the promoters want people who pay,' he acknowledges.

Oakenfold once told me that Alfredo was a genuine pioneer, a man whose influence on the acid house movement should never be understated: 'Alfredo is the man who started it, he deserves all the credit,' he insisted.

When I quote Oakenfold's words back to Alfredo as we talk, he sounds humbled, and takes a moment to gather his thoughts before replying.

'I'm proud. I never thought that I would become this. I'm happy but I'm surprised that things went this way,' he eventually responds. 'People could say, "Alfredo is not at the top of the table", but I've been at the top of the table. Maybe I didn't react in the most intelligent way to stay at the top of the table, I don't know. But I feel proud of what I have done.'

'Some of the biggest and best DJs come to my shows in Ibiza, people I really respect… I think I've really proven all the haters wrong.'
Paris Hilton

Outside Amnesia in the early hours of Friday morning, the scarlet gleamings of dawn cast a roseate flush over the huddles of smokers sprawled out across the asphalt, their supple young bodies glowing with the lustre of tanning oils and fresh sweat. Up on the walls above them are the posters for the club's seasonal attractions: Sven Väth's Cocoon, the so-called 'underground' nights HYTE and Music On – and a billboard with a huge photograph of an American socialite turned celebrity disc jockey, Paris Hilton.

Naked and kneeling, Hilton casts a flirtatious glance over her shoulder as she promotes her weekly Foam and Diamonds party, at which the hotel heiress would spurt a cannon full of suds over her adoring supplicants at the climax of the night.

When Amnesia first recruited Hilton to front a weekly party in 2013, it was seen as the ultimate sell-out – the fabled nightclub where Balearic history was written, the place where Alfredo schooled Oakenfold and where Papa Sven revived the techno faith, was giving up the decks to a vapid reality-TV starlet who played populist US-style EDM spiced up with the occasional rock classic like 'Wonderwall' by Oasis. 'With Paris Hilton DJing at Amnesia, Ibiza is turning into Las Vegas,' grumbled Carl Craig.[41]

Some critics suggested it was proof that anyone could succeed in the high-concept, pre-programmed, press-play EDM sphere, as long as they had the right gimmick. But others argued that it was nothing more than yet another lurid manifestation of the island's gaudily painted nightlife. 'I remember UK and Australian dance music bloggers referring to her residency as if it was the end of the world, but if they were out here in Ibiza they'd have realised that her party was and still is nothing more than an additional option among many,' says Johnny Lee.

The hotel scion tried to be modest, admitting that she could understand why people thought she was a privileged fraud. 'You know, I could totally see their point. If I hadn't been to one of my shows before and I saw "Oh, Paris Hilton is gonna be a DJ", I would understand how people, if they haven't been to one of my parties, would be critical,' she told one interviewer.[42]

She insisted that she had learned her trade, namechecking DJ tech like Ableton Live and Traktor in interviews, insisting that she was always on the Beatport website, searching out the latest tunes. 'All these people that do come to my shows, when they do come, they're like "Wow, I'm so surprised, I had no idea. You're incredible. I can't believe this. This is amazing. I had the time of my life,"' she said.[43]

Mark Broadbent also says he believes that in the context of the Ibiza of the 2010s, the Paris Hilton residency at Amnesia was just another show staged for essentially the same reasons as all the others: 'I don't think it's much different from the Swedish House Mafia or David Guetta or Avicii. She's got just as much right to have a night at Amnesia as they have – she pulls in huge crowds,' Broadbent argues. 'To me, it's symptomatic of what Ibiza is now, and it makes perfect sense.'

French superstar Guetta, who turned electronic dance music into big-time pop with his collaborations with American R&B luminaries like the Black Eyed Peas, Nicki Minaj, Kelly Rowland and Usher, also became the target of online condemnation for a stunt he staged in Ibiza in July 2015. At 4am, at the peak of his Fuck Me I'm Famous night at Pacha, Guetta donned a Native American head-dress and bestrode a horse in an apparent tribute to Bianca Jagger's fabled equestrian appearance at Studio 54 in New York back in 1977.

He certainly made an impact, but perhaps not in the way he would have wished; instead of winning applause for his showmanship, his stunt was seen as a preposterous act of hubris; nightclub history repeating itself as corporate farce. He was condemned for animal cruelty by subjecting the horse to the noise and teeming crowds, and Pacha had to issue a grovelling apology.

Hilton and Guetta took flak because they were seen as symbols of the over-commercialisation of Ibiza, the pin-up girl and poster boy of the big-spending, bottle-buying, VIP-room-lounging elite who had adopted electronic dance music as a fashionable lifestyle accessory and were now poisoning its very soul with their filthy money, or so the critics alleged. (Hilton got it worse because she was female, while Guetta could at least cite credible roots in the Parisian house demi-monde of the nineties.)

There had always been celebrities in Ibiza even before the island had nightclubs, while the eighties had attracted people like Freddie Mercury, Diego Maradona, Roman Polanski and Grace Jones to the dancefloors. (It wasn't always the glamorous ones, however; the only celebs I ever spotted were disgraced glam rocker Gary Glitter and *Coronation Street* soap-opera actor Christopher Quinten partying one night at Ku.) But now there were increasing numbers of oligarchs, tycoons and super-rich entrepreneurs holidaying here too. 'Sometimes you'll be sitting in a bar in Ibiza Town, near the marina, and you'll look out and see five of the 12 biggest yachts in the world moored in the harbour,' says Johnny Lee. 'Make no mistake: this island is a serious hub for serious people.'

An article in *The New York Times* style supplement claimed in 2014 that the island was being reinvented by the high rollers and mega-rich moguls as a kind of competitor to Marbella or Saint-Tropez. 'Another Ibiza is emergent,' it gushed. 'Where the white-whale yachts of the billionaires Lakshmi Mittal, Roman Abramovich, David Geffen and the Saudi royal family are impossible to miss.'[44]

According to Alfredo, the wealthy used to have to find their own spot at Amnesia along with everyone else. Even Prince Albert of Monaco, when he partied there in the eighties, didn't get any royal treatment. 'He never had a private room, we never had reservation tables. I think this is really important. You can sit where the hell you want – yeah, you buy ten bottles of Moët & Chandon, but you have to drink it where you can. That created the whole atmosphere,' Alfredo recalls.

But now the richer punters were demanding the VIP environment they thought they deserved – their own exclusive section of the club with a view of the action on the floor but far enough away from the plebs with their smartphones. They needed a hard-raving crowd, but only as extras for their own drama.

Alfredo wasn't the only veteran who believed things had gone too far in the pursuit of profit. Carl Cox, an iconic presence at Space since the nineties, announced in 2015 that he was finally calling time on his residency after it was disclosed that its owner, Pepe Roselló, would be handing the club over to the Matutes family portfolio. 'Ibiza is spoilt now,' Cox said. 'You can go down to the Hard Rock Hotel and you've got Ushuaïa with its high-end DJs, big bottle-service tables and two-tier VIP areas. Everyone used to be together when they went out and on the same dancefloor... You used to be able to afford to make the most of your money on the island but now you need a lot to enjoy it.'[45] Paul Oakenfold was even more blunt: 'I think the island is a total and utter rip-off now,' he grumbled.[46]

The promoters said they could do little to change the excruciatingly high ticket and drinks prices – after all, the punters demanded a lavish spectacle and the club owners had to make a year's money in just two or three months. 'We tried several times to appeal to the clubs to lower the drink prices, at least for water and beer, but nobody seems to want to take the first step,' complained Cocoon's promoter in Ibiza, Johannes Goller.[47] Any sympathy for the owners waned a little further when Spanish tax officials and anti-corruption police raided Amnesia in July 2016 and discovered €2 million in cash stashed away.

The island's tourism chiefs also became highly sensitive about the island's druggy reputation as they sought to project a more upmarket image. After Michael Posner had a hit with a counterintuitively miserable dirge called 'I Took a Pill in Ibiza', about coming down after a chemically enhanced night out, tourism director Vicent Ferrer moaned that the singer should have focused on Ibiza's 'museums, beaches, culture and gastronomy' instead of MDMA-fuelled raving.[48]

Some observers worried about the possibility of luxury seafront developments swallowing up the remnants of the old laid-back Ibiza, replacing it with upmarket hotels, homogenised leisure complexes and golf courses. Others, like Mark Broadbent, believed that the whole concept of clubbing on the island had become just another form of mainstream entertainment, no longer 'counterculture' in any way at all.

'What we did has become the sound of the high street – it's everywhere, everyone's into it,' Broadbent argues. 'The clubs are busier now than they've ever been, but the bigger ones are just full of people standing facing the DJ and taking photos. They're normal people, they're not total freaks. They're not drug lunatics who've been asleep on the beach all day and only wake up at night.'

The phrase 'it's not as good as it used to be' had been a perennial refrain in clubland since the early days of acid house in London back in 1988, when the original Ibiza contingent expressed their resentment about the late-coming 'acid teds' in their lilac hoodies and Kickers gatecrashing their scene and ruining it. Whether this kind of resistance to change is simple human conservatism or the preservation of essential values depends on one's viewpoint and place in time.

Jamie Jones, one of the Ibiza darlings of the 2010s, who arrived on the island for the first time as a seasonal 'worker' at the age of 19 and then hustled his way into a DJ residency at Manumission before eventually getting his own headline night at DC10, admitted that the island's future was uncertain, but urged the moaners to shut up and enjoy the pleasures that it could still offer.

'The powers that be wanted to turn Ibiza into the new Saint-Tropez. It's a balance between progressing the island as a place for the wealthy and for Ibiza still to be the clubbing capital of the world,' Jones said. 'But I do hate it when people say, "Oh, it's not like it used to be." If you can go now, you'll still have an amazing time as a passionate clubber. When you step off that plane, you'll still feel something special.'[49]

In the summer of 2015, Jesus M. Sobrino, CEO of the Matutes family's Palladium Hotel Group, which ran the Ushuaïa club, gave an interview to the Ushuaïa magazine about the amazing success of Ushuaïa. After listing the number of pyrotechnic devices that had been set off during the season, as well as the cumulative weight of the confetti and the total length of all the streamers that the venue had used, Sobrino explained how Ushuaïa had 'truly been a game-changer for Ibiza'.

Repeating the company's brand slogan for the clubbing resort, Sobrino said that Ushuaïa was an amusement park for adults – a place that could offer its clients 'the correct balance of open-air live music experiences, extraordinary food and beverage outlets, luxury accommodation and a real lifestyle experience'.[50]

Extraordinary food and beverage outlets aside, Sobrino's interview highlighted a shift in public discourse. Even at their most avariciously commercial, Ibiza's clubs had usually dressed up their intentions in Smiley-faced rhetoric. But when Ushuaïa became the latest big player in Ibiza nightlife in 2011, it made no secret of the fact that it was going for upscale, aspirational values – a break with the faux-hippie spin that had prevailed in Ibiza clubland's self-promotion for the previous couple of decades.

Ushuaïa, with its immaculate professionalism and spectacular, pyrotechnically charged poolside shows featuring celebrity DJs like

David Guetta, Steve Aoki, Avicii and Armin van Buuren, had identified a crucial fact: 'underground' credibility wasn't necessarily the way to ensure a substantial return on investment. The music worshipped by hardcore clubbers and zealous journalists at magazines like *DJ* and *Mixmag* might generate revenue from the faithful, but it would not be enough.

'The thing is, the underground ravers and the worker crews out here in Ibiza are really passionate about their dance music. They're fanatics, and whether it's online or via word of mouth, they do all the talking. They create the trends and the culture, but unfortunately they don't tend to spend much money,' explains Johnny Lee. 'While transient EDM fans are happy to fly in and pay €80 to see a David Guetta show, most underground heads want to be on the guest list and they never buy many drinks.'

In a sobering report for the *Guardian* in 2014, writer Ben Beaumont-Thomas was given a guided tour of Ushuaïa by its artistic director, Yann Pissenem, who confirmed that hardcore techno devotees didn't spend much money in his club, but wealthy Emiratis, Russians and Chinese did. 'If I want to make an underground party, I can do it in my garage with a few friends; Ushuaïa is a business,' Pissenem said. Beaumont-Thomas then delivered a chilling evocation of disco hell: 'As I walk around Pissenem's vision of "an amusement park for adults", early-twenties ravers fringe the pool while sugar daddies relax with premium vodka in ice buckets, as Armin van Buuren plays a trance remix of "Let It Go" from [Disney children's film] *Frozen*.'[51]

The tension between creativity and commerce had long been a central theme in electronic dance music, like everywhere else in the arts. While discussing the corporate sponsorship of Berlin's Love Parade, German DJ Westbam once argued that without wealthy patrons, Michaelangelo would never have painted the Sistine Chapel. But how much was too much? How far was too far? Was there a line, and who would really know when it had been crossed?

I wanted to put the question to one of the world's most astute Ibiza-watchers, Ben Turner, a former editor of clubbing periodical *Muzik* who later helmed Pacha's promotional magazine and co-founded the International Music Summit, a roving symposium for industry insiders. Turner first visited Ibiza in 1993 after being captivated by *A Short Film About Chilling*, the documentary that was shot during my own first visit to the island. He had been back several times a year every year since then.

'In terms of music, what Ibiza has done is incredible. It has projected underground music and leaders within that music globally as superstars,' he tells me as we sit down to talk in Ibiza Town one afternoon. 'It's the only place in the world apart from Berlin where the underground sits parallel with the mainstream.'

That was the good news, but Turner had more to say.

'I've been coming here and working here for 20-plus years but I must confess that this is the first time that I've felt worried about the future of the island,' he continues. 'It is thriving – it's thriving at the top end of the scale with millionaires and billionaires, booking tables, buying bottles. They're not dedicated electronic music fans, they're following a trend. And we're all to blame – we've all created this culture, we've been pushing so hard for it.'

A crucial turning point came with the arrival of two icons of American bling, P Diddy and Paris Hilton, Turner suggests. These were not celebrities in the old-school Grace Jones or Freddie Mercury sense. They were creatures of a contemporary culture of fame who lived their lives in the lens and had no shame or reticence about displaying their wealth; indeed, it could be argued that conspicuous consumption helped to fuel their careers. But they also fell in love with Ibiza, and they went on to tell their peers what a great place it was to spend a hedonistic summer.

'It was those two really who helped make the shift, their obsession with the island,' says Turner. 'They've been here every year since, and they created this huge fascination, this huge celebrity following – everywhere they went on the island, there were cameras.'

Shaky video footage from the mid-2000s showed millionaire hip-hop entrepreneur Diddy raving on the dancefloor at the DC10 club way after the sun had risen, surrounded by drug-spangled clubbers and clearly lost in the music. 'My first time in Ibiza – the island just took me,' he recounted later.[52] Diddy also rocked up at Manumission in 2003 to perform his naïvely enthusiastic tribute to house music, 'Let's Get Ill'.

Turner put Diddy on the cover of the Pacha magazine. 'I had to chase him all over the island to get this interview because he really symbolised this new interest in dance music,' he recalled. In the years that followed, Diddy went on to record with some of the brightest talents in the genre – Deep Dish, Felix da Housecat, Stuart Price, DJ Hell – and completed an Ibiza tribute album with tech-house DJ Guy Gerber, which he said he originally wanted to call *Ketamine* but ended up being called *11 11*. Whatever Diddy found in Ibiza, it seemed to genuinely mean something to him, and he fell far deeper into the fantasy than all the other American hip-hop stars who dropped a pill or two and started plundering Euro-trance riffs to energise their tunes.

Diddy and Hilton introduced the island to a new constituency of wealthy globetrotters who expected luxury everywhere they alighted, argues Turner: 'Those two, with their network and their social world, from the Hamptons to Saint-Tropez, the yachts they came in on, the parties they had on those yachts, it just opened up attention from people in those kinds of resorts where house music was not relevant; they were all listening to R&B. Through their passion for it, which was very genuine, suddenly the yachts started coming. The Saint-Tropez crowd became aware of Ibiza and the Americans followed.'

This was not how people like Ben Turner first arrived on the island, however. Like most of us, he came on a relatively limited budget, not on a yacht. This he remembers.

'I was 16 when I first came here and watched the sunset at Café del Mar and it completely changed my perspective on life and on music, and I've come back every year since,' he says. And he worries that future generations of electronic music devotees might eventually be priced out of having the same experience: 'You need places where you can bring your own drinks and listen to DJs for free or go to cheap clubs; at that age you're scared to go into Pacha or Space because of the cost.'

Turner was a true believer in the magic of Ibiza's nightlife – he even edited a book about it, back in the nineties – but I got a sense of real concern about whether what had once been a fragile and imperfect kind-of-almost-sort-of-maybe-democracy was increasingly becoming a hegemony of the rich.

'I still love the island, but I just think it's gone too far,' he explains. 'The new success stories are all geared to that high-end spender. Ibiza has always had this social mix and it's always been quite well-balanced, but I think that balance has tipped in favour of the wealthy, unfortunately.'

'The island has changed a lot – but we've changed a lot too.'
Richie Hawtin

The sun is up but we're not sweating any more as the breeze sweeps across the terrace with its tropical foliage and ochre-daubed walls, shaded from the fierceness of the midday heat by flowing drapes and verdant palms. Bikini-clad girls in feather boas and cowboy hats are sketching out butterfly figures with their fans, buff Spanish boys are rocking their Antonio Banderas look in skin-hugging Moschino tops, and dreadlocked ravers in superfly sunglasses are bouncing on their toes to carefree piano riffs alongside lithesome young Brazilians pouting and posing in leather hotpants and techno-hippies in fractal-print shirts and tie-dyed harem pants

'I feel right, the music sounds better with you...' Cheers go up again and again as the planes scream upwards and away from the airport and that Stardust-Chaka Khan riff plays on and on. Inside the club meanwhile, the ceiling lights sparkle overhead like a faraway galaxy and heels clatter in time on the tiled floor to the darkest of dark techno. We arrived here somewhere around breakfast time, and by the time we eventually leave, time itself will have lost any meaning. It is 1998 and we are in Space; for us at least, these were not the worst of times.

Because for a few wonderful years in the happy-go-lucky aftermath of the rave era, losing yourself on the terrace at Space was one of the most euphoric experiences that could be had during daylight on the European continent. It was also a place where, as the club's owner, Pepe Roselló, often liked to say, 'there are the most beautiful people per square metre in the world'.

Roselló opened Space in 1989 with what he claimed was the idea of creating a place where everyone was equal on the dancefloor, where there were no VIPs, no cameras were allowed, and freedom reigned. 'I am anti-bourgeois… I understand that music makes us equals,' he insisted.[53] No cameras, total equality, one nation under a groove – it didn't last long, but life's like that…

A couple of decades later, above that same tiled floor in Space, Richie Hawtin appears to be floating inside some mysterious kind of rocky grotto like a sorcerer conjuring his spells beneath a turbid moon-disc that glows green and then white with artificial translucence, the techno aesthete handing down truth and discipline to his island domain. Baneful flashes of light and bursts of smoke spew forth as if we're caught in an electric storm on some distant planet as the drums power on and on and on and on and on… My notes scribbled half-blind in the darkness of Hawtin's ENTER party that night are almost unintelligible: 'Senses are distorted, reality has dissipated, everything is alien, yellow searchlights swinging low strafing the crowd, red bursts now as if there was some weird volcanic eruption… Hawtin is punishing, relentless.'

A couple of days beforehand, I was interviewing Hawtin at the pool bar of the Gran Hotel near the marina in Ibiza Town. In black vest and shorts, with a bleached-blond fringe and his old Plastikman tattoo on his arm, he was toned and lean and ready for the season. He politely obliged a group of tourists who interrupted him in the middle of the interview and asked for a souvenir photo together.

What he didn't tell me – with the charming modesty of a British-born Canadian – was that earlier that week, he had been given an honorary doctorate by the University of Huddersfield for services to music technology. Fittingly, it was presented to him by Patrick Stewart, who played Captain Jean-Luc Picard in *Star Trek: The Next Generation*, a crucial influence on the youthful mind-opening of this techno voyager. 'The significance of receiving my honorary award from a man whose performances had been inspiring to me as a technology and computer obsessed adolescent cannot go unsaid,' Hawtin wrote in a statement afterwards. 'Often myself and many other young techno producers would try to imagine how the music of the future would sound. Shows like *Star Trek: The Next Generation* gave us the visual cues and helped our imaginations soar.'[54]

I didn't ask him about this, because I didn't find out about it until later. Instead I asked him about his friend Ben Turner's concerns about the future of Ibiza.

'The island has changed a lot – but we've changed a lot too,' Hawtin responded. He seemed to be choosing his words carefully; maybe he always does. 'When I came in the early 2000s with Sven [Väth], techno wasn't so big on the island. The internet wasn't so prevalent, YouTube didn't exist, there weren't so many people taking photos, so we had our freedom. I can only talk from my perspective, but it felt like an island of freedom.

'I don't feel as free on the island as I did, but I think that's for many, many different reasons – obligations, technology, expectations from the crowd. But I look around and I see people coming for the first time, going out and enjoying the freedom and the hedonistic lifestyle that I've already gone through, and that's incredible. In that way, yes, it's still a magic island. That's all still there but there are a lot of other things overshadowing it these days.'

Any attack on the integrity of the 'Ibiza spirit' was immediately repulsed by the true believers. When a BBC documentary in the mid-2010s asked whether the island had lost its magic, Clara da Costa flashed back on social media: 'Ibiza will never lose its magic, it is an island full of beauty, love, energy and creative beings which is continuously evolving.'[55]

The veteran Boy's Own DJ Terry Farley, an island regular since the

Ibiza 90 jaunt, was a little more sceptical when he responded to da Costa's comment: 'Ibiza is a wonderful place but the clubs and restaurants have been complicit in abusing the clubbing tourists for far too many years now… most people who are clued up have had enough,' he wrote. But others then chipped in to insist that although the big-ticket nightclubs had lost their soul, there were still off-the-track, word-of-mouth parties where the magic could thrive. 'People really do have to avoid following the usual paths,' one insisted.[56]

It's not as good as it used to be… Like all of us, Richie Hawtin had heard this kind of complaint many times in many places before: 'I'm sure there were people having the same discussion 20 or 30 years ago,' he said.

There probably were, and some older Ibiza veterans even felt that the island's best years had ended in the seventies, long before it became a raving destination. Some of them set up a website called Ibiza Times to eulogise the characters who had brought a certain finesse to the good old days. 'Many Ibiza legends and artists will tell you that the best time on Ibiza was from 1966 till maximum 1975,' it insisted.[57]

And maybe *all* of it was true, maybe *our* time was always the greatest – whoever we were and whenever it was – the time when we looked younger and lived looser, before we started to feel that whatever we had experienced so intensely had somehow become transformed into an oversold facsimile of the 'real thing'.

That Ibiza myth which had enchanted so many had been embellished over the years by a cast of the most colourful characters – by Raoul Hausmann and Bad Jack Hand, by Tony Pike and Freddie Mercury, by Pink Floyd and Wham!, by Alfredo Fiorito and Paul Oakenfold, by Sven Väth and Richie Hawtin, amongst all the others. But perhaps as importantly, it had been enhanced by all those unknown or forgotten bohemians and artists and writers and hippies and ravers who passed through, spreading the wild tales that brought others here in search of what their predecessors had found. But would all of them have ended up here if the best the island had to offer was an 'amusement park for adults'?

I thought about what Alfredo had told me a couple of days earlier, about how he was not so despondent about Ibiza's future: 'I think Ibiza can maintain its spirit because it already maintained its spirit for the last 30 years or more,' he had insisted. 'I think there's something about the island that keeps this feeling, despite the development and commercialisation. Why are people still attracted to come here generation after generation after generation? It proves that the magic is still there.'

Was Alfredo right? Could something as fragile and indefinable as 'magic' really hold its own against tough-minded capitalist realism, against the profit logic of VIP rooms and luxury hotels? Many of the big-name international DJs were so wealthy and cosseted by this point that they could not have been expected to have any frame of reference to enable them to understand how expensive it had become for an ordinary person with even a half-decent European salary to go and party in Ibiza for a week or two, let alone to live the Balearic dream for an entire summer. Completely disconnected from the realities that most people inhabited, the star DJs' world was closer to that of merchant bankers. It was not just about ludicrously overpriced bottles of water, it was about the fact that ordinary clubbers were being fleeced by almost everyone at every turn and that young free-spirited creatives like the working-class Brits who helped to pioneer this whole acid house caper might never again be able to afford to spend their formative summers on the island, living cheap and raving hard. Because as Ibiza went upmarket, the 'magic' was being sold off like London apartments to offshore account-holding billionaires.

'What needs to be maintained is the diversity and the uniqueness of the island, because what happens to so many places is they become homogenised,' argued Hawtin. 'The little beach bars, the freedom to have surprise events and free parties on the beach and not just institutionalised nightclubs where you're paying for a ticket – enough freedom for a bit of craziness.'

Enough freedom for a bit of craziness... maybe, in the end, this was one of the best definitions of the Balearic magic that we were likely to find. But as we sat there in that hotel in Ibiza Town, those idyllic little beach bars were being shut down by the police and the developers were scheming over their grand plans to monetise our collective fantasy.

In places rendered increasingly unrecognisable by gentrification, there comes a point when it's time for the free-thinkers to move on. Not long afterwards, Hawtin announced that his ENTER club would not be returning to do another summer season on the island. In 2016, Space closed down too, and was relaunched the following year as Hï Ibiza, a companion venue to Ushuaïa – but not before it celebrated the end of 27 delirious summers under the flightpath on the Playa d'en Bossa strip with a monumental 20-hour finale featuring more than a hundred DJs. 'It's not just about a club closing. It's about a part of our life closing,' one of them, Steve Lawler, told the BBC.[58]

As the marathon session came to an end, just before Carl Cox played the final song, Angie Stone's 'Wish I Didn't Miss You', Space's 80-year-old boss, Pepe Roselló, picked up the microphone and delivered his last testimonial to all those who had found happiness on his dancefloor over the decades: 'Your emotions and love will remain here forever.'

Other clubs would take its place in the life of the culture, of course, and new people would be drawn to Ibiza by the myths and the mayhem, just as we had been years before. But now it seemed that no one could really predict with any kind of certainty exactly how much freedom they might find when they got there.

4

Electric Dream Machine

Las Vegas

GAZING DOWN FROM ABOVE, the gargantuan speedway arena looks like a phantasmagorical encampment nestling deep in the desertified wilderness, a pop-up land of make-believe conjured from light and sound. Under the waxy glow of a gibbous moon, Ferris wheels spin geometric patterns like huge op-art installations next to stages that resemble cyborg spaceships, CGI-generated pagan temples and mutant fortresses; one after another they flush with colour, as bursts of flame billow upwards, LED displays flicker, fountains spurt jets of water and searchlights strafe the terrain. A fire-breathing metal octopus blazes infernally while a huge billboard spells out the plea: 'Love and care for one another.'

The three-day Electric Daisy Carnival just outside Las Vegas was perhaps the ultimate raver's theme park of its time, the quintessential EDM extravaganza and a symbol of how dance music had finally become a mainstream youth culture in the US, some two decades after it happened in Europe. As the gates opened in the ferocious heat that day in June, in surged the carnival's dayglo disciples, this fresh-faced flock of more than 130,000 youths who had flown or driven across country to be here this weekend and arrayed themselves in their most flamboyant glad rags for the occasion: a group of boys got up as Superman with their girlfriends channelling Wonder Woman, three lads with fluffy bunny ears and rainbow flags, a couple hiding their faces behind *Planet of the Apes* masks, someone dressed as a bishop holding up a big cardboard cross embellished with the old-school American rave slogan 'PLUR' (peace, love, unity and respect), and hundreds of scantily attired teens in bikinis, sparkly lingerie and tiny tutus, recklessly baring their buttocks to the unforgiving Nevada sun.

Many of them moved through the arena in little tribes clustered around home-made totems that looked like a weird form of naïve American folk art. There were illuminated lanterns with slogans like 'Good vibes' and 'The rave never stops', drawings of hearts and Smileys, wacky aliens and kooky animals, placards with rallying cries like 'Put your fucking hands up!' or congenial entreaties like 'If you're lonely, dance with us'. Some of their T-shirts also offered enthusiastic declarations of intent for the weekend ahead: 'Let's get weird!' 'Let's get lost!'

On the main stage under vast projection-mapping screens, American duo The Chainsmokers were bashing out that brashly capricious EDM blend of aggression and sentimentality – gnarly basslines, serrated noise-riffs, plaintive pop vocals, mawkish trance interludes and belligerent hip-hop-style ranting. As they bounced around like boxers in the ring, wraiths in fluffy moonboots lifted their smartphones to snap mementoes and steroidal bros raised their brawny fists in unison like a raging mob of shirtless American footballers, braying impatiently for the drop.

But populist EDM wasn't the only sound on offer in this clamorous hippodrome in the wilds of Nevada; nearby stages were throbbing to bolshy dubstep, syrupy trance and even the deepest of house music. In a huge tent over on the other side of the speedway, the Nigeria-born Lebanese DJ Nicole Moudaber was dragging a motley horde of vivacious freaks, tough-looking LA queens and hard-jacking technoheads deep into a shimmering whirlpool of hypnotic syncopation that summoned up visions of Berlin's Panoramabar.

With their devil-may-care outfits and handmade placards, many of the Electric Daisy Carnival faithful really did contribute to the experience rather just consuming it like a product they had bought. These were the people who Pasquale Rotella, the founder of Insomniac, the company that had been running the event for 20 years by that point, described as his festival's 'headliners'. Insomniac even made a film about them, *Under the Electric Sky*, showing how some travelled hundreds of miles to the festival to escape from small-town conformity. 'When we're all together, we can express ourselves,' one says in the film.[1] These were the partygoers who, Rotella insisted, were the real stars of his show, and without whom it would not exist.

'The idea came from the California underground rave scene, when the dancer was just as important as the DJ at the party,' he explained to me in Las Vegas a couple of days before the 2016 Electric Daisy Carnival got under way. 'This was before the term EDM came about and before dance music crossed over and was commercially accepted. When that happened, people wanted to treat it like rock 'n' roll, where they're a fan of a DJ and they just go stand and watch them – and that's not what dance music was about. The people were and still are as important as whoever is on stage. It's almost as if they are performing for the DJ as much as the DJ is performing for them – and they're also performing for each other.'

Rotella was one of EDM's prime instigators, and his story was a classic American Dream narrative, perhaps appropriately for someone who once said his hero was Walt Disney. He grew up relatively poor, the son of Italian immigrants, but went on to become America's pre-eminent party entrepreneur, marry a Playboy bunny turned reality-TV star called Holly Madison, and run what *Rolling Stone* called a '$47 million EDM empire' after selling half of Insomniac to the giant events corporation Live Nation. But he remained keen to show respect for his roots and prove that he wasn't just in it for the money. 'I'm still just a guy from the dancefloor – I'm another raver. That's where I come from,' insisted the forty-something promoter in his black baseball cap and hooded Nike jacket. 'I think that the way to have success in this [EDM] world is to not lose yourself and do it for the original reasons, which is to bring people together. You've got to pay attention to the spreadsheets but you don't live or die by the spreadsheets. You have to be a businessman, but if you've never been a fan, some things can fall to the wayside.'

The teenage Rotella became a rave convert back in 1990, when it was still a little-known phenomenon in the US. But his was not a story of chancing upon some clandestine gay house dive or picking up the cosmic transmissions of a radio auteur like The Electrifying Mojo. The

American rave scene developed largely outside the black/gay disco-influenced traditions of New York and Chicago; house music never really broke out of its subcultural big-city undergrounds in a country and at a time where music with such connotations was never likely to achieve mass acceptance. Instead, American rave was strongly influenced by the British scene and the full-on mentalism of UK hardcore. Indeed some of the best-known of the big American parties were inspired by their promoters' own transformative experiences of going to raves in Britain, such as Frankie Bones' outlaw Storm Rave bashes in Brooklyn and the cyberdelic Toon Town parties in San Francisco.

American ravers also took some of their stylistic cues from British E-heads as they developed their own image, what became known as the 'candy raver' look – ballooning, wildly over-flared trousers known as 'phat pants', fluffy backpacks, cartoon-character T-shirts, multicoloured bracelets – and their own way of moving on the dancefloor, a gawky teenager's gambol-and-skip of a dance that complemented the kindergarten image.

Rotella loved all this. He loved the empathic vibes and the bonkers music and the wacky clothes; in the early days, he would go to parties in LA all dressed up in a top hat and baggy overalls with a backpack filled with lollipops in the Dr Seuss-influenced style of the times. But even as the biggest event of the era was staged in Orange County, California in 1993 – Rave America, organised by Gary Richards, later to become another key player in the rise of EDM and a competitor to Rotella – the scene hit a downturn in LA following a series of police busts.

This only inspired Rotella to start running his own outlaw parties to fill the emotional gap which had opened up in his weekends. 'I wanted to bring back the days when I was happiest, and the only way something was going to happen was if I did it myself,' he explained. 'When I started, the event was an extension of me, it was everything that was in my head, it was the event that I wanted to go to.'

Rotella's tenacity and vaulting ambition was to sustain him through the decades that followed and lay some of the groundwork for what would eventually become EDM. His first Electric Daisy Carnival was held indoors, at the Shrine Expo Hall in downtown LA in 1997, with a computer-warped bees-and-flowers flyer promising 'The Greatest Show on Earth'. That meant a single stage, a screen showing trippy visuals, around 5,000 ravers, no alcohol and a humid atmosphere that 'distinctly smelled of Vicks VapoRub', according to journalist Kiko Miyasato. The partygoers were candy ravers in childish costumes, flying on MDMA and sucking on babies' dummies, Miyasato recalled: 'It was a sea of pigtails, JNCO [ultra-flared] pants, stuffed-animal backpacks, Adidas shell-toe sneakers and visors, Looney Tunes T-shirts, Kangol hats, oversize track suits, rainbow-colored accessories, pacifiers... and lots of smiles.'[2]

Rotella had adopted the Electric Daisy Carnival name from raves organised by an LA character called Steve Kool-Aid – Stephen Enos, who went on to become a private chef for tennis stars Venus and Serena Williams. Enos would later take Rotella to court over the trademark, one of several bruising legal encounters that the Insomniac boss endured as he became increasingly successful, including an indictment for alleged involvement in a bribery-and-embezzlement scheme with the manager of the LA venue he was using for his parties. These charges were eventually dropped in 2016, but Rotella pleaded guilty to a conflict-of-interest misdemeanour and had to pay $150,000 in compensation and serve three years of probation.

Before Rotella's first Electric Daisy Carnival, the LA rave scene of the mid-nineties still had something of an outlaw vibe, according to Miyasato: 'Parties popped up in abandoned warehouses downtown, privately owned farms and the middle of the Mojave Desert,' she recalled. 'Turntables, strobe lights, fog machines and other equipment ran off generators. To find the parties, you had to call a hotline or be in the know, and go on a treasure hunt-like search around the city to finally acquire the address of the party.'[3]

Rotella sought to professionalise the concept and raise the production values of his shows each year. His early headliners at the Electric Daisy Carnival in LA were relatively cutting-edge, with house and techno icons like Carl Craig, Green Velvet, Miguel Migs, Doc Martin and Felix da Housecat, ambient DJs like Mixmaster Morris and various drum and bass mavens behind the decks, and it was only around the mid-2000s when a more recognisably big-arena soundtrack started to emerge with names like Ferry Corsten, Paul Oakenfold, Kaskade and Paul van Dyk taking prominent positions on the Electric Daisy Carnival flyers. Most of the events didn't even make Rotella much profit, he said, at least not at first, although he insisted that he didn't care much about that: 'I am committed to this because I love it so much,' he asserted. 'This is what makes me happy, and even when struggling financially, I was happy. Money can make things easier, but if you have enough, you're good.'

His perseverance finally paid off big-time when EDM became an all-American youth culture explosion at the end of the 2000s. But paradoxically it was a mortal tragedy in LA that would draw media attention to how big the scene had become, and then take Rotella to what was to become EDM's spiritual home, Las Vegas.

He managed to stage his biggest ever Electric Daisy Carnival to date at the Memorial Colosseum football stadium in LA in 2010, but its success was overshadowed by the death of a 15-year-old girl who had taken MDMA. It sparked a moral panic in the US media, which suddenly realised that a mass-market dance-drug movement had emerged in the US, as if by stealth, unnoticed and largely unreported in the mainstream press. The scandal and its political repercussions caused the Electric Daisy Carnival to quit LA and move across the desert to the Las Vegas Motor Speedway.

'We don't use the word "rave" anymore.'

US dance music events promoter

It took more than two-and-a-half decades for dance music in the US to get from underground clubs like the Warehouse in Chicago and the Paradise Garage in New York to the colossal arenas of stadium EDM, exemplified by the Electric Daisy Carnival in Las Vegas and Ultra in Miami. Along the way, the route from marginal subculture to entertainment business was littered with the detritus of busted booms; there had been a series of anticipated commercial breakthroughs for the scene over the years, but until the end of the 2000s, all of them proved unsustainable.

The start of the nineties saw the first house hits in the US: upbeat, poppy tracks like Deee-Lite's 'Groove is in the Heart' and C+C Music Factory's 'Gonna Make You Sweat'. But the pop hits did not achieve critical mass and the rave circuit remained fragmented across the huge land mass of the United States, a country which did not have a creatively minded and publicly funded national music broadcaster like Britain's BBC Radio 1 to unite it aesthetically, and no internet through which people could make common cause and propagandise their culture, even though rudimentary pre-web emailing lists like NW-Raves, MW-Raves, NYC-Raves and SF-Raves did emerge as the nineties progressed and the scene slowly developed nodes of activity all over the country. Incidentally, Brian Behlendorf, who started SF-Raves, was also one of the creators of the Apache HTTP server, the most widely used web server software in the world; back in the early nineties, rave culture and the California tech scene were deeply intertwined. 'There was this missionary sense of, "You're inventing the future at your day job, and you're inventing the future at the stuff you do for play,"' Behlendorf told writer Michaelangelo Matos. 'A lot of people that I met at parties and at the SF-Raves lists were also programmers I ended up working with.'[4]

Mass-access broadband internet would become one of the key factors that fuelled the popularity of EDM. But in the America of the nineties, ravers were anomalous figures, recalls Liz Miller, who started her career handing out flyers for parties in Colorado so she could get in free, and eventually ended up becoming the head of artist relations at dance-music digital supermarket Beatport.

'We really were an underground community,' says Miller. 'Even if you were on vacation with your parents somewhere and you would spot another raver in a Walmart, you would exchange this knowing glance. You definitely felt extremely connected.

'It was a community but there wasn't much information; people weren't really online and all you knew was just what you could read in media outlets. I knew nothing of Ibiza. I knew nothing about the "summer of love" in England.'

Tommie Sunshine (Thomas Lorello), a charismatic rave DJ and party head from Chicago who had been one of the few white teenagers who used to go to listen to black DJs like Ron Hardy in the eighties and went on to collaborate with Felix da Housecat on his classic *Kittenz and Thee Glitz* album, suggests that this lack of information was one of the factors that caused the scene to remain fractured and marginal for years.

'Living in Chicago, in order to find out more about the people who came from our city, we had to go buy British magazines for $12 to read interviews with Marshall Jefferson, with Adonis, with Farley Jackmaster Funk, because no one here gave a fuck about what they were doing,' Sunshine explains. 'Which is mental – and it was that way all the way through the nineties. It was the only way we could find out about anything.'

The second coming of rave in the US in 1997 also saw its first rebranding – as 'electronica'. This attempt to redefine the music as a more MTV-programmable, college radio-friendly phenomenon was focused on British outfits like The Prodigy, the Chemical Brothers and Fatboy Slim, who it was hoped would become album-selling rock 'n' roll-style stars with long-term careers rather than 'faceless' trackheads making tunes for the clubs under bewildering arrays of aliases.

They were also mostly white; black originators like Juan Atkins, Derrick May and Jeff Mills were never really considered commercial prospects by the record companies hoping to profit from the hoped-for electronica boom. Live shows by The Prodigy and Fatboy Slim meanwhile had enough heterosexual thrust to entertain rock-raised kids who might never consider getting into music with gay disco roots. The musicians despised the term, of course: 'I hate this whole electronica thing!' Liam Howlett of The Prodigy ranted to me when I asked him about it at the time. 'The whole thing is just so hyped, it's crap.'[5]

But even this paler rebranding was seen by some commentators as a pernicious threat to rock's values of 'authenticity' – and perhaps, according to one panicked op-ed in *The New York Times*, even a precursor to the death of humanity in music itself. 'Techno-heads embrace a future in which the authentic gives way to the synthetic, the idiosyncratic voice to the noise and glut of the mass mind,' critic Michiko Kakutani fretted.[6]

The year after the electronica hype, I was commissioned by the *Washington Post* to write an article explaining why it had 'failed' as a commercial proposition in the US because only The Prodigy and the Chemical Brothers had managed to make the top-200 bestsellers list in 1997. The editor of the US edition of *Mixmag* at the time, Darren Ressler, told me he had been through it all before: 'In 1992, I saw the dance departments at major labels go wild. The word "techno" was suddenly on everyone's lips, and after releasing tons of mostly horrible compilations, everything went underground again. Still, the upside was that the seeds of the culture were planted.'[7]

Tamara Palmer, an editor at the California-based dance zine *Urb*, argued that a techno 'cottage industry' was developing across the US, a cultural network that was growing organically with little connection to the mainstream record industry. It was also noted that when the Sex Pistols toured the US back in 1978, they were sold as the latest British pop sensation, but *Never Mind the Bollocks* only reached number 106 on the US album chart – and then punk rock remained an underground movement in America for the next 13 years until it finally reached the mainstream with Nirvana's *Nevermind* in 1991. Maybe, I speculated recklessly, teenage US ravers might one day 'mutate the gene to breed an intrinsically American strain of electronica'.[8] It would actually take a lot longer than I imagined; Skrillex was only ten years old at the time the article was published.

Despite the anticlimactic conclusion to the short-lived excitement about electronica, raves continued to thrive across the country, although the authorities were well aware by now that they were fuelled by illicit narcotics. Back in 1971, when President Richard Nixon launched the futile and destructive 'War on Drugs', he declared: 'America's public enemy number one in the United States is drug abuse. In order to fight and defeat this enemy, it is necessary to wage a new, all-out offensive.'[9]

In 2002, Senator Joe Biden became the latest politician to echo Nixon's battle cry as he proposed a piece of legislation which he named the Reducing Americans' Vulnerability to Ecstasy Act. The RAVE Act was based on Biden's view that 'most raves are havens for illicit drugs' and was intended to impose massive fines on promoters if narcotics were seized at their parties. Glow sticks, Vicks inhalers and even water bottles were all described as 'drug paraphernalia' in the prologue to the draft law.

The legislation was eventually adopted as the Illicit Drug Anti-Proliferation Act in 2003, and had a chilling effect on major promoters. The leading rave organisers had already started to go legit in the late nineties, tired of dodging busts and seeking long-term career security. Now they reacted by abandoning the word 'rave' altogether, rebranding their events as 'dance music festivals' in an attempt to minimise the drug connotations and ensure that they could get permits. 'We don't use the word "rave" anymore – it's as simple as that,' one major promoter in the US told me. 'It pigeonholes the scene for its detractors, who all remember the RAVE Act.'

For the authorities, after a series of drug-related fatalities, raves had become synonymous with death. So the promoters stepped up security regimes, brought in new safety measures and began to hold events in more orthodox venues like sports stadiums, where crowds could be controlled more easily to satisfy official concerns about unruly E-heads running wild. It seemed to work; Pasquale Rotella's Electric Daisy Carnival drew 6,000 people in 2002, but numbers rose to 29,000 in 2007, and three years later, the daily attendance at his meticulously organised festival-not-rave had reached 99,000. The music would soon get itself a new name too – EDM.

'People from this generation learn computers in school like we learned to write. Can you imagine the music that these kids are going to make? The way they are going to use modern technology is going to be mind-blowing. This is only the beginning.'

Renaat Vandepapeliere of R&S Records, 1992

'Hear me now!' Skrillex shouts out in his skittish teenagerish voice, rocking up and down on the balls of his feet, darting back and forth behind his console as alien emoticons flash grins and grimaces from the screen and the twitchy little showman swings his shaggy dreadlocks and leaps up to dance maniacally for a few seconds on a micro-stage that's been constructed for him by the decks.

The music he's playing is similarly jittery and restive – he has this attention-deficit-disorder/frantic-YouTube-surfing approach to DJing that creates the disorientating feeling of tumbling uncontrollably through a hyperactive video game as the soundtrack switches from minute to minute and the tunes flash past faster than a Ramones album so there's no time to like or dislike any of them before the next one begins as the feverish turbo-digital rush keeps racing *onwards onwards onwards...*

Dubstep, reggae, trance, metallic Belgian techno riffs and gangsta rap refrains are all jammed into the mash-up as he accelerates through more than 60 tracks before his set ends – his own collaborations with the Ragga Twins, A$AP Rocky and Damian Marley, remixes of Avicii and Benny Benassi, snippets of Kanye West and Steve Aoki with Diplo, vintage a cappellas from Michael Jackson, Salt-N-Pepa and dirty-talking Chicago diva Sweet Pussy Pauline... 'I'm totally exhausted,' a friend remarks when the little Californian leaves the stage as his headlining slot at the Exit festival in Novi Sad finally comes to an end. 'I feel like I've just heard all the dance music that's ever been recorded, *all at once...*' 'This is the sound of a generation gap opening up,' suggests another friend. 'It's like there's now some kind of electronic music for people younger than us that I don't have the references to understand.'

Indeed, Skrillex seemed to be able to channel the frenzied jumble of the globally networked world as if it was natural to him, making him a perfect auteur for the 'digital natives', those who grew up in the always-online era. 'I think there's a whole new voice and a whole new energy, aesthetically and culturally, coming from the internet, but you can feel it all around,' he once said. 'The internet is weird, and people use it in freaky ways – we're going to have to go through this learning curve as a civilisation about what it is to have these things.'[10]

Born in California in 1988 – the year acid house broke in Britain – Skrillex (real name Sonny Moore) had been the singer in an emo band called From First to Last before becoming a DJ and producer. He started to make primitive tracks using cheap software, initially inspired by Aphex Twin and Squarepusher and other 'bearded bedroom geeks' from Britain's Warp Records, as he put it. 'From First to Last got a big [record label] deal, but I left that band because it wasn't the music I wanted to do,' he said. 'I was just making electronic music for fun after that. I hit a point in my life where I was cool with being broke and having a real cheap apartment.'[11]

His first release as Skrillex came in 2009, and its success came as a total surprise to him. As a child who was bullied at school and who only found out that he was adopted when he was 16 – even though everyone around him apparently knew – he said that all he had ever really wanted was to do 'crazy, fun shit', and to be happy.

Skrillex's trick was to combine the brobdingnagian basslines of the British dubstep sound with the rowdy urgency of hip-hop, the itchy glitchiness of Aphex Twin and the gloopily emotive melodies of trance, adding some punk-rock energy and an impish pop sensibility that worked in America – and to do all this at exactly the perfect moment, when the US was good and ready for a freaky white-boy electro star, an alternative dude who could unleash the drop.

According to Liz Miller, who worked with him at the Big Beat record label just as his career started to take off, Skrillex was the opposite of what she derisively calls 'the opportunistic businessmen who see an opportunity to make money as a rock-star DJ'. He just happened to be doing what he wanted to do in the right place at the right time, Miller insists: 'When you meet him, you know he is a *musician* – he would be doing this even if no one was listening.'

He was also a naturally exuberant performer, a crucial element to success on the EDM circuit, where stage shows were often as important as the tunes being played – as well as being someone who delighted in unexpected collaborations. In 2015, he went from headlining Ultra in Miami with guest appearances from pop idol Justin Bieber and Diplo, with whom he had recorded the international hit 'Where Are Ü Now', to playing a riotous back-to-back set with underground darling Kieran Hebden of Four Tet a few days afterwards at a sweaty little club under a pub in London.

But as the most publicly recognisable face of EDM, Skrillex was also the target for critics who saw him as an envoy from the aesthetic dark side, a commercial interloper from the rock arena who turned dubstep into 'brostep', a caricature of dance music for frat boys 'rolling hard' on 'molly', as MDMA powder was known on the US scene. 'As the EDM juggernaut rolls on, Sonny has become a symbol, for everyone who desperately wants to show that they're more-underground-than-thou, for a perceived destruction of dance culture,' journalist Joe Muggs suggested.[12]

Even Skrillex's former advocate Joel Zimmerman, a tetchy Canadian producer who called himself Deadmau5, argued that the Justin Bieber collaboration was a sell-out. 'It's not that I have a problem with Skrillex and those guys, I have a problem with they enable themselves and they put themselves in these positions to be part of *bullshit*,' moaned Zimmerman (whose gimmick was performing in an outsized Mickey Mouse-style head). 'Who aspires to be part of bullshit? It fucking blows my mind. It's like what, you didn't get paid enough?' he demanded.[13]

The acronym EDM may have first been used for electronic dance music in 1980, on the back cover of a single called 'European Man' by British postpunk synth-pop band Landscape (best known for their later hit 'Einstein A Go-Go'). From around the start of the 2010s, it was employed as a catch-all term by the US music industry for *any* form of contemporary electronic dance music – although in Europe, EDM was understood more specifically to mean the more populist sounds made by producers like Skrillex or Steve Aoki.

American EDM seemed to be made up entirely of dazzling sheeny surfaces – the music of a world without shadows and an eternal taurine-fuelled present where the sun is always shining and the party is always pumping; a music which is constantly telling you what a good time you're having NOW. Like the fast-cutting, FX-overloaded Hollywood movies directed by Michael Bay, it offered perpetual instant gratification rather than the gradual build-ups and extended narratives of house and techno. 'Digital maximalism', the writer Simon Reynolds called it, a music designed to be perpetually *in your face*. EDM basslines were monstrous constructions, fine-tooled for ultimate aggressive impact, sounding like spaceships crashing through the molten core of burning planets, or the last desperate mortal croaks of tortured frogs, or the massively amplified dry-heaves of a raver gone queasy while coming up on a pill.

As well as dubstep, its influences included the lustrous electrosonics of Daft Punk and the Harley Davidson growl of their French compatriots Justice, while its aggressively catchy vocal hooks channelled dewy-eyed eighties pop and schmaltzy nineties trance. It also had enough macho vigour to appeal to teenagers who grew up on rock or hip-hop; its roid-rage bellicosity made it perhaps the least gay form of dance music ever invented. All the disco traditions seemed to have been hacked away and replaced with an alternative version of history that started with Keith Flint of The Prodigy screaming about being a twisted firestarter. It was a vision of dance music in which Frankie Knuckles and Larry Levan had never existed, let alone the great gay disco producers of the seventies like Tom Moulton or Patrick Cowley. 'America has never been comfortable with the disco roots of dance music,' noted Detroit DJ Alan Oldham. It was a product perfectly modelled for white American youth.

The EDM sound entered the US mainstream gradually in the 2000s, after rappers started making tracks with lyrics about getting high on MDMA and then began to emulate the big-room trance riffs of European commercial rave hits. Audible markers of change came when Kanye West sampled Daft Punk for his track 'Stronger' in 2007, and then two years later, French DJ David Guetta started fashioning hits like 'I Gotta Feeling' with American R&B stars the Black Eyed Peas. 'I remember hearing "I Gotta Feeling" on the radio for the first time and thinking to myself: "This is house music! On the radio! In America!"' recalls Tommie Sunshine. 'In 2009, America woke up to what the rest of the world was listening to for 20 years, which was a music created *here* – that's the part of it that's so crazy.'

EDM utterly rejected the concept of subtlety; not for nothing were its modulated oscillator wobbles and portamento bass drops often used as soundtracks for video games and YouTube channels aimed at pre-teens. European techno sophisticates found it easy to mock when the Disney corporation released an album of EDM remixes of themes from family movies like *The Lion King*, *Toy Story* and *Frozen* in 2014, commissioned from big hitters like Avicii, Armin van Buuren, Axwell & Ingrosso and Kaskade. The following year, the more juvenile side of EDM appeared to have hit its aesthetic nadir at the Tomorrow-land festival in Belgium, where the DJs played in a kind of Disney World castle and Guetta aired a remake he had produced of the hokey old children's singalong 'If You're Happy and You Know It Clap Your Hands'.

But that wasn't the only grisly aural atrocity at the festival. At one point in his set, the American DJ Steve Aoki shouted out: 'Do you trust me, Tomorrowland?' – then pressed play on a remix of Celine Dion's 'My Heart Must Go On', the theme song from the 1987 Hollywood blockbuster *Titanic*. 'Everyone was singing along and laughing at themselves at the same time. It was an incredible feeling. I just stood there with my arms out and revelled in the vulnerability of it,' Aoki told *Mixmag* afterwards, luxuriating in his own daring, as if playing one of the biggest-selling songs of all time was a triumph of rebellious audacity to be ranked alongside the insurrectionary works of the Sex Pistols or Pussy Riot. 'I'm having fun and I'm just going to keep on having fun. I don't care if I ruffle a few feathers,' he declared.[14]

It was a long way from the ideological purism of those who saw themselves as upholding the tradition of the New York, Chicago and Detroit originators, and who looked upon EDM as some kind of viola-tion of essential values. 'EDM is a corporate marketing ploy designed to capture and monetise youth culture,' argues Marea Stamper, alias The Black Madonna, who was a raver in the American Midwest in the nineties before becoming an inspirational, politically conscious DJ on the global circuit. 'It's really a brand as much as it is a sound. It's another movement to gain control of the buying dollars of a very important demographic.

'It's kind of perfect because it's permanently orgasmic, infinite euphoria, but I think it's driven from the top down, not from the bottom up. It's completely repugnant.'

EDM stars found this kind of abrasive criticism baffling; they couldn't understand what they had done that was just *so damn wrong*. 'Back in the day when we had success as Swedish House Mafia, we were sad. We were like, "Why were people attacking us for doing well because we just kept making the music that we wanted?"' asked Swedish DJ Axel Hedfors, alias Axwell. 'We never adapted to be mainstream, it was the mainstream that discovered us. For us, we were always wondering why people within music attack others within the scene. It's one big question mark for us, even to this day.'[15]

Richie Hawtin tried to reach out across what looked like an emerging generation gap in dance music, releasing a track by Deadmau5 on his Plus 8 label and doing a high-profile interview with Skrillex when he guest-edited an edition of *Mixmag*. Despite our aesthetic differences, we all come from the same roots and we're all in this together, Hawtin seemed to be saying. 'To disassociate yourself with people just because they make music in a different way or because they have 20,000 fans instead of 5,000 fans [at a gig] really isn't credible,' he explains. 'Take Skrillex for example – Sonny is a really cool kid. The music he makes is not my cup of tea, but I'm interested in sitting down and chatting to him and finding out where does he comes from, why does he make music like this? Somehow we're connected because we have a love of making music through technology so we are bound together, so let's find those common similarities.

'We've been creating a foundation for this music for 20 years and now it's out there for anyone to reinterpret or reconfigure into their own version,' Hawtin continues. 'As much as some people don't want to admit it, when you hear Skrillex or other forms of EDM, there are sounds that may have been sequenced in a different way but can be found in my early records or Underground Resistance records. It's a new generation and a new interpretation of this music.'

There was also another point of view – that EDM was a conceptual rupture in a narrative that had been going on for far too long using the same paradigms. Since the innovatory turmoil of the nineties saw the creation of hardcore, jungle, drum and bass, 2-step and UK garage in a few short breathless years, and then the emergence of dubstep, grime and micro-genres like minimal, bassline and UK funky in the 2000s, house and techno had settled into a relatively stable format, developing through modest creative increments and technological enhancements rather than making great leaps forward. It was time for a few young punks to rip up the template again, some people argued.

'Here in Berlin, electronic club music culture is mainstream,' says Robert Henke of Monolake, who was one of the creators of Ableton Live, the software that Skrillex and other EDM producers used. 'People go to a techno club as a touristic event just as much as they go to the television tower or the opera. That's not underground, that's not "different" – that's assimilation on the highest level possible. You go to a middle-class chic restaurant and minimal techno is playing as background music. Or you go to a fancy hotel and they have a DJ spinning boring house music in the lobby. It's just the normal background noise of the twenty-first century. But you couldn't imagine hearing a Skrillex track in this context – it's far more radical.

'You cannot avoid acknowledging that there are a shitload of interesting things going on in his music, despite the things that the style police could question. There are a lot more ideas in an average Skrillex track than in an average minimal house track, which repeats again and again,' Henke continues. 'Obviously the musicians he references as influential are exactly the same ones as we reference as influential, but he is looking at it from an American perspective and transforms it into something that is compatible for people who listen to rock and grunge, by applying a certain way of presenting himself and his music that it becomes attractive to kids who want to revolt against their parents. I find this interesting because in the last 15, 20 years in

Europe, electronic dance music became a normal commodity for our generation.'

Henke, who was in his late forties at this point and had long been one of the most significant figures in Berlin techno culture, saw EDM as a necessary disruption: 'I don't like it mostly and I find it exhausting, but at the same time, pushing things to the limits and really forcing it beyond what's pleasant is the motor for something new to arrive.'

'Every fantasy reflects the place and time that produced it.'

Hari Kunzru

With its constant random cacophony of slot machines burbling, cash tills jingling, drunken gamblers carousing, musical fountains blasting power ballads and street-corner Elvis impersonators groaning about how they're all shook up, Las Vegas was the perfect place for something as garish as EDM to thrive. No glitz was too over the top in this city where excess was actively encouraged, even venerated.

Some people claimed that with the rise of EDM, Vegas had become the Ibiza of the Americas, but to European eyes, the suggestion appeared ludicrous – the Balearic island looked as edgily bohemian as Berlin compared with the tawdry glory of the gamblers' mecca. Both places were holiday destinations where fantasies were made real; both had club scenes that could boost the careers and fill the bank accounts of the top players – but in Vegas, there were not even symbolic attempts to pay lip service to acid-house hippie roots. Here nightlife was a purely business proposition, and its hedonism was untainted by any kind of countercultural contaminant; this was clubbing with all its DIY elements stripped out and replaced with commercial artifice. Like Ibiza, Vegas had its myths, but no one in their right mind came here expecting any kind of spiritual awakening, and even some of the wilder tales told about the city had only a tenuous relationship to the truth, as the guidebook writer Tim Dressen pointed out: 'Las Vegas is a city of legends – most of which are complete bullshit.'[16]

The hotel clubs on the Strip, the high-concept EDM megadiscos like

XS and Hakkasan, were set up to attract American youth who weren't as keen on gambling as their parents' generation and had little interest in the old-school showbiz revues of Celine Dion or Mariah Carey. The Vegas club owners didn't embrace EDM because they loved dance music – they did it, as they do everything, because they love dollars. 'They're constantly trying to engineer the experience for you to indulge – to feel good and to want to spend money doing that – and they finally figured out that they could monetise the energy and the spirit and the sensory overload of electronic music,' says the veteran Los Angeles house DJ and radio host Jason Bentley, who had played at the Electric Daisy Carnival since its early years.

Before the late 2000s, there wasn't much house or techno to be heard in Vegas, although the early US electronic duo The Crystal Method came from the city and named their first album after it. There were a few club nights in the city and the occasional rave, but the major nightspots mainly programmed R&B, hip-hop, chart pop and retro sounds. Mash-up king DJ AM (Adam Goldstein) became perhaps the first Vegas superstar DJ, holding down a lavishly paid residency – a figure of $1 million was rumoured – at the Pure club at Caesars Palace hotel on the Strip, until he died in 2009 as a result of his excessive drug consumption. DJ AM's uproarious crowd-pleasing sets cut and scratched together hip-hop and R&B tracks with snippets of classic songs from musicians as disparate as Guns N' Roses, Michael Jackson, Joan Jett and U2. 'Every club in town wanted DJ AM, and if they couldn't get AM, they wanted someone who sounded like AM,' says Warren Peace, a Vegas-based DJ who was a resident at XS when it first opened.

The scenery started to shift after Paul Oakenfold started a three-year residency at the Rain club in the Palms hotel in 2008. Oakenfold's Planet Perfecto night, with its stage show by Cirque du Soleil, was described as a nightlife game-changer by the *Las Vegas Weekly*, which ranked the British DJ as one of the top-ten greatest headliners in the city's history (Liberace topped the list, followed by Elvis and the Rat Pack). 'At the time electronic music really wasn't the sound of what was going on in Vegas, it was more a rock/hip-hop sound that was really popular, and

Top 40 obviously,' Oakenfold recalled later.[17] According to the *Las Vegas Weekly*, Oakenfold's nightclub spectacular showed the Strip hotels how lucrative an EDM show could be, and 'paved the way for headlining DJs who now command six-figure paychecks for Vegas residencies'.[18]

Oakenfold was followed by Kaskade (Ryan Raddon), who established a residency at XS in 2009. Kaskade was an unusual character, a teetotal Mormon from Chicago who used to go out to dance to Frankie Knuckles while he was still at high school but went on to become one of the biggest EDM stars of his generation. 'The people that were attracted to this music were very forward-thinking, progressive-minded people,' he once recalled of his formative years on the Chicago house scene. 'The fact that I didn't party [drink or take drugs] back then didn't matter to these people. These were weirdos, freaks, geeks, whatever. They were not people that were going to judge me.'[19]

After the financial crash in the US in 2008, nightclubs became increasingly vital to the Las Vegas economy. 'Suddenly people didn't have as much money to spend on gambling, so revenues fell and venues started looked for other ways to draw them back, and electronic music came at the right time,' says Kent Otto, editor of the Electronic Vegas website. Bottle service was a key profit-driver as some punters blew thousands of dollars a night on booking tables and guzzling down heavily marked-up booze, while the success of residencies by DJs like Oakenfold, Kaskade and Afrojack led to a bidding war between the clubs on the Strip for the biggest names, with promoters offering huge sums to secure exclusive contracts.

When Hakkasan opened in 2013, the competition became more frenzied still. The Hakkasan Group was controlled by Sheikh Mansour bin Zayed al Nahyan, a billionaire member of Abu Dhabi's ruling family. To non-Emiratis, Mansour was probably best known as the majority owner of Manchester City football club, where he spent lavishly to recruit star players; the Hakkasan nightclub in Las Vegas did the same with DJs. The *New Yorker* reported that before it opened, the club sent personalised pitch books to Tiësto, Calvin Harris, Deadmau5 and Afrojack, who were all playing at XS at the time, in a bid to lure them away:

'The books described the perks that a Hakkasan residency would offer, including a chauffeured Maybach limousine, access to a fleet of private jets, and a two-storey SkyLoft suite with a butler. Hakkasan was also offering more money.'[20]

Hakkasan was a temple to the gods of conspicuous consumption. On New Year's Eve 2014, it offered its customers a special $500,000 package; those who paid would see their name flashing up on a screen during the midnight confetti drop and be given a 30-litre bottle of Midas champagne, a gold disc signed by Calvin Harris, Tiësto or Hardwell, diamond cufflinks and a diamond necklace.

For ordinary punters, there were no such perks, however; they had to line up for hours in a wearisome queue that snaked right out into the lobby of the MGM hotel if they wanted to get in. When I went down there one night, there were a few Hardwell enthusiasts in the queue, some of whom had brought a sign with the DJ's name spelled out in silver foil in the hope of waving it at him later that evening, plus various glammed-up club boys with razor crops and sunglasses-after-dark, a few shiny-suited gents and voluptuous ladies with clothing cut to flaunt it, but most of the prospective punters seemed to be straight male Americans in sneakers and jeans, dressed as if they were going to their local bar rather than one of the world's most exclusive nightclubs.

The line inched forward slowly for two hours before it reached the security check, with the bouncers treating the customers with measured disdain throughout, as any anticipatory buzz dissipated into the sickly-sweet perfumed air that was pumped out by the hotel to mask the cigarette smoke. Inside, the club looked impressive enough, but I couldn't help thinking that this was not the best way to build a vibe.

For the DJs however, it was like Christmas every weekend, with hit-makers like Calvin Harris and David Guetta being paid as much as $400,000 a show by the Vegas clubs, according to rumour. 'These guys are rock stars. They're like royalty. You should see Calvin when he walks into the DJ booth. It's like he's a god,' local promoter Bo Karlen told me. But Karlen cautioned that only the top-ranking names could fill the clubs on the strength of their fame: 'I think there's only a handful of guys, maybe five or ten of them, who really pull their weight to make the money here.'

The experience of playing to a Vegas crowd was different too – these were hedonistic holidaymakers who were only in town for a few days and wanted to party as hard as possible before their money or their luck ran out. 'When you play here, you are playing to people who are ready to lose $5,000 dollars in one night, people who are ready to sleep with anybody – people who are *ready to go*,' explains Warren Peace. 'That is why people love playing in Vegas, because all these guys and girls want a story to tell. They all want to grab someone and take them up in their hotel room and do drugs and do the nasty thing and then go back home on Tuesday and tell everyone about it. They want those stories, they want to go back home and say, "Dude, listen to what I did!" You don't get that anywhere else, only in Vegas, and that's why it's a party at a higher level.'

A character like Steve Aoki made a lot of sense down on the Las Vegas Strip, where the clubs catered to tourists seeking to lose the plot in the most ostentatious way possible. This long-haired son of the restaurant chain mogul Rocky Aoki had spent his teenage years playing in hardcore punk bands (reportedly he was also something of a political radical back then). He started to DJ in the 2000s under the name Kid Millionaire and went on to prove himself a savvy pop entrepreneur with his Dim Mak label, which released records by Bloc Party, The Kills and Infected Mushroom.

Aoki also became an EDM archetype, best known for goofy onstage antics such as lobbing cakes in his fans' faces and crowd-surfing in an inflatable dinghy. The former socially conscious punk had turned out to be a sharp businessman, and the main product he was selling was himself: 'When you come to a Steve Aoki show, you get a Steve Aoki experience,' he declared.[21] In 2015, *Forbes* magazine claimed, he earned $18.1 million.

Aoki flew in to Vegas from Ibiza for a gig during Electric Daisy Carnival weekend at the snootily vulgar Jewel club, a class-structured environment where the wealthiest watched the proceedings from their private sanctums, the wannabes partied in bottle-service booths by the dancefloor and the plebeians huddled in a circular bar enclosure behind them, roped off from the action closer to the stage. It seemed likely that some of the Electric Daisy Carnival crowd – the ones who weren't conventionally chic or glamorous, the misfits and misshapes from provincial America – might not have felt too welcome here even if they had been old enough to get in.

The gig illustrated how distant the Vegas version of EDM had grown from rave culture. Aoki was as much a performer as a DJ, and his show was like a kind of vaudeville revue for the smartphone generation. He leapt up on a plinth in front of the decks and threw disco shapes with his long bendy body, invited women up to dance with him, fired dry ice over the dancefloor from twin pistols delivered to him by two Robocop lookalikes, and even stopped the music completely to do a call-and-response session with the audience: 'Say *hell yeah*! Say *fuck yeah*! Say *Steve Aoki*!'

As Aoki rollicked around, the soundtrack restlessly scampered between genres and eras – an old Backstreet Boys hit erupted into a banging techno bassline, Jimi Hendrix's 'Purple Haze' rode a dirty hip-hop groove, 'Smells Like Teen Spirit' was stripped and chewed up into rattling trap. And as he ratcheted up the insanity, the young bucks in the booths ordered more bottles of Grey Goose vodka from the busty blonde waitresses in their tiny scarlet dresses, the slim-cut suits poured more champagne for their entourages, and the brashest of the lads jumped up on the banquettes to windmill their arms and roar like raging bulls in sheer drunken elation: 'Hell yeah, Vegas!' '*Steeeeeeve!*'

Aoki was an object of derision for those who believed that EDM DJs were a disgrace to their profession. 'You are not a fucking DJ. You're an overpaid, untalented, cake-throwing, performing monkey,' techno and house DJ Seth Troxler ranted.[22] But the Californian saw himself as a free spirit, an iconoclastic maverick: 'The haters and the trolls have always used me as an excuse to make fun of something that is out of the ordinary, something that doesn't necessarily make sense to them,' Aoki once wrote in a lengthy defence of his wacky stage persona. 'For whatever reason, I have always been a target that people love to attack. From not being American enough as an Asian kid growing up in an all-white neighbourhood, to not being indie enough for the die-hard hipsters in my twenties and now today, not being a "real DJ" for the electronic music purists.'[23]

Amit Duvdevani from the Israeli trance duo Infected Mushroom, who were signed to Aoki's Dim Mak label, also believes that the cake-tossing Californian was a talented trouper: 'Steve is a phenomenal performer; this is how I see him,' Duvdevani explains. 'I love him as a guy. I don't relate to his music so much, but as a persona on stage, besides the cake and all that stuff, he always knows how to make people go crazy.'

And Las Vegas loved Aoki too; for as long as he was making the town money, anyway. Vegas had loved Frank Sinatra and Elvis Presley too, while they were still around. You could still hear their songs playing in casinos along the Strip in the 2010s – and see huge billboards for retro revues by singers like Donny and Marie Osmond – but the crooners were no longer the dominant cultural force that they once had been here; their time had passed, and the DJs were now the ones who brought in the dollars. It seemed clear that the Vegas EDM boom would continue until it was no longer profitable, then the hotels and the casinos would move on again, unsentimentally chasing down the next revenue stream. 'The thing you need to understand about this town is that it's always strictly business,' I was told by a local nightlife photographer. 'We never do it for love.'

'Any teenager goes for a living form of music, the most energetic form of music.'

Guy-Manuel de Homem-Christo, Daft Punk

The eerie five-tone sequence from *Close Encounters of the Third Kind* chimes out around the huge tent, and as the bright white lights go up on a glimmering pyramid on the stage, two helmeted figures in leather suits appear silhouetted in the dry ice and a stuttering Vocodered voice announces their arrival: *'Da-a-a-a-ft Puuunk!'*

The distorted voice resolves into a cyborg melody and the French duo blast into the staccato glam riff of 'Robot Rock', sending the over-crowded tent into a state of delirium. It was a moment that was to shape the future of dance music in the US: Daft Punk's remarkable performance at the Coachella festival in California in 2006 – a shock-and-awe bombardment of sound and vision, hit after sparkling hit – helped to set the template for the EDM show. Here at last was a way to turn two diffident chaps poking at laptops into exotic starlike beings through the transformative power of technology.

'Daft Punk's pyramid lit the fuse for the LED arms race that would fuel the rise of the EDM genre,' suggested one journalist.[24] Another went even further: 'Daft Punk's 2006 Coachella set is to the explosion of dance music in the twenty-first century what the assassination of Archduke Franz Ferdinand of Austria is to World War One. It was the spark that ignited the fire.'[25]

The French duo's illuminated pyramid inspired Skrillex's onstage spaceship and Deadmau5's cybernetic cube set-up, as well as many of the other high-tech EDM spectacles that would follow. Indeed, Skrillex has recalled how deeply he was affected by seeing Daft Punk live at the time: 'I didn't have a drink, no drugs. But I was high out of my mind. It changed my life.'[26] Their show also convinced Steve Aoki that he had witnessed the future of dance music: 'This is how you present it – with production,' he realised as he watched.[27]

Daft Punk had started their visual adventures a decade earlier, when they first took to pranking around in masks for photo shoots in an attempt to create some kind of new visual aesthetic for dance music. 'The playing with masks is just to make it funnier. Pictures can be boring. We don't want all the rock 'n' roll poses and attitudes – they are completely stupid and ridiculous today,' Thomas Bangalter told me when I interviewed them in 1997. (Neither he nor his partner Guy-Manuel de Homem-Christo wore a mask during our conversa-tion.) 'This is new music, so it's a new way of doing things,' Bangalter insisted.[28]

The madcap stage antics and dazzling visual shows that were

developed by EDM DJs who were influenced by Daft Punk helped to obscure the more banal reality of men on stage who were doing little more than pushing buttons on a console. These were no longer geeky boffins; the visual extravaganzas had made them… *techno supermen!*

'Having a show has become very important because you have people who have hit songs who are not necessarily performers,' explains Liz Miller. 'Someone like Skrillex is very comfortable being on a microphone, jumping into the audience, being a rock star, being a frontman, so he's a very entertaining performer to watch. He probably doesn't need an alien ship on stage – he just wants one! But you have other artists who may be pretty shy; they may be production geniuses but before they would be the people who sat behind the star and you would never know their names. Now you're asking them to be the star of the show and that's not necessarily who they are, so a good manager or record label would say, "Well, let's make a show."'

As well as deploying the visual aids, DJs started to *move* like performers, too – dancing around theatrically throughout their sets to energise the audience, or making exaggerated hand gestures and fiddling ostentatiously with the controls on their consoles as if they were painters touching up the last brushstrokes on a masterpiece – all in an attempt to show that *this is live!* and that they were 'artists', not just press-play automatons rebroadcasting other people's music.

The cliché of the vain, arrogant EDM DJ was adeptly parodied by American comedian Andy Samberg on the *Saturday Night Live* TV show; in the skit, Samberg's shaggy-haired, preening character Davvincii, some kind of bastardised mutation of David Guetta and Avicii, waves his arms around extravagantly as he pushes a couple of buttons and then pumps his fist to the beat while men in suits hand him bags of cash.

A few EDM DJs even performed in costume; at the Electric Daisy Carnival in Las Vegas, I saw a Belgian chap called The Magician who had a wand in the top pocket of his sparkly red-and-silver-striped jacket and could do conjuring tricks while he was performing. In contrast to the veteran house and techno DJs who buried themselves deep in the wordless entrancement of the mix, the EDM guys also loved to get on the microphone and *talk* – demanding that arms be raised, or announcing their latest releases, or hyping their social media accounts. At the end of his set at the Electric Daisy Carnival, Dutch DJ Don Diablo – wearing a jacket and headphones branded with his own logo – even stopped the music to give a goodnight-and-farewell speech as if he was Bono or Mick Jagger. 'Tonight we are all one!' he declared, then strutted to the front of the stage and bellowed in his best rock-god voice: 'You are the best, *thankyouverymuch*!'

Some of the major EDM stars' sets were actually pre-sequenced because they needed to synch up the track times to their visual shows, so the lasers were triggered just when the bass dropped and the aliens popped up on screen just when the spooky FX started playing out. Deadmau5 busted up the conspiracy of silence about this when he posted a recklessly honest rant on his website entitled 'We All Press Play', in which he explained how his live sets were constrained to a rigid timeline so 'all the visuals line up nicely and all the light cues are on and stuff'.[29] This was simply standard practice for top EDM DJs, Deadmau5 insisted; any scope for improvisation was severely limited by the necessities of the show. 'A lot of people think that I am creating music on the fly, when I'm literally playing all the versions that you get on the album,' he also admitted.[30]

This was not the only ill-concealed secret of the EDM scene. It had become increasingly imperative for DJs to have hit tunes as promotional tools to get them lucrative gigs, but it also gradually became known that not all of them actually made the tracks that were credited to them. Some DJs, because of their lack of talent or technical ability, employed what were called 'ghost producers' to create all or part of their recordings. The website EDM Ghost Producer, for example, touted its wares with the slogan: 'Purchase unique tracks and release them as your own!'

The practice was endemic, from the top stars to the so-called 'credible underground', insiders claimed. 'Some people just aren't very good at putting together sounds and making things sound right – but have really amazing ideas and work really hard on the music they do with the engineer. But there are other people that just have the money to buy the tracks, and that's kind of a virus in the industry right now,' said DJ Maceo Plex, who admitted he had done some ghost producing in the past. 'If you think that a lot of these big commercial people make their own music, you're living on another fucking planet!'[31]

But for the men at the top, the spoils were unimaginably vast. Swedish twenty-something Tim Bergling, alias Avicii, reportedly lived in an opulent $15 million pad in Hollywood, although he didn't spend much time there because he was always on the road. A revealing profile in *GQ* magazine in 2013 described the private jets, the limousines, the adoring crowds chanting *'A-vi-cii! A-vi-cii!', the* young girls throwing their bras at the stage and the endless bottles of Dom Perignon being sprayed around that constituted Bergling's surreal version of real life.

Bergling explained that he planned out most of his set before a gig so it was guaranteed to get the energy pumping, and devoted the majority of his onstage time to bopping around and mouthing the lyrics to his own hits to enthuse the crowd. 'I'm not really doing much, you know, like technically it's not that *hard*,' he admitted. He also confessed that he had never taken Ecstasy because he was too busy getting famous to have the time to get high: 'I mean, I want to take it,' he said. 'But I'm sort of afraid of anything that makes you feel out of control.'[32]

Earning millions but not having enough time to enjoy life's pleasures was not a recipe for happiness, as it turned out. Burned out by his punishing tour schedule and relentless binge-drinking, Bergling announced his retirement from touring three years later, saying he wanted to live like a 'real person'.

Indeed, the lifestyle of a perennially mobile, time-zone-defying, up-all-night-sleep-on-the-flight superstar DJ was not necessarily good for one's mental health. Dutch trance veteran Armin van Buuren admitted that he had to seek help for depression after being voted number one in the world in *DJ* magazine's annual poll for a fourth time. His poll triumph should have been a cause for celebration, but the pressure brought him down; he felt compelled to read all the social media comments about himself but couldn't cope with them if they weren't positive, couldn't deal with the feeling that he had to find a way to keep himself in the top spot the following year too. 'A lot of DJs have nervous breakdowns,' he said.[33]

'I think it's too easy for a lot of people from my generation to say "It's not the same as it used to be" – well, nothing's the same as it used to be.'

James Barton, President of Electronic Music, Live Nation

In the days running up to the Electric Daisy Carnival in Las Vegas, Pasquale Rotella's Insomniac organisation also hosted EDMBiz, its annual convention for the high rollers and aspiring entrepreneurs seeking to siphon off the rewards of what had become a global culture worth more than $7 billion, according to one estimate. EDMBiz, held amid the faux-Roman kitsch of the Caesars Palace hotel complex on the Las Vegas Strip, was a reflection of the corporate dominance of EDM. It was like the Davos of American dance music, where bigshots from companies like Spotify, the BBC, *Billboard*, Live Nation and sundry Hollywood management agencies came to shoot the breeze with big-name DJs while hopeful supplicants bearing business plans and USB sticks full of tunes tried to hustle up their big break.

Previous conventions had been energised by the fervid optimism that accompanied the rise of EDM, but the 2016 pow-wow was overshadowed by gloomier themes – the recent collapse into bankruptcy of dance-music events conglomerate SFX Entertainment and worries that the spectacular growth of the EDM phenomenon had finally reached its limit in the US.

One of the panel discussions, entitled 'After the Drop', involved a lot of soul-searching about whether the EDM 'bubble' had burst. Sebastian Solano of ID&T, which staged mega-festivals like Tomorrowland and Electric Zoo and was bought out by the ill-fated SFX during the company's wild spree of acquisitions before it went bust, suggested that many people had become infected by gold-rush fever and had simply lost the plot. At the core of the problem, Solano said disconsolately, was that he started off throwing parties but ended up doing spread-sheets: 'It became about money only. Too many decisions were made for the wrong reasons.'

But any idea that PLUR had vanquished the dark forces of Wall Street was banished by the next couple of panels, during which we were told that EDM teens were a marketer's dream because they were essentially a bunch of heedless spendthrifts who were mesmerised by the glittering trinkets of corporate capitalism and expected their heroes to be sponsored avatars. 'This millennial generation, they want to be connected to a brand,' a speaker insisted at one point. If they were to be successful, DJs must think like marketing executives and create their own brands, as well as developing eye-catching stage shows and engaging social-media presences, we were also told. As if to illustrate how it could be done, a Skrillex associate called Marshmello was sitting in the middle of some of the panellists with an oversized marshmallow-shaped tub jammed on his head to disguise his identity, looking like nothing less than a human brand.

There was also a fair bit of EDM-will-never-die boosterism, exemplified by the corporate-raider bullishness of the 'entertainment vice-president' chap from Hakkasan who bizarrely insisted that 'Vegas is synonymous with being the epicentre of nightlife worldwide', and then went on to promise/threaten his competitors: 'We have a very aggressive expansion plan.'

A couple of years beforehand, music writer Trent Wolbe had reported from EDMBiz that the postpunk/underground techno idea that 'selling out' was a *bad thing* was an alien concept to the EDM generation. 'If the EDMBiz conference confirmed anything, it's that the genre is a business first, and an artistic endeavour second – and I don't think there's anything wrong with that,' Wolbe said. 'Electronic music still remains one of my deepest loves, and the fact that it's highly commercialised just means I get to hear more of my favourite sounds in more contexts than I ever did when I was an angsty teen downloading 64k Orbital MP3s over a shoddy 28.8k USRobotics modem.'[34]

This was the angle that EDM executives loved – it's bigger so it's better, it's everywhere so the 'fans' are much better served by its easy-access ubiquity. Everything available anytime everywhere – everyone wins! (Although the will to action caused by the lack of availability had been one of the propulsive forces in many of the most vital cultural developments of previous decades, from punk rock to acid house.) Wolbe ended his article with the approving signoff: 'EDM has become the first "voice of a generation" that openly accepts a partner all other types of music bristled at: unabashed capitalism.'[35]

Of course rave culture had always been driven by entrepreneurs of one kind or another – some of them legal, some on the wrong side of the law; some of them idealists, others profiteering opportunists, and a few of them genuinely piratical characters with a swashbuckling disregard for health, safety and sanity. It took a certain kind of daring to become a big-time operator in the chaotic and sometimes dangerous after-dark world, and people's motives for getting involved differed according to their personal imperatives – from British millionaire James Palumbo, the former Eton schoolboy and merchant banker with no particular interest in dance music who succeeded in turning London's Ministry of Sound into a nightlife empire, to Dimitri Hegemann of Tresor, who saw club culture as an artistic mission, to someone like Pasquale Rotella, constantly chasing his dream of building a disco Disneyland.

The early raves around the M25 motorway in Britain in 1989 – mega-parties like Sunrise, Back to the Future, Energy and Biology with their laser shows, funfairs and bouncy castles – were in many ways aesthetic precursors to EDM extravaganzas like the Electric Daily Carnival, Ultra or Tomorrowland, although a key difference was that they were illegal. Sunrise's founder, Tony Colston-Hayter, a former professional gambler who started out selling slot machines while he was still at school and briefly became public enemy number one in the British tabloid press in the summer of 1989, was as keen as someone like Pasquale Rotella to stage the most spectacular party for as many people as possible: 'I didn't see why it should be kept just to a special few,' he once said.

Colston-Hayter could easily have gone on to become a mainstream promoter, although it didn't turn out like that. The man who was once described as 'Acid's Mr Big' by the tabloids briefly returned to the headlines in 2014 when he was convicted of masterminding a plot to steal £1.25 million by hacking accounts at a British bank. He claimed that he only got involved in the fraud to get money to fund his drug addiction; the judge jailed him for five-and-a-half years.

A police mugshot showed him looking seedy and unshaven, a sad distortion of the youthfully arrogant, cheeky-faced twenty-something who had once delighted in bamboozling the police and staging some of the most magnificent illegal parties of Britain's 'summer of love'. Colston-Hayter had always been an unashamed capitalist and saw his raves as 'the ultimate hedonistic leisure activity' with no political significance – an ideological stance that might have made him a welcome guest at EDMBiz – but instead, he ended up broke and in jail.

Some of the leading promoters of that era used their entrepreneurial talents in a much shrewder way than the ill-starred Colston-Hayter, however. James Barton was a teenage ticket tout from Liverpool who became an acid house promoter and then progressed to running the immensely popular Cream club and its Creamfields festival in the nineties. He ended up selling the company to Live Nation, relocating to LA and becoming the entertainment events giant's President of Electronic Music, tasked with guiding its expansion into the EDM sector and cutting deals to acquire holdings in companies like Pasquale Rotella's Insomniac and Gary Richards' Hard Events.

Barton was named the 'most important person in EDM' by *Rolling Stone* in 2014 and topped the *Billboard* magazine list of 'EDM power players' the year afterwards. He had always been one of the most business-savvy of the British club promoters, but he was also a man who understood the need to maintain certain standards of aesthetic credibility in order to safeguard the value of his brand. He argues – unsurprisingly but earnestly – that the options on offer in the 2010s were far superior to anything in the much-mythologised glory years of the late eighties and nineties.

'I'm in my late forties and I first discovered the music in 1988. I couldn't put on the radio and hear this music then or go into a mainstream record store and buy these records. It was so underground, we spent a lot of our time in shitty warehouses or crappy nightclubs or driving round the M25 trying to find a party,' Barton explains. 'I think today's electronic music fans are so much better served. The shows are incredible, the investment is huge – if you are 19, 20, 21 today, compared to 1989 or 1990, there's so much more on offer: you've got easy access to the music; you've got so much choice of so many great events.'

When I ask him if some of the magic of those buccaneering years might have been lost along the way as the scene became institutionalised, he disagrees.

'I think if you get a kick out of being chased by the police and the excitement of climbing through a window into a dodgy warehouse – yes, you're not going to have that same amount of vibe and anticipation if you're walking up to a very well-organised, controlled festival. But I don't think people want to deal with that shit,' he argues. 'When I tell my daughter what I used to have to do to listen to the music, she looks at me like I'm from a different planet. Young people now are just so much better served.'

But ensuring order while maintaining credibility could be a powerful challenge. Hardline security measures at dance music festivals, intended to create the impression of a strict anti-drug regime in order to appease the authorities, could severely limit the freedoms that such events were supposed to offer. At the Electric Zoo EDM festival in New York in 2014, partygoers were obliged to watch a video warning about the perils of 'molly' after two people died after taking MDMA at the event the year beforehand, while security officials monitored video feeds from robotic cameras and six drug-sniffing dogs and dozens of medical staff were on patrol, checking people for signs of drug use such as dilated pupils – in addition to the regular airport-style searches at the gates. Even staff and trucks were checked as they entered the site to prevent drugs being smuggled in before the festival, reports said. 'Organisers have turned this year's event into a dayglo version of North Korea. It's all a farce because EDM and ecstasy are essentially soul mates and the saucer-eyed dancing on display showed that to still be true,' a *New York Post* journalist noted cynically.[36]

One couldn't, however, accuse James Barton of lacking ambition for the culture that had become his life's work. When I asked him about the future, he outlined a potential scenario in which the rave insurgents of yesteryear go on to control the music business – a future in which 'people of my generation get to 65 and we're running the media outlets, we're running the record industry, we're running the touring and the live industry'. It was a vision of a world in which the EDM entrepreneurs get to dictate terms to the pop-culture corporations – one in which the upstarts become the establishment.

According to Barton, it was these men and women, the ones at the top, who were going to decree the destiny of dance culture: 'Where we go next is in the hands of a few key people – it's in the hands of the musicians and the producers, it's in the hands of the agents and the managers, and it's in the hands of the promoters, and it's up to us to make sure we continue to plot a path which gives us sustainability and also gives us a seat at the table with what I perceive as the old guard – the rock 'n' roll people, the pop people,' he said.

For people like Richie Hawtin and John Acquaviva, sustainability was also the key to the future, although they preferred to operate on a smaller scale. They believed that their career longevity had only been possible because they had remained true to their definition of the core values of techno – aesthetic integrity and artistic independence. 'Why are people coming in and trying to buy up electronic music? Because it's like nothing else; it's unique. For the first 20 years, electronic music held on really tightly to its own internal power, which is its integrity and authenticity,' Hawtin argued.

As well as being DJs, producers and record-label owners, the two Canadians had taken the culture's entrepreneurial impulses to another level and become venture capitalists. Acquaviva was a managing partner and Hawtin the chairman of the advisory board of Plus Eight Equity Partners, a firm that was named after their nineties record label and invested in developing imaginative music technology businesses.

They had been early investors in the Final Scratch DJ software and the Beatport website when it started, although they sold up when they felt it had got too mainstream.

'Rich and I, when we're participating in something, we always try to find that balance between altruism and capitalism,' explains Acquaviva. 'We both do what we want. He releases music that he wants, not what the market wants. We like to make people think. We're not here to pander to people. But when business gets bigger, you give people what they want, and that's what EDM is.

'When we started, we didn't need more than a bit of gumption and desire because it was new and fresh for the taking in 1990. Now there's a lot more cost. It's not as organic and sincere. Everyone's got their marketing plan.'

So it seemed, at least in Las Vegas anyway. One afternoon, in a break between the panel discussions at the EDMBiz convention, I went down to the Liquid 'beach club' at a nearby hotel behind the Strip, although there was no actual beach there; it was just one of those daytime pool parties organised by the big hotels to monetise the afternoon hours. I wanted to find out what one of the younger American DJs thought about the marketing of EDM, and how he planned to plot his course through the shark tank. I was meeting Jason Blau, a 25-year-old who performed under the name 3LAU and had grown up in Vegas, where he was seen as the little prince of the mash-up, beloved for his *Dancefloor Filth* mixtape series, a local hero who was instantly mobbed after he finished his set by giggling girls in bikinis and eager boys demanding a communal selfie to post on social media.

It was a bacchanalian tableau down by the pool, all those strapping young Americans ripped to the tits on beer and vodka, screaming for *more more more* and looking like something that Brueghel might have painted if everyone was wearing swimwear and slathered with suntan lotion, thrashing and splashing in the pool in front of the DJ booth like ferrets in a bathtub. As Blau worked the crowd with his populist EDM tunes – 'Let's get fucking crazy!' he shouted – his father was dancing right behind him, rocking hard to his son's rhythms. It was a genuinely touching scene; you could see the dad's pride in his boy's achievement, his delight at being able to share the moment – but like the middle-aged clubbers grooving to Alfredo's tunes at Pike's in Ibiza, it was also another indication of how rave culture had now spanned two generations.

When I talked to Blau afterwards at the hotel bar, he spoke in crisply sober terms about how a young DJ should conduct himself in order to be successful, using the kind of language about building a 'brand' and a social media personality that would have been incomprehensible when people like James Barton were dodging the police to get into illegal raves back in Britain in the late eighties or when Larry Levan and Frankie Knuckles were spiking the punch with tabs of LSD to get the dancers going at The Gallery club in New York more than a decade before that.

But maybe this is a bit uncharitable – times change, and customs with them – and Blau was spot-on when he started talking about the future of EDM, arguing that whatever happened to any particular style, dance music would continue to regenerate itself – just as it always had, whatever it had been called over the years: 'EDM is just a bit of jargon, it's a buzzword,' he pointed out. 'When people say the EDM bubble has burst – well, the word might become unpopular but dance music will not.'

Back at EDMBiz that afternoon, I got talking to Tommie Sunshine, who was holding court by the coffee counter, with his flowing mane of Woodstock hair and dark sunglasses looking like nothing so much as Jeff Bridges' last-of-the-hippie-believers character The Dude from *The Big Lebowski*. Alongside Frankie Bones, Juan Atkins and Richie Hawtin, the forty-something DJ was playing at what was the 20th Electric Daisy Carnival that year, as part of Pasquale Rotella's anniversary tribute to the US scene's pioneers.

Never less than loquacious, Sunshine had got himself on a serious roll, talking about how DJs used to be the 'wizards behind the screen' but had now become the focus of attention and had to caper like prat-falling clowns to provide picture memories for smartphone-wielding onlookers. 'Now there are people who are sponsored by 7 Up, people that are doing M&Ms commercials, they're doing these big branding events but at the same time they're trying to be credible in the "underground" – whatever the fuck that means anymore. But the weird thing is we're living in a time when you can actually *get away with that*,' he marvelled. 'That's *mind-blowing* to me!' All the same, he didn't seem downcast about it at all – quite the opposite. He was expecting a counterblast to challenge the orthodoxies of EDM.

'What's going to happen is there's going to be this whole new underground in response to it, because if I was 17 years old, you couldn't get me to stand at a main stage at a festival. I would be like, "This is horseshit! This is just pop a cappellas played over nonsense!"' he declared. 'I think there will be kids who'll come along and rewrite the techno handbook, rewrite the trance handbook, and they'll completely turn all of this upside down – which is great, because that's what moves the music forward, not grumpy 45-year-old assholes who complain about how bad it is now and how good the old days were.'

As I wandered through the festival grounds at the Electric Daisy Carnival that weekend, amid the chuntering dubstep basslines and savage shrieks of digital noise, I scanned some of the ravers' faces for a sign, remembering what he had told me and wondering if any of them might lead this uprising, and when it might begin.

5

House Nation

South Africa

A SPECTRAL APPARITION RISES from the clouds of dry ice billowing through the humid Cape Town air, pipe-cleaner limbs contorting wildly as he leaps and prances to a zigzagging drum groove that sounds like hammers battering out a metal tattoo on a tin roof. This undulating wraith, or DJ Spoko as he is known, flashes a toothy grin from beneath his baseball cap and scarlet bandana and pokes a skinny finger towards the sky as his comrade Mujava teases out the wonky synth melody from one of South African electronic music's biggest international hits – the one they made together, 'Township Funk'.

This pandemoniacal display on the terrace of the grand Edwardian city hall building at the Cape Town Electronic Music Festival was a masterclass in what Spoko was calling 'Bacardi House'. With its clattering percussion, urgent snatches of chant and lurid melodies, his vivacious sound was one of several indigenous South African variations on the house groove that had developed since liberation from apartheid in the nineties. Geographically isolated from the global electronic mainstream, the southernmost African country had lovingly embraced house music and created its own unique cultures around it. Some South Africans liked to boast that their country was the biggest consumer of house music in the world; true or not, it was certainly a place where a prodigious variety of new forms had emerged, both populist and left-field. As the great South African DJ Black Coffee once put it: 'We have 11 languages and all these languages have different cultures and all these cultures have different sounds and different styles of singing.'[1]

This wealth of talent in a country of around 53 million people was remarkable, rising from a traumatised society which had somehow survived the horrific brutality of apartheid but remained massively unequal, racially divided and disfigured by poverty, violence and political corruption.

DJ Spoko was just one example of how all this was possible – a story of how young South Africans employed a mixture of do-it-yourself inventiveness and entrepreneurial verve to make themselves heard. Born Marvin Ramalepe in the rural north of the country, Spoko began making music after he moved to live with his father in the Atteridgeville township, west of the country's administrative capital Pretoria. Using his father's personal computer and a pirated version of the early music software FruityLoops, he and his friend Mujava (Elvis Maswanganyi) started trying to emulate the hip-hop sounds they loved. They failed – but in the kind of serendipitous accident that has led to so many musical breakthroughs over the years, they ended up creating something else entirely, a kind of raw, minimalist electro-funk with all the blinding brightness of a flashing strobe.

'Something went wrong, but it still sounded good,' Spoko recalls. 'So I said, we can't be no Dr. Dre, we can't be no Snoop Doggy Dogg, we've got to be ourselves. At the time we couldn't play no synthesizer so we were just making drum music. No bass, just drums – bang! I just banged those drums. Hard! We would put five kicks together to make sure this shit is distorted, so we can feel it. And five snares, so we can make sure this shit is crazy.'

His father was unimpressed with his punkish efforts: 'My old man would say, "You're making noise, you make me want to go stay in a hotel." Even my neighbour said, "Can't you play something soft?" I said, "I hate soft music. I just love noise."'

Spoko's township friends were also dismissive of this peculiar brand of house music that he had developed by accident, with its militaristic snares and off-kilter tonalities: 'People would come to my crib and listen and say, "This is shit, Spoko, you've got to play something that is real." But I say, "This is real to me. It's new, I like it."'

He first started to attract some local renown when he began to test out the music he calls his 'poison' at a neighbourhood shebeen. He then spread his sound throughout Atteridgeville by giving out tracks to minibus-taxi drivers to play as they plied their routes – a method used by many young producers in the townships where the drivers sometimes function as local taste-makers, playing the hottest tunes to entertain their passengers. 'So when they go to town and come back to the hood, they'll be pumping my shit. If they've got something they like, taxi drivers are going to turn it up. Schoolkids would overload in the taxi because the driver has my songs,' Spoko says, savouring the memory of how his ugly 'noise' became a local sensation.

He also generated income by selling job-lots of ten tracks at 100 rand a time to what he describes as local 'gangsters' as soundtracks for their parties. His shady patrons even gave his music its name: Bacardi House, because it was perfect raving gear for dancers wired on strong booze. Not that Spoko had much choice in the name; the way he tells it, the bad boys made him an offer he couldn't refuse: 'I said, "OK, OK. If you like it like that, it's going to be like that." Even if I wanted to give it another name, I couldn't. I just had to bow to them – "OK it's Bacardi, guys, I feel you!"' He chuckles at the recollection: 'So since then, it's been Bacardi.'

Spoko was a voluble, jocular kind of character but with his cap pulled low and his bandana trailing beneath it, partly concealing his face, he could move through a crowd like a phantom, as if raindrops couldn't touch him or even douse the spliff perched smouldering between his lips. There seemed to be little doubt that the young Marvin Ramalepe was an unusual teenager; he picked up the nickname Spoko – 'Ghost' – while growing up in what was known as the Ghost Town neighbourhood near the Atteridgeville cemetery: 'Maybe they were dissing me because I was a thin young boy and I liked to walk through the dark alone to get some fresh air and do some thinking. They would say, "You are like a ghost, man – a ghost!"'

His gang tattoos also attested to some darker times in his youth that he only vaguely alludes to: 'Kids in my hood say they want to be like me. I say, "No don't be like me, I am a bad man. Go to school, get educated,"' he tells me. His computers were apparently stolen several times by people needing drug money. But for Ramalepe – King Spoko, the War God, as he has sometimes called himself – adversity seemed to be an everyday perennial that existed to be overcome, again and again: 'Music – you've got to be willing to die for it,' he says. 'It's like a black hole you fall into. It's crazy; one minute you're up, the next you're down, it's heaven and hell – but *I must do it.*'

His sidekick Mujava had his times of suffering too; just after 'Township Funk' was released by Warp Records in Britain in 2008 and started to attract international attention, he had a mental breakdown and was forcibly hospitalised. In a poignant scene in the South African music documentary *Future Sound of Mzansi*, Mujava evoked echoes of *One Flew Over the Cuckoo's Nest* as he recalled how anyone in the mental institution who spoke out was heavily sedated in order to silence them: 'When you talk for yourself, make them angry, they inject you with lots of medication... I used to tell them, "I am Mujava." I used to tell them I was famous and my music is popular overseas...'[2]

Perhaps it's not surprising that South African electronic dance music developed so differently and inspired such unusual characters in an environment that would seem alien and confusing to many western Europeans. But what was truly astounding to an outsider like me was its ubiquity – because South Africa really was a house nation.

'If you drive across the country, you'll realise the power of house music,' says Culoe de Song – real name Culolethu Zulu – a DJ from KwaZulu-Natal province, an hour and a half outside Durban, who made melodic tribalistic house and dressed like a hip priest in a long sombre coat and dark fedora.

'A lot of the house music that people love here has a lot of soul, with lyrical content and melodies and a groove. It's deep and quite intense for a mainstream sound,' he explains. 'Originally it was this cool thing; if you were into it, you kind of belonged to this secret society – it was not your normal nine-to-five guy who watches prime-time. It was vibe-seekers, people who love the cool stuff – the underground, the drug world – people who want to express their freedom. It was like an alternative community of some sort.

'Then it just went really ballistic across the country, although it wasn't supported by the mainstream scene or the celebrity culture, but by the people. So when it got really big, even guys like me in remote areas could access it.' Culoe de Song was from one of the country's 'homelands', nominally independent or partly self-governing territories set aside for black ethnic groups under apartheid. 'There was no "scene" there. If someone got a CD we would get a tape of that and it would be passed on, or I would just tape things off the radio.'

Away from the bohemian downtown scenes in Johannesburg and Cape Town, there were huge raves attracting thousands of dancers in black townships like Soweto, playing purely deep house. 'They're not playing stadium house, but good, tasteful deep house – the deeper the better,' explains British producer Charles Webster, who became one of the most popular DJs on the South African deep house circuit after his soulful anthem 'Better Day' was a national hit in the late nineties. 'The people really know their music; if the DJs play too hard, people leave the dancefloor,' Webster says.

During the nineties, cult record shops in Johannesburg like Soul Kandi and House Afrika developed into record labels that nurtured the early South African house producers, while the new youth radio station YFM offered a broadcasting outlet for domestically made grooves. 'YFM played house music most of the time and that was unheard of on radio before,' says Vinny da Vinci (Vincent Motshegoa), one of Johannesburg's first house DJs, who also co-owned House Afrika. 'People gravitated to it in a big way… it was like a calling.' Heather Mennell, the former editor of the South African edition of *DJ* magazine, remembers it as a revolutionary moment: 'It was a huge expression of hope and freedom.'

The fervour for deep house turned foreign DJs like Charles Webster, who had enthusiastic but relatively small cult followings elsewhere in the world, into genuine stars in the country. Ethnomusicologist Gavin Steingo remembered talking to US producer Little Louie Vega of Masters at Work after he went to play in South Africa for the first time in 2000. 'He expected to have to take a taxi. He got to the airport and there were bodyguards waiting for him. They took him to a stadium, where he played for 20,000 people,' said Steingo. 'He was a major celebrity there, and had no idea.'[3]

Part of the reason for the popularity of deep house was political. Arriving not long before the country's liberation from apartheid in 1994, it was perfectly placed to occupy the cultural free spaces that opened up as white minority rule finally ended.

'A lot of electronic music is party music, and for the last 20 years we've had a big reason to celebrate,' says Nthato Mokgata, alias Spoek Mathambo, the Soweto-born producer and vocalist who became one of the most inspirational performers on the country's avant-garde electronic scene. 'Being a democracy for a first time, that creates a culture all of its own, people being free to move around where they used to not be able to.'

The subtitle to *Future Sound of Mzansi*, the feature-length documentary that Mathambo co-directed in 2014, was 'Welcome to the Apartheid After-Party'. He argues that electronic dance music was the soundtrack to liberation for the country's youth in a similar way to how techno became the new pop culture of reunified Germany after the fall of the Berlin Wall.

'A lot of the music culture and party culture comes directly from the fact that it is a freedom party – not just any party, but a freedom party,' he explains. 'It's not just the freedom to express oneself but the literal thing of being able to go to different places at different times because there were curfews before that. Because of their race, people wouldn't be allowed into certain establishments.

'It's a very functional, real freedom, not just freedom of expression. Being able to be in the street, 2,000 of you with a sound system without the army shooting you down – that's what it's about.'

These were exhilarating times with a genuine sense of new possibilities emerging. 'For a few years after the end of white rule in 1994, Nelson Mandela's visionary leadership encouraged the hazy belief that a political miracle had occurred and that a new South Africa had been born, exorcised of the torment of the past,' wrote *Financial Times* correspondent Alec Russell in his book about the post-apartheid era.[4]

Public space had even been even designed to keep races apart and stop people from gathering, says urban planner Zahira Asmal: 'During apartheid, three black people standing on a corner together talking was considered a demonstration.'[5] So after the night-time curfews imposed on black people by the apartheid regime to quell unrest were lifted, there was an outpouring of repressed energy.

'Before 1994, if you lived in a township, there was a curfew. By seven or eight everyone was off the streets, and the streets were patrolled by police with Casspirs [armoured vehicles],' explains Duncan Ringrose, the former director of the Cape Town Electronic Music Festival. 'Then 1994 came and suddenly you didn't have to be in your house at night, and you could make some noise, so the street bash culture just exploded. It was this eruption of celebration and it spilled out onto the streets with sound systems.'

Even before the end of apartheid, house music had begun to take root after pioneering DJs like Vinny da Vinci, Graeme Hector (alias G-Force) and Rozzano Davids started converting clubbers in Johannesburg and Cape Town to the sounds of Chicago and Detroit. In the early nineties, Cape Town's first raves with suitably starry-eyed names like World Peace Party were held in industrial areas on the outskirts of the city, while LSD and smuggled supplies of MDMA began to energise the emerging scene at clubs like Eden, which was located in an old ice cream factory. ('Why did we call it Eden? Because we wanted it to be a massive E den,' promoter Jesse Stagg explained.[6]) All of this was largely ignored by the authorities, who were struggling to contain the bloody unrest of the time, recalls one of the original Cape Town ravers, Roger Young. 'The cops didn't know how to deal with it,' he says. 'It never really was a problem until around the mid-nineties, when parties started being shut down. They were busy with trying to suppress the violence, so they didn't really care about us dancing in warehouses.'

Young, a white South African, remembers how witnessing even a slightly racially mixed crowd raving together for the first time felt liberating: 'I grew up in a fairly segregated environment, so to see that – oh shit! People are dancing, and all the other stuff is going away…'[7]

Rave culture, with its implicit message of tolerance, suggested to him at least that another way might be possible.

'It was the new South Africa. Mandela had just come out [of prison], black and white people could mix now freely, whereas before it was illegal,' recalls Rozzano Davids. Before that, the police would often harass people at the atypically mixed although predominantly non-white club called The Base where Davids used to play hip-hop and acid house in central Cape Town: 'Our white friends would have to go to the door and keep the police from coming into the venue,' he says. 'But after 1990, after Mandela was released, we could party in peace.'

Despite that, South Africa's early house clubs were never really all that integrated; the youth culture of the time could not help but reflect its social environment. Indeed, even more than two decades after the end of the apartheid regime, many of the same divisions persisted. The political system might have changed, but the social boundaries that it had enforced so harshly were harder to break down.

'Kwaito was our first freedom of speech.'

Black Coffee

Before the popular ascendance of deep house, kwaito ruled the club scene. Kwaito is South Africa's low-slung, pitched-down reinterpretation of house, a slo-mo hip-shaking style that originated in the early nineties at around the same time as the first raves, between the release of Mandela and the end of white minority rule. According to its founding myth, it began when DJs like Oskido (Oscar Mdlongwa) and Christos Katsaitis took the innovative step of pitching down American house tracks to around 100 beats per minute to better fit South African clubbers' dancing style.

'Before kwaito, we used to play a lot of house: the late Frankie Knuckles, all the big Chicago tracks,' Oskido explained. 'It was hard for us to get that music – there were only a few selected shops. Christos was my friend and he used to import records, but those records were too fast. We decided to reproduce them, slowing them down. That's how [Oskido's mix-CD series] *Mixmaster* came about: I was reprogramming the music, slowing it down. Eventually, we started putting our own lyrics on it, talking about things happening in the township.'[8]

It was a bold move that took the music beyond its US roots and helped to lay the foundations for a host of localised variations. Oskido, Katsaitis and Don Laka cut tracks for their Kalawa Jazmee label that imitated their US heroes, but with more laidback grooves and vocals in South Africa's own languages, while bands like Boom Shaka and Trompies became kwaito's first stars, with songs that seemed to express the optimism of the end of the apartheid era in titles like 'It's About Time' and 'Celebrate'.

Under apartheid, politically-inspired songs were often banned, so musicians sometimes sought to disguise their messages. One of the best-known examples was 1989's 'We Miss You Manelo' by Chicco, ostensibly a song about a teenage runaway, but which was recognised by most people who heard it as being a plea for Mandela to be freed. Kwaito however was full-on escapist party music, although Kalawa Jazmee bands and DJs often played at African National Congress rallies, and one important early kwaito track – Arthur Mafokate's 'Kaffir' from 1995, with its message from a black worker to his white employer urging: 'Hey boss, don't call me kaffir' – showed that it could very occasionally be a critical force.

In Gavin Steingo's book about kwaito, he argues that the music might have been resolutely unpolitical but it sounded like 'the promise of freedom' amid the harsh social realities of the immediate post-apartheid era, its high-living ebullience creating an 'alternative sensory reality'.[9] Black Coffee insists meanwhile that its power derived from the knowledge that it was a genuinely autonomous black South African movement: 'Kwaito was our first thing that was never controlled by anyone,' he explains. 'It was something that was ours. It was born on the streets. It was about whatever the artist wanted to talk about.'

Black Coffee (Nathi Maphumulo) was one of a generation of South African DJs who was raised on kwaito. He was also one of a series of unique characters who helped South African dance music to push forward creatively through the 2000s, and he became a genuine phenomenon in the country – a deep house celebrity with an independent attitude and a sense of moral righteousness. There's a remarkable scene in a Resident Advisor documentary about his career when he revisits his old township school; the pupils in their uniforms who have gathered in the schoolyard in anticipation of seeing some unnamed returning alumnus burst out in screams of star-struck joy when this DJ icon appears in front of them. It was hard for a non-South African to grasp exactly how popular a figure he was in his own country. 'I've worked in many townships with Black Coffee and it's like working with Michael Jackson – honestly, it's incredible, wherever you go, all the small kids jump on him. He's a massive idol,' says Valentino Barrioseta, who ran the Cape Town-based Bridges for Music charity. 'The whole country lives and breathes house music and every kid wants to be a DJ like Black Coffee.'

Black Coffee grew up in a rural township outside Durban and dreamed of becoming a DJ, but a serious injury at the age of 13 initially looked certain to end his ambitions. As his neighbourhood celebrated the release of Nelson Mandela in 1990, a speeding car careered into the crowd, killing two people and injuring dozens of others including the young Nathi Maphumulo, causing him to lose the use of his left hand. But despite his disability, he persevered and succeeded – an indication of his strength of character.

Growing up in his township, far from the city, he used to have to milk the family cows every morning before going to school and spent his hours daydreaming of an escape into the enchanted but seemingly unreachable world of music. 'A township is a place strategically built by the South African government to put black people, and make sure they don't amount to anything,' he once explained. 'The hardest thing to do was leave and find opportunities, so kids get caught up in the township, where there's nothing to aspire to be. The people who did well were people who stole for a living. They were the most stylish, and they were the people you'd look up to. They were the people who were having a bit of fun with their lives. So it was a far-fetched dream for me to come out and find a platform.'[10]

He started out by making imitations of records he liked but couldn't get, before developing his own emotive style of deep house. He was offered a recording deal by Sony early in his career but preferred to remain independent and set up his own company instead. 'I knew what I wanted, and that freaked a lot of people out,' he says.

What was intriguing about Black Coffee was that he really seemed to believe that his example could be a practical inspiration; the break-through that he achieved in overcoming adversity and asserting his independence could convince other young people who grew up in the townships to strive for better futures. In the hedonistic nocturnal world of club culture, it's rare for a DJ to express any ambitions towards moral leadership, but this was South Africa, and different rules applied.

'As South Africans, I think we still have a sense of responsibility,' he responds when I ask him if he believes that house music should have some kind of social conscience. 'We want to do better for the country we come from. By doing better and helping other people, we can make things better.

'In my country, we are still dealing with a lot of insecurities. Just as people, we still think so little of ourselves. The problem is that we are so traumatised by the past; people never believed in themselves – we were *told* not to believe in ourselves. That is why change is needed. Otherwise we're always going to be stuck in a black hole where the old government still has control because we're still afraid of them.

'We need to get away from everything they told us, get out of that old cycle and believe we can do more. I do all I can to preach that. Every little opportunity I get, I try.'

If Black Coffee was the idealistic superstar, Spoek Mathambo was the restless maverick, the cult figure with a taste for the weird and an eye on the future. His nickname meant 'Ghost of Bones', and was adopted from a television sitcom called *Emzini Wezinsizwa*, about migrant workers living in a Johannesburg hostel. Inspired by Fela Kuti, Stevie Wonder, Prince and Iggy Pop, his music veered all over the place, picking up traces from American hip-hop, British postpunk, European techno and South African kwaito, amongst many other things. He called it 'township tech', but that offered little suggestion of its scope and ambition.

'I'm a boy from Johannesburg, not London or Hong Kong, so my music is infused with a lot of African tradition – mythology, musical tradition, rhythmic sensibility. That's there, but so is Warner Brothers and Hollywood and hip-hop and rock and avant-garde jazz. So I'm a mixture of all these sensibilities,' he explains.

Mathambo's background was similarly diverse. He grew up in Soweto in the eighties during the state of emergency but went to a mainly white school. He also lived in Sweden and married a Belgrade-born musician, Gnucci.

'I'm from the generation that grew up during the change,' he says. 'I spent the first few years of my childhood with army tanks rolling down the streets and smoke bombs going off, people getting kidnapped and shot – the state of emergency started in the year that I was born. So the tension in society and the explosion of that tension into total energy and excitement, then disappointment about new governments and cor-ruption, is all there in the huge explosion in creativity in fashion, art and music that I've experienced and been a part of.'

He got some early exposure working with Waddy Jones, later to become better known as Ninja from South African rap/rave band Die Antwoord, then recorded in a couple of multiracial duos as Playdoe with electronic producer Sibot (Simon Ringrose), and as Sweat X with another local innovator, Markus Wormstorm. Mathambo's own debut album, *Mshini Wam*, took its title from 'Umshini Wami' – '*Bring Me My Machine Gun*' – the Zulu war song favoured by the military wing of the African National Congress.

'Spoek is like a machine. He's constant, people can't keep up with him,' says Cape Town musician Jake Lipman, alias JacobSnake, who drummed on some of Mathambo's records. 'Essentially, that guy is… He's a genius, you know? He's like a flaming ball of creativity. His reference points are so interesting, and he's managed to amalgamate and mesh so many different reference points together. He's constantly evolving and constantly changing.'

His electrifying cover version of Joy Division's 'She's Lost Control' was a crucial illustration. In the disturbing video that accompanied the release, a white-suited Mathambo declaims his reinterpretation of Ian Curtis's lyrics through a megaphone in a cemetery as zombiefied children jerk like marionettes and blanche each other's faces with flour and milk; the video ends with Mathambo curled up foetus-like and dirt-spattered in the graveyard mud.

He says that he likes 'dark and edgy' postpunk music because it has a tension and anxiety that chimes with contemporary South African society. 'I wanted to juxtapose what was happening in South Africa in electronic music with what was happening in the UK with the postpunk movement in terms of social climate – how the doom and the darkness can also create a positive reaction, a feeling of energy rather than just a feeling of wanting to drop your head and cry,' he explains.

In a country with no shortage of musical innovators, none were as effortlessly eccentric as Richard Mthetwa, alias Dog, although better known as Nozinja, a forty-something former mobile phone repair shop entrepreneur who invented the frenetic, cartoonish style that came to be known as 'Shangaan electro'. Nozinja's early tracks were accompanied by bizarre low-budget videos that he made himself; in the clip for his song 'Nwa Gezani' from 2009, he bops around stoutly in a businessman's suit and tie with what looks like an enlarged, super-saturated postcard of bright yellow tulips in the background, interspersed with shots of women frenetically shaking their bottoms in crazy-coloured *xibelani* skirts.

Nozinja has sometimes performed in a psychedelic leotard and vest with multi-hued cummerbunds ranged across his tubby belly and hot pink costume feathers attached to his biceps. His music was also a madcap combination of the traditional and the futuristic, irrepressibly shiny and open-hearted with twitchy lo-fi melodies skittering around the beat as it zipped along at a speed of around 180 beats per minute – a pace only previously attempted by producers of full-on hardcore styles like gabba and footwork.

For Nozinja though, this was nothing particularly unusual. When I ask him how his music got so manic, he responds as if it was a matter of fact that should be obvious to anyone: 'It's fast because that's how the Shangaan dancers are dancing – I didn't choose to be fast; I had no other alternative than to make it fast,' he says.

'What I did was to fuse two different genres of music and play them with different instruments. I took old South African disco bubblegum music – just the basslines they were using – and I took Shangaan drums and melodies and I fused them together. But I didn't play them on the original live guitar that comes from Shangaan. I used marimba instead.'

Shangaan is the name of Nozinja's tribe, one of South Africa's many ethnic minority groups, and one that he argues is relatively marginalised. He says he wanted to preserve and promote traditional Shangaan musical culture but update it for a new generation brought up on kwaito and house; in this sense, his sound was also a spiritual descendant of the upbeat 'Shangaan disco' tracks that were made in the late seventies and eighties.

'People knew that Shangaan is one of the 11 official languages in South Africa but they never knew about our culture, our dance,' he explains. 'We have taken it and modernised it. The elders will sometimes complain, they will tell you, "In our days, we didn't do this, we didn't dance this fast, we didn't play with computers."' But for Nozinja, this was just the kind of backhanded encouragement he needed to go even further out, to ratchet up the velocity and make those chattering marimbas pulse even more frantically.

'I always tell people, "Don't do something that anybody else is doing,"' he says, laying out his personal manifesto for musical progression, one which could equally apply to many other South African producers: 'Don't come with somebody else's idea, because you can never be that man or woman.'

'There is music being made here that doesn't exist and couldn't exist anywhere else on the planet.'

Jumping Back Slash

A slight young man in a denim shirt and sunglasses saunters through the rural Zulu township of KwaDabeka, about 20 kilometres inland from Durban, past a sign with a Bible quotation announcing that you are now entering a 'godly suburb', past the chickens clucking in the unpaved yards of government-built bungalows, down a gentle slope to the corrugated iron shack where he makes his music. As Lwazi Asanda Gwala walks, a filmmaker's camera follows him as he recalls how his mother's boyfriend first got him a computer program to make music when he was around ten years old. 'When they broke up, I still had the CD with me, but I didn't have the computer,' he recalls.[11]

Gwala held on to the disk with the software, waiting and waiting until he got access to another computer and could finally get to use the program again. When he did, a few years later, he started trying to fuse hip-hop, house and elements of traditional Zulu maskandi rhythms, added a low, menacing bass hum to the mix, and a new style started to take shape. *Gqom*, it became called.

Gwala is now better known as DJ Lag, one of gqom's originators, and he argues that the sound was a new amalgam that could only have been created by young black South Africans: 'This is our identity,' he says. Gqom, which translates from Zulu as something like 'bang' or 'ricochet' and is pronounced with a tongue-challenging postalveolar click, was a kind of tranced-out jump-up sound with a compulsive offbeat syncopation that could be ominously deep but at the same time retained the raucous youthful exuberance of the township lads who invented it. Moody drones surge below the percussion as one-note semaphore riffs signal hypnotically and barely identifiable snatches of voice are pitched down or distorted until they sound like the frantic yelping of a hound or the growling of a lion. Claves chatter dementedly while tom-toms cascade downwards.

'It's a very dark, intense, steel-cladded variation of South African house. It's music for wild rave parties,' I'm told by Menchess (Menzi Ntuli), a member of Rudeboyz, one of the pioneering gqom crews from Durban. 'Deep house is mainstream now. This is more crazy, not as sophisticated, more raw and pounding. It's in a different world on its own.'

Although gqom's early history is blurry, its originators generally agree that it first emerged from Durban around the start of the 2010s, recorded using pirated software, shared on social media and by mobile phone, and popularised by minibus-taxi drivers who blasted the sound to attract young passengers to ride with them. Many early tracks were only identified by a mobile phone number or a Blackberry Messenger pin code, enhancing the sense of utter disorientation produced by the music itself. But although it seemed to have appeared from some alien reality, gqom was actually a kind of feverish hardcore reimagining of kwaito, Afro-house and what was known locally as 'broken beat'. It took all of the South African genres that preceded it, smashed them into pieces and then reassembled them into something new.

'It's all the music that came before it distilled into this dark, weird, broken sound which is very minimal but can sound quite big with all the echoes and the reverbs,' says Gareth Jones, alias Jumping Back Slash, a British-born but South Africa-based producer who worked on material for Spoek Mathambo's Fantasma project and whose thrilling tribalistic house style has drawn inspiration from gqom.

'Obviously they're hearing Black Coffee and all that Durban house sound with the drones, the reverb and the mental syncopated shakers, but they're taking away its smoothness,' Jones explains. 'They go "fuck it" and they strip out the vocals, take out that four-on-the-floor kick drum and start giving it that broken rhythm. Then they add that drone and that one-note repetition that goes on for about six minutes.'

Exploration of the unknown possibilities of cheap, second-hand or seemingly obsolete tech has been a constant factor in the development of electronic dance music. Just as the early Chicago producers created acid house by tweaking new sounds out of the Roland TB-303, which was originally marketed as a practice aid for bass guitarists, Durban's young gqom producers teased their music out of whatever equipment they could get their hands on.

'These kids don't have a studio, they have a cheap laptop and they have a cracked version of FruityLoops, and just like grime in the UK, it's boys having a bash. It's real grassroots underground culture,' says Jones. 'In a way it's like a punk scene – it's black and it's centred around electronic music, similar to how grime was like a punk scene. It's music that challenges you, makes you think. It's the real thing, full stop.'

The availability of inexpensive mobile phones and the spread of internet access was a crucial factor, which meant that as well as promoting their music via the minibus-taxis, as DJ Spoko did in Atteridgeville, gqom producers would brutally compress their tunes so they could upload them more easily to South African file-sharing sites like KasiMP3, which became the repository of a vast archive of DIY dance music.

When they first started cutting tracks, many gqom producers had no greater goal than to be local heroes in their own neighbourhoods around Durban. DJ Lag says he didn't even have that ambition: 'I was not trying to be popular at all,' he insists. 'When I started being famous around Clermont, my township, I was really surprised that what I was experimenting with with beats came to be loved by people, and I still cannot believe that it is actually happening.' A few months after we spoke, I watched him electrify the dancefloor at the Unsound festival in Poland – the township lad from Durban, turning the Central European dancers all the way out.

The unruly sounds of South African subgenres like gqom or DJ Spoko's Bacardi House have sometimes been explained as part of a continuum of DIY electronic dance genres from the less salubrious urban areas of the world – a kind of sonic kin to various other boisterous booty-shaking styles with a kleptomaniac attitude to sampling which utilise cheap software to fuse rave's energy and rap's aggression, such as Venezuelan changa-tuki, Brazilian baile funk or Angolan kuduro.

But there's also a sense that South African sounds like gqom could never have emerged anywhere else. 'Kwaito isn't kwaito unless someone's rapping in Zulu on it, so you can't make it in the UK; the same with Afro-house, the same with gqom – even the mad Afrikaans redneck music, it could only come from here because of its history,' argues Jones.

The gqom scene, according to Durban lore, was also an MDMA-fuelled raving subcult. In the music's early phase, several gqom tracks praised the joys of Ecstasy, or 'qoh', as they called it. 'It goes hand in hand with gqom music,' a producer from the Formation Boyz crew said. 'Once you take qoh, you just go out of space.'[12] Some of the best known were Rudeboyz' 'Mercedes Song' and 'Mitsubishi Song', both references to car-logo imprints on Ecstasy pills, at least according to the publicity material for their release.

'It's entirely up to your interpretation. A Mitsubishi can be a car but it can also be a pill,' laughs Rudeboyz' manager Tsepo Khonyane when I ask him about this. 'Ecstasy is very popular in Durban. It's not that gqom emerged from Ecstasy – it's the nature of the sound: it's very dark, it's very intense, it's very drum-based, so these people who are into that Ecstasy culture prefer sounds that will play around with their mind, you know?'

Khonyane says that the Ecstasy connotations made radio stations wary about playing gqom, so producers started to avoid overt drug references. There was even a short film about the township raving scene, entitled *U'Qoh*, which was made to warn about the perils of Ecstasy and shows a youth getting spiked with MDMA at a party, collapsing on the dancefloor, then being carried home unconscious by his mates to his weeping mama. But the comments on some gqom songs on video-sharing websites like YouTube offered a more positive appraisal of the drug: 'Qoh qoh qoh – qoh qoh qoh!!!!!' one enthused.

The drug references inspired a journalist from the South African *Mail and Guardian* newspaper to venture out to expose what he described as the 'pervasive nihilism' of gqom in 2014. He ended up at a daytime rave in a hilltop neighbourhood somewhere outside Durban, in a kind of makeshift one-room club built of concrete blocks where the latest gqom MP3s were banging hard.

His scandalised dispatch began by portentously invoking Alexander Shulgin, the 'godfather of Ecstasy', who resynthesised the long-forgotten chemical compound MDMA in the sixties: 'In the undulating ghettoes of Durban, [Shulgin's] legacy of experimentation lives on

– albeit a little more loosely – among a generation of youth who may have never heard his name,' he wrote.[13]

With a kind of perverse fascination, he went on to report that the vibe inside the club was 'dark, and yet engulfing and electric', describing some of the qoh-crazed ravers as almost feral in their sexual abandon. A dealer he met then offered him a peace-and-love pitch about MDMA that was reminiscent of the old British acid house-era tales about how E cured football hooligans of their aggression. 'If someone is on qoh, even if you step on their toes they won't beef with you. There's just this overwhelming kindness that envelops them,' the dealer insisted. 'In my opinion, it should be freely available at the store, like liquor.'[14]

Obviously most club cultures are also drug scenes – this is the perennial narcotised reality of underground nightlife across the world – but there was no evidence to suggest that Durban's gqom freaks were any more off their heads than ravers of a similar age in Berlin, Paris or London. And the salacious qoh-rave exposé – with its promise of drugs, sex and wild dancefloor action – was as much an advertisement for the genre as the tabloid reports about acid house in Britain back in the late eighties, when the shock-horror headlines actually helped to encourage the country's youth to partake of the forbidden pleasures of the night.

More importantly than all of this however, the scene gave Durban's gqom generation an outlet to express themselves through a DIY culture that charmed its spells from the cheapest of technology. As one of the Forgotten Souls crew put it: 'Music is not about the equipment you have, but the creation in your head.'[15]

'No one can say, "I have the formula" – there is no such thing right now, there are no rules saying what you can do or not. This is a new society and you can create what you want, and that is what's making it exciting.'

Culoe de Song

Clouds of pungent smoke drift languidly over the low-rise concrete buildings of Gugulethu, one of the impoverished townships that sprawls outwards to the east of Cape Town. The heavy smell of barbecued meat in the air is almost potent enough to be intoxicating, as people rush to and fro with plates heaped high with choice cuts for the grill and bottles of bring-your-own hooch.

For years, the streets of Gugulethu had no names, just the initials NY – standing for 'native yard' – and a number. Many of its original inhabitants were forcibly moved here in the sixties when Cape Town's multiracial District Six neighbourhood was razed by the apartheid regime.

Mzoli's grill restaurant on NY115 in Gugulethu had become something of a local institution, attracting hungry carnivores of all races from all over the city to chow down on steaks, ribs and sausages, guzzle beer and party hard to the DJs who pumped their house beats into the afternoon sunshine. I was there with Andile 'Max' Stemela and Sello Mangwana, a kwaito duo known as Ruffest, who had brought some new tunes to give to the restaurant DJs to play, because Mzoli's, like the minibus-taxis and KasiMP3, was also a place where fresh hits could be promoted.

We sat down to chat just across the road at a shebeen called Esikomu, among tables packed with revellers scarfing down grilled meat and pouring endless glasses of brandy and vodka. Ruffest, like so many others, started out cutting rudimentary tracks in township bedrooms using FruityLoops, but the duo got their break when they were selected to take part in a two-week government-funded training course for emerging musical talents run by kwaito originator Oskido. At the end of the course, which taught them business and marketing skills as well as studio techniques, the participants were given either recording equipment or DJ tech to further their careers.

Ruffest went on to feature on a sizzling 2012 album by electronic beatmakers LV on London's Hyperdub label, but even this marginal cult success didn't come easy. Stemela was once a dancer, but was now in a wheelchair – he refers to it as 'my BMW' – because his legs were paralysed when he was shot during a gunbattle between rival gangs in the nearby Nyanga township. 'I was caught in the crossfire, in the wrong place at the wrong time,' he says. 'But I did not stop, I did not give up, I said this bullet that hit me will not stop my dream of being a musician.'

More adversity, more struggle... 'Kwaito is all about happiness, celebrating being African,' says Mangwana. 'Most artists who are starting sing about ladies, sing about booze, sing about nice times – the good things in life. But as you grow, you see that you can't just write about fun all the time; there has to be a message...' He pauses and looks glum for a minute: 'Kids should want to be the next Ruffest or even the next president, but they are just destroying their lives and killing each other...'

I remembered what DJ Roach from the veteran Cape Town breakbeat label African Dope had told me earlier that week: 'Creativity thrives on suffering, and there's a lot of suffering here, especially in the townships, so that's why you have so much creativity.'

Back in the city centre that evening, the Cape Town Electronic Music Festival was starting to gather pace at the City Hall. It was on the balcony of this building, in February 1990, that Nelson Mandela gave his first speech after his release from prison, an event that signalled that the demise of the apartheid regime was not far off. In a powerful, dignified address, Mandela called on all South Africans to join together and push forward towards freedom and democracy, to end white rule and build a new society. 'Our march to freedom is irreversible,' he declared. 'We must not allow fear to stand in our way.'[16]

Outside on the City Hall terrace, Jumping Back Slash is bombarding the crowd with immense gqom-influenced beats and rolling drums layered with warped-out samples, while inside, DJ Fletcher from African Dope fills the old colonial hall with the stately riffs and booming sub-bass of electronic reggae. As Fletcher rocks the digi-dub, a snatch of Jamaican vocal echoes upwards towards the high stuccoed ceiling: 'Oh my suffering...'

Cape Town is South Africa's legislative capital and the country's third most populous city after Johannesburg and Durban. In the city centre, stallholders were hawking African textiles, Mandela T-shirts and Bafana Bafana replica football tops to the tourists while upmarket coffee shops and pavement gold traders plied their wares to their respective social constituencies. Near parliament, where gaggles of homeless people were squatting on blankets in the street, squinting in the midday sun, there was a statue of Boer War hero and former prime minister Louis Botha in military uniform on a steed rampant with the inscription 'Farmer, Warrior, Statesman' – although it was defaced by activists later that year amid a furious debate about whether such monuments to white rule should still be standing.

The mellifluous calls to prayer from the mosque nestling among the vividly painted housefronts of the Bo-Kaap district were an indication that the city was very much a multicultural place, although the million-dollar mansions in Camps Bay on the other side of Table Mountain, with their high gates and 'armed security' warning signs were completely socially disconnected from townships like Langa and Gugulethu. 'You have this artificial paradise on one side and enforced poverty on the other,' notes DJ Roach.

Without any naïve 'rainbow nation' delusions, the Cape Town Electronic Music Festival was trying to channel the surging energies of the country's dance culture and bring some of its disparate creative communities together. That meant township auteurs like Spoko and Mujava as well as forward-thinking white South African beatmakers like Felix Laband, who created his own evocative strain of politically conscious, kwaito-tinted electronica that collaged the jibber-jabber of politicians and the burbling of evangelist radio preachers; a music which Laband once described as 'the sound of the seven o'clock news in both heaven and hell'.[17]

Duncan Ringrose, the Cape Town Electronic Music Festival's director in its early years, was a white boy who got his early musical inspiration listening to hip-hop, which might be unremarkable in the US or Europe but was hardly 'normal' in South Africa in the apartheid era. For him, the festival was kind of a mission, although it was all about the music at the same time. 'I could not just put on a "festival",'

Ringrose says. 'What this country has been through and the amount of sacrifice and suffering that South Africans have witnessed first-hand, I don't think you should be in this country if you're not contributing.

'The music is the tool but the end goal is trying to create social cohesion – connecting people, building communities and breaking barriers. Even if I wasn't in the music industry, that end goal would still be there. It just happens that I love music and it's what I know, and it's become a vehicle for what I want to do in the broader picture of society.'

Not for the first time, I was struck by the decency and thoughtfulness of some of these South African club people, the way they felt they had to try to come to terms with their own history and find some way of helping to create a better future. Ringrose admitted of course that the audience at the festival was still largely white, and that was an inevitable result of generations of trauma and oppression. He added that this was something that couldn't be solved with a couple of decades of universal suffrage and a few banging tunes: 'We try to contribute by doing what we do, which is music. But it's not an easy road because we operate in the most hedonistic industry on the planet – it's not known for its social conscience.'

He also acknowledged that the Cape Town beat freaks digging their abstract electronica and the township kids raving to deep house rarely if ever came together. 'It's still very segregated – in terms of class as well as race,' he says. 'I think there's still a large part of white South African society that's still in denial about what went down here. It's easy to say that Nelson Mandela came and made everything cool and we're now all OK with each other, but there is still a lot of anger and a lot of things need to be worked through.'

A crucial element of the festival's mission was the series of workshops and lectures that it organised, both in central Cape Town and in the townships. The festival headliners didn't just fly in, play their records, then take their fee home; they also had to communicate directly with the locals and leave some knowledge behind.

In 2015, Four Tet and Detroit's Octave One were doing workshops at the Gugu S'Thebe Cultural Centre in Langa township. Apart from the new shopping malls and the police station, the cultural centre with its respectful displays of African art hanging in the hallways looked like one of the most modern buildings in this dusty low-rise neighbourhood. Nearby in makeshift shacks made from corrugated iron, tarpaulin and planks of wood, people were cooking on open wood fires, although many of the rundown shanties had been replaced by rows of low-rise state-built RDP (Reconstruction and Development Project) cottages, their concrete drabness enlivened by the gloriously kitsch murals of the hairdressing kiosks dotted along the roadside and a few more opulent two-storey houses with high walls and barred windows built by wealthier residents.

Langa was almost 100 per cent black. More than 20 years after liberation from apartheid, South Africa's blacks, whites and 'coloureds' (as they were defined under the racist system) still often lived apart – partly a legacy of the laws that designated and enforced different areas for different racial groups to live in, physically entrenching post-colonial oppression. Under apartheid, black people over 16 had to carry passes at all times, internal passports to prove where they were allowed to be, or else face arrest. The legislation was only repealed in 1986.

When we arrived at the cultural centre, a crowd of local township DJs and Cape Town hipsters had already gathered in its outdoor amphitheatre and a precocious schoolboy was rapping on the low concrete stage over a rowdy electro beat: 'I'm the king of the jungle!' he declared with a confidence way greater than his years. He even introduced himself: 'My nickname is Michael Jackson and I live with my grandmother and my two brothers and my two sisters. I'm ten years old.'

It was a charming moment, and Lenny Burden of Octave One was clearly thrilled to be there: 'The music we started to make in our mama's basement got us all the way to Africa. It's incredible!' he enthused. As he and his brother Lawrence demonstrated how they created their live sound from their complex jumble of boxes and wires, cranking up some old-school hard-jacking house and building the intensity as the snares started to roll, feisty little 'Michael Jackson' leaped back onto the stage for a valedictory shimmy.

The Cape Town Electronic Music Festival had close links to Bridges for Music, a charity dedicated to bringing some kind of social responsibility to the blithely heedless world of electronic dance music. Bridges for Music's first project was to build a music school in Langa to teach entrepreneurial skills as well as production techniques. The charity was started by Valentino Barrioseta, who previously worked as the marketing manager at Amnesia in Ibiza, and he used his Balearic connections to convince high-profile DJs to give up some of their earning time to spend a few philanthropic days in South Africa.

'I feel that there are a lot of amazing souls and talent in this industry but they are trapped into things that don't really make any difference to the world, full of egos and hedonism, and I was right at the epicentre of that in Ibiza,' Barrioseta explains. 'I thought, how can I put my energy into something that might make a difference to someone, or at least highlight the positives of dance music?'

Barrioseta convinced Skrillex, Richie Hawtin, Black Coffee and Swiss DJ Luciano to become patrons of the charity. Skrillex and Hawtin also did lectures in Langa and played a Bridges for Music free party in Soweto, way out of their normal comfort zone, in a place where few people knew who they were. It's an experience that a superstar DJ must rarely encounter, and which Hawtin relates back to his early clubbing days, when he used to cross the river from his home in Canada to rave to Derrick May's sets at the Music Institute club in Detroit.

'There are moments like when I was in Soweto where it really comes back to that deep, basic level of how powerful music can be, and how it can have this effect of bringing people together – arm in arm, smiling, laughing and dancing together,' Hawtin recalls.

'My brother and I walking into the Music Institute in Detroit, we were the only white kids there. We were younger than everyone and we were a bit naive – should we be there or shouldn't we, who knows? – but we felt somehow this sense of belonging, those intimate feelings of when the scene was small and if you liked this music, you were part of it. That purity of feeling was there in South Africa, and that was mind-blowing.'

Skrillex was so charged up after speaking in Langa that he went on afterwards to jam with Cape Town DJ Fosta at his township home, then invited the South African to play with him at the Glastonbury Festival. When I asked Fosta about Skrillex, he responded simply and warmly: 'Sonny has a great heart.'

The Californian EDM producer also said he felt a special sort of energy at the Soweto gig: 'People in the townships didn't necessarily know who Skrillex was or what I was doing and then you had white kids from across the tracks that came over who before were too afraid to go, or think about going, into these areas,' he recalled. 'So culturally, because you had these people intermingling, the locals dancing with the other kids, people meeting, kids linking up, local producers linking up with the middle-class South African white kids, it was like breaking stereotypes with music.' The experience made him so excited about the possibilities that he ended up giving away a USB stick of unreleased tracks to local producers to sample or remix as they wished: 'Have it! Do what you want with it! Spread it around!' he enthused.[18]

Barrioseta says that this was all part of the plan – to show the stars another side of South Africa and hopefully inspire them to want to do good as well as get paid. 'We didn't want to just throw a big party for white kids, which is what happens if Richie Hawtin or Skrillex or any of these guys comes down here. It might be a sold-out show but it's 8,000 white kids; the DJ flies in, plays, gets two or three hundred thousand dollars and flies out again not knowing anything more about the real issues in the country or the amazing talent in the townships,' he explains. 'So we show them in a very tangible way how they can affect people.'

After Bridges for Music's initial success in South Africa, Barrioseta started to target wealthier markets in Europe and the US. 'The whole EDM industry is lacking this social responsibility, so we want to create a platform to allow big artists and festivals to utilise their fan base to help create positive change,' he says.

'But the biggest challenge that we face is the headspace that people have in this industry – everyone is completely snowed under, everyone is over capacity, and at the end of the day, if you are waiting to have enough spare time or spare money to do good, you will never do good. That's the reality, because you will never have enough spare time or spare money. But every now and then, you find someone who is really committed and is really willing to make a difference – although it doesn't happen that often.'

As the sun began to descend over the township roofs that day in Langa, Four Tet's Kieran Hebden played a tune he made with his old school friend Burial, a blissful impressionistic watercolour of a sound-sketch that might have been perfect for a balmy evening at the Café del Mar in Ibiza. But despite the glorious sunset – and Barrioseta's Amnesia connections – it really did feel that we were a world away from the moneyed hedonism of the White Island.

'South Africa's negotiated transition from white rule to democracy was one of the wonders of the late twentieth century. But it was only the first chapter of the post-liberation narrative,' Alec Russell wrote in his book about the country. Russell was brutally direct about the obstacles that stood in the way of any kind of 'happy ending' for South Africa, not least among them what he warned was 'the near impossibility of overcoming the nightmarish legacy of an abhorrent system'.[19]

Back in 1995, a year after the first democratic elections, Nelson Mandela had also spoken frankly about the challenges ahead: 'There is no short cut to the country of our dreams,' he warned.[20]

While I was talking to Jake Lipman in downtown Cape Town and asked him whether he thought dance culture was a positive force in the new South Africa, he responded so vigorously that he almost knocked our coffee cups off the table: 'Definitely. It *is*. One hundred per cent, it *is* a positive force in this country,' he insisted. 'It allows people to express themselves in a positive way. How can it not be good?'

But I wondered whether the gauzy utopianism characterised by old Chicago house anthems like Joe Smooth's 'Promised Land' and CeCe Rogers' 'Someday' had any kind of resonance in South Africa, all those blissed-out clichés about brothers and sisters joining hands and transcending racism and injustice, or the old slogans like the Americans' 'peace, love, unity and respect' and the rave mythologies of tolerance and togetherness – could this culture really play any significant unifying role here, where the population was 80 per cent black but whites still owned most of the land and the major companies?

'It should have that function in South Africa in terms of unifying people, but due to the country's social structures, it doesn't,' responded Spoek Mathambo when I asked him what he thought. 'People who enjoy the same music should be able to dance to that together under one roof, but because there was this entrenched system for such a long time separating people because of their race and their class and their culture, that isn't a reality.'

Mathambo took a couple of seconds to think and then concluded carefully: 'There is a culture which is developing that is starting to change that, although it's on a very small level. Hundreds of years of separation can't be broken down in 20 years. The past still casts a shadow.'

Interlude

Pirates of the Black Sea

ON A SANDY STRETCH OF LAND on the eastern shore of the Black Sea, far from the nearest city, in what was once the ancient kingdom of Colchis, a new republic had been established – a republic that would shine brightly for ten days only, sun-soothed by day and sonorously illuminated by night, until it finally evaporated into the subtropical air, all its energies spent in the quest for pure bliss, leaving no trace of its marvellous existence behind. Or at least that was the plan.

Kazantip was the most notoriously bacchanalian festival in the former Soviet Union, the Burning Man of the old Communist East. It had gained renown over two decades as a beachfront extravaganza on Ukraine's Crimean peninsula, attracting thousands of Russian and Ukrainian youths with its promise of hardcore techno, free expression and limitless intoxication in the sun. 'It seems to me that the closest description to the festival's image among ravers is the work of the Soviet writer Sergey Mikhalkov, *The Festival of Disobedience*, where a city is described in which children were left without adults,' explains Ilia Voronin, the editor-in-chief of *Mixmag Russia*. 'It really was a unique festival with a cultural ecosystem. Partly Burning Man, partly rave, partly some analogue of Ibiza.'

Kazantip was also a self-proclaimed 'republic', with its own president, foreign minister and constitution, although it only existed for a few weeks each summer. To gain entry, one had to purchase a Kazantip 'visa' – a symbolic gesture of commitment to the cause and an indication that this was autonomous territory where normal rules didn't apply. The Kazantip Republic, or so its propaganda material claimed, was a 'real alternative to reality'. In other words, it was one of those bizarre phenomena that have occasionally been thrown up by the rave scene over the past few decades, in those moments when the freewheeling do-it-yourself ethos of the culture has empowered the craziest of characters to step forward and set the agenda with little care for material rewards, moral conventions or the consequences for human sanity.

It started in the early nineties as a get-together for windsurfers on the Kazantip headland on the coast of the Sea of Azov. The location gave the event its name, and it went on to develop into a full-on rave festival which lasted for almost a month each year, occupying the turbine hall of the unfinished Shcholkine nuclear power plant, where construction work had been abandoned after the 1986 Chernobyl disaster.

Kazantip then moved to the beachfront village of Popovka on Crimea's Black Sea shore, where a reporter from *Vice* once memorably if somewhat inaccurately hyped it as a debauched free-for-all, full of half-naked Slavic lovelies and vodka-crazed mafia dons who came for the alfresco sex as much as they did for the music. But it was actually rather more like a techno holiday resort with a touch more sartorial flamboyance and a pervasive feeling of nonchalant beatitude, as journalist Will Lynch reported for *Resident Advisor*: 'People slip into an emotional state that's a notch above the usual festival glow – a sustained, hedonistic zen that comes from weeks of marinating in this weird environment.'[1]

The Kazantip Republic's 'president', Nikita Marshunok, was the kind of man who could inspire his flock to follow him across borders with a pledge of paradise at the end of the journey. 'He is a very charismatic person. A real leader. He's able to infect people. Probably he could become a quite good politician if he wanted,' says Voronin.

But after several years of rapturous summers on the beach at Popovka, Marshunok ran up against some real-world political problems when his little unrecognised statelet became the casualty of a much more serious border-shifting manoeuvre, after Russia moved to annex Crimea in March 2014.

Now there were gunmen and tanks on the streets and checkpoints at the new 'border', and the festival's Ukrainian regulars started to feel they might be distinctly unwelcome amid the upsurge of nationalist chauvinism. According to rumour, the new Moscow-backed officials in Crimea or some of their pet crime lords then put the gangster squeeze on Marshunok for more cash if he wanted to continue using Kazantip's regular site in Popovka. The President wasn't amused, complaining of 'extortion, blackmail and abuse' by the Crimean authorities and 'threats from Russian special forces and commissioning/racketeering institutions'.[2]

There was hope that Russian metals tycoon Mikhail Prokhorov, a billionaire who owned one of the Kazantip stages as well as the Brooklyn Nets basketball team and had reportedly known Marshunok since they were young hustlers selling acid-washed jeans in the Soviet Union in the late eighties, might intervene to save the event. But that didn't happen, and the Crimean authorities banned Kazantip altogether. 'They want to turn our town into a haven of criminals and drug addicts,' explained chief prosecutor Natalia Poklonskaya. 'Kazantip is famous for rampant crime, prostitution and drug addiction.'[3]

But Marshunok had already made his own move, resolving to shift Kazantip out of embattled Ukraine and eastwards across the Black Sea to the former Soviet republic of Georgia, where the government was desperate for tourist cash and offered him a slice of coastline in the rustic resort of Anaklia, which was centred around a little village where cows wandered freely across the scrublands in front of incongruously opulent five-star hotels.

Georgia seemed like it could be a perfect location for Kazantip; after all, it had a laid-back approach to bureaucracy, its hospitality and cuisine were legendary throughout the former Soviet bloc, the weather was hot and the booze was cheap. There was also a vibrant new underground techno movement emerging among progressive, European-oriented youths in the capital Tbilisi, at clubs like Mtkvarze, Café Gallery and Bassiani. But what President Marshunok perhaps didn't take into account was that Georgia was also a deeply conservative Orthodox Christian country with punitive anti-narcotics legislation which meant that party chemicals could be hard to score.

Immediately after it was announced that Kazantip was coming, ethno-nationalist groups started to hold demonstrations, incited by the Georgian Orthodox Church, which said the festival was an insult to the country's Christian traditions. One archbishop even declared that the Kazantip Republic had a series of ministries dedicated to promoting nefarious practices, among them the Ministry of Masturbation and the Ministry of Homosexuality and Untrimmed Body Hair. I wondered what he made of article six of the Kazantip 'constitution', which declared that one of the constitutional responsibilities of each citizen was 'to believe in the unreal and to believe in miracles'.

When I turned up at one of the religious protests outside the state chancellery in Tbilisi, a young man was holding up a home-made banner comparing Kazantip to Sodom and Gomorrah, while a few paunchy priests lolled about in the evening sun and a bearded fanatic ranted through a megaphone about gays, Muslims, paedophiles and decadent Western pop music. 'Young people nowadays know the biography of Michael Jackson, but nothing about our history and our kings because they are brainwashed – and now they want to be part of this sinful thing!' he moaned.

It might have seemed like a skit from *Monty Python's Flying Circus* if the Orthodox Church hadn't been the most powerful and respected institution in the country. I had a word with one of the protest organisers, Josip Manjavidze, who ran some kind of moral vigilante group that called itself the Alliance of Patriots; a man who had previously been arrested for attacking a gay rights rally and was now urging the government to ban Kazantip. He told me in almost medieval terms that the festival was a 'scourge' that must be exorcised for the sake of the population's physical and mental welfare.

'Kazantip means propaganda for the use of several very serious psychedelic drugs, propaganda for free sex, propaganda for the revival of ancient orgiastic rituals. Such a demonstration for this ideology on a large area of the seafront will have a harmful influence on the moral foundations of society,' Manjavidze warned. 'What normal person would be for this? How could anyone approve of it?'

Psychedelic drugs, free sex, orgiastic rituals – well, it certainly sounded promising to me. There was also a rumour that the devilishly talented Ricardo Villalobos would cast his wicked spell over the party at some point, although Manjavidze didn't mention anything about that. Not long afterwards, I was on my way, approaching the Black Sea coast through the humid subtropical darkness as searchlights swept across the beachfront in the distance. As I crossed a stiletto bridge, I could see a rave village lit up in pulsating pink and purple lights with welcoming messages playing out in English and Russian over a video wall: 'We don't suffer from madness – we enjoy it!'

Geodesic domes hung with drapes clustered along the palm tree-lined promenade, glowing red in the night air, each of them a bar with its own vibe and tunes, playing everything from hard techno to eighties retro. The Kazantip freaks were already cutting loose; one man cavorted on a podium by the shore wearing a Caucasus highlander's shaggy fright wig and surf shorts, while his girlfriend rubbed up next to him in hotpants with a horse's head mask covering her face. Someone poured a round of vodka shots; someone else passed around a bottle of mineral water laced with some kind of MDMA analogue. Then somewhere around the bar on the edge of the dancefloor as the drugs began to take hold, looming out of the night came a man dressed in a Hawaiian shirt, amber Ray-Bans and a fishing hat, his cigarette smouldering in a long, slender holder – an improbably realistic Hunter S. Thompson impersonator, like a Ralph Steadman caricature come to life. This ersatz Dr Gonzo shook my hand and reassured me in heavily Russian-accented English: 'Don't worry, this is Kazantip!'

The next afternoon, I sat down for a while with Kazantip's 'foreign minister', a dark-eyed, intense young man in shorts and toe-boots called Oleg Mishuris from Vinnytsia in Ukraine, who insisted, without any irony, on referring to Marshunok as the President and Kazantip as the Great Nation throughout our conversation, and got a bit irritated when I described it as a festival.

'Kazantip is not a festival. It is *not* a festival! We hate this word,' he grouched. 'Maybe I should feel insulted when I talk with foreign media and they do not know what Kazantip is. It is a Great Nation, not a festival. If someone says it is a festival, they can maybe give up their visa and go away.'

Mishuris told me that the whole event was actually a kind of role-playing game which was much more about creating a free space for unrestrained social interaction than about music or dancing. It was an interesting take: raving as a large-scale, unmonitored psychosocial experiment – throw all these volatile elements together, step back and enjoy the spontaneous combustion.

'It can be compared, not in terms of history or size but in terms of ideology and concept, to Burning Man,' he continued, citing the legendarily uninhibited annual be-in on the Black Rock Desert playa in Nevada. 'Burning Man is also not really a festival; it's a gathering of people. They have no "line-up", they have no stages, just a gathering of people who want to play the game. You are going there and you play the role you like, what you want to be – the choice is yours – and they create an atmosphere where you are immersed in this. It's the same with the Kazantip Republic.'

Even the protesting priests, who by now had pitched up at the Kazantip site in Anaklia and were holding another rally outside in a last-ditch attempt to banish this pernicious foreign perversion, were playing their role, according to Mishuris: 'They have another game and the name of the game is the church. The name of the game is not religion; religion is no game, I take it very seriously – I believe in God. But the church, for me, is not really religion. The modern church is just about power and money.'

But unfortunately, the attendance at the Anaklia event fell way short of what President Marshunok and his ministers were expecting. Local traders had also hiked their prices to cash in on the 'wealthy' foreign tourists, while some Russian women complained of being sexually harassed and there weren't enough drugs to fire up the dance.

The opportunities for free expression were further limited by the abundance of policemen, who drifted like grey ghosts around the huddles of ravers chatting and chilling until nightfall and even patrolled the beach in sand buggies to ensure there was no doping or fucking in the dunes. But there were moments of vividness, like when dancers climbed to the top of ladders on the beach and set off flares in the Ukrainian colours, filling the sky with blue and yellow plumes of smoke, and when they baffled the locals by staging a pyjama-clad afternoon parade though the village, and when they frolicked barefoot in the sand to roiling acid loops as lasers reflected off the waves crashing onto the shore, bouncing the glittering neon beams back into the cosmos.

During the daytime, Marshunok pootled around the promenade on a Segway, and each evening, after a gong was sounded to mark the sunset, he offered a gnomic homily to his Great Nation, his beloved citizens who he said looked like nothing less than 'aliens who fell from the moon' to the bewildered Georgian villagers.

Even in adversity, Marshunok was still trying to rally the faithful. Kazantip was a 'perfect social model', he insisted, and he said that he still had hopes that he could convert the unbelievers to his cause. 'I think it's possible to do a mental revolution – in Georgia and in the rest of the planet,' he asserted. 'We can do it.'[4]

The head of the Georgian tourism authority, Giorgi Sigua, was fired for bringing Kazantip to the country – although to his credit, he didn't go quietly, accusing the church of trying to pressurise him and of holding back the country's economic development by imposing moral conditions on foreign entrepreneurs. Too much church influence on the state would result in the country 'becoming Iran', Sigua warned.[5] It was one of the most sensible things that anyone said during this time of immoderate idiocy. (In the years that followed, Sigua would go on to launch the GEM Fest dance festival on the Anaklia site, without the protesting priests.)

As recriminations swirled though the local media in the aftermath of the Kazantip debacle, the Georgian economy minister pompous-ly declared that the festival had failed because it was inimical to his nation's culture. But in the sense of staging a grand public showdown between liberal values and religious conservatism, and of highlighting how unelected moral custodians worked to stifle progress in the post-Soviet space, Kazantip had been a spectacular success.

Unsurprisingly, Marshunok did not return to Georgia the following year, but the Great Nation's next destination turned out to be an equally politically toxic choice. In February 2015, Kazantip ran up against the disapproval of conservative authorities yet again when it tried to pitch up on the Cambodian island of Koh Puos and the local government promptly banned it, explaining that it involved 'indecent activities'.

Later that year, the Kazantip Republic finally returned to Crimea – but not for long. After a series of arrests and drug seizures at its homecoming event entitled Befooz, the Russian authorities who now ran the peninsula banned the festival again. 'It's a question of national security,' declared chief prosecutor Poklonskaya, as if a temporary outbreak of peace, love and techno might shake the foundations of Moscow's rule.[6] In yet another outburst of unintentional surrealism, the disputed territory had ousted the imaginary republic.

The case of Kazantip was an example of the utopian rave dream coming up against inconvenient realities and finding itself suddenly impotent. Marshunok's grandiloquent rhetoric about creating a 'perfect social model' had been rendered meaningless by realpolitik, religious power-players and murky vested interests.

A few months after it was banned, a fire broke out at one of the Kazantip buildings by the beach in Crimea. The site was gutted after the emergency services initially refused to come out to fight the blaze, telling callers that 'this hotbed of evil' should be allowed to burn.[7]

Temporary Autonomous Zone

France

'THE RENDEZVOUS POINT HAS BEEN SET for Angerville, in Essonne. The convoy is leaving from there, heading south,' announced a terse communiqué from the shadowy organisers of FrenchTek 23, an illegal 'Teknival' set for a secret location somewhere in central France at the end of April 2016.

The message calling on the outlaw clans to gather in this small French town signalled the start of a 12-hour mystery tour that ran deep into the night as the organisers tried to keep the destination confidential to prevent the outlaw rave from being busted before it got underway. The police made it clear that they were ready for action too: 'The security forces will have the capability to react and apply the laws governing this kind of event: drug controls, roadside checks, confiscations of sound equipment,' they warned.[1]

There was a brief stand-off along the road when police seized the keys to a truck that was transporting a sound system, but eventually the motley convoy of cars, lorries, motorbikes and camper vans was allowed to pass, and after darkness fell, it had made its way more than 100 kilometres south to Salbris, where around 15,000 ravers and dozens of sound systems had started to gather for the largest illegal outdoor party in the country for years.

Towers of speakers were stacked up like prehistoric monoliths – walls upon walls of sound boxes, one after another, right across the site, like a post-apocalyptic reimagination of a Jamaican soundclash – while tents were set out by ravers clad in hoodies and scarves against the nocturnal chill. A police helicopter cruised overhead and several hundred officers remained on standby, but they didn't move in to close it down; the local authorities had capitulated to the force of numbers and allowed the party to go ahead. It was a triumph of countercultural solidarity, claimed one jubilant member of a sound-system collective called Synoptik: 'The Teknival is the spirit of liberty,' he declared.[2]

As well as being a weekend-long rave, FrenchTek 23, with its clenched-fist logo and its 'Raveolution' slogan, was also intended as a show of strength – a protest calling for the repeal of France's anti-Teknival legislation and an end to the police harassment, sound-system seizures and punitive fines that had troubled the outlaw free-party scene in the country for years. 'Hounded by varying forms of repression at the whim of our rulers, sometimes to the brink of collapse, we've taken some blows but we are still standing, still proud. But now enough is enough!' the organisers proclaimed in a statement issued before the event.[3] Near the site, someone had also affixed a home-made banner to some bushes with a message for far-right politicians who had been stoking up disapproval: 'The Teknival pisses on the Front National.'

From Croatia's idyllic Adriatic coastline to the haunting volcanic landscapes of Iceland, from the Great Wall of China to Mount Fuji in Japan and the ancient Mayan city of Tulum in Mexico, all across Europe and the Americas, through Asia and Australia and even sometimes in the more liberal states of the Middle East, dance music festivals were a growth product of the 2010s. From high-concept, high-budget spectaculars like the Electric Daisy Carnival, Tomorrowland and Ultra to mission-oriented events like Movement in Detroit or the Cape Town Electronic Music Festival, and smaller-scale, specialist 'boutique' affairs where the organisers styled themselves as 'curators', there was no shortage of choice for the hedonistic adventurer. A festival offered a chance to catch up with all the most in-demand DJs of the moment in any chosen genre in one place at the same time. It was the ultimate raver's holiday jaunt, delivering the promise of a few days in an altered state amid a sheltered community of like minds, with a few lurid tales and maybe even a suntan to take home as souvenirs.

For those who saw such events, with their wristbands, security teams, steel fences and sponsorship logos, as soulless business ventures, there were the free techno festivals known as Teknivals. The perpetual refuseniks of European rave culture came together each year at these raggedy jamborees held in the far-flung fields and forests of France, Italy, the Czech Republic, Poland, Romania – in fact anywhere they could dodge the law for a few days, park their trucks and set up their speaker stacks, bust out the booze and the drugs and blast some brain-scrambling beats.

The scene had made its deepest impact in France, where the first-ever Teknival was held back in 1993. The initial impetus came from Spiral Tribe, the militant sound-system crew who had left Britain for mainland Europe after being charged with 'conspiracy to cause a public nuisance' for allegedly organising the country's biggest and most noto-rious illegal party, a week-long gathering of more than 25,000 ravers at Castlemorton Common that sparked a nationwide moral panic in May 1992.

Four Spiral Tribe members were among the defendants who were acquitted of the conspiracy charges after a trial estimated to have cost the state around £4 million, but by that time they had already organised the inaugural Teknival in Beauvais in northern France. The following year, in 1994, they moved on to the Czech Republic, where hundreds came to rave for days on end in a provincial field against an apocalyptic sculptural backdrop of decommissioned Soviet MiG fighters and other second-hand Red Army hardware installed by itinerant salvage-art col-lective the Mutoid Waste Company.

The Teknival was perhaps the closest thing to anarchist philosopher Hakim Bey's idea of a 'temporary autonomous zone', an ephemeral pirate cantonment on land briefly liberated from the forces of control – a concept that was often used to theorise the rave scene in Britain in the late eighties and early nineties when parties were staged in disused warehouses, factories, aircraft hangars, quarries and open fields. 'The TAZ is like an uprising that does not engage directly with the State, a guerrilla operation which liberates an area (of land, of time, of imagi-nation) and then dissolves itself to reform elsewhere / elsewhen, before the State can crush it,' Bey wrote.[4]

After ravers started to use his idea to validate their culture, Bey went on to clarify that corporate-sponsored parties did not fit his definition: 'If

Pepsi Cola is involved then that is by definition from the very start to the very finish not a Temporary Autonomous Zone,' he insisted. 'Maybe it's a zone and maybe it's temporary. But it sure isn't fucking autonomous.'[5]

The Teknival circuit had roots in an older countercultural movement dating back several decades – the free-festival circuit established by post-sixties hippies and 'New Age travellers' who traversed the lanes of rural Britain in their antiquated buses and caravans, setting up camp and celebrating when they could, especially around ritual dates like the Summer Solstice. The rave scene then inspired a spectacular outbreak of chemically enhanced hedonism across Britain in the late eighties, but it also attracted people who saw it as a countercultural way of life, not just a bit of weekend lunacy. They drew inspiration from its do-it-yourself ethos, but quickly became disillusioned with the venal and unscrupulous promoters who they believed were seeking to dominate and profit from the scene. When some of the early house and techno sound-system collectives started to throw free parties at the Glastonbury festival, on travellers' sites and in the inner-city squatlands of Britain's major cities at the start of the nineties, they began to make common cause with the older generation of hippie nonconformists and travellers who had been politicised by years of police repression, and a new renegade alliance was forged.

Spiral Tribe's founders had some experience of the hippie free-festival scene but were also energised by the primal rush of acid house, developing a lysergically inspired, eco-spiritual philosophy of the techno sound system as a tool to invoke elemental life forces, breach the boundaries of consciousness and reconnect with the earth. They looked different too, like an itinerant band of techno stormtroopers with their black combat fatigues, heavy boots and shaven skulls, and their music was harder than the rest, a raging torrent of high-velocity noise that was well described by one of their slogans: 'On top non-stop.'

As the Spirals travelled back and forth across Europe in the mid-nineties, staging Teknivals as they went, hardcore sound-system crews started to emerge all over the continent, emulating their British mentors' stern sartorial style, acid-tekno sound and mutinous *make-some-fucking-noise* attitude. 'Everyone started shaving their heads and wearing combats and having it severely, all these little tribes cooperating, all cellular but all allied,' Spiral Tribe's co-founder, Mark Harrison, told me at the time.

France was where their message seemed to resonate most deeply. Paris in the early nineties already had a thriving illegal rave scene driven by postpunk attitudes and 'a desire for joyful insurrection', as film director Xanaé Bove put it in a documentary about the era, *Ex-TAZ*.[6] Spiral Tribe found that they could tap into this ready urge for anarchic self-expression: 'The momentum really built up in France – suddenly we were getting four to five thousand people within one hour of storming a site,' Harrison said. 'The French police didn't have rules and regulations for it and they had never seen anything like it.'

Even two decades later, many French ravers still saw the Spirals as the instigators of a new era in their country's alternative culture: 'They are respected by a lot of people who see them as the beginning of their movement,' explains French author Guillaume Kosmicki, who published a book of personal recollections of the scene entitled *Free Party*. 'They travelled a lot in France, they made a lot of contacts, created a lot of nodes. There were a lot of sound systems in the nineties, but their message and image made them different.'

By the time of the 14th Teknival in May 1996, near Vitry-le-François, south of Reims, it was clear that the French authorities had got a bit more clued-up about what was going on. On a hill not far from the site, riot police from the CRS security force had unloaded shields and batons from a cavalcade of white transit vans, primed to move in as soon as they got the command.

But they were already too late. A guerrilla settlement with its own main street, generator-powered electricity, entertainment, catering, refreshments and shelter had already sprung up after the first sound systems started to roll into the nearby fields under cover of darkness. Most of them were French, but the biggest of them all, occupying the prime position on the main drag with its own bar and record stall, was the Spiral Tribe rig.

The sound system I had travelled there with, a British crew called Desert Storm, was switching from blissed-out trip-hop and jungle while the sun shone, to fierce techno and tweaked-out acid after dark fell. By night, the site was swathed in an eerie, mystic glow as lightning flashed across the treetops and plumes of orange smoke rose from wood fires while the sound of thunder rolled deep under the frenetic ululations of the 303s. For the next few days, reality would be suspended and time would lose all meaning.

The Spiral Tribe ethic appealed to people who wanted to live outside the bourgeois norms of 'the system' and escape the strictures of work, rent and orthodox consumerism – as well as attracting drug-guzzling anarchists for whom nightclubs were way too *straight*. At another Teknival in July 1996, in a field near the village of Hostomice in the Czech Republic, I got talking to a young Austrian in a Spiral Tribe T-shirt, who nostalgically recounted his acid house conversion experience, but then explained how he had quickly become disillusioned with what he came to see as the commercialised conformism of house clubs, and how that feeling of ecstatic distinctiveness had evaporated as the first innocent months of bliss passed. Then the Spirals turned up in Vienna and set up base at an art squat, banging out parties there each week. For my Austrian acquaintance, this was the moment of revelation; the deranged intensity of the Spirals' music laid siege to his consciousness: 'I had not heard or felt anything like it before,' he said. He was re-energised, started getting his own sound system together and running his own free raves, another Teknival convert burning with the zeal of the new believer.

By the late nineties, some of the sound-system crews had already started purpose-building their own music for Teknivals – grimy, low-tech productions which took influences from dystopian hardcore tracks such as 4Hero's 'Mr Kirk's Nightmare' and off-kilter free-party anthems like Aphex Twin's 'Didgeridoo', from the belligerent sonic onslaught of Dutch gabba and from the ascetic starkness of the techno released by labels like Underground Resistance and Rising High. This harsh, nervy and sometimes sinister sound with its punishing martial kick drum was calibrated for maximum disorientation of the senses amid the intoxicated madness of a Teknival. Some of the releases from Spiral Tribe's Network 23 label, made by crew members under names like SP23, 69db and Crystal Distortion, were even recorded on the road, in a mobile studio mounted in a circus showman's trailer that they towed around Europe. There were also crews that specialised in live improvisation with relentlessly savage acid-tekno sets running for hours on end, from day into night and all the way back into the light again.

'From the Middle Ages onwards, the carnival has offered glimpses of the world turned upside down, a topsy-turvy universe free of toil, suffering and inequality. Carnival celebrates temporary liberation from the prevailing truth and the established order; it marks the suspension of all hierarchical rank, privileges, norms and prohibitions.'

Reclaim the Streets manifesto, 1999

Just as in Britain in the nineties, the increasing popularity of the French Teknivals brought them into the conflict with the law, and the authorities sought more powers to clamp down on the illegal ravers who had become known in France as *teufeurs*. After right-wing MP Thierry Mariani proposed an amendment to French security legislation decreeing that any large-scale party had to get permission at least a month in advance, thousands marched in protest in Paris, Lille, Lyon, Marseille and Nantes, while CRS officers wielding batons broke up another rally in Toulouse. But again, just as in Britain, where there were several demonstrations against the planned legislation that became the 1994 Criminal Justice and Public Order Act – with its clause that envisaged sanctions against outlaw raves playing 'sounds wholly or predominantly characterised by the emission of a succession of repetitive beats' – the protests failed to change French lawmakers' minds.

The 'Mariani amendment' came into force in 2001, prohibiting unsanctioned gatherings of more than 500 people, and the year afterwards, clashes erupted at a roadblock that had been set up to stop convoys of ravers reaching a Teknival on the Col de Larche mountain near the Italian border. Police officers fired tear gas to force back the *teufeurs*, who pelted them with bricks and stones, although the riot squads eventually retreated, allowing thousands to set up camp for the weekend.

The new legislation did not inhibit the free party movement from growing and attracting new recruits – people like Florentin Arnaud, one of the younger generation of French sound-system activists. Arnaud was a member of Dominotek, a Toulouse-based crew established in 2008, several years after the Mariani amendment came into force. Dominotek saved up money to assemble their sound equipment, equipping their rig piece by piece, and staged small parties around their hometown of Toulouse in the south. They were never, not even once, given an official permit to hold an event. 'There were always problems with the security forces,' Arnaud explains. 'Sometimes we got beaten, sometimes we got zapped, sometimes we got arrested, but we never submitted.'

Arnaud describes free-party values as 'an openness of spirit, helping each other, the pleasure of sharing' – values that he, in turn, sought to pass on to newcomers to the scene even younger than himself. But like many on the French scene, he too saw the parties as part of a political struggle; a perpetual battle against 'freedom-killing laws that try to murder our culture'.

Vincent Tanguy from the Brittany-based 716 sound system describes the French scene as an autonomous libertarian movement with the do-it-yourself philosophy as its ideological core – even though, he admits, its values were always under threat, and not only from the authorities. 'DIY is the essence of the movement but as with everything, the Teknivals and the free parties have created their own idols and their own star system,' Tanguy explains. 'A lot of people don't want to understand it but just to consume it.'

Because of its anti-authoritarian stance and countercultural roots, the free-party scene was about as political as rave ever got, although at heart, it was still all about the pursuit of pleasure. In Britain, anti-rave legislation and years of showdowns with police had nurtured fiercely defiant attitudes and a sense that the techno-travellers' lifestyle itself represented a kind of social resistance, but the sound-system crews saw conventional politics as a meaningless establishment charade. Some French ravers became campaigners however, prepared to negotiate with officials, lobby politicians and engage with the media in an attempt to create space for their scene to survive, and possibly even thrive.

In March 2017, more than 180 sound systems held simultaneous protest parties on the streets of seven cities across France, attracting an estimated total of around 25,000 ravers to rally against alleged repression and, as the slogan of the demonstrations put it, to 'dance for freedom of expression'. Ahead of the rallies, the organisers' press statement delivered a series of demands to the French authorities: 'An immediate and definitive end to seizures of sound equipment; the cancellation of the Mariani amendment; an immediate end to abusive procedures against organisers and participants; the possibility of access to unused and usable public land for our festivals.'[7]

By this time, there were as many as 800 sound systems in France and about 4,000 parties each year, with attendances ranging from 50 people to tens of thousands, estimated Samuel Raymond, the coordinator of Freeform, an organisation set up to campaign for the rights of free-party sound systems. (Freeform was funded, somewhat ironically, by the French youth ministry.)

Raymond had the necessary credibility to speak on behalf of the scene – in the early nineties, he had hung out with the British free-party sound system Vox Populi and campaigned against the Criminal Justice Bill in London, and he had been among the ravers at the first-ever Teknival in Beauvais in France in 1993. He explained the incredible popularity of free parties in his country as the result of a strange mixture of repression and tolerance towards rave culture, which drove sound systems out of the cities and into the wide-open spaces of the French countryside, where they could disappear into the bucolic agrarian landscape.

'If you go back to the early nineties, I was a rave party organiser, and the authorities would fight against all these young people who were doing this, but they would still try to do it,' Raymond recalls. 'But as there was no space to do this [in city-centre clubs], they started to organise free parties. Until 2000, you didn't risk any seizure of your sound system, so it was really easy to go in a field and make a party.

'So the authorities created a space for it by on the one hand being very hostile against techno music, and on the other being quite tolerant about free parties. Also because France is a big country and a rural country, there is a lot of space in the countryside. Germany is the same, but in Germany it didn't happen like that because there was space for techno parties and for techno music, so they didn't have so many free parties.'

Guillaume Kosmicki believes that this was part of a generational attempt to find a cultural cause worth believing in. 'The music in France was not so exciting before the arrival of the free parties. The only music that was free was the punk movement, and that was finished for a long time. There were no social movements with music,' Kosmicki argues. 'I think French people needed to find a way to express political ideas and express their freedom; I think we didn't know it, but we were waiting for this, because for a long time, society was sclerotic.

'That's why it works in Italy too, because in Italy the political context is very intense – there are squats, there are anarchists, and the free parties were an answer to that energy,' he continues. 'In France too there is a context of squats, there is a context of political engagement – it is political engagement which does not have anything to do with political parties, but it's part of the life you are living outside of society.'

The Mariani amendment didn't stop the free parties happening but it did change their character, Raymond suggests. 'The scene was going a bit crazy. There were a lot of parties with 10,000 people, 20,000 people without authorisation, so the government took quite a strong step,' he says. 'But this left the scene in quite an interesting state because this [official attendance limit of] 500 people gave quite a space for it to develop. If the law says 500, it can go up to 1,000, the police are not really strict if everything is OK, they won't count people. It means that the scene has been very active because it is quite easy for people to organise a small party in a field or a farm.'

For Vincent Tanguy, the Mariani legislation also signalled the beginning of a new phase in the free-party movement. 'The amendment sounded like the "end of playtime" to many people, something that took away all the illusions of the generation that saw the beginnings of the free parties. There were demonstrations, [protest] raves, confrontations, but the law was adopted,' he says. 'In my opinion, the law enabled the restructuring of the scene and the resizing of the parties for a while, in order to better hide from the law.'

Downscaling helped some of the organisers reassert a measure of control over a scene that had become a chaotic sprawl, and gave them the opportunity to think again about how to move it forward, argues Kosmicki. 'Around 1998 it was the worst moment – there were too many people, too big events and no control. In the beginning, you could explain to the newcomers how they can act to respect the environment, respect nature, but then nature was being completely trashed by these events,' he says.

'After the law, a lot of people quit this movement, a lot of parties were cancelled, and for four or five years there were just very few, so the sound systems could think about how to organise those events better. A lot of people who didn't understand what a free party was got out of the scene because of all the problems with the law and the police. The big dealers, the criminal organisations profiting from the free parties, got out of the scene after the law too, because there was no security for them after that. I am not against drugs, but when things are becoming too big, all the bad elements of society come too.

'So I think it's a bad thing and a good thing in a way, this law, because it changed a lot of things, and the movement could begin again in a new form after that, slowly but with a new assurance.'

Twice a year, around May Day and in mid-August, the French authorities started to provide the *teufeurs* with sanctioned sites to hold large-scale Teknivals, such as the Laon-Couvron military base in northern France in 2011, where sound systems set up under leaden skies on the airstrip's asphalt, incongruously surrounded by fences, barbed wire, soldiers and policemen – a 'free' festival under strict surveillance. 'When you arrive, you think, wow, what is this – a state carnival?' commented one astonished young raver.[8]

Critics sarcastically described such officially approved events as 'Sarkovals', after the right-wing politician Nicolas Sarkozy, who was the country's interior minister for several years during the 2000s. Some sound systems boycotted the Sarkovals altogether; for Tanguy, they were the antithesis of the free-party philosophy: 'When the government is helping you and finding a location for you and doing everything for you, there is a huge problem – there is no longer any self-management. You are no longer credible if you speak to your people about free-party ideals, because you have become a dependent of the state,' he says. 'I'm completely against this way of operating, which to me would be synonymous with the death of the movement, because we would no longer be alternative but instead would be gobbled up by society.'

Discontented with the legally sanctioned Teknivals, which they saw as an attempt to co-opt and neuter their culture, and frustrated with what they claimed was the duplicitous attitude and delaying tactics employed by officials when negotiating about the May Day and August sites, which left them too little time to stage the events as they might have liked, the free-party crews announced in 2016 that they were ceasing to cooperate with the authorities. 'The sound systems said, "No, we cannot work together any more,"' says Raymond. 'No, we don't want to have this party legally, and we will do it without you. There will be no negotiation.'

The success of the first illegal Teknival of the non-cooperation era, which drew 15,000 ravers to Salbris on May Day weekend in 2016, served to embolden them. As August approached that year, they were getting ready for a second unsanctioned extravaganza. The general destination was announced as Occitania, a vast swathe of southern France stretching from the Atlantic to the Italian border. A list of the 42 sound systems expected to play at the Teknival was published, and a flyer with a graphic image of a rampant techno cyborg and the slogan: 'The sound of resistance.'

'It would be easy to treat us as "stupid and irresponsible" again, especially in the current climate of terror. Our response is simple: we are brave, we are united and we are in solidarity. We will remain steadfast no matter what happens.'

French Teknival communiqué, August 2016

Twilight had already faded to black as our ancient pastel-green Mercedes truck growled and strained its way through the rugged passes and around the serpentine bends that led across the Midi-Pyrénées towards the Teknival that Friday night in August.

I was travelling with Djé and Emmanuelle, who lived in the truck in the grounds of a rambling house owned by another sound-system activist. The ageing vehicle had been converted to accommodate bunk beds, a cooker and their two large dogs, and was also loaded with a voluminous stash of aromatic, fruit-infused bottles of rum that they intended to sell at the Teknival. We had taken the long way round on our route from Toulouse; free-party people often avoided major roads because of fears about being stopped and hassled by police who took an instinctive dislike to the unconventional appearance of trucks like ours, which was decorated with trippy swirls of monochromatic graffiti. Djé also had to stop and get out at various points along the way to tinker with the engine and realign the headlights, his fingernails stained with engine oil, another sign that an existence outside bourgeois conventions had its hardships as well as its pleasures. There was a brief supper of packet noodles by the roadside, then we pressed on again into the gloom.

Around 5am, as we neared a village called La Cavalerie, not far from the town of Millau, we saw a long line of glowing red and orange lights on a hilltop above. But it soon became clear that this was not the party; instead it was a lengthy queue of ravers' hatchbacks, camper vans and trucks backed up solid for about a kilometre along the road that led to the entrance to the site. Some people had jumped out to have a smoke or take a piss while they waited, while others lounged in open car boots, swigging nonchalantly from cans of beer. Then, suddenly, when a bit of free space opened up along the grassy verge by the road-side, Emmanuelle manoeuvred the truck past the static queue, past a brace of police cars at the entrance to a dirt track heading into the fields below, and downwards onto the Teknival site.

Immediately we were assailed by an onslaught of scything metal tekno and dazzled by the glare of the lights from the sound systems and the torches held by the ravers milling randomly along the path. With rigs and tents and bars and stalls set up along winding lanes in a lightly wooded valley, and weird natural rock formations poking out of the hill above like extraterrestrial sculptures, it looked like some kind of otherworldly village, one whose inhabitants would roister and make merry for a few short days and nights before vanishing again, almost as if the whole thing had never happened.

Over the course of the previous couple of decades, Teknivals had become a kind of parallel European party circuit, a well-established alternative to the commercial festivals that the *teufeurs* despised. Despite some of my aesthetic differences with their music, I had to admire their dedication to their cause. Sound-system activists had to be electricians, mechanics, chauffeurs, cooks and DJs, all at the same time over the course of a chaotic weekend – a commitment that would not offer them any salary or pension, just a chance to get together with like-minded friends and get seriously twisted for a few days every so often. This little self-policing community was one of the closest things to anarchy in action I had seen, even if it was ultimately reliant on the authorities if fire or some other mortal disaster struck. For the *teufeurs*, this was their paradise, the alternate reality they worked so hard to spirit into existence. 'It's magical that people can still come together and organise themselves to celebrate together like this,' one of them remarked to me as the morning sun started to rise above the fields, obviously feeling the bliss.

Before the weekend, a local state official had described the *teufeurs* as 'stupid and irresponsible', and warned that the event would be 'a wild festival that plays Russian roulette with people's lives'. But because the Teknival quickly reached critical mass, with around 15,000 ravers on site by Saturday morning, the authorities had little choice but to allow it to go ahead. One of the organisers gave a defiant statement to the French news agency AFP: 'Tekno people are emancipated and independent people; that's what causes the fear,' he declared. 'We are continuing and will always continue to claim our right to party.'[9]

The police, although armed with guns, were keeping a relatively low profile, mainly checking documents at the entrance to the site, breathalysing drivers and occasionally searching vehicles. There were only three arrests over the weekend, and the most significant official intervention came when the authorities delivered truckloads of free bottles of mineral water to prevent dehydration in the broiling afternoon heat – a commendable gesture that I could never have imagined being made at an illegal rave in Britain.

Somewhat symbolically, it turns out that the site is known as '1789 Arbres de Liberté', its trees originally planted to commemorate the bicentenary of the French Revolution. The vibe is abundantly permissive, with an atmosphere of shameless druggy lawlessness despite the police helicopters that circle overhead from time to time, offering a droning counterpoint to the music. 'We are one tribe and they are another tribe, and they are afraid that our tribe is not under their control,' one raver remarks as he gives the flying cops the finger from a safe distance.

In every clearing in the woods, through every gap in the trees, there seems to be another rig playing industrial drum and bass or cartoonish old-school hardcore or shiny cybernetic techno-trance. 'Warning, warning, warning!' a raggamuffin cry goes up from the Mental Resistance system, while the Dominotek crew from Toulouse are blasting out squiggly acid, and across a shady grove just further on from them, a DJ on the Baba Punk Monsters rig rinses out a tech-house stomp for a full ten minutes before the groove dissolves into abstract electronic noise and a stentorian voice proclaims: *'This is your sound system speaking. I am now in control…'*

The music feels like it has diversified since the Teknivals of the late nineties, when raucous acid tekno ruled – I even heard some jacking house music and a track by Berlin dub-techno masters Basic Channel – but the dominant sound was still that massively detuned 909 kickdrum, repeated to oblivion at a hectic pace. And when the beat is pummelling away at an unsyncopated 170 beats per minute, it's pretty much impossible to dance in any conventional way, so the *teufeurs* don't so much boogie as *swarm* around in front of the towers of speakers like agitated bees, some of them even shoving their heads into the sound bins to get a full-force blast, or standing awestruck in front of the stacks as if they were demonstrating their obeisance to some pagan god of noise.

Some of the tunes are rhythmically obtuse and physically demanding, like Aphex Twin's more lysergic moments, forcing dancers to contort their bodies into inhuman shapes as they try to mimic the eccentric flow of the drum patterns; others feature disturbingly wonky melodies that sound like bad-trip reimaginings of 8-bit video-game soundtracks. One tune is made up of little more than a bass kick, a dry reptilian rattle of snares and an eerie, persistent keening that sounds like an android sailor blowing his harmonica in the depths of a K-hole, its atonal coda getting progressively woozier as it lurches back and forth. This, for me at least, was classic Teknival music, uncompromisingly peculiar and utterly disorientating.

Many of the sound systems are impressive constructions with lighting gantries, banners and bars, brought in on huge lorries that nestle at rest behind the trees, but some are no more than little pillars of speakers set up by enthusiastic amateurs who seemingly just want to be part of the whole thing, as much as they can. Unlike most places on the club circuit, the DJs go relatively ignored; they usually play from discreet plastic tables by the side of the rigs, while the dancers' ardour is wholly focused on the sacred speaker stacks in front of them and the frequencies they are broadcasting.

Many *teufeurs* are clad in the now-traditional *on-top-non-stop* Spiral

Tribe techno-traveller style of combat fatigues, shaven heads and heavy boots, or crusty dreadlocks and piercings, although some have dared to dress more flamboyantly, like the chap wearing a suit and a frilly New Romantic shirt. But a lot of them just look like teenage ravers anywhere in the world, wearing brand-name sportswear and showing off their first tattoos in the sunshine. For some of these novices, the free-party scene can prove to be a rite of passage that helps to shape an alternative consciousness that endures long into adulthood, believes Guillaume Kosmicki: 'It's an initiation; you learn a lot of things in that world. You learn to live in nature in hard conditions, you learn to make fire, you quit the cities, you quit your parents, you quit everything, and you go and learn about life.' Some of the sound-system veterans who Kosmicki interviewed for his book about the free-party scene had tears in their eyes when they recounted how it had changed the course of their lives, he says. This was their Woodstock, their glimpse of utopia, their self-defining moment of liberation.

Columns of cars continue to roll in all Saturday afternoon, a few of them from as far away as Spain, Italy and Belgium, churning up the reddish-brown dust that swirls around constantly over the dirt track as the encampment spreads out further over the stony fields, right up to the hilltop and those strange rocky outcrops ranged along the skyline. Pirate flags and Smiley pennants flutter in the light breeze above some of the camper vans as time dissolves into an endless *now*.

As dawn breaks on the third day, I watch a young couple pick their way through the long dewy grass in the early-morning mist, hoods up but smiling at each other beneath the dark cowls, tenderly and maybe expectantly, as they wander hand in hand away from the raucous clamour of the sound systems and slowly back towards their tent, ready to lie down together for a few hours before starting all over again.

7

The Party at the End of the Road

Israel

BY MIDDAY THE SUN IS SHINING DOWN more fiercely than ever and there's a writhing, feral mass of bodies locked into the relentless pulse of the machines, stomping up a dust cloud from the gritty earth. The music breaks down into alien cries, insect screams from some Burroughsian nightmare, before celestial *kosmische* chords sweep it back up into the light and that motorik bassline hammers in again. They are all here now under the op-art canopies, the wildest and most expressive of the trancers, getting sweatier and grimier as the long hours pass, hurling their torsos forward in wayward, heedless lunges or pinging from spot to spot like fleas, skipping and frolicking, or just standing rooted to the earth with their arms outstretched in awe, conducting the heavenly vibrations as they blaze through their consciousness... *Karahana*, they call it here, that moment of perfect intensity, the point when all the madness coils up into itself then bursts outwards in one huge raging tornado of energy that envelops everything and everyone around it. On the edge of the crowd, as the synthetic melody dissolves into ornate whorls and curlicues of sound like the baroque tendrils of a fractal pattern, I watch a man's eyes roll back in his head as he lifts his face towards the sun and reaches out to grasp the heavens, as if he could pull down paradise itself.

'Balagan!' one trancer shouts to his friend – *chaos!* – both of them stripped down to their shorts, eyes wild with psychotropic fervour and faces streaked with the red and purple paint they've all been spraying all over each other in the churning melee down at the front. Between the speakers, the music feels like a series of power surges, bursts of static shock and random jolts of current, and the ground is churned up like a herd of hooved beasts have been rutting around frantically in the dirt.

On the open-air dancefloor now there are men with pointy beards and tall wizards' hats; there's a character prancing about in a white hazmat suit with red and green lights mounted in its hood, a stilt walker dressed up like Willy Wonka shouting inaudible messages through a home-made loudhailer as if he was a psychedelic town crier, and a beefy fellow with his bald head painted lime green pouring water over everyone around him to cool them down. Some dancers have stripped down to underpants and Jesus sandals, ponchos slung over their tanned shoulders as protection against the sun; a couple of lads are even wearing their girlfriends' floaty dresses with incongruously clumpy boots. A few have prepared themselves some suitably curious headgear in advance, like the home-made gold Mickey Mouse head one is wearing, while others have improvised, like the young man who has decided it would be a fine idea to hollow out a large watermelon and jam it down over his skull like a motorcycle helmet. The music is weirder and darker now, the sound of rocket ships flashing through asteroid storms, videogames glitching out, mainframes malfunctioning, galaxies exploding. At some point, from somewhere out of this electric blizzard, comes what sounds like the sampled voice of the philosopher Alan Watts: 'There is no such thing as tomorrow. There never will be, because time is always now...'

At six in the morning, the Sea of Galilee had looked as milky as a cup of the sweet chai they were selling on the festival stalls, as the early mist hung over the lake deep beneath the Golan Heights, more than 200 metres below sea level. A woman in a brightly woven headwrap burned incense in a chalice as she sipped her coffee and smoked a daybreak spliff, while a lone swimmer bobbed in the waters and a half-naked man in a carnival mask squatted on the beach nearby, barking at a dog.

Now the lake was shimmering turquoise and harsh rays had lit up the raggle-taggle hamlet that had sprung up both inside and outside the wire fence that encircled the party. The Doof festival was almost an institution here in Israel, the country that had unexpectedly become a global leader in the arcane world of psytrance; its organisers had moved from staging illicit raves in deserts and forests back in the nineties to legally occupying this beachfront idyll by the Sea of Galilee for several days each year since 2004.

The site is just a short drive from the Syrian border and beyond it, the brutal war between Bashar al-Assad's government forces, rebel insurgents, Islamic State militants and their various foreign sponsors, while to the south, along the road back to Tel Aviv, stretches the ominous concrete wall dividing the Israelis from the West Bank and the Palestinians. But in a testimony to the weirdness of everyday existence in Israel, this paradisiacal enclave felt utterly separated from the seemingly perpetual conflict around it; this was a place where politics was rarely mentioned and geographical limitations seemed to temporarily dissolve – and perhaps that was part of the attraction. 'Israel can get claustrophobic. It is so small you can drive right through it in a few hours, but when you get to the end you have to turn round and go back again. You can't go any further,' one Doofer told me. 'That's why we need some sort of release like this.'

Wandering through the site, it looks like a nomadic caravan come briefly to rest amid the dazzling bougainvillea, palms and eucalyptus trees. The disparate ethno-mystic emblems of the psytrance tribe are proudly displayed on banners, flags and drapes – mandalas and Om signs, Bob Marley and the elephant-headed god Ganesh, Zodiac symbols and marijuana leaves and mushrooms. Only the brawny Russian-speaking security guards serve as a stern reminder that we are not cast adrift in some techno-hippie utopia.

Some of the Doofers look like veteran lysergic explorers – the sort of grizzled heads who might have inside information about the most obscure parties in the wilds of South-East Asia or data on the latest 'research chemicals' from the psychedelic frontiers. Many of them have arrived all dressed up for this carnival of the senses; among the stereotypical psytrance hippies in their low-slung harem pants and dreadlocks – at least one of them droning away on a didgeridoo – there is a huge hulk of a black-bearded pirate with a silver ring through his nose, an eyepatch and a bandana, and a girl in combat boots and a khaki Hiawatha dress brandishing a wooden staff topped with a voodoo skull.

There are also lean and muscled young men who appear to have just finished serving with the Israeli Defence Forces, walking with a military gait and that look of disciplined intent in their eyes.

These Israeli psytrancers clearly take their festivals very seriously indeed; waking up after a brief nap, I see that three gazebos and a couple of barbecues have sprouted up on the few remaining metres of empty ground next to my tent. Many of them have set up set up intricate canopies, lugged in crates of water, braziers and camping stoves and sun loungers and hammocks and all kinds of other household supplies. On the beach, a few are even running refrigerators and little sound systems from portable generators.

Some have also established secluded havens for themselves amid the mass of campers, setting their tents in tight tribal circles inside huge multicoloured windbreaks; behind one of them, languid youths pull on hookah pipes as a lanky hippie patters away on some bongos, while from another rises the pungent aroma of grilling meat. Within these temporary refuges, people talk of epiphanies and freak-outs and heroic doses, about who lost it and ripped off all their clothes on the dancefloor or which DJ took them beyond the peak of the possible. Some are hoping for a repeat of the 13-hour downpour at the previous year's festival, when only the most hardcore of the Doofers revelled in the swampy pit of a dancefloor as rain battered the site, but it was not to happen.

The trancers don't have the beach all to themselves, however; as well as several enclaves of ordinary tourists enjoying the Galilee sun, there is what appears to be some sort of religious education tent set up by the festival's perimeter fence, with books and pamphlets and a poster of a venerable white-bearded rabbi passing on his wisdom to a respectful student. As clouds of dope smoke drift through the scalding air, a middle-aged Orthodox Jew looks out at the wayward youths with their cryptic tattoos and shakes his head slowly in perplexity.

I remembered something that one of the Doof festival's organisers, Zohar Abiri, had told me a few days earlier: 'The message of the old generation was "life is not about partying". It was not a part of the culture to be liberated and free and happy, because it's such a heavy country,' she had said. 'A closed-minded society is scared of a new generation that is open-minded and questioning. They think happiness is dangerous.'

'The psychedelic revolution never stopped, but just had to travel halfway around the world to the end of a dirt road on a deserted beach where it was allowed to mutate and grow without government or media pressures.'

Goa Gil

Psytrance had been conceived many years earlier, on another beach over 4,000 kilometres south-east of Galilee, on the shores of the Arabian Sea. Once it had been known as Goa trance, but in the years before that, when it all started, it didn't really have a name at all.

For hippies seeking a sublime location for consciousness expansion or escaping the demise of the sixties dream, the former Portuguese colony of Goa was the ultimate refuge – socially tolerant, spiritually resonant, incredibly cheap and, back then at least, pretty much off the map for the straight world. This was the cosmic oasis at the end of the hippie trail, a place that offered the promise of both enlightenment and quality dope. All it needed was a suitably psychedelic soundtrack, and the hippies brought that with them.

Gilbert Levy, a teenage head from San Francisco who used to run with the Family Dog collective on the acid rock scene in the Haight-Ashbury district, arrived on the overland trail via Amsterdam and Afghanistan, seeking asylum from Western reality. He moved around India, hitchhiking between temples and becoming a guru's disciple in Kashmir, studying yoga, meditating three times a day and hanging out with the wandering holy men known as sadhus. He got himself a new name too – Goa Gil.

When Gil first made it to Goa in 1970, a significant hippie colony had already been established there and had begun to stage its own entertainment. 'The first parties were just a campfire on the beach with

acoustic guitars, somebody with maybe a flute or a little hand drum,'
he recalls. As the seventies progressed, Gil and others started getting
bands together to do rock 'n' roll jam sessions at the parties; they would
also play tapes in between their sets – 'anything from the sixties, acid
rock and Jimi Hendrix, the Beatles, soul music or John Coltrane'.

By the early eighties, new sounds had arrived that would simultaneously disrupt this lysergic idyll and create the basis for a global
subculture with the Goa experience as its mother lode. Nomadic
characters like Fred Disko and Dr. Bobby (the father of Canadian
techno-pop producer Tiga), and yet more obscure individuals with
names like German Paoli, Swiss Rudi and French Fabien started to mix
postpunk electronic music from cassette decks at the all-night beach
parties each winter season. This was initially considered by some of
the hippies to be as blasphemous as Bob Dylan going electric in 1965.
'The music lost some essence of what hippieism was about,' argued
Goa veteran Steve 'Madras' Devas.[1] Some less peaceable heads even
attacked a sound system to stop what they called the 'machine-gun
music' at one party.

Goa Gil however decided to abandon his rock 'n' roll jam band and
switch to the new electronic dance sound: 'People couldn't understand
it; they thought it sounded robotic,' he remembers. 'Sometimes we
were playing and there were even threats from some people, other
people came up *begging* for Grateful Dead, begging for anything but
this music. Heavy Deadheads even used to put a Walkman on during
the party to listen to Grateful Dead on their headphones.'

Ray Castle, a punk scene veteran from New Zealand who went on
to become one of the most important DJs in Goa in the late eighties,
says that freaking to electronic music while peaking on LSD was simply
a superior experience to watching a rock band on stage – it took you
right inside the vibe, right into the heart of what he calls 'a mystical
dance dharma zone'.

'People were going all night on acid and they had a continuous flow
of music that people were playing off tapes and that was more fun than
standing around looking at a band jam. It's the difference between a

stage show and a channelled gathering which is not focused on a performer – it's about participation rather than being an observer in an audience,' Castle explains.

'There was no focus on the DJ – you'd go to one of these parties and you wouldn't even know where the DJ was. They'd be sitting behind a palm tree or something. It's not like now where they're up on stage and everyone's looking in one direction at them like they're a rock star and they're acting like they're playing live but they're just pushing buttons. It was Sensurround sound; the speakers were all over the place so you didn't know where the music was coming from, so people got into this experiential freeform dancing on acid to this weird continuous flow of drum machine-driven sounds, the new electronic music which was fresh then, and it was a whole new way of dancing and exploring one's inner self on hallucinogens.'

Some of the Goa regulars spent summers in Ibiza to escape the rainy season, and several of the dancefloor anthems were the same in both places, like The Residents' 'Kaw-Liga', a favourite of Alfredo at Amnesia as well as at Goa's full-moon parties. But the two scenes were conceptually different; there were no upmarket nightclubs like Pacha or Ku in Goa, and no charter flights bringing in planeloads of British holidaymakers – at least not at that point. The drugs made a crucial difference too, argues Castle: 'It wasn't an Ecstasy scene in Goa, it really was an acid scene, which made the difference from a nightclub playing house music in Ibiza, London or New York. This was real acid disco.'

And the acid disco maestro was a self-effacing Frenchman known only as Laurent, who is said to have arrived in Goa in 1984 from Paris, where he had been doing parties on a barge on the Seine, then reportedly lost his return plane ticket and never went home. Laurent helped to define the new sound, setting some of the sonic parameters for what one day would become Goa trance. Mixing up everything from industrial funk to postpunk, electronic body music, Neue Deutsche Welle tracks, synth-pop and even a bit of Hi-NRG, he wove a psychedelic tapestry of sound, creating a night-long narrative out of disparate music in a similar way to what Alfredo in Ibiza, Larry Levan in New

York and Ron Hardy in Chicago were doing at around the same time in the mid-eighties, although with different ingredients, influences and imperatives.

The music was played on twin cassette decks, and later on DAT, because vinyl couldn't survive the heat and the dust. Laurent would even re-edit tracks on the tape machines, cutting out vocals he didn't like and rearranging sequences to extend instrumental passages, a bit like the Chicago house originators but with more low-tech equipment. His favourites came from the darker side of the spectrum – the Belgian powerstomp of Front 242, along with tracks by Yello, Cabaret Voltaire, DAF, Blancmange, Front Line Assembly and Sven Väth's early releases as OFF, but also peculiar electro mixes of bands like Alien Sex Fiend and the Bollock Brothers – anything that he felt would enhance the trip.

'Because of the drugs, the mind-blowing locations and the tribalistic nature of Goan beach parties, he could make tracks feel and sound different,' wrote British DJ Dave Mothersole in a rare and evocative eyewitness account of the late-eighties Goa scene and the enigmatic Laurent. 'Playing for anything up to ten hours at a time he would move from dark, hard hypnotic beats during the night, to sweet, uplifting, sun-kissed grooves in the morning. From Skinny Puppy and Nitzer Ebb to Koto and Laser Dance; from 100 to 150 BPM; from nightmare-ish and scary to blissed out and glorious.'[2]

Castle calls the style 'maverick space-groove invention', and it went on to absorb the weirder elements of acid house, Belgian New Beat and Frankfurt trance, again in parallel to what DJs like Alfredo were doing in Ibiza but without the sunny pop vibe or the blacker influences of funk and soul.

Laurent quit DJing for unknown reasons around 1994 and retreated into obscurity, occasionally popping up on internet forums to post long lists of tracks from his Goa heyday, but never revealing his surname. In his only known interview, after he had already quit playing music and apparently taken up gambling to make a living, the reclusive innovator gave a brief and matter-of-fact explanation of how his sound sourced its magic: 'Here you make parties for very heavy tripping people who have been travelling everywhere,' he said. 'You have to take drugs to understand the scene here, what people are thinking.'[3]

'Laurent is a very distinguished legend but a very modest character; he only did it for free, it wasn't a commercial thing for him,' explains Castle. 'But he wasn't the only one. There were basically just a whole lot of fanatics who would search these unique pieces of music down, record them on tapes and bring them to Goa and then everybody would copy all this stuff.'

The music would be sequenced to trace the contours of a trip, getting stranger and more intense as the night deepened. Some of the more sensitive acidheads were sometimes freaked out by the sonic FX of 'car crashes, people screaming, glass shattering, machines guns and explosions, beasts and monsters roaring', according to another veteran Goa DJ from the US who went by the name of Chicago. But as the sun rose, the mood elevated into rapture: 'We all remember crying in front of the speakers, tears of joy, with goosebumps, shivers… ecstasy – a strong feeling of oneness and togetherness with each other and the magnificent nature surrounding us,' he recalled.[4]

For Castle, this was all the result of sonic and chemical experimenta- tion at a unique moment in cultural history that could not be repeated: 'It was a kind of movie soundtrack for you to have your trip in. It wasn't perfectly mixed music because it was off tapes, but it was mystical, exotic and evocative,' he says. 'We were in India, this mystical ancient culture, but we were listening to this high-tech industrial cutting-edge music. And no one had any idea this was going on.'

But they soon found out. Acid house and the rave scene brought a new wave of travellers to Goa, and they were not backpacking along the hippie trail and through the Hindu Kush any more, they were arriv- ing by plane – although they were, in their own way, trying to lose themselves in order to find themselves, just as the hippies had done. For the ravers who embarked upon a spiritual quest after Ecstasy opened up questions in their minds that Western consumerism could not answer, Goa seemed a logical destination. But the world had shrunk and India had modernised since the sixties; now it was much easier and required less commitment to make the same cross-the-world trek that Gil had done 20 years earlier.

Among those who arrived were musicians like Sven Väth, who recorded some Goa atmospheres for his 1992 *Accident in Paradise* album and would develop the Frankfurt trance style with his Eye Q label. The 'Back from Goa' mix of his track 'No Fate', with its multiple layers of chattering 303s, didgeridoo and sitar effects, was his tribute to the full-moon parties. 'The Goa sound is a very special deep trance,' Väth said at the time. 'It's a serious thing. These people are not kids, this music is a part of their lives.'[5]

Even more significantly for the scene's future, former Killing Joke bassist turned ambient house record producer Martin Glover, alias Youth, a collaborator with Alex Paterson of The Orb, also took a trip to Goa. Youth was captivated by the style that had been developed by Laurent and the other full-moon DJs: 'You'd see them under a cloud of dust mixing from two cassette decks. I've never had anyone blow my mind like that guy [Laurent],' he said. He identified the Goa scene as part of a countercultural continuum stretching deep into the past: 'It's not just a place, it's a state of mind and it's an old tradition which goes back to the Stonehenge free parties, the beatniks of the early sixties, the poets, the first acid technicolour parties of the sixties, the poets and artists of twenties Paris, it's an ancient timeless tradition going back to the Eleusinian mysteries and magick and all that,' he insisted.[6]

After returning to London, Youth started making music with other Goa converts, tracks that were purpose-built for the parties on the Arabian Sea shore: bubbling cyborg acid lines, portentous riffs and squibbles of melody like electronic calligraphy over a strident, elementary beat, with sampled snippets of voices delivering otherworldly messages. Goa trance was born.

The Goa trance style was pioneered by Youth's label Dragonfly, which he set up in 1993, and by TIP Records, which was co-founded by Raja Ram, the former flautist with psychedelic rock band Quintessence, and Ian St Paul, an Ibiza veteran from the Amnesia eighties who had previously run the seminal acid house club Spectrum with

Paul Oakenfold. To DJs like Oakenfold and Danny Rampling, who also championed the new style in their broadcasts for BBC Radio 1 and put together the pioneering mix CD *A Voyage Into Trance* for Dragonfly, the early Goa trance tracks by The Infinity Project, Hallucinogen, Man With No Name and Total Eclipse sounded like an exciting break from the nightclub orthodoxies of the time. Indeed, it felt like acid house all over again, but this time with a lot more acid. Goa veterans also started to do parties in southern England using the aesthetics they had brought back from their trips to India: fluorescent décor, psychedelic imagery, black lights and prodigious doses of LSD.

But in Goa itself, as increasing numbers of raving tourists joined the old-time trippers on the beaches during the winter season, intrigued by the tales of this tropical paradise which were now being reported by the European pop media and promoted by DJs like Oakenfold, Rampling and Väth, the scene started to creak under the pressures of its own popularity.

'Before it was only for people who used to travel to India looking for magic, going there to find themselves through gurus or meditation or yoga. Goa was under the radar. Not a lot of people knew about it and the parties were just for a few hundred people. They were free and the cops would not really hassle them too much,' says Ray Castle. 'But it all got out of hand in the nineties after Goa became a musical genre, and all of a sudden it was on the radar and the parties and sound systems got bigger but so did the problems with the authorities and the cops.'

The number of foreign tourists arriving in Goa more than doubled between 1985 and 1995 – and would double again in the decade that followed – meaning that very soon it was no longer a clandestine freak enclave. A curfew was imposed on all-night open-air raves, the police stepped up drug busts and shakedowns for bribes, and local bar owners started to take over control of the party scene from the hippies. As with the expansion of Ibiza's clubs and the development of touristic infrastructure when increasing numbers of ravers joined the party on the Balearic island, the creeping commercialisation of Goa began to dilute its hippie essence. The Ibiza scene would mutate and survive, but the Goa veterans found the changes difficult to endure. When the journalist Erik Davis published his captivating report about 'the technofreak legacy of golden Goa' in 1995, it already seemed like an elegy for what had been lost. 'We came here so long ago,' Goa Gil told Davis dejectedly. 'It was like the end of the world. And now the whole world is at our doorstep. The communications lines are open. Where do we go from here?'[7]

Amid the decline of the 'hippie Raj', some of the psychedelic nomads scattered to places like Koh Phangan in Thailand or Byron Bay in Australia, as Ray Castle did, establishing new outposts of fluorescent activity wherever they ended up. In the process, Goa trance became a global subculture, but one which no longer existed in its pure and original form in its birthplace. The Goa experiment, an attempt to sustain a countercultural community off the grid, lasted only a few decades. But how brightly it burned, and what strange wonders it left behind.

'Raving can be viewed as a transcendental mind-altering experience providing psychic relief to alienated people in a secular, repressive and materialistic society.'

Russell Newcombe, drug policy expert, 1995

Goa Gil went on to become one of the international superstars of psytrance. The hoary-dreaded yogi with the laidback Californian accent and intuitive talent for a good soundbite was still playing his trademark 24-hour sets at festivals all over the world right into his late sixties. Before starting each gig, he would set up an altar with pictures of his gurus, sprinkle holy water from the Ganges and recite a mantra. He was accused by some critics of setting himself up as the high priest of trance, of making a career out of the Goa tradition and of playing malevolent, borderline psychotic 'darkpsy' music, but admired by others as a survivor who didn't desert the cause – the man who set out on the hippie trail and never went home again. When Albert Hofmann, the beloved chemist who first synthesised LSD, appeared with Gil at a psytrance festival in Basel, it was yet another endorsement of the American DJ's status as the grand old man of contemporary psychedelic music.

Gil regarded his parties as a form of 'active meditation', a spiritual ceremony rather than a rave. 'It is redefining ancient ritual for the twenty-first century,' he insists. 'With music, you can take people to the highest level if you do it consciously. When I play the 24-hour sets, I take them through the whole night and into the next afternoon, and the longer the trance goes on, the stronger it gets. I am trying to create an alternative to the Babylon system – not unlike what we did in the sixties, when the first explosion of consciousness happened.'

Some very extravagant claims have been made for the spiritual significance of psytrance, several of them perhaps influenced by the ingestion of lysergic acid. 'Psytrance is an arrow in human evolution pointing in new directions, showing and demonstrating new ways of living,' declares the introduction to the book *Goa: 20 Years of Psychedelic Trance*. It describes the scene as 'a ray of hope on the horizon of a controlled world where the human and spiritual elements have turned to grey'.[8]

The rave as quasi-religious or neo-pagan ritual is one of the recurring themes in psytrance discourse. 'Our intention is to create a modern day temple, a positive space created with love, where we can join as one tribe to journey deep into trance just as our ancestors did long ago,' Chris Deckker, who ran the Return to the Source parties in London, once wrote in a kind of manifesto for the scene. 'We view the dancefloor as a sacred space, a place to connect with our power.'[9]

Julian Reyes, the producer of a documentary called *Electronic Awakening*, went further: 'Electronic music is modern shamanism; it is the evolution of ritualised drum circles. The music is a key that digital shamans utilise to move, inspire, teach, and heal others. From a global perspective, electronic music is spiritual technology that can help humanity open metaphysical doors to a realm of infinite possibilities.'[10]

Claims like this are among the reasons why psytrance was sometimes mocked by the house and techno fraternities, who saw it as some kind of embarrassingly unhip cousin, barely to be considered part of the same global electronic dance music family; a delusionary white-dreadlocked cult with a mentally unhealthy obsession with LSD, a fluo/fractal visual aesthetic that was as kitsch as the cover of a fantasy fiction book, and a sonic style distilled from all that was not black, all that was not *funky*.

Many of the trancers, for their part, considered the house and techno scenes to be commercial sell-outs with no spiritual or ecological awareness. Their conception of raves as space-age rites was significantly influenced by the American ethnobotanist and philosopher Terence McKenna, who was liberally sampled on psytrance tracks both before and after his death in 2000.

McKenna became a kind of Timothy Leary for the psychedelic fringe of the techno generation in the early nineties, at a point when a certain kind of clubber who had surfed the rush of the original rave scene was seeking to put these life-changing experiences into some kind of spiritual context. A feeling this powerful must have greater significance, they reasoned; it couldn't just be a technologically updated, chemically enhanced *Saturday Night Fever*, could it?

The psilocybin-inspired philosopher seemed to appear at exactly the right moment, preaching the idea that rave culture was a contemporary version of the ancient dance-drug rituals of tribal shamans, his theories providing a tailor-made context for the ecstatic impressions of questing clubbers. In his book *Food of the Gods*, McKenna set out his theory that from prehistoric times onwards, psychedelic plants had played a vital role in the development of human consciousness. If such plants were reintegrated into society in contemporary shamanic rituals – *raves!* – they could avert the ecological crisis facing humanity by facilitating an evolutionary leap to a higher level of consciousness. 'With electronic culture you can create shamans for the interplanetary village and this to my mind is the function that rock 'n' roll played in the sixties and that house music should play in the nineties,' he argued in one interview.[11]

McKenna admitted that he didn't have all the answers: 'If you think I'm a guru, you haven't taken enough psilocybin,' he once quipped.[12]

But some people did consider him a kind of teacher who could offer a deeper understanding of rave culture. Among them were The Shamen, a former psychedelic rock band who had been transformed by their experiences at acid house clubs in London. 'The acid house and rave scene was very hedonistic back then and in truth many people didn't really understand why they were enjoying the culture in the way that they were; they were just doing it. Terence's ideas definitely fulfilled a role,' explains The Shamen's rapper Richard West, alias Mr C. The band invited the ethnobotanist to deliver a narration on 'Re:Evolution', a track on their *Boss Drum* album, which went double-platinum after its release in 1992.

It was one of those moments that could perhaps only have happened in the early nineties: after a run of big hits, The Shamen, who were one of the most successful bands in Europe at the time, decided to release the distinctly uncommercial track as a single, even though it was little more than eight-and-a-half minutes of speechifying about the benefits of psychedelics and McKenna's concept of an 'archaic revival', set to a somewhat abstract electronic backdrop – and it reached number 18 on the British pop charts. 'We were able to push the views of Terence into the mainstream of society,' Mr C says proudly.

But it was psytrance which offered the most fertile terrain for McKenna's ideas to take root. Psytrance combined romantic spiritual yearnings with a desire for technological progression, remixing McKenna's shamanic tropes and samples from Eastern religious philosophies into a garish high-tech collage of recontextualised psychedelia. Aliens and astronauts, Ganesh and Shiva, they all danced together in the psytrance cosmology. 'The psytrance party allows the commingling of age-old ecstatic techniques with attitudes and technologies that reject tradition in the name of an open-ended, novelty-seeking alternative popular culture,' suggested Erik Davis.[13]

The Australian academic Graham St John, who has studied psytrance culture in more depth than most, describes it as 'a globalised optimisation of the post-sixties quest for experience', founded on a core of bohemian wanderers who travelled in self-imposed exile from an unforgiving Babylon, not only physically journeying across the planet in search of temporary havens but mentally too, fuelled by psychedelic drugs, deep into inner space. St John suggested that trancers 'imagine themselves as alien to the popstream, adopting the recombined insignia of ancients and extraterrestrials, the monstrous and the fabulous, the outlaw and outrageous'.[14]

A lot of the music reflects this – with its florid synth runs and mind-melting FX, it sometimes sounds like the aural equivalent of a Salvador Dali painting, enhanced by suitably portentous samples from *2001: A Space Odyssey*, *Dune* and *The Matrix*, recordings of NASA space launches, Timothy Leary speeches or any number of vintage documentaries about tripping on acid. Darkpsy, one of several psytrance subgenres that branched out from the Goa template as the scene matured, takes this feeling of utter mental disorientation yet further, conjuring a demented vibe of diabolical possessions and alien visitations.

Psytrance is also a long-form immersive experience, as days and nights of open-air communing at festivals coupled with the exertions of non-stop dancing break down barriers, with people sharing chillums and offering each other drops of liquid acid to energise the atmosphere even more. This was undoubtedly a scene you had to commit to – chemically, sartorially, physically and attitudinally – or you remained an outsider, a square who would never really get it. Some of the festivals also tried to stay true to hippie ideals, like the annual Boom in Portugal with its alternative energy sources, 'healing area' for sweat lodges, meditation and yoga, and 'mental sanctuary' for people having a bad trip. Boom organiser Diogo Ruivo described the festival as 'a ritual of liberation' in which people could 'join the flow of cosmic consciousness'.[15]

In his book about dance music and spirituality, *Trance Formation*, US academic Robin Sylvan argued that global rave culture was not just a spiritually charged scene but a 'significant religious phenomenon'. Raving could help people to transcend the ego, feel part of a larger whole and 'connect to the sacred', Sylvan suggested. As evidence, he cited the Berlin Love Parade, the Burning Man festival, and a rather earnest-sounding event that he attended in a church in San Francisco which began with 'guided meditation' before turning into a full-on dance session, then ended at dawn with the partygoers all lying on the floor, listening to Bach fugues being played on the church organ. For Sylvan, the rave experience could act as a gateway to the divine, 'a stimulus to explore more traditional forms of spirituality and religion'.[16]

More hedonistically minded and secularly inclined clubbers might have found such assertions easy to ridicule, but from the early days of acid house onwards, a significant minority had been enraptured by the mystic visions generated by their ecstatic experiences on the dancefloor and sought to investigate them further, which is why some of them ended up travelling to places like Goa or exploring yoga, meditation, Eastern spiritual practices and pseudoscientific alternative therapies.

Dance culture generated such powerful and seemingly life-changing experiences but its ideology was infinitely malleable and subject to individual interpretation, so it was hardly surprising that some believed it must have higher meaning – or that spiritual entrepreneurs saw it as a potential market for their wares. In the US, with its strong traditions of born-again evangelism, cheerleaders for Christianity were also active on the margins of the rave scene, like GodsDJs.com, a self-styled 'Christian EDM community' which also sold downloads of faith-inspired electronic music via its website, or the dancefloor missionaries of the Jesus Luvs Ravers crew, who travelled around American festivals and targeted partygoers who might be convinced to see the light. Jesus Luvs Ravers was run by Goshen Sai, who said he found God after suffering the comedown from years of being a hard-partying 'wild man'. Sai saw himself as a missionary who would 'harvest' damaged souls: 'Father, send me the ripe ones,' he would pray as he scoped out potential recipients for Christ's ministry on the dancefloor. 'These festivals are the moments that most ravers live for. It's their utopia. They are so hungry to experience heaven that a demonstration of God's supernatural love is not only welcome, but desired and greatly appreciated,' he declared.[17]

Away from the more predatory schemes of the evangelists, there had always been strong echoes of the black American churches' gospel tradition in many deep house and garage tracks, like Tony Humphries' joyous mid-eighties mix of the Joubert Singers' 'Stand On the Word', which was originally recorded for worshippers at a church in New York before becoming a dancefloor anthem. Devotees of clubs like the Paradise Garage are often reported to have described the experience as 'going to church', while Frankie Knuckles even called the Warehouse in Chicago 'a church for people who have fallen from grace'.[18] DJ Pierre, who was a member of the Phuture trio who created the original eighties acid house anthem 'Acid Tracks' and then became the master of dark hypnosis with his Wild Pitch mixes, was one of several American producers to publicly embrace Christianity; in 1996, he even recorded a song about his conversion, 'Jesus On My Mind'.

But Detroit veterans Robert Hood and Terrence Parker went further still, becoming ordained Christian ministers. Hood says he saw his DJing, and his gospel-influenced techno recordings under the name Floorplan, as a chance to preach the faith in unusual circumstances. 'When I'm studying the Bible and I'm reading about Jesus as he went from place to place, he didn't just minister to the people who were saved. His job was to spread the gospel to the sinners and to reach out and touch them and welcome them,' Hood explains. 'I'm a disciple – a disciple as in an agent of change, a vessel, a living witness who can tell people they are welcome in the family of God. That's what Jesus would have me do. I'm a representative of the Kingdom of Heaven, so it's my job to preach the gospel of love to the masses.'

Hood even tried to bring some spiritual enlightenment to one of the world's most hedonistic nightclubs, Berghain in Berlin, by playing one of his most explicitly religious tracks – a rollicking-in-the-pews workout called 'We Magnify His Name' – early one Sunday morning.

'I was contemplating whether or not I was going to play it because the Berghain sound is brutal, but the Holy Spirit said, "I created you to make this record. I put this vision and idea in your spirit to create it, and now you are to play it,"' he recalls. 'The Holy Spirit told me to play "We Magnify His Name" and play it loud and make the people feel the spirit in it. So it was like a church revival on Sunday morning at Berghain at 7am, and it was beautiful. The spirit and the anointing, you could feel it sweeping through the place, and the people could feel the message.'

Just as Hood sought to somehow infuse dancers with spiritual vibrations, so did some of the psytrance DJs like Goa Gil. But raves have never been an easy medium through which to convey any idea more complex than the wilful pursuit of pleasure. Hood's sonic sermon might easily have been lost on its intended recipients as they roiled in the humid darkness of Berghain's turbine hall, while not every psytrance devotee saw their movement as an essentially spiritual practice, as Gil once acknowledged. He suggested approvingly that some people went to psytrance festivals to 'commune with the universe or experience the full depth of their consciousness' – but admitted that others just wanted to get off their heads and have a good time.[19]

'These travellers by nature were people looking for freedom. They finished the army, took a big trip and discovered this new kind of freedom. And they got hit by this music exactly when they were celebrating this first feeling of freedom. So it was good chemistry, because they wanted to extend that feeling of freedom when they came back.'

Eyal Yankovich, Israeli DJ and founder of HOMmega Records

In 1988, Israeli citizens were allowed to apply for Indian visas for the first time. Like the impact of the fall of the Berlin Wall on German techno, it was one of those historical coincidences that had unexpected cultural resonance. Young Israelis who had just completed their mandatory military service started to use their demobilisation bonuses to head out to India on holiday, eager for the sort of experiences that would put them in another state of consciousness. Some of them ended up in Goa.

There was already a postpunk industrial and electronic body music scene in Tel Aviv in the eighties, but by the summer of 1990, the first

Goa-inspired full-moon parties were being staged in forests and on beaches around Israel, a country with a generous supply of wilderness, although the brutal conflict with the Palestinians meant that it was heavily policed.

'I had finished the army; I had been in a combat unit, a paratrooper unit. We were the first generation to go into Lebanon, and I think it had something to do with that because the first people who organised the parties had the same background. They were in combat units then they went to the Far East to rave for a year or so, then came back and did the parties,' recalls film director Isri Halpern, who went to some of those first trance events.

'It was amazing, hearing that music for the first time; it was a different sound. I thought, "Finally I am experiencing something that is happening *now*" – not something that was from the sixties or the seventies. It was something that was right now, right at this moment – and I'm there. So it was very exciting – it looked different, you had the ultraviolet lights, and the music was different. It sounded like nothing you'd ever heard before. In the eighties in Israel, everybody was dressing in black like they were depressed, then all of a sudden people were jumping around, wearing colourful clothes, taking drugs and really *dancing*.'

Halpern's recollections of how these Israeli Goa heads brought the party home with them somehow echo the stories told by the young Brits who returned from Ibiza in 1987 and tried to recreate the Balearic vibe in rainy London. And inevitably, the first Israeli trance parties were followed by the first Israeli trance tracks, by outfits like SFX, a project launched by Yaniv Haviv, Avi Nissim, Lior Perlmutter and Guy Sebbag, who would go on to rename themselves Astral Projection and become leaders of the genre. Two decades later, the slimmed-down Astral Projection duo of Nissim and Perlmutter remained scene heroes.

SFX had met at the Penguin Club in Tel Aviv; they were originally into postpunk electro-pop but were converted to acid house by the rudimentary experiments of Psychic TV's *Jack the Tab* album, and used the money generated by their early releases to travel to Goa. Crucially, they saw trance as a continuation of industrial electronica, Belgian New Beat and Detroit techno, not as a descendant of disco like American house music. 'We can say that trance music is the reincarnation of new wave music and the dark eighties we liked so much,' Nissim once said.[20] Indirectly influenced by the mysterious Goa DJ Laurent and his peers, the Israelis, like Youth and his associates in London, would take the scene in their own direction.

And then, like almost everywhere else in the world where this culture has taken root, came the first crackdown. In 1992, Nissim and Sebbag were arrested at a club called Impulse in Ramat Gan near Tel Aviv and charged with drug possession. The subsequent trial put the entire scene in the dock, with police witnesses claiming that all trance DJs were essentially drug dealers and the clubs were narcotics distribution points. They were both acquitted for lack of evidence, but had to pay their own court costs. 'I have to say we did feel a bit triumphant, but we felt a bit screwed by the system,' Perlmutter recalls. 'It was a rough ride, and pretty scary, [Nissim] could have gone to jail just for playing our music and being in the wrong place at the wrong time.'

As the police became more assertive, a moral panic erupted, but one with specifically Israeli characteristics. Like everywhere else in the world, it centred on the drug menace, but the trance scene was also seen as a potential threat to the battle-readiness of the nation's youth. LSD and MDMA would sap the martial spirit, making it harder to sustain the indomitability of the Jewish state, it was argued by conservatives. A generation of fluo-clad freaks would be too fucked-up to fight. 'They were just afraid of losing control over the kids,' says Perlmutter. 'Afraid the kids would feel a bit too free and run off to India instead of the army.' A couple of Israeli newspapers even sent reporters to Goa for New Year's Eve in 1995, and they dutifully filed shocked dispatches about the deviant drugged-up activities of the country's impressionable youth.

'A lot of young people were going to Goa and there were reports that they were losing their faith in Zionism and Judaism, losing their religion, and that was a quite frightening thing for the government in the nineties, which was a very tense time in Israel with all the suicide bombings,' says Elinor Carmi, a scene veteran and author of a book called *TranceMission: The Psytrance Culture in Israel 1989–1999*. 'So it was seen as a kind of threat to the fighting spirit, but it was also a threat that people were believing in something else and not only in the country.'

It was not the first time that nightlife had been described as a national security risk; journalist Nissan Shor's book about the clubbing history of Israel, *Dancing with Tears in Our Eyes*, documents moral panics dating back to the early rock 'n' roll years and the opening of the country's first discotheques. The phenomenon of young people heedlessly going out partying when the country was on a perennial state of alert sparked debates in the Israeli parliament about the degradation of Zionism and the threat to the nation's future, according to Shor. Although clubbers were not necessarily anti-establishment, nightlife was often seen as intrinsically transgressive: 'In Israel, youth is perceived as a building material for the young state's foundation, and it must not be tempered with such foolishness as music and fashion,' he says.

The nineties were a perfect time for the psytrance scene to thrive, Shor believes. 'It was an era of transition – the first Intifada broke out in 1988, extreme violence towards the Palestinian population which led to the Oslo [peace] agreements in 1993, and then a communal feeling of a new era has come – cable TV started its broadcasting and also the first commercial TV channel,' he explains. 'It was like a burst of optimism and a sense of connecting to the Western world.'

The Israeli media's scandalised reports about the early raves, just as in Britain in the late eighties when tabloid headlines screamed about the evils of Ecstasy, only increased the fascination. All-night partying, mind-bending drugs, bizarre rhythmic music – for many young people, this was an advertisement, not a public health warning. 'The police tried to fight it, but that made it more fascinating for the young genera-tion and it became part of the culture,' says Amit Duvdevani of Israeli trance duo Infected Mushroom, one of the bestselling bands in the country's musical history. 'That's why there are so many producers coming out of Israel.'

But the scare stories also mobilised moral and religious campaigners who sometimes wielded significant political influence, and the police began to raid parties wherever they could find them. Isri Halpern's documentary film *Psychedelic Zion* captures the feeling of the Israeli trance generation under siege in the late nineties, telling the story of Peace & Love Productions, three optimistic but somewhat naïve working-class youths from provincial Tiberius united by the love of LSD and psychedelic dance music who set themselves up as illegal rave promoters. 'Our goal is very powerful; it's spiritual,' one of them declares at the outset of the tale, unconsciously echoing the philosophy of Goa Gil.[21]

This was a key moment when people from outside Israel's Tel Aviv-based cultural elite managed to gain influence over a pop-culture scene, suggests Elinor Carmi. 'In terms of class, it was the difference between Ashkenazi, who came to Israel from Europe and mostly have whiter skin and have been running the country for most of the time and are usually associated with the techno and house elite, and Mizrahi, who came from Arab or African countries who have darker skin and were the ones who were mainly dominating the psychedelic trance scene,' Carmi says.

'Psychedelic trance was one of the only music subcultures where they had the chance to be in influential places, like being artists or party organisers. It attracted people who were considered lower class – they call them *arsim*, which I suppose is the equivalent of "chavs" in Britain – and who would never be allowed to get inside techno or house parties in Tel Aviv because they would never pass the selection at the door.'

The democratisation of druggy bohemia – and of pleasures previously only available to the urban bourgeoisie – was crucial to the trance scene's development, agrees Halpern. 'It started with the "sophisticated" Ashkenazis in Tel Aviv but it quickly spread out and the provincial youth picked it up in places like Tiberias which were kind of out of the loop,' he says. 'What I liked about it was that before, most of the youth culture was brought to you by the mass media – "this is what's happening in America, this is what's happening in Europe" – but this was the first thing that came from the roots. The media didn't know about it and when they did find out, they didn't know how to deal with it. They didn't know what it was about. For many years it was under the radar and it grew and became huge.

'The scene then was very mixed – you would have Arabs and Jews and religious and non-religious people,' he continues. 'But although it was very mixed, there was very little violence, and it was a very safe environment for girls because it wasn't about sex, it was about drugs, so they would not be harassed.'

A pro-trance commentator in the Tel Aviv newspaper *Ha'ir*, using utopian rhetoric similar to the kind of talk that was commonplace during Britain's 'summer of love' or the American raves of the nineties 'PLUR' era, claimed in 1998 that this was a truly egalitarian movement: 'Trance cuts across ethnic and economic classes. Whoever took part in one of the raves last summer surely noticed an amazing thing: that everyone was there. Druggies from India and greasers from the suburbs, girls from development towns with their tank tops and platform shoes dancing alongside buttoned-up BA students. This is the true power of the rave: it creates an unstoppable surge of humanity. At the raves there is no fighting, no arguments; the atmosphere is saturated with love.'[22]

I was told a similar peace-and-unity story by a trancer at the Doof festival by the Sea of Galilee almost two decades later: 'The people who criticise psytrance should all come here and see Israelis and Arabs on the same dancefloor, all happy together and with no problems between them.' But Nissan Shor was not convinced that all these loved-up dancefloor vibes resulted in any more tolerance within Israeli society. 'It's fair to say that in trance parties you could find people of all races and colours, including Arabs, which is rare. But it has no influence on the "outside" world,' Shor argues.

Psychedelic Zion framed its narrative with news clips of Palestinian uprisings, the aftermath of suicide bombings, grim-faced politicians making speeches and soldiers marching with flags, then cut to footage of wild-eyed, long-haired ravers in crazy-coloured clothes going mental in a field, suggesting that trance was some kind of release mechanism amid the militarised uncertainty of everyday life. 'Most countries aren't like us. You wake up in the morning and wonder, will a war break out today or not?' one of the Peace & Love Productions trio comments in the film.[23]

The documentary also tried to show how Israel in the late nineties became a psytrance superpower, the world's biggest consumer and musical exporter of the genre. At one point, Halpern turns his lens on a bunch of provincial schoolchildren who have just been to a classmate's bar mitzvah. Asked what kind of music they were dancing to, the kids all yell back at the camera: 'Trance! Acid!'

The arc of the film follows the classic acid house trajectory – enlightenment, euphoria, crash and burn. The Peace & Love Productions crew chase around the Sea of Galilee in convoys looking for places to set up their rig and let rip, like a scene from the orbital raves around the M25 in Britain in 1989 – and like the British rave organisers, they are eventually thwarted by raids and arrests. The film also depicts officials holding crisis meetings about trance parties, and police showing off seized hits of LSD and describing rave organisers as 'some of the most serious criminals in the country'. Anyone who had read the British press coverage of the early rave scene would have found such rhetoric familiar.

After a police decision not to grant them a permit to hold a party, the Peace & Love Productions trio took their case to the Israeli supreme court – but they lost, went bankrupt, and had to go back to their day jobs, their psychedelic dream finally over. 'I'm disappointed in my country, the "establishment",' one of them says dejectedly.[24]

Despite this, the film's director argues that trance did manage to give young Israelis some kind of new perspective: 'This massive dose of MDMA and LSD that went through a whole generation here opened up the country,' Halpern insists. 'It's a different Israel now – more liberal, more open. So I think it did something really good for the psyche.'

Another landmark moment came in 1997 – the Drugless festival, which was organised by an entrepreneur called Asher Haviv, supported by an Israeli anti-drug organisation and endorsed by the police. It was staged at the Ganey Huga water park near the border with Jordan, featuring international trance stars like Tsuyoshi Suzuki and Youth.

Drugless was billed as a demonstration of how trancers could rave without chemicals, but after three days of madness, it was described by one newspaper as 'the biggest drug party in the history of the country'.[25] The joke was on the authorities, I was told by one veteran trancer who was there: 'They were shocked by what happened, but they got what they deserved,' he said. 'It was poetic justice.'

It was in this turbulent environment that discontent with the crackdown fuelled one of the biggest pro-rave rallies of the nineties. The Give Trance a Chance rally in July 1998, with a massive sound system and psychedelic sculptures on stage, brought more than 30,000 people to Tel Aviv's Rabin Square for what Halpern recalls as 'a very surreal kind of demonstration', where DJs like Astral Projection and California Sunshine turned the protest into a full-on freak-out.

'This country loads you up so much that it's inhuman. And what are we asking for? That they allow us to break loose once a week,' explained one of the rally's instigators, Drugless promoter Asher Haviv. 'There is not a place in the world where trance is being threatened. Only the state of Israel with its old-time mentality.'[26] Apart from the Rave Against the Occupation organised by peace activists attempting to raise the psytrance standard against the government's military operations in the West Bank and Gaza, which gathered 4,000 liberal party heads outside the Tel Aviv Museum of Art in May 2002 to dance for tolerance and peaceful coexistence, it was one of the few occasions when Israeli trance got overtly political.

By 2007, according to a BBC documentary called *Flipping Out: Israel's Drug Generation*, around 30,000 young Israelis were travelling to India each year in what had become a commonplace rite of passage after finishing their military service. 'Here one can feel normal again... no bombings, no corruption, none of that pressure back in Israel,' one recently demobilised soldier explained in the film.[27]

Amit Duvdevani of Infected Mushroom was one of those who journeyed to Goa after serving in the Israeli Defence Forces. 'I think a lot of Israelis, after they do the army, they want to go and travel and forget about their lives for at least one year,' he says. For Duvdevani, living in Goa for a while proved to be a creatively life-changing experience: 'The whole party scene over there, the people that lived there and the Israelis that came with me – it was one big happy family going half insane or completely insane, so we had the time of our lives and when I came back to Israel in 1996, we started doing Infected Mushroom.'

The experience of compulsory military service was one of the keys to the unusual popularity of trance in Israel, believes Elinor Carmi. 'Most of the people who first went to Goa were in combat military units,' she says. 'So you had so many people who were basically traumatised from the horrible things they had seen in the army, seeing friends being killed, taking part in things they did not necessarily agree with, and they wanted to get away from Israel and the Zionist dream and they finally felt something they could connect to. In a way, dancing and taking psychedelic drugs was this meditative healing process that helped them cope with the things they had gone through.'

Astral Projection took a similar view: 'Things have always been very stressful in Israel, everyday life in our extreme little country, so people really connected with this type of music, it freed them from all that, it let them fly away into a spiritual musical journey that took their minds off current situations,' says Perlmutter.

Despite having written about psytrance in his book about the history of Israeli nightlife, Nissan Shor doesn't actually like it very much. He disdains what he calls the 'vulgar' music, the 'bad hippie clothing', and what he thinks is the belligerent atmosphere at parties. But all the same, like Carmi and Perlmutter, Shor believes that it did serve a social purpose in the context of contemporary Israel: 'It helps you to unload your angers and anxieties, like body slamming in a mosh pit at heavy metal concerts,' he argues.

'I think that the amount of psychological pressure that's put on young Israelis can be translated into forms of cultural unruliness that characterise trance parties – the feeling of no man's land, parties that are happening far from the establishment's reach in the deserts and forests across the country. Like raves in Britain, but with a sense of end-of-the-world despair – let's party till we fall off our legs, because you don't know what will happen tomorrow.'

'Everybody needs a place where they can go insane peacefully.'
Slogan from Israeli psytrance festival Doof

The aroma of eucalyptus started to saturate the air as the afternoon heated up and people wandered around smeared with multicoloured paint and festival grime, glowing with that aura of contented achievement after a long journey that has tested the body to its limits.

On one of the stages on the Doof festival's final morning, someone had been playing a lush downtempo 'psybient' set, a kind of glittery Balearic trance with shuffle beats, tablas and ethno-psychedelic samples, while people sat cross-legged on rugs outside the chai shop massaging each other's shoulders, or did yoga and meditated in the festival's 'Alternative Zone' in a nearby clearing in the trees.

But the music on the other stage was hitting full power again, as an ascetic-looking dreadlocked hippie, stripped to the waist, triggered yawning chasms of noise from the speakers and flailing snares sheared off in all directions while that relentless giddy-up psytrance bassline sent the Doofers bouncing back and forth across the stony ground.

Doof may not have been as big as keynote events on the trippers' calendar like VuuV in Germany, Boom in Portugal and Ozora in Hungary, but it was the longest-running psytrance festival in Israel. It was originally established by three school friends from the city of Rehovot who called themselves Barkash, UV and Zirkin. They had gone off travelling after they did their military service in the early nineties and took the name Doof from the nickname for Australian outback trance parties, 'bush doofs'. These were not your typical DJs; one had a PhD in nanotechnology, another worked as an IT systems administrator for a major company.

'I would like to think that we created something like a community,' Zirkin responds when I ask him what they were trying to achieve in Israel when they returned home from their travels. 'There is a big difference between a festival and a party. It's great to camp with a bunch of people, share the same space and the same dancefloor and the same experiences over several days and slowly develop a relationship. The festival takes some time to gain its power – slowly, slowly it is cooking, building up all the time, and on the last day it blasts off.'

And blast off it did, that last day by the Sea of Galilee. Psytrance was the cult with no self-consciousness, no calculated attempts to project any impression of funky urban cool – and during those final hours, people really did 'dance like there's nobody watching', lost in the uninhibited raptures of *karahana*. While Doof's organisers made no extravagant spiritual claims for their festival, there certainly was a participatory vibe, with people purposefully getting involved in raising the collective mood, creating peculiar little impromptu performances for the dancers around them, staging intricate displays of staff-juggling and poi-spinning and hula-hoop acrobatics, helping to create the party experience rather than just watching the show.

'When everybody meets every year, amazing things happen on the dancefloor,' Zohar Abiri insisted. 'It's family and friends and safety and freedom and love and sharing and interaction and communication – and music of course. It becomes this entity as people come and they meet and it grows and grows.

'We have Arabs on the dancefloor too – not a lot, but we do,' she continued. 'You see coexistence on this dancefloor and it's amazing. It's a lesson for humanity. I am always emotional when I see so much happiness and goodness, so much creation and inspiration – especially in this hardcore country.'

If Goa was once a secret enclave for psychedelic exiles at the end of the hippie trail, the Israeli psytrance scene could be seen as another form of escape – a rather more transient flight from the violent uncertainties of a world much closer to home. It was a chance to get right out of your mind in a dayglo hideaway temporarily established within the perimeters of a militarised state on a perennial state of alert; a place where the pure joy in unguarded togetherness went undisturbed by the discords of reality – for as long as the trip lasted, anyway.

As the festival neared its end and I watched some of the young Doofers pack down their tents and load up their arsenals of utility kit into their backpacks, sated with pleasure from their exertions, I wondered what kind of lives they were going back to now.

The Outer Limits

Shanghai

DOWN THE RABBIT-HOLE WE GO, descending the stairs from the street, feeling our way through the sudden gloom of the claustrophobic dog-leg tunnel and then emerging into the little blacked-out box of a basement with its metal ventilation shafts and exposed wiring ranged out across the ceiling. As our eyes adjust, all that's really visible is the glowing green light of the emergency exit sign: 安全出口. There is no product branding on the walls, no external signals filtering in from the outside world somewhere above our heads; nothing to break the spell cast by the stark, esoteric techno rhythms pulsing around the room. Subterranean, mysterious and austere, the Shelter club in Shanghai was like a compact version of the old Tresor vault in Berlin, a model of what an underground club should be – a place where all kinds of things could happen, and maybe even would as the night moves on.

The Shelter was once a real air-raid shelter before becoming one of the first clubs to open in the Yongfu Lu nightlife zone in Shanghai's French Concession quarter. It was home to the most adventurous musical productions in town – a place where the subcults of dubstep and hip-hop, techno and grime, reggae and footwork were tenderly nurtured like exotic flora by enthusiasts and obsessives deep down below China's most populous city and its streets seething with their irrepressible mercantile energies.

Tonight the party was called VOID, and it was all about the purest of techno. VOID was run by a multinational crew of DJs who saw themselves as guardians of an authentic spirit that must be defended from the forces of uncaring capitalism which would smother its life force with corporate marketing and drain its vital essence.

I went to meet one of them, Ma Haiping, who made records under the name MHP, at the art museum where he worked during the day, and where an exhibition of exquisite Tibetan artefacts was about to open. Wearing a Kraftwerk T-shirt and donnish spectacles, MHP seemed like a scrupulously modest and self-effacing kind of character, but he was also one of the few native Shanghainese electronic dance music producers, and someone who had been involved in many of the frontline developments in the city's techno culture since the turn of the millennium, his career trajectory shadowing the giddy rush of urban transformation.

In the Golden Age of the twenties and thirties, the Yangtze River port city had been a cosmopolitan metropolis and trading powerhouse, attracting mavericks, tycoons, revolutionaries, artists and gangsters – the 'Paris of the East' (or the 'whore of the Orient', as some called it). Recalling the pre-war Shanghai of 1937 in his book *Empire of the Sun*, J.G. Ballard described it as 'this electric and lurid city, more exciting than any other in the world'.[1] Until the forties, it was producing the most significant Chinese films of the era, and its culture of embracing the foreign and mixing it with the indigenous was known as *haipai* – Shanghai style. But after the Japanese invasion and the subsequent Communist takeover in 1949, it became an industrial centre, and when the young Ma Haiping was growing up in the eighties, it was still relatively underdeveloped.

Shanghai's spectacular revival was decreed by the Communist Party at the beginning of the nineties, when it was decided that it would become a futuristic landmark city to awe the whole of humanity – and quickly. 'The speed and efficiency with which the Communist authorities would move Shanghai from mothballed relic of the past to stunning vision of the future would rattle the world,' suggested author Daniel Brook. 'In just 20 years, the city's people would go from commuting to run-down factories by bicycle to riding to the city's new international airport on the fastest train on earth. Makeshift huts would be replaced by a high-rise cityscape boasting more skyscrapers than Manhattan.'[2]

MHP remembers the Communist Party slogans of that period, when the transformation was getting under way – 'Achieve the four modernisations', 'Accelerate urbanisation', 'Change Shanghai every year'. From 1991 onwards, when the free market was permitted to tear through its economy, the city of his childhood started to disappear in front of his eyes and a new one replaced it. Factories were shut down or moved out, astounding new buildings like the retro-cosmic Oriental Pearl Tower sprouted from what used to be farmlands, wharves and warehouse zones across the Huangpu river in the Pudong district, and residential districts spilled outwards as the city expanded relentlessly. 'After that, you didn't even know the streets you grew up with any more, it was so different,' he says.

Chinese writer Mian Mian, the author of novels like *Candy* and *Acid Lover* about sexual adventurism and drug-taking among the urban social misfits of the nineties, has also spoken of this profound sense of disorientation brought on by the city's astonishingly rapid development: 'My memory of the early 1990s was that if I shut myself in for a month, the city would change beyond recognition,' she once wrote. 'Everyone in the city has been reshaped in this metamorphosis.'[3]

MHP first came into contact with foreign avant-garde music in the late nineties, when he heard Throbbing Gristle and Japanese noise musician Merzbow on the influential Shanghai radio DJ Sun Mengjin's late-night show – another of the broadcasters who left a lasting mark on the youth cultures of their countries by creating their own community of sound. 'It was amazing – 11 o'clock at night, almost nobody listening. It was like magic,' MHP recalls. 'I contacted the guy on the radio, he gave me a lot of CDs so I learned about experimental electronic music. We are a Communist country so I totally understood what industrial music was about – the government controlling minds.'

He also remembers going to hear pioneers like Derrick May and Richie Hawtin in Shanghai at some of the earliest techno events in the city, when few others knew or could even comprehend their music. 'When Richie Hawtin came to play, there was nearly no one there. I remember a guy next to me asking, "Is that CD stuck? Does he need someone to fix the mixer?" Because he was playing that minimal stuff.'

MHP's modesty couldn't quite obscure the crucial role he had played in Shanghai's marginal but inventive alternative music scene over the years. He was a member of the experimental electronic band Aitar and the No Wave-style noise-rock quintet Junkyard in the early 2000s, and was also involved in the first of the influential Antidote parties in 2004, with American promoter Michael Ohlsson and fellow Chinese techno producer B6. 'Basically most of the current Shanghai electronic music scene developed out of those parties,' says his VOID collective comrade Cameron Wilson.

His music's vivid, luminous melodies with their retro-robotic Model 500-style basslines won him influential admirers around the world; his *Crepuscular Rays* EP was released on Dutch veteran Orlando Voorn's Night Vision label, while *The Chinese Connection* was issued by Detroit's Cratesavers International. But although he sometimes played records at the VOID parties at the Shelter, he wasn't really a club head; on the contrary, he agreed with Jeff Mills' opinion that 'techno wasn't designed to be dance music, it was designed to be a futurist statement'.

MHP preferred to listen to his own music while driving through Shanghai's riverfront Bund district on a rainy day, scanning the skyline with its mixture of colonial and hypermodern architecture. Techno, for him, was a means to unlock and explore the imagination, and to drift freely through the possibilities that opened up. He collaborated with free-jazz musicians and video artists, and spoke of taking inspiration from science-fiction writers like Philip K. Dick. Techno should be intellectual as well as physical, he believed – and it should always be art, never commerce.

'Now I'm thinking about what Chinese techno music can be. It's not just a simple mix of techno and Chinese traditional music – no, that's the wrong way to do it,' he says. 'Techno music was made by American people but then it went to Europe, and when it was made by Europeans, it was different. Derrick May in Detroit is not the same as Surgeon in the UK, who is not the same as Basic Channel in Berlin. The Detroit guys have their legend, but we have our own story, and we should make our own music in our own way. But it still needs time to develop.'

The VOID crew were hoping to help create an environment in which the music could develop naturally amid the frantic cultural and economic hubbub of this city of around 24 million people. The opening of the Shelter back in 2007 offered them the opportunity to make a start.

'When the Shelter opened it was like a bomb going off, because there was nothing here in Shanghai at that time that was genuinely music-focused. Things did happen, but in isolation. There were pockets of stuff that appeared and then vanished – independent universes that never connected,' says Cameron Wilson, whose DJ alias was Shanghai Ultra although he came from Dunfermline, where once upon a time, when he was a teenager, he made what he claims was the first Scottish gabba record (Unknown Source, *Fear of the Unknown*, a grungey industrial stomp).

The Shelter was determinedly different – it was a stark and gritty European-style club created by and for hardcore dance music aficionados. Tonight before the DJs took to the decks, the VOID crew were screening the Jeff Mills documentary *Exhibitionist*, a masterclass in making music with the Roland TR-909. Wearing a black suit in a white room, Mills' slender, dextrous fingers manipulate the Japanese drum machine as if there was an entire percussion orchestra responding to the flicks of his baton. VOID were trying to show that there was more to techno than just raving, but the fact that there was even a film about Mills' 909 technique also indicated how much the music of Detroit had become the focus of some kind of transglobal gnostic sect.

VOID had already brought in Motor City legends Juan Atkins and Robert Hood, as well as various Underground Resistance DJs, to play at the tiny Shanghai venue. 'We want to get people into it, spread the word, show what's behind it,' says Wilson. That also meant demonstrating techno's ideological integrity: 'VOID will not associate with branding or marketing because it would compromise the message. Even drinks sponsorship, we just refused it. We can't stand it. Sports brands, drinks brands, lifestyle brands, they're all buzzing around Shanghai trying to exploit the culture. They say they understand the cutting edge, but the cutting edge by definition has nothing to do with them.'

His anti-branding polemic reminded me of the Berghain owners' determination to exclude corporate logos from their Berlin venue in an attempt to ensure that clubbers were dissevered from the prevailing materialism that characterised daytime life, and relocated in an alternate reality where such values no longer held the same power.

'For me, techno gives you a way to see the world differently,' Wilson continues. 'Then if you involve brands in it, how is that seeing the world differently?'

The Shelter was founded by renowned local DJ Gary Wang, who pioneered hip-hop in China and won the country's first DMC mixing championships in 2002, and Gareth Williams, a Chinese-speaking Mancunian who married a local reggae vocalist called ChaCha and ran a label called SVBKVLT that released Asian bass and dubwise tracks – a real Shanghainese *haipai* scenario.

'When it opened, there was nothing like it here at all, so it was packed all the time with people just discovering new music,' Williams recalls. 'There were really exciting times in 2008, 2009. People were really positive, thinking the scene was going somewhere great – and it is, but at a much slower speed than we thought then. And now the corporate bullshit has moved in, the branded events, which makes it harder for more independent people like us.'

At VOID, local skate rats in Thrasher hoodies and Adidas sweatpants mingled casually with black-clad disco ladies and Western technoheads in combats. As MHP blasted into a vintage Detroit track, a pair of European hipsters pranced across the dancefloor, lilting and dipping and sketching imaginary arcs with their cigarettes as if they were sparklers, while a group of Chinese lads frolicked in a ragged circle, legs akimbo, throwing out their arms at bizarre angles, abandoning themselves in the darkness to the all-consuming pulse.

Shanghai's new generation of middle-class youth had more disposable income and leisure time than their predecessors, and far more access to global pop culture through the internet despite the Chinese government's Great Firewall, which blocked many Western news and entertainment sites. But it was also clear that despite this, expatriates still made up a significant proportion of the clubbing crowd, particularly in Shanghai, where around a quarter of a million foreigners were living in 2015, according to official figures which included people not considered 'mainland Chinese', from Hong Kong, Macau and Taiwan. Many of the most adventurous promoters were also foreigners.

As a major port, Shanghai had repeatedly served as an entry point for fresh ideas from abroad, according to Anna Greenspan, the author of a book about the city's hunger for modernity, *Shanghai Future*. 'Almost all modern technologies came to Asia via Shanghai. Gaslights were introduced in 1865, the telephone in 1881, electricity in 1882, running water in 1884, and the tram in 1901,' Greenspan wrote.[4]

This relentless desire for new developments also made it a perfect place for new subcultures to emerge: 'It has an energy, a vibe, a dynamism and a tension,' Cameron Wilson argues. 'It's in a cultural state of flux, it's always moving and changing. It's socially very progressive as well, and that attracts a certain kind of people – not only from abroad, but from the rest of China too.'

Yet he admitted that electronic dance music was still a completely marginal subculture here in China's most heavily populated urban environment: 'If you get 300 people at the Shelter, in a city this size, that's just a speck of sand.'

And inevitably, even that would not last, because nightclubs never do. The Shelter opened its doors for the final time on the last night of 2016 after the authorities declined to renew its licence, meaning that after an adventurous nine-year run, it was all over. Gareth Williams announced the news in a wry tone of resignation, offering a fond farewell to all those who had played and partied down there in the darkness: 'Fuck it. Thank you. Love you.'[5]

'China is in the midst of the fastest and most intense process of urbanisation the world has ever known, and Shanghai – its biggest, richest and most cosmopolitan city – is positioned for acceleration into the twenty-first century.'

Anna Greenspan

There's an unruly crush at the steel barriers fencing off the entrance to the rave, where pugnacious security cops are struggling desperately to subdue the frantic punters as they surge forward, waving their tickets and clamouring to be let in. Then suddenly the squabbling crowd of sportswear-clad youths opens up to allow an imperious crew of blinged-out Chinese disco daddies to stroll through like the lords of their manor, their insouciant scowls and dark sunglasses deflecting any attempt at dissent. One of them has a glistering brace of pistols sketched out in diamanté on the back of his hoodie, while his friends sport old-school Stüssy T-shirts, sapeur-style suits and sculpted crops as they swagger past in formation flanked by their ladyfriends in vertiginous heels and shiny hotpants, their faces doll-like in bloodless masks of make-up.

From a distance, the stage looks like a sci-fi castle from a movie-themed amusement park, with its three huge video screens mounted in a spiky silver structure built out of what resemble cast-off parts from a Transformers toy factory. The Dutch DJ Don Diablo is playing what sounds to be a remake of Queen's 'We Will Rock You' and shouting 'Put your fucking hands up!' as old-school Belgian synth-stabs collapse into the boisterous turbo-bounce of EDM.

He then leads the audience in a call-and-response chant – 'House time? Anytime!' – although there's little in his set that could be really described as house in the sense that any of its Chicago originators might recognise it. Instead there is a selection of glossy melodies reminiscent of white eighties pop and a lot of stop-start EDM assault-and-battery. He plays an aggressively banal version of the rave classic 'You Got the Love' and shrieks: 'I want to see some telephones in the air!'

As he signs off by making a heart sign with his hands, a drone swooping overhead flashes back images of the arm-waving crowd onto the screens, giving the whole event an artificial epic feel, like we're all dancing in some documentary film about a legendary cultural happening, not at a sponsored rave on a patch of open ground next to some tower blocks.

Because this *is* a rave, although not as it would have been understood on those fine blurry nights back in Britain in 1989 when the vibe was heightened by the fact that it was all highly illegal and the heat could come down at any time. The heavy security presence at this weekend's Storm festival in Shanghai might have been familiar, but here there are jarring gaps between the DJ sets when advertisements are played out on the screens, causing any communal vibe that has built up to instantly dissipate, ensuring that the party can never amass the cumulative energy to take it to the next level. There is also no sign of any illicit drug use, although there are adverts selling an energy drink called YAO with the slogan 'Stay high'.

Across the arena, punters are assailed by a barrage of branding messages and corporate logos, while what appear to be promotions personnel wander around waving flags bearing the names of headliners Tiësto and Skrillex, as well as adverts for a Chinese radio station. Meanwhile locals who haven't got tickets for the party have clambered up onto metal containers overlooking the perimeter of the site to gaze down in bemused fascination at the noisy UFO that has landed in their neighbourhood, although their view is partly obscured by the portable toilets (which are helpfully labelled 'emiction compartment' in English for foreigners who are too wasted to work out where to urinate).

Stilt walkers in black bodysuits studded with red lights move eerily through the crowd as dusk starts to settle in and Skrillex takes to the stage, the screens flashing out fast-cut images of dancing aliens, explosions, flying saucers and neon slogans insisting that it's time to 'FEEL GOOD'. 'Do you want to get fucking crazy right now?' Skrillex demands, while people wave smartphones and toy light-sabres in the air, the bass belches and grizzles and a gruff sample exhorts us: 'Don't stop, work that pussy!'

Tiësto closes the night with a slick melange of EDM and trance tropes and the occasional nostalgic refrain dragged up from house history. He's briefly joined by Chinese pop singer Jane Zhang for a rendition of their collaborative track 'Change Your World', which was recorded specifically to promote the event and to market electronic dance music to Chinese youth with its bilingual lyrics and easily mastered melody for karaoke singalongs.

This Shanghai Storm event had no connection with the American outlaw raves of the same name run by Brooklyn breakbeat don Frankie Bones in the early nineties, of course; in fact its full name was actually Budweiser Storm, like a sponsored extreme sports tournament. The showpiece Tiësto-Zhang performance had also been engineered to promote Anheuser-Busch's beer brand, part of a strategy to consolidate Budweiser sales in China by associating it with what was hoped would be an exciting new EDM youthquake. I watched an unintentionally revealing promo film about the making of the track, featuring both stars talking earnestly about their corporate engagement as if it was a breakthrough in Sino-Western cultural relations facilitated by the elixir of diplomacy that is beer. 'I think what Budweiser's doing is amazing for dance music and for the culture,' Tiësto (Tijs Verwest) suggests in the video.

Even the spooky stilt walkers at Storm were part of a 'dancing aliens visit Shanghai' theme which the organisers were hoping to monetise, I found out later when I read a profile of the festival's promoter Eric Zho in the local English-language media. 'With a themed festival, we can have a lot of fun in marketing messages to the mass consumers, and if done right, we can launch toys and other merchandise with the alien theme,' Zho explained in one of the most unapologetically capitalistic interviews I have ever read with anyone involved in dance culture.[5]

Zho described his EDM festivals as 'product lines' and said that underground music was a potential ancillary market that he was 'testing' with the help of sports goods manufacturers Adidas. 'We are in the business of selling an experience to our consumers, not just bringing the best music to them,' he explained.[7]

His company was behind the idea to localise EDM – 'make it available for mass media consumption', as Zho put it – by pairing up Western DJ heroes with Asian stars: Avicii with Taiwan-based singer Wang Leehom in 2014 and then Tiësto with Jane Zhang the year afterwards. The strategy seemed to be to import a pre-fabricated EDM template, but make it less 'foreign' by bolting on some Chinese characteristics in order to sell it to a potentially lucrative new market, rather than trying to cultivate something from the grassroots, which would have been a far more unpredictable venture.

Inevitably, dance music veterans were cynical about such an obviously mercenary intervention. A columnist on the China Music Radar website argued that the glitzy meaninglessness of EDM could fit into Chinese mainstream nightlife, but might never achieve any genuine cultural significance: 'Scenes take years and years to gestate, to grow and to reach critical mass. It is rare (in fact we can't think of a single example) to see private and corporate money actually "creating" one,' the writer noted.[8]

The first Western electronic musician to play in China was Jean-Michel Jarre, who did shows in Beijing and Shanghai as far back as 1981. DJ stars had been playing club sets in the country since the nineties, when Paul Oakenfold made his first working visit to Shanghai. Beijing also had an annual EDM fest on the Great Wall featuring the likes of David Guetta and Armin van Buuren, but Oakenfold got there before them too, doing a show at the centuries-old ramparts in 2002 – although the first ever Great Wall rave actually happened four years before that, organised by a Swiss-led expat crew called Cheese, with the DJs playing in a turret.

The day before Budweiser Storm, Oakenfold was back in Shanghai, playing at Luce, one of the upmarket nightclubs favoured by nouveau riche Chinese and wealthier, less aesthetically discerning expats. The main room was packed with smart young fellows in dark suits and their painted molls, all seated at tables, on each of which was an illuminated Perspex box, glowing in the pink and neon-blue lights and stacked with bottles of booze – high-end vodka and champagne, plus Chivas Regal with green tea as a mixer (a contemporary Chinese favourite).

It almost looked like a nightclub scene from a Hollywood period picture about Shanghai's decadent thirties, but there was something missing – there was only a tiny rectangle of space in front of the DJ box that served as the 'dancefloor'; the entire remainder of the club was occupied by the tables and the suits and the bottles. As Oakenfold dropped his bangers, there was almost nowhere to dance.

This was by no means unusual. Upmarket clubs in Shanghai often engaged prestigious Western guest DJs, but the vibe was all about conspicuous consumption, not sweaty raving. The Linx club even had a VIP area that was periodically raised up by hydraulic pumps so the less wealthy could watch their betters sipping their champagne in the air above them. Waiters put on a little show every time someone ordered a particularly expensive bottle; sparklers sizzled in jeroboams of top-marque fizz and showgirls pranced around to pay the appropriate respect to the big swinging dick who was paying the bill. Linx was reported to have once engaged actress Nicole Kidman just to sit in its VIP area; punters were apparently charged thousands of dollars to book tables near her. The Mint club meanwhile had a 17-metre-long aquarium with miniature sharks and a VIP terrace with views of the Shanghai skyline.

The DJs who got booked to play at such places were often selected according to their rankings in international popularity polls, particularly the annual *DJ* magazine list, which had become a kind of prescriptive text for some of the country's promoters. 'The Chinese club industry has calcified around the *DJ* magazine top 100 DJs ranking,' says Andrew Bull, the director of Shanghai-based marketing firm Shine Communications. Bull knew what he was talking about; he was a veteran DJ who had played at the celebrated Disco Disco club – the 'Studio 54 of Hong Kong' in the late seventies and early eighties, according to legend – and he was responsible for organising Oakenfold's first gig in Shanghai.

'The club owners really buy the *DJ* magazine top 100 – it's a ranking that is taken to be the gold standard,' Bull explains. 'They're like, "I've got the number five", "I've got the number 23", "I've got the number 61". The numbers give them everything they need to know. It's become like a Bible for them.'

Extravagant displays of wealth at nightspots in chic neighbourhoods like the Bund were also not unusual, says Reggie Ba-Pe of STD Promotions, which ran the Arkham club, one of the city's more musically adventurous venues.

'I remember once this new club opened up called Ibiza – the most terrible name – and they gave us a spending budget to book artists for them,' Ba-Pe recalls. 'There was a guy sitting there at a table with a hundred bottles of champagne in front of him – literally a whole table of champagne and buckets of ice, sitting there in the seat closest to the dancefloor, smoking a cigarette with a few models around him, not giving a fuck about the music. It's a show of status – "I've got all this, sitting here smoking my cigarette with my bitches, I'm the fucking man!" I'd never seen anything like it before in my life.

'So there's this whole other side of Shanghai, this over-indulgent scene of showing your wealth and going to parties and buying a hundred bottles of champagne *just because you can*. If you go to the outskirts of the city, you can see some of the worst slums, but when you get to the Bund, it's as self-indulgent and debauched as it can be.'

Not everyone on the Shanghai scene was so quite tough on these ostentatious spendthrifts. Rainbow Gao, a veteran Chinese club promoter in her early fifties, was a child in the harsher years of the People's Republic, during Mao Zedong's Cultural Revolution, when millions were brutally persecuted, forcibly displaced, imprisoned, executed or starved to death. Gao says she believes that all the conspicuous consumption was at least partly the result of decades of deprivation.

'Chinese people like to show off because we have been poor. It's like a psychological imbalance,' she suggests. 'Everything is new, and right now most Chinese people only think about making money. But people have started to travel, so it is slowly starting to change.'

Gao founded The Mansion, a five-floor 'cultural centre' in a villa on a housing estate not far from Shanghai Zoo which she insisted was not a nightclub, and where she lived with her DJ boyfriend and daughter. The green-walled building stood out among the sober houses on the estate, with its cheerful red door decorated with a Chinese lantern, its bulging mirrored window and backyard swimming pool with an artificial mini-beach on which visitors could relax.

As well as being a weekend party venue, The Mansion was also a kind of hostel where anyone could stay for free if they pitched in to help keep the place going. There were rows of bunk beds, chill-out areas, a karaoke and games floor, while down in the basement disco area, purple plush banquettes lined the graffiti-spattered walls.

'It's not a club – we never call The Mansion a club. It's much more than that. We organise an electronic music party every weekend but this is not the major idea,' Gao explains. 'I'm trying to create a community. People can stay, relax and exchange ideas. We are trying to develop everybody's creativity.'

Gao had an interesting past. Growing up in the northern port city of Tianjin, her father was jailed during the Cultural Revolution and only released after Mao died. She studied biophysics while simultaneously working as a model, ran a bar in Beijing, and started one of the country's first international modelling agencies. She also claimed to have organised the first-ever outdoor rave in the Chinese capital, featuring a French psytrance DJ. But throughout all her endeavours, she came up against the same obstacle, she says – misogyny: 'I always had a problem, as a pretty girl with some knowledge who was really active: that guys control the market, and if there is someone I want to work with, they just want to get me in bed.'

As well as The Mansion, Gao programmed the electronic music stage at Shanghai's Midi Festival and the Yin Yang Music Festival on the Great Wall outside Beijing. She had little time for flashy ventures like Budweiser Storm: 'Storm is like the outdoor version of a Chinese commercial club, so they target the people who follow the American bullshit and the superstars,' she says. 'We don't want our festival to be expensive or show-off, but for everybody to experience. That's why we allow people to bring their own food and drink, and also to camp.'

Critics claimed that The Mansion's DJs were naïve dilettantes and its party-goers clueless young hedonists – 'frazzled tweakers', one journalist called them. But a measure of bickering and backbiting was inevitable in a small scene like the Shanghai alternative club circuit, and Gao had her admirers too. 'She's trying to build a scene here; it's a grotty business, but any independent spirit here will come from people like her,' suggested Andrew Bull.

She certainly had big dreams: 'In my lifetime I cannot make money out of this, but I can help China develop its culture and creativity rather than only making money. Maybe in 40 or 50 years – after I'm not here anymore – maybe China could lead the world.'

Her words reminded me of something that the author Mian Mian – who was also a party promoter at one point – had said about the destiny of those who had tried to push the social boundaries in China on the cusp of the millennium: 'All we can do is make the road easier for the next generation. This is our fate.'[9]

One of Gao's heroes was veteran punk rocker He Yong, who had played at the democracy protests in Beijing's Tiananmen Square in 1989 and whose doomy, anti-authoritarian song 'Garbage Dump' was one of the starkest pieces of socially conscious Chinese rock of its era.

Gao was once on the committee of a state-backed rock festival when it booked He Yong to perform, but after the punk rocker made a dangerously political quip from the stage, he was temporarily banned from performing live. His mental health deteriorated and he was hospitalised for a while. By the time he came to stay with her briefly at The Mansion, he had fallen on hard times after going through a period of heavy psychiatric medication.

'Twenty years ago he was a dreamer: creative, insightful, brave and compassionate,' Gao wrote in a poignant article afterwards. 'Seeing him like this broke my heart. Life is vulnerable, natural disasters can kill, but only politics can truly destroy you.'[10]

'Here, inside a cluster of brick warehouses at the end of a dirt lane, hundreds of thousands of discs by foreign artists, both major and minor, are piled in cardboard boxes and wicker baskets stacked several metres high. Li wades through the CD sea like a beachcomber, looking for favoured titles. He buys the discs by the hundreds for 12 cents each, then sells them back in Guangzhou for $2 apiece. "This," Li says, glancing up from his treasure hunt, "is my paradise."'

'Zombie Discs', Time, January 2003

Many of China's first electronic music producers started to discover the genre in the same way: through the millions of unwanted or deleted CDs and cassettes from the West that were bulk-dumped on the country in the nineties as a cheap way of getting rid of them. Their plastic cases were saw-gashed or holed to indicate they had no commercial value, but the music usually remained audible. After they were shipped into ports like Guangzhou, they ended up being sold off on the black market in a country where access to Western music had been limited for decades; even as late as 2001, only 700 foreign records were approved for import. The condemned discs and tapes became known as *dakou* – cut-outs. 'Before, the only way people knew foreign music was through books. But with *dakou*, we could hear it,' said Guangzhou-based music writer Ou Ning.[11]

Suddenly all kinds of sounds were available – an unfiltered torrent of utterly foreign music, delivered with little social or historical context to enable people to make any sense of it. 'It sounded cool, but what *it* was wasn't clear,' as author Jonathan Campbell observed in his history of Chinese rock.[12] But despite the effort involved in sifting through these huge piles of unfamiliar discs and tapes to discern some kind of meaning, *dakou* helped to energise the Chinese alternative scene in the mid-nineties, inspiring new bands and independent record labels.

'*Dakou* CDs enabled musicians and audiences in China to listen to music that was either censored or deemed too marginal by China's music distributors. Examples of titles range from the new wave of Joy Division to the industrial sound of the German band Einstürzende Neubauten and the digital hardcore of Atari Teenage Riot,' Dutch academic Jeroen de Kloet wrote in an article about what he called the '*Dakou* generation'. '*Dakou* CDs are, however, not necessarily alternative: Celine Dion and the operas of Wagner have also appeared on the market. But the more alternative titles were picked up by rock musicians and audiences, and consequently became tremendously nutritious for Chinese rock culture, as they opened up a musical space that did not exist officially in China.'[13]

The mass dumping of CDs also helped to create a huge pirate

distribution network across the country. China had an enormous, vibrant urban shadow economy – informal markets, street vendors, pedlars, hawkers, scrap merchants and hustlers of more nefarious products – and a verve for copying foreign imports. *Shanzhai* was the slang word for counterfeit goods, particularly mobile phones and other electronic devices, which didn't even try to pretend that they weren't fakes – a kind of DIY entrepreneurialism dedicated to mass-producing semi-imitations or mutant adaptations of desirable consumer items.

But even before *dakou* CDs reached the streets of China's major cities, there were bootleg cassettes for sale on Shanghai's black market, says Shelter club founder Gary Wang, who bought his first hip-hop tape on impulse in 1988 without even knowing what kind of music was on it.

'There was a bunch of college students who made pirate cassette tapes with black-and-white covers and every weekend they would go and sell them on one corner downtown,' Wang recalls. 'One weekend I went there and by accident I picked out Run-DMC's *King of Rock*. I had no idea what kind of music it was, or who Run-DMC were, but the sound just had a really big impact on me. From then I started to look for any black music. I picked up anything with black people on the cover, but I had no idea that it was hip-hop. After a year, I read an article in a music magazine and found out what it was.'

But whether the influence of renegade phenomena like *dakou* could help to nurture original forms of Chinese electronic music that were more than just copies of Western styles remained unclear. In the 2010s, there were still relatively few Chinese producers, despite the fact that the music had been around, on the country's avant-garde fringes at least, for over two decades.

Some put it down to the enormous pressure that Chinese youth were under to study hard, conform and succeed, especially because – due to the state's one-child policy, which was enforced until 2016 – almost everyone was an only child and had to carry the entire weight of their parents' hopes and expectations in the country's brutally competitive economy, where messing around with beats wasn't seen as a reliable route to affluence.

'The parents and the school always put a lot of pressure on the kids. They're kind of brainwashed,' says Wang. 'Same with my parents. I had a really unhappy middle school and high school period, the most unhappy time in my life for sure. I'm lucky, I went to Japan [to attend college] and I'm able to do what I like to do, but most kids probably don't have that type of opportunity, so for them it's difficult.'

There was another major factor that defined the contemporary musical environment in China, Wang argues: history. Specifically, the years of isolation, political repression and economic hardship during the Cultural Revolution, which continued from 1966 to 1976. 'At that time we completely closed up the whole country; we didn't let people out, we pretty much didn't let people in, and there was no information about anything. We didn't know what was going on in the rest of the world, including in music,' he explains.

'So basically we lost this era, which was a great era for music – rock, soul, funk, all of it – we had zero connection to it. You can find funk from Thailand or Iran from that time, but you can never find Chinese funk, because it didn't exist. So this to me is very, very important, because we are lacking that influence. We don't really have anything to start from, no foundation at all. Now we have the internet, but learning everything at once is not necessarily as good a way to learn; with cultural things you need to take your time to build it and develop it.'

The 'early adopters' of electronic music in China were often the intellectuals, the relatively well-off aesthetes who saw techno as art. Some of the best Chinese electronic music was also decidedly intro-spective, not pumping club gear, suggests Michael Ohlsson, the founder of the Dada club, which operated in both Beijing and Shanghai. 'In Beijing in particular there's a lot of drone techno, shoegazer stuff, arty postpunk vibes,' Ohlsson says. Indeed, it was very hard to imagine sen-sitive Chinese producers like MHP screaming out 'Do you want to get fucking crazy right now?' like Skrillex.

Another example of this more cerebral approach was Beijing-based Shao Yanpeng, who had also recorded as Dead J and released some of his scintillatingly severe techno on Berlin's Tresor label. Shao came from an avant-garde background, and was also a sound designer for theatre productions and exhibitions. Among his inspirations was the changing face of Beijing's urban architecture amid its ongoing capitalist boom – not the kind of subject that often troubled EDM DJs. 'My album in 2011 was named *Ting Tai Lou Ge*, which is an old Chinese phrase to describe the architectural landscape,' Shao says. 'The phrase also means unreal landscape in the imagination. Those giant weird new buildings in China are the modern form of *Ting Tai Lou Ge*.'

Shao, who also made a film called *Date* about electronic music in Berlin, featuring interviews with Thomas Fehlmann, Robert Henke and Manuel Göttsching, first found out about the genre though *dakou* CDs. But he cautioned that people like himself were rare in China, and that most of the country's electronic music producers had either studied or lived abroad.

'Chinese people are not quite used to this kind of music culture. A lot of reasons: language, culture history, government policy,' he says. 'You know in China we are not able to access YouTube, Facebook or even Soundcloud. From this aspect, China does not belong to the information system of the world.'

His fellow Beijinger Howie Lee (Li Huadi) – who had studied in London – was one of the few Chinese producers cranking out heavy-duty bass music for club dancefloors. Lee actually started out by playing punk rock, which had been a fertile genre in the capital in the nineties. 'When I was a teenager, I played in a punk band. I had a lot of anger, I wanted to rebel, I was angry about how society was fucked-up,' he recalls. 'Punk has a lot of energy, a lot of anger, and it's easy to play. I was very young…'

He also believed that Chinese electronic dance music was still at a very early stage of development in the mid-2010s: 'Most people think it's a Western import because there are not many Chinese musicians doing it and they don't really understand what it is. They think it's EDM, or just strange music. But you must understand that a few years ago, mainstream people did not understand rock music, so it's going to take a while because electronic music is a new concept for them. Karaoke is way bigger than clubbing, that's for sure '

With a Beijinger's city pride, Lee insisted that the music being made in the capital was better than anywhere else in the country because the urban environment was more *hardcore*, although Shanghai, around 800 miles south, had a more active club scene because it was wealthier. 'Beijing is super harsh – lots of smog and shitty northern people,' he explained. 'It's not a stable place – Beijing is always changing, politically as well, because the drug issue is very intense, so politically there is big pressure and they have crackdowns on clubs.'

Lee was making compulsive post-dubstep bass beats with distinct Chinese characteristics – jingling melodies, digital chimes and bells, snatches of vocal refrains from old records and cut-ups of ancient elemental riffs. Most other Chinese electronic music producers were still trying to create copies of their Western heroes' work, he complained: 'They need to break the rules, not be so conservative.'

But even so, just as the music was no longer wholly controlled or defined by Americans or Brits or Germans any more, it could never be completely Chinese either, he insisted. 'Electronic music doesn't really belong to anyone now,' he said.

'China is the final frontier of EDM global domination.'

Eric Zho, Budweiser Storm festival promoter

They were gathering that sunny Shanghai morning at the Hyatt on the Bund, a suitably salubrious environment for the tanned tycoons and keen-eyed entrepreneurs of global electronic dance music who accumulated air miles like others pick up discount coupons from supermarkets. Some were in sleek suits, others in T-shirts and jeans, some sporting asymmetrical hipster cuts and tattoos, others balding and paunchy. Like the EDM equivalent of colonial emissaries, they had come to find out how to exploit what it was hoped could one day be the world's biggest electronic music market – China. The slogan of the event: 'Awakening the dragon.'

The International Music Summit was an itinerant dance-music business forum that took place in different locations throughout the year and across the globe. Moving from Ibiza to Los Angeles to Singapore, IMS was an arena in which schemes were hatched, hands were shaken and deals were sealed. In the Hyatt's lustrous atrium, delegates gathered in huddles, swapping gossip and business cards, and as I waited for the first session to start, I overheard a few of them trading updates: 'We brought him in and he did good business for us'; 'However you want to position it, it's OK with our brand values'; 'That might require a different contract'.

IMS had been founded by BBC Radio 1 DJ Pete Tong and journalist Ben Turner several years earlier, at a point when the music's credibility seemed to be on the downturn. 'We felt it was time to put a business focus back on electronic music,' Turner explained. 'When we launched it in Ibiza in 2007, everything was negative. The industry was depressed. But in two years it went from being rock bottom to being a global genre – and it hasn't looked back from that point.'

Turner's opening speech to the first IMS to be held in China put the glittering prize right on the table: 'There are 1.3 billion people here so the opportunity is huge. It's important for us to grow this market in the right way.'

It seemed to be one of the core beliefs shared by many of the people who attended international conclaves like this: growth is good. Electronic music should keep on expanding, keep on becoming more popular, keep on colonising new territories. Whether constant growth was creatively beneficial wasn't questioned, and no one asked if sponsorship had a positive effect, or if global brands should be involved; it was simply assumed that they must be part of all this. Turner, an evangelist for the music with a commitment stretching back decades, had stressed that things should be done *in the right way*, although here in the bubble world of techno-capitalism, it really wasn't all that clear that there was any consensus about right and wrong.

But maybe I was being a little naïve about all this; it was just globalisation in action, after all. As Andrew Bull had told me: 'It's corporate business now, it's not like a couple of guys who've just come back from Ibiza and think they've seen the future.'

It was certainly a long way from the anti-corporate rhetoric I had heard from the VOID boys down at the Shelter. Many of the delegates at IMS had a totally different vision of the scene, one in which companies like Anheuser-Busch were philanthropic patrons, the Medicis of the global dancefloor, giving all those young Michelangelos the chance to do their funky thing. This at least seemed to be the pitch from Anheuser-Busch's global head of music, Clarissa Pantoja: 'It's all about the values that are behind this culture, which are the same values that Budweiser shares,' Pantoja told her audience at the Hyatt. 'We really want to be involved in the culture, not only bringing the brand, not only bringing the experience, but also things like the collaboration between Tiësto and Jane Zhang, which is bringing the local culture and electronic music together.'

But there was a problem. Several problems, in fact, and not all of them involved the Communist Party of the People's Republic of China. Some of the delegates seemed to be hearing for the first time that if you wanted to do business in China, you needed to speak to your audience in Chinese; most people in the country couldn't even find the big EDM tunes online if their titles were only written in English. And most potential punters hadn't even heard of the West's DJ heroes. 'They can play for 100,000 people at a festival in Europe but when they come to China, nobody knows who they are,' admitted Eelko van Kooten of Dutch EDM label Spinnin' Records.

Then there was the official blacklisting of musicians who had expressed what were seen by the Beijing authorities as politically toxic opinions, particularly about Tibet. 'Any artistic group or individual who have ever engaged in activities which threaten our national sovereignty will not be allowed in,' the Chinese culture ministry once warned.[14] Kraftwerk were denied visas because they had once been listed on the bill for a Free Tibet festival, and Björk was banned after shouting out 'Tibet! Tibet!' at the end of a song called 'Declare Independence' while she was performing in Shanghai.

'To even apply for a permit [to hold an event], you need to understand which artists are blacklisted, which artists are not,' Eric Zho told the IMS delegates. 'They publish this information only to established promoters at the beginning of each year. So if you're not in that group, you will never know that so-and-so took a photo with the Dalai Lama for example and thus became banned.' It also wasn't always clear how the laws would be enforced in practice; while the Rolling Stones were told they couldn't play 'Honky Tonk Women' and other songs with 'suggestive' lyrics at their first Chinese gig, Public Enemy were allowed to get away with performing 'Fight the Power'.

Although it was hard to imagine that most premier-league EDM DJs would ever make the unfortunate 'mistake' of ending their sets with a call for Tibetan liberation, there was another issue too: censorship. 'You want to release a track? The government has to hear it first,' warned Zho. According to media reports, the Chinese culture ministry forbade around 120 songs in 2015 for promoting obscenity, violence or crime or violating public morality, most of them by hip-hop bands. Critics said it was part of a wider trend towards censorship as President Xi Jinping sought to extend the regime's control over the cultural sphere, and in 2016, the authorities stepped up efforts to control what music was made available online. 'This edict is the latest strike in a multi-year campaign to "cleanse" both the internet and culture more broadly of material the ruling Communist Party might deem a threat to China's stability,' Reuters reported.[15]

Bizarrely, at around the same time, Chinese propaganda officials also decided to release their own funky little cartoon hip-hop video featuring the sampled voice of President Xi; an attempt to woo the WeChat generation with positive messages about reforms intended to fight corruption and poverty, albeit couched in stiff Party language. 'Let the people's wishes become our action,' Xi declaimed over the track. 'An arrow will never return once it's shot by a bow.' It went out under the decidedly unfunky title 'The Reform Group is Two Years Old', which attracted a fair bit of mockery on Chinese social media. Perhaps it just needed a Tiësto remix.

Some of the IMS speakers were savvy enough to understand that if dance music was to really take root in China, it needed to be adopted by the country's youth on their own terms. A pre-packaged import shipped over in an attempted act of contemporary cultural colonisation would not be enough. 'If China is to have longevity, it has to have its own scene,' argued Mark Lawrence from the Association for Electronic Music. During a break in the speeches, I chatted to Janis Chang, an executive at Chinese record label Taihe Rye, who told me she was hoping for a domestic DJ icon to emerge and rally a new generation to the cause.

'We need to create one local hero so the concept of dance music will speed up,' Chang declared, frustrated with some of the speakers' bland confidence that they could impose their own values on her country. 'Foreigners have their own concept of cool, and we have our own local taste. The concepts are very, very different. So just having Tiësto work with Jane Zhang on one song won't work. We need to do something *here*, create a local culture and a local hero. If we don't create something and just do promotion, it will never work.'

Andrew Bull joked during one panel that in order to build a market, karaoke-friendly EDM tracks could perhaps be created for KTV lounges, the popular nightspots where people went to sing along to the latest hits. Mark Lawrence immediately quipped back: 'I think Frankie Knuckles just turned in his grave.'

What wasn't mentioned by anyone that day was Ecstasy, the wicked ghost at the corporate feast – as if a deluge of Bud, or perhaps a torrent of Chivas Regal and green tea, could supply enough narcotic vigour to get a nationwide party started. Because drugs were a highly sensitive topic in China, one that could blow the whole caper. As everyone hoped that no one in authority realised, they were also one of the vital forces that had helped to evangelise the culture in the first place.

Turner had told me a few months earlier that he believed the situation for dance music in China was full of opportunity but essentially fragile, and that the whole scene could be shut down abruptly if the government decided that there was any threat to social stability.

'There's potential but it's also on a knife-edge,' he said. 'They're on the cusp of big brands wanting to spend but they're so scared of the drug culture around it, and it all depends on how it's presented and positioned. The interest is huge but everyone's so scared of the drug side of things.'

The Chinese Communist Party already knew about MDMA, and had done for years. After an Ecstasy cult emerged in major cities like Beijing, Shanghai, Guangzhou and Shenzhen in the late nineties, the authorities cracked down hard with a coordinated anti-drug campaign focused on dance clubs. Many clubs were raided and shuttered and ravers arrested as police tried to suppress the demand for 'head-shaking pills', as they were sometimes called because of tranced-out Chinese ravers' idiosyncratic dance moves. 'A nationwide anti-drugs campaign has targeted mainly dance halls, night clubs and other entertainment places where drug users and dealers gather. Against this backdrop, the "head-shaking pill" dealers and addicts have gone underground,' an official communiqué noted in 2002.[16]

But in the years that followed, China emerged as a major covert producer of the chemical precursors used to make MDMA, as well as an exporter of new dance-drug analogues that were sold around the world as Ecstasy substitutes, according to Mike Power, author of the book *Drugs 2.0*. 'China is crucial to the modern dance-drug complex,' argues Power. 'It is the source of many of the hundreds of novel psychoactive substances that have contaminated MDMA supply chains worldwide.' And it was inevitable that some of these substances would end up on the domestic market too.

Club busts continued intermittently over the years that followed as part of the authorities' attempts to stamp out vice and narcotics, but it was never quite clear what would get raided and when. In February 2016, a few months after the IMS forum, riot police busted a rave called The Real Deal that was being held in a tunnel near an IKEA store in Shenzhen, sealing off the entrances in the early hours of the morning and taking almost 500 people into custody for drug testing. Over 90 came up positive for narcotics, more than half of them foreigners, police said. But because the tunnel raves had already been going on for several years before the bust, it appeared to be an indication of a somewhat arbitrary approach to law enforcement. 'Cops knew those parties. They came before and just had a look; they didn't care. This time they wanted to catch people with drugs,' said one online commentator. 'The legality of any party in China is almost impossible to judge,' warned another.[17]

In the space of just a couple of decades, China had undergone what journalist Evan Osnos described as 'a transformation one hundred times the scale, and ten times the speed, of the first Industrial Revolution'.[18] But this transformation had left a lot of uncertainty about what could be permissible and what could be forbidden, while new political diktats could lead to unforeseen clampdowns. This meant that the status of dance music events remained ambiguous and mutable, as I realised when I spoke to Chinese promoter Miao Wong, who started one of the country's first electronic labels, Acupuncture, and staged the INTRO festival in Beijing.

'I think it's very unclear, what is possible and what is not possible,' Wong explained. 'Take our festival for example – we did it for three years and then the authorities realised there is a so-called "new" type of music festival, an electronic music festival, and they don't want that, because of drugs. Then it became hard.'

In 2013, INTRO was held in what had been China's largest steelworks on the western fringes of the capital, where thousands of people partied amid the industrial detritus, abandoned machinery and decommissioned smokestacks – but the year afterwards, the event was abruptly cancelled. Another unpredictable factor was institutional wariness about large gatherings of young people, Wong said: 'That is the problem that all the music festivals in China are facing.'

I remembered what another Chinese promoter had told me: any developments in electronic dance music culture would be dependent on the country's economic vitality and on Communist Party policy – forces beyond ordinary people's control: 'The biggest problem is the government, which overly controls anything culture-wise, and the second biggest problem is that we are not able to change it,' he had cautioned.

Osnos wrote that the collision of two powerful forces, authoritarianism and aspiration, was crucial to understanding contemporary China. There was the Party's dedication to perpetuating its reign, and the people with their 'hunger for new sensations, ideas, and respect', as well as their belief that they could transform their lives amid this dawning era of opportunity.[19]

For Miao Wong, that hunger was fuelled by watching videos of European rave carnivals like the Berlin Love Parade – and while she understood the limitations of operating in her own country, she still believed that she could find space amidst the official restrictions to make some of her fantasies real.

'We know that something like the Love Parade is not possible in China – ever – but we think we can do *something*,' she insisted. 'Everything is always uncertain here – but yes, I do think the future is full of opportunity.'

I hoped for her sake that it was true.

9

Aliens in the Desert

Dubai

WHEN MEHDI ANSARI FIRST VENTURED DOWN into the basement of the Holiday Inn Al Barsha, he knew this was the place he had been looking for. It was a half-forgotten room underneath a sports bar in an unremarkable four-star hotel next to a cacophonous highway, and the management appeared to have all but given up thinking what they could do with it. But Ansari knew: he could start the club he had been dreaming of since he arrived in Dubai from Tehran, and create his own world of sound deep below the streets where the Emirati city's hegemony of commerce and conformity would cease to reign, for five hours every Thursday night at least.

'Somebody told me there was something under that hotel so we went there and asked: "I know you have something down there, I want to see it." They said: "It's nothing, we don't have a nightclub, forget about it,"' Ansari recalls. 'But we went down there and when they opened the door, I was like, "Yes! This is the place!"'

'But they didn't want to give it to us; they were not answering our calls, not agreeing to arrange a meeting – because we were nobody, you know?' Ansari persisted; he had discovered his underground haven and wasn't going to give up on it easily: 'I found where the owner of the hotel's room was, so I snuck in, knocked on the door and said: "You are not doing anything with that room, so why not give us a chance? You have nothing to lose, so give us this opportunity." And it worked.'

That was back in 2012, and over the three years that followed, the delightfully outspoken Iranian DJ and his friends managed to turn this neglected basement with its black concrete walls into an unlikely outpost of underground dance music in the Middle East. Analog Room, they called their party, and they brought in guests like techno veteran Delano Smith from Detroit and Berghain resident Nick Höppner from

Berlin in an attempt to raise a standard for the music they believed in. British acid house innovator A Guy Called Gerald (Gerald Simpson) used Ansari's Roland 808 and 606 machines to play live; Derrick May returned again and again because he loved the vibe in the little room. Even after its three-year run in the customised Holiday Inn basement bar finally ended, Analog Room continued to thrive in other lovingly adapted spaces around the city.

'There was something we wanted but it didn't exist, so we had to invent it. The whole reason for doing this was to improve the culture of the city, to improve the scene, to play people something they never heard before, to surprise them,' Ansari explains. 'I have to do what I believe in, I don't give a fuck what other people think. We were going deep, because we're into art music, educating people and creating a culture.'

Art music... educating people... in the sparkling bubble of Dubai nightlife, this wasn't exactly a populist pitch for the custom of wealthy expats seeking to spend some of their tax-free salaries having a jiggle to Beyoncé on a boozy night out. But down in the Analog Room basement one Thursday night, it appeared that Ansari and his friends had succeeded in creating some kind of community, however transient, through the sheer strength of belief. Radiant waves of mellifluous techno pulsed deep and low as abstract projections played over the dark walls and clusters of mirrorballs twinkled overhead in the darkness; immaculately suntanned girls in floaty floral dresses and glittery heels swirled lithely around the floor while boys in tight T-shirts swung their gym-toned arms to the rhythm. Behind the decks was Ansari, who played under the name Shemroon, and Adam Rahman, a technohead expat from Chennai in India who also ran his own parties in Dubai called Warped. Some devoted souls had even driven for an hour and a half from Abu Dhabi to be here; they made the journey back and forth every week, I was told.

As this was Dubai, a Muslim state that relied on foreign labour to help create its riches, there were of course some peculiar local characteristics – everyone looked like they could have come from anywhere in the world, their accents European, South Asian, American, Australian, while upstairs in the hotel lobby, young Western women in diaphanous party outfits chosen for the baking heat mingled with Muslims in cover-all abayas; none of them took the slightest bit of notice of each other. Because hotels were almost the only places in the Emirati city that were permitted to sell alcohol, such incongruities were not exactly unusual here. 'The licensing laws are restrictive, and you have to finish at 3am on the dot,' one of the Analog Room crew remarked. 'It's not like London or Berlin when you can get around it somehow, but we do our best – sometimes we do a boat party after the club, from 4am to 10am.'

By two in the morning, Ansari had started to build a seething break to its climax as the last hour of the night got underway and the dancers of all races and nations were whooping and cheering, their arms raised towards the basement ceiling as they surged and eddied around the DJ booth. 'Sometimes I get really hopeless about the scene, but then I remember why I want to do this,' Ansari had told me. It was all about moments like this.

Analog Room seemed to be one of those unusual clubs in off-the-circuit cities at that time, like 20/44 and Drugstore in Belgrade or Mtkvarze and Bassiani in Tbilisi – or the Shelter in Shanghai – where hardcore enthusiasts strived to promote the music they loved because they wanted to share it with their crowd, who might not have even heard it before but trusted them because of their immaculate taste and commitment to their cause. Ansari was one of those indomitable characters – a person who once filmed himself driving around Dubai with a 606 and a 303 mounted on his car's dashboard, blasting acid tracks as he twisted through the traffic. It was an aesthetic mission, a calling even, for people like him – to make alien flowers bloom in the desert.

'We are just trying to do something good, not to do business,' he says. 'Hate me, love me, I don't care – this is what I believe is right. Maybe I make it harder for myself by the way I talk sometimes, but still I don't care. I believe in this.'

He gives an ironic smile and then concludes: 'It's the worst-case scenario in the world to do an underground club in Dubai, but we have to do it.'

'Dubai is built on dreams. In only a few years, all this rose from the sand...'

Anthony Bourdain, No Reservations

Dubai was perhaps the most bizarre metropolis on earth, a city built upwards from the barren deserts of the Gulf, one of the most extreme physical manifestations of the audacious notion that nature could be subjugated by mankind and money. Along the 12-lane highway that roared through the city, dazzling swarms of blocks were lit up in gaudy pinks and purples and pulsating electric blues; skyscrapers and ziggurats and asymmetrical twin towers nuzzled up face-to-face to each other's lime-green neon-lit façades, an aesthetically promiscuous display of hectic postmodernism in which all imaginable architectural styles existed simultaneously in the same place.

The highway was lined with huge billboards advertising designer goods, luxury cars and upscale property developments with names like 'Sparkle Towers' – and every so often, a huge image of Dubai's emir, Sheikh Mohammed bin Rashid, pictured against the backdrop of the city that his family built. In the gaps between the blocks, there were also meticulously laid-out gated communities and parks designed to be picture-postcard perfect, and even a few mosques, although there was really only one god here.

And almost all of it was new. As recently as 1960, Dubai had just 60,000 inhabitants who lived in an area of just two square miles; the United Arab Emirates itself was only established as an independent state in 1971. Now there were more than two million people living in Dubai, in this surreal cityscape where construction workers were constantly breaking new ground.

'The city is always changing. You can wake up in the morning and there will be a new building next door,' I was told by Shadi Megallaa, one of the city's finest DJs. 'You never get used to it – it's strange and it will always be strange.'

In a transient urban landscape where expat workers came and went according to their contracts, Megallaa had watched the decades pass and the city grow up with him. His family moved to the United Arab Emirates not so long after he was born in 1979, and this was his home – but he wasn't an Emirati citizen, and possibly never would be.

'I'm an alien,' he says. 'I'm from Egypt but I never really lived in Egypt. No matter where you're from, they don't naturalise anyone in the UAE. You can live here for 50 years and you'll still be an expat. So I have no identity. I am not Egyptian because I never lived there. When I go to Egypt, they ask me, where are you from? And here I will always be a foreigner. So where the fuck am I from?'

He wasn't alone. In this through-the-looking-glass environment, the aliens far outnumbered the citizens; by 2015, fewer than 15 per cent of Dubai's inhabitants were Emiratis. The biggest communities among the foreigners were the Indians and Pakistanis, most of them labourers brought in to build a state that would never grant them citizenship. In Dubai, unless someone was wearing Emirati national dress, a typical first question really was: 'So where are you from?'

Like schoolchildren everywhere, Megallaa grew up with the pop songs they played on the radio; in the eighties in the UAE, that meant Madonna, Prince and Michael Jackson, he says. He first came into contact with underground dance music when a schoolmate's elder brother went to university in Britain and brought home a selection of happy hardcore mixtapes: 'It was unreal, I'd never heard anything like it,' he recalls. 'It wasn't the music so much, more the energy.' While studying at the University of Kansas in the US, he travelled to hear British DJs Sasha and John Digweed play at Twilo in New York – 'that was life-changing' – and then returned to Dubai in 2000 and starting DJing himself. But although he had changed while he was away, the city hadn't, at least not musically: 'The music you could hear in clubs was just bad hip-hop and eighties. It was like it was stuck in a timewarp; you would hear the same songs you heard when you were at school.'

For Megallaa, the transformational moment came when what he describes as the city's first underground club opened in the early 2000s. Called the Terminal because it was situated near the airport, it had the same kind of spirit as Analog Room, he suggests. 'I think this was the most significant thing that ever happened in Dubai nightlife. Before they took it over and made it Terminal, it was a rundown bar for cab drivers to drink – very ghetto, in a two-to-three-star hotel. It was just four black walls, no tables, nothing. And it wasn't just house and techno, they booked Gilles Peterson and Questlove from The Roots. That was unheard of in the city. At the time it was revolutionary, because Dubai wasn't really on the map then like it is now.'

'Very ghetto' isn't a phrase you often hear spoken in connection with Dubai; most people's initial impression is of some kind of Gulf Vegas – brash and flash, punctiliously sanitised and stringently policed. Waiting for Megallaa to get back from a boat trip one humid evening, I watched the pleasure cruisers and gin palaces roll in to the Dubai Marina, a watery clearing in a forest of skyscrapers, disgorging portly oligarchs and their lithe young ladyfriends, with servants scurrying along behind them carrying their bags.

As a pair of neon-blue pyramids lit up on top of one of the towers and palm trees started to twinkle with fairy lights in the dusk along the promenade, hordes of South Asian labourers lined up stoically for their minibuses as their shift building the next glitzy skyscraper came to an end. I was glancing through a satirical column in local club magazine *Infusion*, which described Dubai as 'a city where the rich get richer, the stupid get stupider and the arrogant get more arrogant'.[1] It was intended as a joke – maybe…

'When people ask me what Dubai is like, I say, "Imagine living in a mall,"' says Salah Sadeq, who came from Bahrain and ran the Techfui label, another of the fine DJs from the wider Middle Eastern region who spent several years playing underground dance music in Dubai. 'Here it's all about commerce. Every little thing you do, you pay for. The minute you leave your house, you're spending money. Even in Bahrain, you can have a good walk, pass by a park, stop by someone's house, drop into a restaurant – here you can't do that. It's built like that; it's a money-making machine.'

So was Dubai's club culture, insisted Mehdi Ansari. 'The city is a gathering of multinational people, more than 200 nationalities, and the reason most of them come here is the same – they come here to work and make money and not pay tax, to live in a good apartment and to have a fancy car,' he explains.

'So the basis is money, and when they want to go and party, they want to show their money off, they want to go somewhere where they know the songs, they want to sing along with Rihanna or David Guetta, they are not here to rave on. None of them are artists or musicians. So that's why the scene here is very "business". It's about getting in the rich people who want luxury to buy tables and bottles.'

But some expats who had made the city their home were keen to defend it. When Britain's *Guardian* newspaper mocked the Dubai authorities' attempts to create a Shoreditch-style hipster quarter – the D3 'creative neighbourhood' – and described it as a soulless caricature, one commentator on the newspaper's website snapped back: 'Is it London? New York? Of course not – but for a 40-odd-year-old country, there are plenty of people having a decent pop. Scratch below the cliché and you might see that.'[2]

It was hard to believe that you could ever find anyone who was genuinely committed to this synthetic metropolis unless that person enjoyed the privileged and subsidised status of an Emirati national. And yet such people existed, people who believed they could build something here that was not a luxury apartment block or an upscale auto dealership flogging Ferraris and Maseratis to the tycoons. Something that appeared to be unachievable in this desert of the imagination, where all that grew was concrete, steel and glass – a genuine living culture.

'Dubai is about lavish display. They're not bashful about it, they put it right in your fucking face,' admits Megallaa. 'But the world perceives that Dubai is all just like the Burj Khalifa. There is that, but there is so much other stuff going on underneath. People like me want to do something here because we love it and we care about it – we want to be part of something important here.'

Megallaa was a long way from the Dubai cliché of the improvident philistine. As well as house and techno, his vinyl collection stretched from calypso don The Mighty Sparrow to Parliament to legendary Egyptian singer Umm Kulthum, and he had made an absurdist psychedelic electro album that sounded like Future Sound of London channelling *Maggot Brain*. His dream was to open Dubai's first dance-music record shop – and after many months of hard striving, he eventually managed to make it happen.

What was often overlooked was that the city could actually be an oasis of liberty for musicians from stricter Islamic countries in the Middle East. I once heard the BBC World Service interviewing an Iranian couple who produced ethno-dance tunes under the name 25band, and who had fled across the Gulf to the UAE to play their music and escape the restrictions imposed by the Islamic Republic. 'When we left Iran, we lost something but we gained something. We miss our families, but here we have freedom, we can make our music, exactly the music we want,' said rapper A-del.[3]

Dubai has been described as a 'tribal autocracy' with an omnipotent if relatively benevolent leader and power passed down through the generations by its leading families. 'We have no political parties, no political problems,' an Emirati businessman once told Reuters.[4] But this lack of political liberty was compensated by certain social freedoms that were prohibited in many other Middle Eastern states. In Dubai, women were relatively unoppressed by regional standards, and the media relatively uncensored compared to countries like Saudi Arabia; the environment was far more peaceful than in Iraq or Syria, and alcohol was available in sanctioned outlets to ensure that foreigners felt relaxed enough to bring their expertise to the Emirati economy and help everyone get rich. 'These social liberties compensate those who might grumble about a lack of a political voice,' suggested former Associated Press correspondent Jim Krane in his book about the city.[5]

Krane compared Dubai to a city-state built on trade, like Venice in the twelfth and thirteenth centuries: 'Dubai, like old Venice, survives as an island of enlightenment in a sea of religious fundamentalism. Both cities provoked a backlash for their tolerance. Venice was pilloried by the papacy for trading with Muslims. Dubai gets excoriated by Muslim hardliners for catering to Christians – and a hedonistic lifestyle replete with pork, alcohol, and prostitution.'[6]

Dubai would never have the nocturnal intensity of somewhere like Beirut, where people partied harder to zone out the fears and frustrations of living in perpetual chaotic uncertainty. But the Emirati city was a place where some people could realise dreams that could never be contemplated under more repressive regimes, where self-expression was sometimes only possible in secret.

'I learned to lie when I was six,' Mehdi Ansari told me when I asked him about his childhood in Tehran. 'I was asked to lie by my parents because we should not tell anyone that we have satellite or we have a video player. We were seeing that our parents looked different when they go out of the house. My mother covered up outside. It makes you very strong, if you don't lose yourself.'

Even in the Islamic Republic, you could get recordings of Western pop, and Ansari worked his way through R&B and metal into house and techno. 'People would come from abroad and give us CDs and we would download things as well. Deep Dish were popular because they were Iranian guys,' he says. 'We would hang out, smoke joints and listen to music and party. We were never an Islamic Republic family; we were a Persian family. This was underground life in Iran.'

He and his brother Salar began to DJ, make beats and host clandestine parties despite the risk of arrest, imprisonment or punishment by lashing by a regime that considered after-hours socialising with the opposite sex morally unacceptable, let alone booze and narcotics. 'People do their thing in Iran and they are not complaining because they're afraid of getting killed, but they are still living their lives,' Ansari explains. 'They are so much into music. They dance, they do drugs, there are great parties and great artists – they have so much soul.'

His Analog Room partner Siamak Amidi was also from Iran and

used to stage secret parties in Tehran in the 2000s, at private houses or in rented chalets at holiday resorts on the outskirts of the capital, attracting anything from a few dozen people to a few hundred while constantly trying to evade the attentions of the police.

'We had to be careful because it was illegal,' Amidi recalls. 'At that time in Iran, it was going through these very serious political changes, a more moderate president was elected so it was getting a bit softer, but also the hardliners were putting in a lot of effort to crush that. So it was very difficult and dangerous; we had to be careful not to go too big.

'If you got caught, you could potentially end up in a very serious situation. Drinking is forbidden, mixed parties are forbidden, loud music was forbidden. You could sometimes buy the police – pay some money – but sometimes you couldn't. You could end up getting lashes or end up in jail for several months. I personally got arrested three or four times for throwing parties and had to go to court – I got lashes, and I was in jail for some time.'

Amidi was probably one of the only DJs in the world who could say that he had been sentenced to a flogging for staging a party. But at the time, he insists, it didn't seem like such a big deal.

'When you're growing up there, you understand the dangers fully,' he explains. 'You have two choices – either you live life the way they want, with the ideologies they are dictating to you, or you say, "Fuck it, I'm going to do whatever I want and I'm going to deal with the consequences." For me, at the time at least, and for all the people I was hanging out with, it was not pleasant, but obviously we knew what was going to happen to us if we got caught. But for us it was worth it to do serious parties – and the parties we were doing were really quite serious.'

Serious indeed, and not just musically – despite the total prohibition imposed by the Islamic regime, with its 'morality police' constantly on the watch for infringements of religious law, Tehran's underground scene was neither teetotal nor drug-free.

'Drugs are everywhere in Iran – traditional stuff like hashish and opium,' Amidi says. 'So drugs were always available – psychedelics,

MDMA, marijuana, everything. And we had a hugely mixed crowd: gay people, lesbians, everyone. It was the ultra-liberal side of Tehran society. It was the complete opposite of the ideology that was ruling Iran.'

But the things that people like Amidi and Ansari wanted to achieve were not really going to be possible under Iran's religious autocracy, they realised, and they eventually made the decision to move abroad and study in the UAE. Although Dubai's regime appeared to some Europeans to be offering a tawdry imitation of 'freedom', it could look different if you were seeing it from another perspective.

There were contradictions, of course. Kissing in public could be sanctioned with a fine and sex outside marriage carried a prison sentence, but prostitution flourished. Alcohol was on sale at hotel bars, but drug possession was punished with a mandatory four-year prison sentence without the benefit of a trial, as British drum and bass DJ Grooverider discovered when he was arrested while carrying cannabis in 2007; he served ten months in jail before being pardoned. Traffickers could be executed, although this was rare.

Paradoxically, the ban on illicit substances was actually a positive attraction for some expats who had racked up deleterious cocaine habits during their raving days on the European club scene. 'I wanted to get away from all that because I was just getting smashed all the time and I just couldn't avoid it,' one told me. For him, Dubai's booze-fuelled nightlife offered a chance to keep on clubbing without the potentially debilitating temptations: 'There was no gear here, so I just fell in love with the place.'

Others simply came to ensure their economic survival, however. As I spoke with one foreign DJ in an airy Western-style café not far from the Palm Jumeirah, a preposterous frond-shaped archipelago of land reclaimed from the sea and dotted with luxury resorts and residences, a man was methodically sweeping up the sand outside the window – one of the legion of impoverished foreigners doing the menial jobs that kept the city functioning. These were the people who built the roads and then cleared the pavements, who cleaned the offices of international companies and looked after their employees' children, who delivered the food that they ate and then took away the garbage afterwards – the unknown thousands who prevented the fantasy from evaporating into the heat of the Gulf.

Amnesty International and Human Rights Watch often criticised the UAE for the exploitation of migrant labourers and the abuse of female domestic workers, as well as the arrests of government opponents. The construction labourers were the expatriates who didn't get to share in the property-brochure dream of a luxuriant seafront paradise.

'Dubai isn't kind to these men. It gives them no recognition. Their feats of construction don't mean they share the wealth their projects generate,' Jim Krane wrote. 'Instead, Dubai hides them from view. Most eat and sleep in hardscrabble labour camps in the desert, with a distant view of the skyline that they've sacrificed so much to build.'[7]

'Dubai is very peculiar.'

Ellen Allien

The receptionist at the Jumeirah Beach Hotel had some unexpected advice for me: 'Turn left outside the door and get in a golf cart.'

I had been obliged to use some unorthodox methods to get to parties over the years – calling dodgy promoters from payphones at motorway service stations for directions to illegal raves off the M25 in Britain, helping to dig a dirt track to enable sound-system trucks to get into a field at a Teknival in France, creeping delicately over potentially mined wastelands after the curfew in post-war Bosnia – but no one had ever asked me to get in a golf cart.

But of course this was Dubai, and they did things differently here. The golf cart puttered away from the hotel – a grand folly of a building designed to look like a glass wave rolling in from the Gulf – and down the winding path that traversed a semi-circular spit of land protruding into the sea, past moored yachts and private-beach sun loungers towards the pleasure palace lit up in glowing colours at the end. Along the way, a couple of Russian blondes were giggling by the side of the path as they took pictures of themselves against the backdrop of the seven-star Burj al-Arab hotel, which looked like the sail of a monstrous dhow rising out of the night like a leviathan from the surf.

The club was called 360, a reference to its panoramic views of the Dubai seafront. Up on the top-floor balcony, Finnish DJ Kiki from Ellen Allien's BPitch Control label was playing lush, liquid techno to the tiny dancefloor. A whip-thin glamour queen in a sheer silk dress pirouetted across the floor, swinging her hair as if she was screen-testing for a shampoo advertisement, as her consort, an aristocratic-looking little chap in an open-necked shirt with a string of love beads around his neck and butter-soft leather loafers, gazed adoringly upon her feminine form.

This was a tonier crowd than the technoheads who sweated it out down in the basement at Analog Room, but despite its spectacular viewing platform, 360 was by no means the most upscale club in town. The same night, Deep Dish DJ Dubfire was playing at Provocateur, which sold itself as 'the first luxury electronic music venue in the city', according to *Time Out Dubai* – a decadent fantasia of a place that looked like an oligarch's twisted vision of a cross between a Knightsbridge private members' club and a licentious duchess's boudoir.

In the downstairs bar at 360, I meet Mike Bufton, alias Mr Mister, the British promoter of tonight's Audiotonic party. Bufton started out playing on pirate radio in Slough but moved to Dubai in 2006, seeking the kind of opportunities that were unavailable in Berkshire. 'I wanted to find something different,' he says. 'I heard that Dubai was a very forward-thinking place.'

Bufton launched a radio show to 'preach the underground thing', turned Audiotonic into one of the city's best-known club nights, picked up several 'best DJ' awards from local media, and in the meantime, became something of an advocate for the charms of the city.

'I love Dubai. I love the safety. I've got two kids, schooling is amazing, safety is amazing – I can send my wife home pissed and I know she'll get home safely and I won't have to worry,' he explains. 'The government here are amazing; the ethos here is appreciate life, but if you're living in the UAE, don't fuck around. If you're going to fuck around, then you're going to get punished for it.'

Bufton insisted that Dubai got a bad press for human rights violations, and was more tolerant than it was ever given credit for – a Muslim country in the Middle East where you could party until 3am with a beer in your hand and never worry about being arrested by religious police or kidnapped by Islamic militants.

'The locals are so accommodating. It's an amazing place. The UAE is a beautiful place. To the haters, honestly: bollocks!' he says. 'If you're here in a place like the UAE, why flout the rules? You're here in a place where you can be free, you can do what you want to do.

'Intelligence here is super-strong – they know everything that's going on. Or at least I hope they do, with the whole ISIS and al-Qaeda thing – it's on our doorstep, it's so close. But the rulers of the country are on it. They're so on it, man.'

As Dubai became a popular tourist destination for the kind of people attracted by its offer of sun, sea and shopping, the club scene grew to cater for their nocturnal desires. But it was a costly business – like the Chinese promoters obsessed with their *DJ* magazine top 100 rankings, the biggest venues in the UAE wanted the biggest names on their bills, and the competition to secure the most in-demand Western DJs drove prices way up.

'Now it's known that big promoters and hotels will throw money at DJs to try to grab a slice of the market. Competition is very, very tough,' says Charl Chaka, the South African editor of Dubai nightlife magazine *Infusion*. 'When it's Dubai, the agents put an extra zero on the asking price – it's a well-known fact. And the DJs are eager to cash in; I don't blame them.'

Adam Rahman puts it more simply: 'People hear Dubai and think money.'

According to Rahman, some venues were spending up to €50,000 on headline DJs – and the flashiest of them all, the Blue Marlin Ibiza UAE, didn't even charge people to get in to its parties featuring international crowd-pleasers like Sven Väth, Dixon and Jamie Jones.

'Imagine – they are paying Sven Väth all this money and it's free to get in. It's *free!*' marvels Rahman. 'But they have people dropping silly amounts of money inside – I'm talking 40 grand for a table. We did a party with Marco Carola there and I was looking at the table plan and I was amazed – both tables nearest to the DJ booth had gone for 40 grand each. I was like, *what?* I have never heard of somebody at a techno party dropping 40 grand on a table.'

Getting into a Blue Marlin Ibiza UAE party might have been free but it wasn't necessarily easy, even for someone like Rahman, who was a well-known DJ on the scene. While Berlin clubs sought to attract free-thinkers, the Emirati venue wanted to ensure that it brought in enough free-spenders. 'You have to plan in advance,' explains Rahman. 'You get lunch booked in advance to make sure you're assured entrance because they are very, very strict on the door. It's crazy. But you get used to it and you adapt or you don't go.'

This was only one of many differences between the club cultures of Europe and the Gulf. Dubai had a reverse season – winter for outdoor parties, summer indoors to escape the withering heat, and a few weeks off for the Muslim fasting month of Ramadan. 'There is no nightlife for a month during Ramadan, but because there are so many expats here, they allow you to go to a bar after seven o'clock after the fast is broken, which I don't think is allowed in many other Muslim countries,' says Rahman. 'I think Dubai gets a bit of flak about that from the rest of the Islamic community but it can't afford to close the doors because it would drastically affect their tourism and the foreign workers they need.'

Not every international DJ who played in the city was seduced by its affluent allure. 'Dubai is very peculiar,' says Ellen Allien. 'Everything seems so fake and it stinks of money. I hardly got an impression of the culture there. I just saw these hordes of people who had moved there to make money, only to blow it all again.'

But as well as the restrictions, being stuck out in the Gulf presented novel opportunities, insisted *Infusion* editor Charl Chaka. He had recently returned from playing at a rave called Bedouin Tech, organised by veteran Burning Man party collective Disorient at a desert campsite in the wilderness about an hour's drive from the city, where fire jugglers and fluo-painted libertines danced barefoot through the night on the warm sands.

Chaka was clearly feeling the afterglow: 'There was maybe 300 people there and it was very intense. There was an open bar, art projects, yoga sessions, healing sessions – really something different,' he said. 'I was playing on Saturday morning at 11am and there were all these camels coming in around the campsite. I was looking at them and thinking, I'm in the Middle East on a campsite in the desert with camels running around me and I'm playing house music… it was amazing.'

But a crucial difference that affected the overall vibe of Dubai nightlife was the fact that the clubs were drug-free – no pills or powders to raise the collective pulse to another level.

'In Europe, if everyone's fuelled on gear on the dancefloor, it absolutely goes off. But here, you can only get to a certain peak, so the dancefloors never go off like they do in Europe. It's a totally different scenario,' one expat clubber told me. 'Here you get that last couple of hours when everyone's fucked on booze and they're all going crazy, but the rest of it is a warm-up. People come out to the club at midnight and literally at two fifty-nine, the doorman comes to tell you to turn it off. There's no "one more".'

The lack of drugs meant that the Dubai club scene could only rise so far, he argued: 'If this city had chemicals and was cooler, it would be right up there, because the clubs are state-of-the-art.'

At 360, I met a British DJ called Mark Pickup, who was also head of sales at *Hype* magazine, which was *Mixmag*'s commercial partner for the UAE. He explained to me the complexities of producing this hedonist's handbook in a Muslim country. 'We have to stick to certain rules when publishing the magazine,' he said. 'We can't have any reference to alcohol whatsoever or any photos of anyone smashed. We have a team that goes through the magazine before it's published to ensure that there's no reference that can upset any locals. Politically as well – we can't write anything political, although we wouldn't do that anyway. No drugs references whatsoever, obviously.'

The clubbers snapped in *Hype* looked suitably zany without being obviously intoxicated, and appeared to come from all over the world. As Salah Sadeq had told me: 'People talk about melting pots – Dubai is the real thing.' There were of course no pictures of Emirati men in their flowing white kandura robes or women in black abayas (in fact there was very little that gave a visual hint that the magazine was published in the Middle East), but that didn't necessarily mean that none of the locals ever went clubbing at night, said Pickup.

'I have a friend who's a police officer by day but he plays percussion in nightclubs in the night-time,' he said. 'The Emiratis don't go out in their national dress – they're not allowed to. But they do go out in their normal clothes. That's why you can't take photographs in a lot of nightclubs – Emiratis don't want to be photographed drinking at a party.'

If one of the typical questions you asked someone in Dubai was 'Where are you from?', another was 'How long will you stay?' Because this was another of the city's peculiarities: a sense of human transience to complement its ever-changing skyline. Even long-term expatriates who had made homes and careers for themselves in the UAE tended to leave eventually. But in this pervasively materialistic environment, built on the benevolent authoritarianism of its ruling dynasty and the relentless toil of its labouring underclasses, some people said that they owed the city a lot for giving them a chance to achieve things that they might never have been able to do in their homeland.

'Dubai is the land of opportunity,' argued Chaka. 'It's given me the opportunity to do something that's always been my dream. I feel blessed to have that; not everybody gets it. It's given me a standard of living that I really couldn't get anywhere else in the world doing what I want to do, and I wake up every day a happy man. I'm living the life!'

He also felt proud that he had helped to nurture this unlikely oasis of dancefloor hedonism in the Gulf – part of an audacious social experiment that rose from the arid sands and whose destiny in this turbulent corner of the world could never be certain.

'It's exciting to be a part of it. It's almost like you're writing nightlife history here – in the Middle East, where it's least expected. It's cool, it means I've done something with my life, you know, done something positive. And I'm grateful for that.'

Despite all this, Chaka said he didn't expect to stay here full-time forever. Neither did Mehdi Ansari, the Persian with the high ideals and the hard-jacking 303 on his car dashboard.

'Dubai is not me, I am not Dubai-style. I am from Tehran. I am the son of the mountains and the trees and the rivers and the vibe of the city – the real city, not a highway with some houses around it and some palm trees that they brought in,' Ansari said as the light dimmed in the courtyard of the coffee shop where we were sitting, amid the intensively tended lawns of a faux-suburban 'village' with twin facsimiles of New York's Chrysler Building gazing down incongruously in the distance.

'This is a very good environment for people to start their story, and I have enjoyed my time here,' he said. 'But definitely, I am looking forward to going somewhere I feel better.'

10

The Promised Land
New York

AND HE'S OFF DOWN THE LITTLE RUNWAY, that taut-muscled one in the white PVC shorts, back and forth across the illuminated perspex catwalk under the huge mirrorball at the centre of the room like it was fashion week in Milan and he was right in the focus of every photographer's lens. Move one: a twist and a shimmy, a feint and a pout; he throws some shade to the side, then turns back again, face all arrogant and dismissive; takes a second walk at it. Move two: hands caress the air, a coquettish arc with a hint of a maybe-smile. Then, and only then… *sha-blam!* – he throws himself to the floor in an audacious dead-drop dive, swirls round 360 degrees and then steps back up again, sashaying on and away off the catwalk as if *nothing unusual happened here*, casting an insouciant glance backwards to the onlooking crowd to remind them that he aced the move. As he exits stage left, the song keeps on asking us: 'Don't you? Don't you? Don't you? Don't you? Don't you want some more?'

At a Pride week ball in New York City, everyone's ready to flaunt what they've got. There's the man in blonde wig and leotard, thigh-high plastic boots and red suspenders, and the Rick James and Donna Summer lookalikes, and that powerfully built fellow in white lipstick and a checkerboard onesie with a huge pink-and-blue frou-frou concoction on his head, who later that night changes into a body stocking with a ruff decorated with fairy lights and accessorised by a Smiley-face handbag. The voguers are taking turns on the runway now, the dancers from the ballroom houses out to show and prove, the acrobatic spins and graceful dips and skittish little flounces getting wilder as the excitement rises. The ball commentator, our master of ceremonies for tonight, gets back on the microphone again: 'I don't care where you're from, I don't care what you do, I don't care how much your parents earn – we are all one family here!' And then he gestures to the DJ, MikeQ, and a demented cut-up of what might once have been Tyree Cooper's Chicago house stomp 'Acid Crash' hammers out of the speakers like a team of industrial panel-beaters knocking hell out of sheet metal.

Anyone who went searching for the soul of dance culture would inevitably end up in New York at some point and, despite the decades of gentrification and socio-economic cleansing that had eviscerated Manhattan club life, might still have found it here among these ballroom kids with their tough backgrounds and unconventional dreams, for whom music was life and the soundtrack of the city was always *house*.

A couple of days before the ball, I was down on one of the Brooklyn piers talking to MikeQ – Michael Cox – the charming, soft-spoken young DJ who was getting ready to churn up the mellow evening air with a firecracker set that deconstructed all kinds of musical references from New York's glorious nightlife heritage and re-energised them for his own generation's scene – the kiki scene, they called it, an offshoot of the ballroom vogueing circuit for younger dancers.

'The core of the scene is that it's about being a community, a family,' he tells me. 'The ball is where you can go and be who you want to be – it's a sanctuary for people who need somewhere they can go to be themselves, somewhere they can be creative, somewhere they can be a star.'

On the kiki scene, MikeQ was definitely a star. He first saw people vogueing at a gay club in New Jersey when he was still at high school back in 2003; this was more than a decade after the media excitement over Madonna's hit 'Vogue' and *Paris is Burning*, Jennie Livingston's glitterball-vivid, emotionally captivating documentary about the ballroom stars of the late eighties. MikeQ wasn't a dancer and he didn't walk the balls, but he did join one of the vogueing houses, those little ballroom families with their exotically aspirational names referencing the fabulous worlds of couture and high glamour, each with their own house 'mother' or 'father' to look after their flock.

He also got hold of some cheap software to fashion his own home-made mixes, snatching sounds and vocal samples from the house tracks he loved and posting the results on a scene website. 'I'd chop things up like the a cappella of [vogue star] Kevin Aviance saying "cunty!", or "Work This Pussy" by Sweet Pussy Pauline, and just try to make them my own. I would also have MCs come over to my home and record them.' Establishing his own Qween Beat stable of DIY track-makers and recording for respected underground dance labels like Fade to Mind in the US and Night Slugs in Britain, MikeQ became an exemplar of the new-school ballroom style, where the past was reimagined to create a sound that was resolutely modern.

His open-air set that evening, with the Manhattan skyline shimmering enticingly just across the river, gave an indication of what that meant: new music studded with a rich array of quotations from queer New York's clubbing history – the searing Wild Pitch riff from Joint Venture's 'Master Blaster', the hyperactive clatter of Todd Terry's drums, Tronco Traxx's ball banger 'Walk for Me' and the magnificently over-the-top drag diva Moi Renee shrieking: 'Don't you hear me calling you, Miss Honey? *Miss Honey!*'

But MikeQ's music was not just a mashed-up homage to the past, it was something fresh; all of his sources had been vigorously repurposed with a young man's venturous irreverence and raw-boned verve, cut to fast-firing jump-up beats that sometimes sounded like they owed more to hip-hop or even ragga than to disco. He has spoken about how the boisterous Jersey Club sound, with its jittery snares, scuttering breakbeats, choppy samples and automatic-fire handclaps, had an influence on the way he created his tracks. Like Jersey Club, his music was less about slick production and much more about making a truly *fierce* impact that would inspire competing dancers to ever more audacious feats of agility.

But even so, all the echoes from another era couldn't help but remind me of the words of New York writer Chi Chi Valenti which were adapted by Malcolm McLaren for his 1989 ballroom tribute *Deep in Vogue*: 'Sometimes, on a legendary night like the closing of the Garage, when the crowd is calling down the spirits – listen, and you will hear the footsteps of all the houses that walked there before.'[1]

'My personal favourite song in ballroom would be "Love is the Message", of course. There's a historical sense when you hear that song, it takes you back down this long path of all the battles and all the rivalries and all the controversies and all those moments that ballroom stands for. That song has a true symbolic essence and that's why it is still the soundtrack for the house and ballroom community because that's what we try to pass along – that love *is* the message, that even though we all hurt and we all hurt people, we still need that love.'

Chi Chi Mizrahi of the House of Mizrahi

'*Uno, dos, tres, cuatro!*' The spooling shudder of a record rewinding cues up the deathless prelusive call-out from MFSB's 'Love is the Message' – the ultimate New York gay club anthem since its original release in 1973 – and as the orchestral strings commence their sweet, low glide down over a chopped-and-pumped ballroom beat, a lithe young man in a soft leather jacket and box-fresh sneakers throws impetuous vogue shapes on a subway platform as a train rolls into the station and then a pair of youths whirl and dip and contort their bodies with the fluid energy of dolphins on one of the West Village piers. The adrenalised remix of MFSB was by MikeQ, and the voguers were dancing in the opening sequence of *Kiki*, the 2016 documentary about the new-school ballroom community directed by Swedish film-maker Sara Jordenö and co-written by scene veteran and rights activist Twiggy Pucci Garçon.

Kiki was released around two and a half decades after *Paris is Burning*, the film that had so radiantly illuminated a previous generation of ballroom icons (and in which 'Love is the Message' had also featured, in its original disco format). But although so many years had passed – years which had seen some crucial advances for lesbian and gay people in the US – many of the problems that these young dancers faced remained the same as those their predecessors had endured. Gay marriage rights had been won, but New York's black and Latino transgender teens remained marginalised, perpetually living on the edge of jeopardy. *Kiki*, a more overtly political movie than *Paris is Burning*, tried to show how they were often rejected by their parents, ostracised by their communities or schools, left homeless and poor, forced to turn to prostitution to make a living and pay for their hormones if they were transitioning or their meds if they were HIV-positive – and constantly at risk of attack by random aggressors or deranged clients.

For some of them, all they had that really meant something were the ballroom houses, the city piers where they hung out and practiced their moves, and the balls – their outlet for self-expression, the magical world of drama and play in which they could be heroes. The film showed the kiki kids' courage in the face of transphobic violence, poverty, drug addiction and sexual exploitation – their determination to not just survive, but to celebrate their lives. Theirs, says Jordenö, was 'an art form of defiance and resilience'. And unlike the political powerlessness of the cast of *Paris is Burning*, there were signs that some members of the new-school ballroom generation had the confidence to take action for change, to become advocates and campaigners for their cause. 'It's important that people see this film and know that we're strong as fuck,' one of them says at one point.[2]

One of the most striking presences in the film was Chi Chi Mizrahi (Francisco Gonzales), an effervescent character and spirited mover whose life changed when a boyfriend took him to a gay club in Harlem when he was 19 years old.

'We walk in, it's completely pitch-black, the bass is booming – it looked like a regular after-hours spot. But around 2am the lights came up and you were able to see who was inside: a lot of queer men of colour, a lot of transgender people of colour,' Mizrahi recalls. 'I had heard of balls before, but the only vogueing I knew of was Madonna, literally – I never knew it was an actual lifestyle and a culture. Just watching people walk runway and strutting up and down and arguing and yelling and being so passionate, seeing people doing all these off-the-wall dips and struts and sashays, I was just mesmerised, I was like, "How can I be a part of this?"'

Gonzales joined the House of Mizrahi and took its name as his scene surname, as ballroom kids often did. Joining the house gave him a feeling of security in a social world that he was only beginning to comprehend.

'To me, a house is family, loyalty, support,' he explains. 'Growing up as a feminine gay man with people who didn't have an understanding of different cultures and lifestyles, I was teased, I was called a faggot, I was called a homo. I knew that I was feminine but I didn't identify as gay because I didn't know what gay was. So the house helped me develop.

'A house is a chosen family, it's a family that you decide to be a part of, with an understanding of the past life that you left – meaning that if you were kicked out of home and you don't have nobody to call family, you can have that family with your gay mother and gay father.'

For Mizrahi, just like his friend MikeQ, who programmed the music for *Kiki*, the cultural history of ballroom was something to be cherished, particularly since so many of those who shaped its traditions died as a result of the virus that wiped out an entire swathe of New York City's nocturnal innovators: 'We are always paying homage to the past and to the people who are no longer with us,' Mizrahi says. 'Paying homage to our history is a must, because guess what? If we don't keep it alive, no one else will, and we will have no way of teaching it to the new people who come into the community.'

When he watched *Paris is Burning* for the first time and learned more about some of that history himself, Mizrahi was devastated by the pain that his community had suffered just so recently: 'I was fucking dumbfounded. I was like, *what the fuck?* It was a mixed message for me. It was like, "Is my life going to be like this being a gay man in this community? Is it going to be full of HIV, is it going to be full of death? Am I getting into this lifestyle that is really fucked up?" It's a hell of a great movie with great quotes and entertainment, but it also shows what it was like to be an LGBTQ person of colour 25 years ago. The fact was that in the eighties, HIV and crack were killing people in our community at an alarming rate.'

Paris is Burning captured an important moment in New York club culture, before Manhattan's nightlife was transformed by gentrification and many of its brightest personalities struck down by the virus. Even then, the documentary's main characters had few illusions about what they were up against: 'You have three strikes against you: you're black, gay and a drag queen,' one of them remarks in the film.[3]

During the shooting of *Paris is Burning*, one of the cast, Venus Xtravaganza, was murdered; in the years that followed, most of its other leading figures died too: Angie Xtravaganza, Willi Ninja, Dorian Corey, Pepper LaBeija, Avis Pendavis, Octavia St Laurent – mainly from illnesses related to AIDS. As Hector Xtravaganza said at his house mother Angie Xtravaganza's wake in 1993: 'My entire gay childhood is disintegrating before my eyes.'[4]

Jennie Livingston's film took some toxic flak from a few critics who accused the director of exploiting black gay culture and turning it into a spectacle for white audiences; the dispute even provoked a second documentary, *How Do I Look*, which tried to focus more on how the participants felt they should have been portrayed. But *Paris is Burning* also served as an inspiration for some gay teenagers who saw it as a window on another possible world. 'When *Paris is Burning* came out I was just a kid in the local choir in my church in New Orleans. I remember how much I loved everything about it: the characters, the costumes, the music,' said Big Freedia (Frederick Ross), a sexually provocative genderqueer singer from the New Orleans 'bounce' scene. 'I couldn't believe there were gay black and Latino men being portrayed like that on screen. It meant a lot to me and in many ways inspired me to do something different and follow my dream, no matter what others said.'[5]

Through the recollections of some of its older characters, the documentary also pointed the way back towards the little-known history of the balls, and to pioneers like Crystal LaBeija, whose disgust at being defeated in a drag beauty pageant in what she believed was a racist rigged vote – a moment captured in the 1968 documentary film *The Queen* – led her to set up what some believe was the first of the modern-day houses, the House of LaBeija. Drag balls had been popular in New York as far back the 'Harlem Renaissance' of the twenties, and some accounts say they were already happening in the city in the nine-teenth century. The emergence of the first houses around the turn of the seventies also coincided with the birth of the gay liberation move-ment, after drag queens stood on the frontline during the Stonewall riots in 1969.

Paris is Burning, Madonna's 'Vogue' and Malcolm McLaren's 'Deep in Vogue' video, featuring the sinuous movements of dancer Willi Ninja, helped bring this underground choreography to mainstream consciousness at the turn of the nineties, but the real ballroom scene was never just a pop fad; it was a way of life and a culture that con-tinued to evolve when the attention moved elsewhere. The style had started when dancers threw poses that emulated fashion models' pos-tures in *Vogue* magazine, but as the years progressed, a more acrobatic, physically challenging 'new way' style of walking the runway emerged with moves like the dramatic *sha-blam* drop-to-the-floor offering an alternative to the more stately, balletic moves of the *Paris is Burning* era.

The music evolved too, as the scene needed soundtracks for ball-room competition categories with increasingly outlandish names such as 'Catboy Sex Siren', 'Butch Face' or 'Soft and Cunt' as well as the more traditional 'Realness' and 'Runway'. A key figure in this progres-sion was Puerto Rico-born Vjuan Allure, who started his clubbing career sneaking in to hear DJ Junior Vasquez play at New York's Sound Factory – a favourite venue in the early nineties for voguers to stage their dance-off 'battles' – even though he was way under age.

'At that time, Junior was *it* and Sound Factory was *the club*,' Allure recalls. 'I loved the harder tracks, the tribal tracks, all the battle tracks he played, not the washed-out club remixes he started making later. I was a dancer, I loved to battle. It was like an addiction – I had to get enough money each week to go to the club, because I had to battle.'

Vasquez's pounding bitch-house tracks like 'X' and 'Get Your Hands Off My Man', or the Salsoul-sampling 'Dub Break' which he recorded as Ellis D, were compulsive incantations for the Sound Factory voguers and the banjee boys, the black and Latino men who preferred 'straight' hip-hop-style clothing. The Sound Factory was also the place where Madonna recruited Jose Gutierez Xtravaganza and Luis Camacho Xtravaganza from the House of Xtravaganza to choreograph and star in her 'Vogue' video and Blonde Ambition tour. Vasquez usually favoured a dramatic, hard-charging style, but as the night became morning, he would often return to some of the classic sounds of New York disco history, and the teenage Vjuan Allure would get bored.

'I wanted a sound that was *now*. I wanted a *hard* sound like Todd Terry, and when they played older songs, I would be like, "*When* are they going to get to the *point?*"' He stifles a mock yawn. 'And that was the whole thing when I started making tracks, I wanted to get to the *point* of the song. There are certain songs in the vogueing scene that have a special break that you really want to dance to, so I started to concentrate on making an *entire song* as hot as that for the dancers. I wanted to get to that point when everyone would be screaming, falling out, *crazy...*'

Allure's music was purpose-made for a very specific environment – rooted in, shaped by and created for a grassroots community which remained invisible to most of the outside world. It was low-tech, gritty and urgent, but also conveyed ballroom's mischievous sense of self-referential humour, as evidenced by track titles like 'Clap for the Bitch', '10,000 Screaming Faggots', 'That Butch Queen Don't Stop' or 'Kunt Darling'.

Allure admits to being influenced by rambunctious breakbeat-plus-808 style of the Baltimore sub-genre known as BMore Club, just as MikeQ credited the Jersey Club sound as an inspiration. But central to all the new-school ballroom producers' work was Masters at Work's 'The Ha Dance', a raw garage dub from 1991 with an industrial-strength cymbal-crash effect and a sample from the film *Trading Places* of Eddie Murphy and Dan Aykroyd yelling out: 'Ha!'

The 'Ha' became woven deep into the sonic DNA of the new-school ballroom sound, sampled and processed and endlessly reimagined by almost every young producer on the scene. Allure has been credited with being the first to remodel the 'Ha' in 2000; since then, he claims to have made scores if not hundreds more reinterpretations of the iconic track. MikeQ's restless staccato versions of the 'Ha' meanwhile stripped it to its propulsive elements and reassembled them into something much starker and incisively compelling.

Allure sometimes used archive movie samples of ballroom icons like Crystal LaBeija from *The Queen* or Angie Xtravaganza from *Paris is Burning*; other times he would use the voices of ball commentators like Jack Mizrahi or Dashaun Wesley. But he would also pick up phrases that he heard ordinary voguers saying at balls and turn them into hooks for his songs.

'There was this one instance at a ball where someone was being judged at one of these contests and one of the judges refused to look at someone, and so she walked up to him and just said, "Look at me, bitch!"' he recalls. 'The reaction was crazy, everyone started to laugh and this phrase swept through the ballroom scene, so of course I picked it up and made it into a track.'

Chi Chi Mizrahi had said it was necessary to preserve ballroom lore to prevent it from being lost forever; in a way, Allure was documenting some of its contemporary rituals as they happened, like some kind of informal dancefloor ethnographer. 'That's how it works,' he says. 'I just make it for the dancers, but it also captures these moments in these kids' history.'

'In a way, I think the club became a cathedral – a cathedral of freedom, music and dance; but above all, it was a cathedral of love.'

Richard Grant, owner of the Sound Factory

And then the huge black stacks of speakers at the corners of the dancefloor seemed to stretch out and rise upwards with some kind of elemental sonic force as the lights burst across the giant mirrorball like phosphorescent tracer fire. The bassline rumbled way down into the deepest root of the spinal cord – and then queerer and queerer, it seemed: the banjee boys all around me, all muscled and glistening, were pumping their bodies up against each other, sweat mingling, shorts and vests drenched with exertion as they chased the rhythm down, their bulging chests and limbs straining to sketch out the contours of the groove. And then everything went black...

With the lights out and the room at the brink of panic, an air-raid siren started to roar up out of the darkness and the shadow-clad musclemen began to clap in unison, their meaty palms slapping against each other as an electronic clave tapped out a click track: *Tik-tik-tik-tikka-tik-tik-tik-tikka-tik-tik-tik-tikka-tik-tik-tik...* The boys were rocking compulsively in anticipation, but whoever was controlling the music wrenched them back sternly, teasing their senses, cutting them back again and again to the brutal severity of the clave as the siren howled down to its last. And then the clave again – *Tik-tik-tik-tikka-tik-tik-tik-tikka-tik-tik-tik-tikka-tik-tik-tik* – and finally the suppressed energy was released, as the bass hammered out hard, hitting the consciousness like a breeze block hurled outwards from inner space, smacking the bodies around me out of shape...

'*Work!*' someone seemed to call from the edge of elsewhere. '*Work!*'

'*Gotta work!*' the voice ordered, clearer and more formidable now. '*Gotta work it to the bone, bone, bone!*'

I can't remember whether I screamed then, but I do know that almost everyone else did. '*Work it to the bone, bone, bone!*' And then the DJ – Junior Vasquez – wheeled the filthy groove back, looped it, repeated it, turned it and us inside out again and again until no one had anything left to give or anything left to feel...

The Sound Factory, on a seedy stretch of West 27th Street where prostitutes plied their trade among the dingy warehouses, was a place where magic like this could happen every weekend, back then. The club opened in 1989, around the same time as Vasquez was recording camp cut-up house tracks such as 'Just Like a Queen' under the name Ellis D. Born Donald Mattern in 1949, this son of a butcher had left his hometown of Lancaster, Pennsylvania to study fashion in New York and worked as a hairdresser before falling under the spell of Larry Levan at the Paradise Garage, and giving himself a new name.

Since it closed in September 1987, the Paradise Garage has become the most iconic nightclub in dance music's history; mythologised, idealised, lovingly eulogised for its sense of musical freedom and adventurousness. 'The Garage was a world unto itself, a utopian community cut off from the surrounding city,' journalist Frank Owen once wrote in an evocative tribute to Levan, who died in 1992.[6] It was one of the few venues to have a musical style named after it – Frankie Knuckles' Warehouse gave us house, Levan's club gave us garage – and its stature has only grown as the years have passed, as it became a kind of ideological totem for those who believe that its values should continue to be the guiding spirit of dance culture.

The Paradise Garage helped to define the nightlife of its time in the city, but the Sound Factory was to establish its own mood for the early nineties. This was 'last great room' of the old-school style in New York gay clubland, according to Frankie Knuckles, who also played there in 1990 and 1991, when he was at the height of his own powers.[7] The Factory was an attempt to carry forward the traditions of the Garage, but it nurtured a more urgent energy that was very much of its own era, largely due to the electric witchery of Vasquez, whose long mesmeric sets attracted some of the most fabulous dancers the city has seen.

And what dancers they were... one morning at the Factory at around 9am, I remember the mood shifting almost imperceptibly as if *something* was about to happen – it wasn't clear exactly what, but the music faded and the lights stopped flashing and some of the most vivacious characters started to form what looked like a guard of honour around a short stretch of the dancefloor and the stately electronic chords of Kraftwerk's 'Trans-Europe Express' began to billow up around us like clouds of cool vapour. This was the cue for the voguers to make their move, gliding down the improvised runway with regal elegance, their arms curving graceful arcs into the air. It was the first time I had seen anything like it, this majestic improvised display of choreographic flair, with the DJ picking out the free-flowing gestures of the most extravagant movers with a flashlight as they paraded through the darkness.

Vasquez's Sound Factory years also coincided with a dazzling run of creativity in American house music – the percussive euphoria and moody, off-kilter sounds of the records released by the Strictly Rhythm label, the propulsive, hallucinatory Wild Pitch mixes of DJ Pierre, the deep, rolling Miami grooves of the Murk duo, the radiant post-disco beats of Masters at Work and the titanic ballroom throwdowns unleashed by labels like Tribal and Twisted. This was music that seemed to be made specifically for the West 23rd Street warehouse – and sometimes it actually was, particularly tracks like Vasquez's mix of Lectroluv's 'Dream Drums' and Angel Moraes' transcendental epic 'Welcome to the Factory', music that was intended to inspire the most delicious sensory abandon. While the productions and remixes that Larry Levan had made for his dancers at the Paradise Garage, like the spaced-out electronic funk of the Peech Boys' 'Don't Make Me Wait', Taana Gardner's 'Heartbeat' or Gwen Guthrie's 'Seventh Heaven', were sensuously psychedelic, the tunes created for the Sound Factory were tougher, faster and charged with primal energy.

In one part of the room would be the white Chelsea lads with their shirts off to display their gym-honed chests, in another were the banjee boys, and then there were the voguers from the House of Xtravaganza (for whom Vasquez recorded his 'X') and dancers like Kevin Aviance, whose 1996 track 'Cunty' became a source of samples for scores of ballroom tunes in the decades that followed.

It became rarer in later years for one DJ to be so identified with a single club, but until the Sound Factory abruptly shut down in 1995, Vasquez – the fierce ruling diva whose booth was his kingdom – refused to play anywhere else. On the last night, he took to the floor himself at the close and danced with his people.

The Factory's demise coincided with the war on nightlife launched by New York mayor Rudy Giuliani, who came to office in 1993, preaching zero tolerance against drugs, prostitution and violent crime and vowing to clean up the murkier corners of Manhattan, like the smut shops and stag-movie cinemas around Times Square. His police commissioner Bill Bratton's 'broken windows' philosophy – sanctioning even the most petty of crimes to demonstrate that no lawbreaking would go unpunished – saw cops rousting rough sleepers and street drinkers and busting the squeegee hustlers who cleaned car windows for spare change, but also acting to curb the excesses of Manhattan nightlife. Over the years that followed, as its rougher edges were smoothed over and gentrification extended into what had been the wilder reaches of the city, Manhattan gradually got safer, cleaner and more predictable, but house music's promised land became increasingly desertified.

The Sound Factory reopened in another space, without Vasquez this time, but was shut down again in 2004 after a drug bust. Vasquez moved on to the Tunnel and then to Twilo, a new club set up in the old Factory space, but by the beginning of the new millennium, his chosen sounds had become brittle-bright instead of deep and hypnotic.

A few years later, he admitted in a confessional article in gay magazine *Next* that he had become addicted to crystal meth – so badly enslaved to the drug they called 'Tina' that he even suffered a seizure at an airport after a party. '*A fucking seizure*,' he said. 'It happened after I played a night in Austin, Texas – I bit my tongue and everything.'[8]

By the time he was playing at Twilo in the late nineties, he was 'belligerent' about his addiction, he said: 'It would be all over the DJ booth, scattered all over the records.'[9] By this time he was also taking Xanax to come down and get to sleep after marathon drug sessions. His bones started aching; he was no longer eating properly: 'Tina brings you down and beats you up... She's a nasty bitch,' he said.[10]

Whether his drug abuse was to blame or not, he would never again recapture the creative vitality of his years at the Sound Factory – and those who were there at the time would never again experience such a potent fusion of sound and human passion. His influence would live on through the new-school ballroom mixes of people like Vjuan Allure, and the club would take its place in the collective memory of the city's nightlife, but after a few brief years of ecstatic glory, his reign was over.

'The contexts from which the deep house sound emerged are forgotten: sexual and gender crises, transgendered sex work, black-market hormones, drug and alcohol addiction, loneliness, racism, HIV, ACT-UP, Tompkins Sq. Park, police brutality, queer-bashing, underpayment, unemployment, and censorship – all at 120 beats per minute.'

DJ Sprinkles, 'Midtown 120 Intro'

There are rarely any lasting memorials to commemorate the spaces that the great clubs once inhabited, where people danced, drugged, celebrated, loved, found themselves or lost their minds. Once the doors close for the last time, the spirit leaves too, and moves on to summon its magic elsewhere, as it must.

Once a year, veteran dancers would return to King Street in New York, where the Paradise Garage once was, to mark the birthday of their beloved Larry Levan and come together once more to play the old tunes and remember the good times, while the street where the Warehouse club once operated in Chicago was named Frankie Knuckles Way in 2004 after a campaign supported by an Illinois state senator called Barack Obama. But such tributes were rare indeed. Dance culture was all about the moment, and a warehouse or a basement was just a space in which that moment happened, for however long it lasted.

But as the decades passed and the internet encouraged the cataloguing and sharing of archival information, the culture began to develop a keener sense of its own history, with an increasing number of specialist websites publishing exhaustive retrospective articles and interviews that chronicled in ever more meticulous detail those peak experiences and the people who made them happen. As some of the veterans of house and techno's early years entered their forties and fifties, their sense of being part of an important cultural continuum also deepened. While such ardent retrospection could sometimes make the past seem so important that it almost overshadowed the future, it could also provide an essential context in which to understand the value of a culture that – before the late nineties anyway – was relatively little documented in photographs or videos and rarely analysed while it was being lived, because it was being lived so intensely.

The Honey Soundsystem crew – Josh Cheon, Jason Kendig, Jacob Sperber (alias Jackie House) and Robert Yang (alias Robot Hustle, alias Bézier) – coalesced in San Francisco in the mid-2000s around a shared mission to promote adventurous underground music to the Bay Area gay scene, to throw some wild parties and check out some hot men on the dancefloor, but also to celebrate and preserve some of the history of the city's sexual counterculture. 'We realised that there were so many untold stories and so much unearthed music related to San Francisco and its queer dance music history,' explains Sperber. 'There were people who wanted to tell stories about a lifestyle that had been buried by HIV and gentrification and the sands of time.'

'This whole generation of artists was wiped out by AIDS,' says Cheon. 'There was this black hole for a time until this other generation came around that wasn't so close to that mass eradication and we were able to process this sensitive history and piece it together, because in the nineties everyone was so distraught, they had watched the virus decimate their whole community.

'We didn't witness this from a first-hand point of view; I wasn't old enough in the eighties to know of people dying of AIDS, but I think that whether it's our responsibility to do this or not, it's what we feel needs to happen and it's important to us to share information about all these people who were lost.'

Journalist Andrew Ryce described one Honey Soundsystem event as 'overwhelming, sexually charged and permissive, with the almost utopian vibe you get from a really good queer party', with a libidinous cast of leathermen, drag queens, a few straight couples and lots of lusty boys getting it on.[11] But the crew also sometimes used their parties to highlight vital moments from queer history, like one event that they themed around Andrew Holleran's classic novel about gay life in seventies New York, *Dancer from the Dance*.

A crucial breakthrough came when they unexpectedly discovered a trove of neglected reel-to-reel tapes, recordings of largely unknown music by San Francisco Hi-NRG producer Patrick Cowley. Cowley was the synth adventurer and sexual hedonist who produced Sylvester's exhilarating disco classic, 'You Make Me Feel (Mighty Real)', but died of AIDS when he was just 32 years old, in 1982. There was so little knowledge about the condition back then, Cowley's doctors couldn't work out at first exactly why he was ill, and he continued to make music until he was too weak to carry on, propped up on pillows in his studio producing records like Sylvester's 'Do You Wanna Funk' and his own *Mind Warp* album in the months before his death.

'Here is someone who was a synthesizer wizard, who was onto some really psychedelic ideas and who was unapologetically talking about his homosexuality at a time when that was not necessarily going to sell records,' says Sperber. 'We loved his music and what it represented in terms of how we could bring people together over how queer people are making the culture, but then there was also the really sad story of someone who lost his life very young. To a lot of people at the time, it was one of the first instances that made them realise that something really terrible was happening.'

Sperber used to play sometimes at a bar called Daddy's in San Francisco's Castro district, where a veteran called John Hedges – 'Disco Johnny' – was also one of the DJs. Hedges, who was *Billboard* magazine's disco DJ of the year back in 1976, had taken control of Megatone Records, Cowley's old record label, after its previous owners died. Now he was getting older, Hedges had decided to move to Palm Springs to enjoy his retirement, and he invited the Bay Area's gay DJs to come to his house and take what they wanted from his huge record collection, which had been mouldering in a basement for several years.

It turned out that as well as the old vinyl that he had stored down there was a series of tapes marked with the name 'Patrick Cowley'. 'We saw these two boxes of dusty reel-to-reels, not knowing what was on them,' Cheon recalls. 'We asked him what he was going to do with them, and he said, "Oh, I'm going to throw those away." So we asked if he knew what was on them and he said no. We said, "We'll take *everything*."

'The titles were so crazy – one was called "Catholic" and one was called "Good Clean Fun". It was in Patrick's handwriting and the songs had these really weird names. We took them over to a studio and had them transferred and then we heard this music and we were like, *"What is this?"'*

Some of the recordings were electronic soundtracks that Cowley had produced for porn films and the music ranged from spaced-out sound experiments to proto-techno tunes, cosmic drugginess and throbbing analogue funk. *Catholic, School Daze* and *Muscle Up* were eventually released by Cheon's Dark Entries label, which specialised in reissuing obscure eighties avant-garde electro-pop and almost-forgotten industrial dance music, one of an increasing number of outlets that were dedicated to excavating dance culture's half-forgotten history and giving new life to music that had seemingly been lost in time.

Until then, the glorious cheesiness of most Hi-NRG meant that a lot of it had never appeared likely to enjoy a major revival moment. But in the mid-2010s, DJs like The Black Madonna started airing some of the old tracks for techno dancefloors, while a bizarre Hi-NRG retro cult managed to survive at Mexico City's Patrick Miller club. Named after Mexican DJ Roberto Devesa, who worked under the alias Patrick Miller, the club was where his flamboyantly attired devotees known as the 'Patricios' showed off their moves in the centre of breakdance-style circles of onlookers to vintage tunes produced by the likes of Patrick Cowley and Bobby O.

But Honey Soundsystem's Patrick Cowley project was about more than just the music itself; it was also about adding another piece to a patchwork of cultural remembrance, memorialising the San Francisco gay scene of the pre-AIDS era – the years in which Harvey Milk became the first openly homosexual public official to be elected in the United States, and the years in which riots broke out when furious crowds marched on City Hall from the Castro district after Milk was shot dead in 1978. 'Rights are won only by those who make their voices heard,' Milk once said. 'Out of the bars and into the streets!' the demonstrators chanted.

'Living in San Francisco, which was the birthplace of so many amazing gay achievements, and hearing all the stories about the riots and the uprisings and what Harvey Milk did, the history is so strong here,' says Cheon. 'We loved everything about that history and we wanted to share that with the people coming to our parties, and I also think Patrick was a gateway into a deeper part of the musical history at a very important time when things were shifting away from disco into more proto-techno electronic vibes.'

It was also a way of paying tribute to all the lives that had ended too soon. In 1982, several hundred people died as a result of AIDS in the US; among them was Patrick Cowley. But the death toll kept on rising each year until it peaked at nearly 50,000 in 1995. By the early 2000s, over half a million Americans had died, leaving a fearsome landscape of grief and desperation.

'The saddest part of discovering Patrick Cowley's music was realising that people were holding onto things because that was what they had left,' recalls Sperber. 'People were keeping collections of that [Hi-NRG] stuff because it was connected with memories of the people who had died – and died instantaneously, too. Your friend is just *gone*. You were going to the club last week, doing acid, having the time of your life at the peak of your youth, and the next week he's dead.

'I grew up Jewish, my mom worked at the temple, and I grew up learning about a lot of ideas around the Holocaust – like the work that is important to do when something of that magnitude happens to a community, and how to remember, and why it's important to remember.'

'There are still these special places in the world, these free places where you can express your sexuality, places where it is still about that unity through music, and places where you are free to be queer, whatever the fuck that means to you.'

Honey Dijon

The night before the annual Pride parade, we're down on the dance-floor at a party called Wrecked at The Bunker in Brooklyn, the borough that had become the new bohemian centre of New York nightlife, which had continued to flourish as much as the law would allow after two decades of gentrification had swept away so many of Manhattan's grand old spaces and scummy after-hours dives. In Brooklyn, techno parties could still run deep into the daylight in old warehouses and other repurposed spaces along the urban canals and in murky industrial zones. All around us, boys are embracing boys, girls are kissing girls, freaky dancers of all races and genders are jacking their bodies hard and a DJ called Matrixxman is rinsing out industrial-strength techno, casting us down into a cavernous tunnel of dubwise reverberations before leading us back up into the light again.

Wrecked was one of the clubs – alongside places like Men's Room in Chicago, Honcho in Pittsburgh, Macho City in Detroit, Spotlight in LA and the parties staged by Honey Soundsystem – that formed part of an emerging alternative queer dance network in the mid-2010s which journalist Andrew Ryce described as 'America's gay techno underground'.[12] It was the queers taking back control over the culture they played a vital role in creating, or so the stories went, and as close to the radical sleaze of Berlin as it could get in the relatively conservative United States.

It was also a counterblast against the 'circuit party' scene – corporate-sponsored mega-events for gay men held all across the US and beyond, promoted by adverts featuring shaved and oiled gym bunnies, where the favoured soundtrack was bright and brash hands-in-the-air house topped with poppy diva vocals; mainstream dance music with a certain methamphetamine drive to its clattering 'pots and pans' beat. 'Circuit music', they called it.

'Our scene was a kind of reaction to the circuit,' says Ryan Smith, who ran Wrecked with his DJ partner Ron Like Hell (Ron Herrera). 'Like a lot of people, we felt there was a void – a lack of gay events with good music. There were techno parties that gay people went to for the music, but gay men weren't the majority. We wanted to bring back that role of gays being more innovative and get away from this rut that gay dance music had been in for probably ten or 15 years.'

This network of like minds was nurtured by an ironically named

Facebook group called Gays Hate Techno, explains Smith: 'We definitely support each other in many senses. From the beginning, it's been like a very strong community. We're trying to build it up from nothing, for all intents and purposes, so we really realise the value of helping each other and promoting each other.'

The DJs who found their natural place on this anti-circuit circuit were mavericks and iconoclasts like Carlos Souffront from Detroit, who says he tries to play techno 'from a postpunk perspective' – an attitude that might have been incomprehensible to the buff circuit boys with their shiny remixes of R&B divas. Souffront, who was also on the bill that night at Wrecked in Brooklyn, had always wanted to go to the kind of club where the soundtrack was intrepid but the vibe was distinctly *queer*.

'The queer parties are the most transgressive parties, the most daring parties,' he says. 'I think that AIDS killed off an entire generation but now it's a time of renewal, it's the first time when I've felt like there's a global simultaneous resurgence of queer dance culture, by and for gay people.

'For me, it was always a dream to be able to cruise *and* listen to good music, because you go to a gay bar and it's just the worst in terms of music. But now it's actually happening *everywhere*. I don't want to make it a queers-only club because I'm all about radical inclusion, but it's the queer people who are throwing the best parties, certainly in the US right now.'

But for the deep house producer and queer artist Terre Thaemlitz, who made records under the alias DJ Sprinkles and described herself as a feminist Marxist, gay clubs were more important as places of sanctuary than they were as forums for celebration. Before the Giuliani crackdown in New York in the mid-nineties and the Disneyfied makeover of Times Square, Thaemlitz used to play at Sally's II, a downmarket joint for transsexual prostitutes and their suitors on West 43rd Street, where Dorian Corey and Angie Xtravaganza from *Paris is Burning* used to perform drag routines. Thaemlitz doesn't believe in the house nation clichés of unity and togetherness, peace and tolerance. This, she has said, is just 'greeting-card bullshit'. She favours a harsher truth – that unstoried clubs like Sally's II were, and continue to be in less tolerant parts of the world, some kind of safe houses, refuges from crisis and fear.

'For me, the "party" itself is one of the least interesting aspects of what happens in a club,' Thaemlitz says. 'The clubs that I think are important are the clubs that have lives extending beyond the events. Like the old Sally's – it wasn't a pleasant place to be, but it was one of the few places where certain types of people *could be*. It was a shelter of sorts for impoverished transgendered people who had often been abandoned or disowned by their biological families, etc. And I think that sort of vital and real functionality is very different from the transcendental promises of pleasure-based dogma. The reality is that there is a necessity for certain spaces for ostracised people.'

But if such spaces could offer the outcasts a chance of asylum, others really did believe that they could make their dreams of liberation come true. When the young Honey Dijon (Honey Redmond) discovered DJs like Ron Hardy and Frankie Knuckles as a gay teenager in Chicago in the eighties, she felt that she had somehow found a better place in life.

'It was like going into another world and another reality that you didn't realise was possible,' Dijon recalls. 'It was literally otherworldly for me. It was a mixture of people and cultures and sexualities that I never experienced before – seeing all these colourful characters all joining together and celebrating their music. It was also exciting because it was the beginning of a cultural movement, so there was so much electricity in the air. There was a sense of connection, camaraderie, sexuality, expression...

'You have to also understand that this music came out of cultures that were oppressed, so it was amazing because it was this space that people could go and be themselves. House is basically the bastard of disco and it was always a black and Latin art form, the music of people of colour, of queer people.'

As well as dancing to house, the Chicago teenager also frequented the influential postpunk/industrial store Wax Trax, whose label released darkside electronic body music and transgressive rock records by bands like Front 242, Ministry, Front Line Assembly, Laibach and the Revolting Cocks. 'Chicago is a segregated city but if you knew the right people, you went to the industrial clubs, you went to the gay clubs, you went to the new wave clubs. Since I never fitted in with any one group, I did all of it,' she says. 'I had friends who were totally into The Cure and Depeche Mode or Nitzer Ebb and Front 242, and friends who were into house music and disco – and all that stuff informs everything today.'

She met her early mentors in record shops – Chicago scene heroes like DJ Derrick Carter and Jesse Saunders, who made the first proto-house track, 'On and On', with Vince Lawrence back in 1984 – and the music offered her an introduction to a world in which an outsider could maybe thrive. For straight youths, dance culture has meaning as a way to release tensions, as a rite of passage, as a musical inspiration, as an alternative to the everyday; for those who aren't straight, it can also offer the possibility of defining your own identity on your own terms and finding the strength to survive in an unforgiving society.

'When I look back at my life, I was lucky, because everything that I was told was wrong about me – at that time I was a black, gay, effeminate person, before I transitioned – it was all a blessing instead of a curse, because I ended up in this world. I was in the right place at the right time,' Dijon says.

But like Terre Thaemlitz, she also cautions that house music's formative years were times of struggle and loss as well as joy and new beginnings: 'Everyone romanticises the past, but the eighties was when the AIDS plague started and so you've got to remember all of this music was happening at the same time as people were dying or being oppressed.'

She moved to New York in the nineties and found another mentor in Danny Tenaglia, whose declamatory tribalistic sets entranced the room at Twilo, the venue on West 27th Street which had once housed the Sound Factory. And eventually Honey Dijon become the most beloved transgender DJ on the global underground, playing everywhere from Berlin's Panoramabar to Chicago's Smart Bar, with an impeccable sense of style that also led to her soundtracking catwalk shows and fashion events for companies like Louis Vuitton and Givenchy.

What made her different also made her special, and what made her special helped to make her successful in this subculture that was willing to accept her as the person she was, she believes: 'I think being a trans person, having been on both sides of the gender spectrum, and being different and not conforming and being queer – all of these things really have given me an advantage because I've seen it from all the angles,' she says.

'My transness definitely informs what I do because it's allowed me to walk in so many worlds. If I was just a regular heteronormative girl, I would not have been able to go to those types of clubs, those queer places where we went to hear that amazing music. And I feel like I carry the DNA of that culture with me. It's awesome, you know.'

'I think music is really, really serious, because it's so personal.'
Frankie Knuckles

A rainbow beach ball bounces high above the heads of the marchers on Fifth Avenue, and for a few moments the plastic globe seems to hang in the air, almost weightless, as if it might stay up there forever – until the dramatic thunderclap drum intro from Funky Green Dogs' nineties classic 'Fired Up' booms out from a sound system and reverberates back off the façades of the surrounding buildings, commanding us to step forward.

There is music everywhere this afternoon, blasting from the Pride march floats – funky house, bumping garage, reggaeton grooves, diva pop, symbolic old favourites like Diana Ross singing 'I'm Coming Out', and swirling disco from a truck carrying an elderly Stonewall veteran who is all dolled up in a white tuxedo, a bow tie and a bejewelled crown, gazing down regally from his rostrum like the emperor of some fantasy republic.

It's June 2016, a fortnight after the massacre of 49 clubbers at a gay disco called Pulse in Orlando, and the mood is one of steadfast defiance. Almost two million people have taken to the streets of Manhattan today, the news agencies are reporting – one of the biggest Pride events anywhere, at any time – and the marchers are all determined to show their colours in all their extravagant splendour, to demonstrate that the values of decency and tolerance can prevail and malignant prejudice must never triumph. There are imperious ladies in carnival headdresses, muscle boys in cowboy chaps with glitter-sprayed buttocks, drag queens in vertiginous PVC boots, bare-breasted burlesque girls in gold lamé, a phalanx of costume-shop gladiators and a platoon of anarchists holding up a banner that warns: 'Queers bash the fuck back.' And then there are elderly gay couples tenderly holding each other's hands and smiling as they survey the thronging masses, and gaggles of excited teenagers on the street corners as the floats cruise by, rainbow flags painted on their smooth young cheeks, snapping pics on their smartphones and chattering like scamps, delighted to be part of this moment for the first time in their lives.

On a side-street off Fifth Avenue, some of the kiki kids have gathered on a sound-system truck run by the Hetrick-Martin Institute, an organisation that was providing support services for vulnerable lesbian, gay, bisexual and transgender youths. At the controls is MikeQ, in denim shorts and a black vest, raising a sonic storm of stuttering riffs and chants, metallic crashes and tyre squeals, bass booms and siren calls. As the float gets ready to pull away and join the parade heading downtown, he cranks up an urgent hotstepping groove and an MC yells out: '*Work it, work it, work it, work it!*'

A couple of hours later, the kiki float finally slides into Christopher Street and motors onwards towards the Stonewall Inn, a site that President Barack Obama had just designated the first US national monument to lesbian, gay, bisexual and transgender rights. In the window of the tavern where the Stonewall uprising began in June 1969 are pictures of the people who died in the nightclub shooting in Orlando, and a placard that urges: 'STOP THE HATE.' As the truck rounds the corner, MikeQ fires into a fierce 'Ha' track while one of the kiki boys vogues deliriously and an MC hypes the rainbow flag-waving crowds by the roadside with a barrage of ballroom glossolalia – and then the siren wails out again, calling down the spirits one more time.

If anyone wanted to know whether dance culture still really *meant something* in the turbo-capitalist EDM era – well, for these ballroom girls and boys at least, it really did.

And they were not alone, it seemed; for others too, this was still a culture with the potential to create beauty and transform lives, to open up free spaces where outcasts were welcomed and mavericks could be heroes – an environment in which the progressive values of tolerance and open-mindedness could be the guiding force. As Honey Dijon put it: 'For me, it's not just about music – it's culture, it's art, it's sex, it's love, it's release, it's freedom.'

Others had spoken in similarly utopian terms: MikeQ described how New York's ballroom houses could provide 'a sanctuary for people who need somewhere they can go to be themselves'; Culoe de Song talked about South African house culture being a kind of alternative society for 'people who want to express their freedom'; Carlos Souffront recalled how thrilled he was to discover 'a collective of all sorts of misfits' in Detroit that would embrace an outsider like him; while French sound-system activist Florentin Arnaud eulogised the itinerant European rave tribes who believed in 'openness of spirit, helping each other, the pleasure of sharing'.

Of course for most people, nightclubs were places to party, to dance to some great tunes, get wasted, get off with someone, have the best night of your life – and this had genuine value too, undoubtedly. Celebration was its own reward. The idealised visions of an emancipated promised land – this lovingly mythologised 'underground' – were not shared by everyone. There were more than enough hedonists who felt no need to seek any deeper sociopolitical significance in their weekend lunacies.

Because while electronic dance music culture had, in some places at least, managed to uphold its bohemian spirit, it had simultaneously become an increasingly standardised entertainment format all over the world. Its nocturnal economy sustained countless DJs, producers and promoters, enabling many remarkable and talented people to earn a living from the music they loved, and yet it was also the foundation for a global marketplace in which entertainment corporations, telecommunications firms, fashion brands and beverage companies competed for influence and bounty.

As it continued to grow around the world, it had managed to survive a series of official interventions intended to quell its wilder excesses, from the anti-rave legislation in the US to the French attempts to stamp out free parties. But increasingly, in the world's wealthier cities at least, it had also begun to feel the pressure of urban gentrification.

When clubs were threatened with closure so the neighbourhood around them could be domesticated, it was often argued by those who tried to resist these shutdowns that nightlife acted as a unique kind of laboratory for artistic innovation. Indeed, clubland had helped to nurture a remarkable variety of new musical forms over the decades, from hip-hop, electro, house and techno to drum and bass, trance, dubstep and grime, as well as their innumerable subgenres. This became even more evident as the culture took on different meanings and assumed new significance in some of the places across the world in which it had made its home, throwing up an abundance of localised mutations, from the convulsive reverberations of Durban gqom to the fierce brightness of the new-school ballroom sound of New York. All nightclubs eventually close their doors, in the end, but the music will be the culture's enduring testament.

By the early decades of the twenty-first century, the greying veterans of electronic dance music were revered as intrepid explorers and the fallen heroes mourned as icons of a glorious movement. But the culture was still being reinterpreted and reinvigorated by newcomers who sometimes paid their humble respects to their illustrious predecessors but inevitably had keener eyes on their own destinies, taking what they needed from this magnificent history and all those who walked those dancefloors before them, and using it to create something that resonated with their own generation.

The past would always be there for all of us, but the future would be theirs, to make of it what they could.

By late afternoon that day in New York, as the parade reached its end, the sound-system floats had begun to play their final songs, one last tune after another. One of the trucks was blasting out a looped diva's wail, repeating over and over again: '*I believe... I believe... I believe... I believe...*'

Down on the pavement, amidst the clamour of the beats and the cheers and the whistles and the laughter, the girls and boys were hugging each other and exchanging kisses, offering farewells and swapping phone numbers and promising to see each other later, as they started to make plans for the night ahead.

Acknowledgements

Special thanks to my dear friends Monika Lajhner and Slobodan Brkić for convincing me that it was possible to attempt the impossible.

Thanks for support, assistance, contacts, good advice, helpful commissions and generous hospitality in many places around the world during the research for this book are due to Zohar Abiri, Dragan Ambrozić, Mehdi Ansari, Florentin Arnaud, Adi Avikzer, Vanya Balogh, Trenton Birch, Kim Booth, Rajko Božić, Nathan Budzinski, Andrew Bull, Todd Burns, Tomma Chaladze, John Collins, Michael Cox, Max Daly, Jon Dasilva, Duncan Dick, Robin Forestier-Walker, Tomislav Grujić, Michael Hann, Sven Harding, Cornelius Harris, June Joseph, Kim Kadish, Hari Kunzru, Alexander Kvatashidze, Jürgen Laarman, Johnny Lee, Caspar Llewellyn-Smith, Carl Loben, Vladimir Lozinski, Billie Ray Martin, Derrick May, Gareth McConnell, Shadi Megallaa, Liz Miller, Nthato Mokgata, Mark Moore, Mariam Murusidze, Magda Nowakowska, Gordan Paunović, Aaron Peters, Felix Petty, David Piccioni, Mike Power, Tobias Rapp, Samuel Raymond, Dave Rimmer, Paul Rimple, Salah Sadeq, Rita Sayegh, Margarita Semenova, Susanne Simon-Paunović, Pamela Smith, Sevi Spanoudi, Marie Staggat, Jonas Stone, Terre Thaemlitz, Andy Thomas, Sven von Thülen, Wolfgang Tillmans, Tijana Todorović, Sasha Toykinen, Ben Turner, Ilia Voronin and Cameron Wilson.

To Keith Robinson – rest in peace my friend.

Much gratitude is due to Bill Brewster, Elinor Carmi, Heiko Hoffmann and Heather Mennell for kindly reading drafts of the manuscript and offering their expert opinions, and to Milica Mančić for invaluable help with translations.

Thanks also to Hannah Westland at Serpent's Tail for initiating this whole project and Matthew Hamilton at Aitken Alexander Associates for vital encouragement and support, as well as to Nick Sheerin for editorial guidance and Patrick Taylor and Neil Burkey for their work on the manuscript.

Finally, love to Alex Collin, to my brothers Richard and Will, and to all the members of the extended Collin clan.

Photography credits

Selected bibliography

Luke Bainbridge, *Acid House: The True Story* (Omnibus Press, London, 2014)

Bill Brewster and Frank Broughton, *Last Night a DJ Saved My Life* (Headline, London, 2000)

Mel Cheren, *Keep on Dancin'* (24 Hours for Life, New York, 2000)

Matthew Collin, with contributions by John Godfrey, *Altered State* (Serpent's Tail, London, 1997)

Felix Denk and Sven von Thülen, *Der Klang der Familie* (Books on Demand, Norderstedt, 2014)

Alice Echols, *Hot Stuff* (W. W. Norton & Company, New York, 2010)

Sheryl Garratt, *Adventures in Wonderland* (Headline, London, 1998)

Dave Haslam, *Adventures on the Wheels of Steel* (Fourth Estate, London, 2010)

Tim Lawrence, *Life and Death on the New York Dance Floor, 1980–1983* (Duke University Press, Durham, 2016) and *Love Saves the Day* (Duke University Press, Durham, 2004)

Michaelangelo Matos, *The Underground is Massive* (Dey Street Books, New York, 2015)

Frank Owen, *Clubland Confidential* (Ebury Publishing, London, 2003)

Dom Phillips, *Superstar DJs Here We Go!* (Ebury Publishing, London, 2009)

Tobias Rapp, *Lost and Sound* (Innervisions, Berlin, 2009)

Simon Reynolds, *Energy Flash* (Faber & Faber, London, 1998)

Tom Rom and Pascal Querner, *Goa: 20 Years of Psychedelic Trance* (Nachtschatten Verlag, Solothurn, 2011)

Peter Shapiro, *Turn the Beat Around* (Faber & Faber, London, 2009)

Dan Sicko, *Techno Rebels* (Billboard Books, New York, 1999)

Mireille Silcott, *Rave America* (ECW Press, Toronto, 1999)

Graham St John, *Global Tribe* (Equinox Publishing, Sheffield, 2012)

There are also more in-depth accounts of the Berlin Love Parade, the Teknival scene and Europe's illegal sound-system raves in my book *Pop Grenade* (Zero Books, Winchester, 2015).

Notes

All the interviews in this book were conducted by the author between 1988 and 2017, except where indicated. Some passages in the text were developed from reports written by the author for the *Guardian*, *i-D* and the *Daily Note*.

Introduction
1. *Chicago Reader*, 22 April 2014
2. *Chicago Reader*, ibid.
3. FACT, 3 September 2014
4. *Shoom Club: An Insight*, April 1988
5. *Daily Express*, 27 June 1989
6. *Daily Mirror*, 29 June 1989
7. *The Sun*, 26 June 1989
8. The National Archives (UK), 30 December 2016
9. Matthew Collin, with contributions by John Godfrey, *Altered State*, Serpent's Tail, London, 1997
10. *Resident Advisor*, 9 October 2013

Chapter One
1. *i-D*, March 1992
2. *i-D*, ibid.
3. Red Bull Music Academy website, 24 May 2016
4. *Record Mirror*, 25 June 1988
5. *Spin*, October 1998
6. *Rolling Stone*, 26 August 2015
7. Dan Sicko, *Techno Rebels*, Billboard Books, New York, 1999
8. Bill Brewster and Frank Broughton, *Last Night a DJ Saved My Life*, Headline, London, 2000

9. Alvin Toffler, *The Third Wave*, William Morrow, New York, 1980

10. *Record Mirror*, ibid.

11. *Record Mirror*, ibid.

12. *Billboard*, 14 December 2015

13. *i-D*, ibid.

14. Felix Denk and Sven von Thülen, *Der Klang der Familie*, Books on Demand, Norderstedt, 2014

15. 313 mailing list, 4 February 1997, archived on Hyperreal.org

16. Charlie LeDuff, *Detroit: An American Autopsy*, Penguin Books, New York, 2013

17. *The Face*, May 1988

18. Mark Binelli, *The Last Days of Detroit*, Bodley Head, London, 2013

19. *The Last Days of Detroit*, ibid.

20. *Magnetic Magazine*, 7 August 2015

21. Red Bull Music Academy website, 2010

22. *The Verge*, 2 June 2016

Chapter Two

1. Westbam website

2. Matthew Collin, *Pop Grenade*, Zero Books, Winchester, 2015

3. *We Call it Techno!*, directors: Maren Sextro, Holger Wick, 2008

4. *NME*, 25 November 1989

5. *Pop Grenade*, ibid.

6. *Pop Grenade*, ibid.

7. Felix Denk and Sven von Thülen, *Der Klang der Familie*, Books on Demand, Norderstedt, 2014

8. Matthew Collin, with contributions by John Godfrey, *Altered State*, Serpent's Tail, London, 1997

9. *Der Klang der Familie*, ibid.

10. *Pop Grenade*, ibid.

11. *Pop Grenade*, ibid.

12. *Pop Grenade*, ibid.

13. *Pop Grenade*, ibid.

14. *Observer*, 18 July 2001

15. *Pop Grenade*, ibid.

16. *Pop Grenade*, ibid.

17. *Der Spiegel*, 2 August 2010

18. *Guardian*, 25 July 2010

19. Tobias Rapp, *Lost and Sound*, Innervisions, Berlin, 2009

20. High-Frequencies website, 10 June 2006

21. *Discopia*, 1 October 2004

22. *GQ*, 25 July 2015

23. Lonely Planet website

24. XLR8R, 28 May 2014

25. *Resident Advisor*, 10 March 2009

26. Deutsche Welle, 30 August 2005

27. Reuters, 9 November 2014

28. Facebook, 10 November 2014

Chapter Three

1. Paul Richardson, *Not Part of the Package*, Macmillan, London, 1993

2. Damien Enright, *Dope in the Age of Innocence*, Liberties Press, Dublin, 2011

3. International Music Summit Ibiza, 25 May 2011

4. *Image et Son*, 1969, quoted in Stephen Armstrong, *The White Island*, Transworld, London, 2004

5. Richard Neville, *Hippie Hippie Shake*, Duckworth Overlook, London, 2009

6. International Music Summit Ibiza, ibid.

7. Grace Jones, *I'll Never Write My Memoirs*, Simon & Schuster, London, 2015

8. *Daily Mail*, 16 August 2004

9. *Pacha: An Oral History*, DJ History website, 2008

10. *Pacha: An Oral History*, ibid.

11. *Pacha: An Oral History*, ibid.

12. Matthew Collin, with contributions by John Godfrey, *Altered State*, Serpent's Tail, London, 1997

13. *Altered State*, ibid.

14. Test Pressing, 20 February 2013

15. *Britain's Balearic Soul*, BBC Radio 4, 27 August 2011

16. *Altered State*, ibid.

17. *Boy's Own*, Issue 5, Spring 1988

18. *Altered State*, ibid.

19. *i-D*, June 1988

20. Dom Phillips, *Superstar DJs Here We Go!*, Ebury Press, London, 2009

21. *Daily Mail*, 1 August 1998

22. *Memory Motel* by Kris Needs, unknown publication / date

23. *Guardian*, 9 July 2000

24. *Loaded*, October 2012

25. International Music Summit Ibiza, 24 May 2013

26. International Music Summit Ibiza, ibid.

27. International Music Summit Ibiza, ibid.

28. Pulse Radio website, 14 July 2015

29. *Ibiza Style*, 12 September 2015

30. *A Short Film About Chilling*, director: Angus Cameron, Channel 4, 1990

31. *Altered State*, ibid.

32. Facebook, 16 July 2015

33. *Superstar DJs Here We Go!*, ibid.

34. High-Frequencies website, 10 June 2006

35. Bridges for Music seminar, Cape Town, 6 February 2015

36. *i-D*, ibid.

37. *Vice*, 25 September 2014

38. *Vice*, 10 July 2015

39. *Pitchfork*, 25 August 2015

40. *In Search of Balearic*, DJ History website, 2008

41. *Thump*, 13 November 2015

42. EDMTunes website, 17 July 2015

43. EDMTunes website, ibid.

44. *The New York Times*, 7 December 2014

45. *Daily Record*, 23 August 2015

46. *Billboard*, 26 July 2016

47. Cocoon website, 10 August 2012

48. AFP, 6 April 2016

49. *Mixmag*, June 2015

50. *IU*, Issue 6, 2015

51. *Guardian*, 7 August 2014

52. International Music Summit Los Angeles, 16 April 2014

53. International Music Summit Ibiza, 25 May 2011

54. Facebook, 14 July 2015

55. Facebook, 30 September 2014

56. Facebook, ibid.

57. *Ibiza Times* website, 21 September 2006

58. BBC News, 5 October 2016

Chapter Four

1. *Under the Electric Sky*, directors: Dan Cutforth, Jane Lipsitz, 2014

2. *Las Vegas Weekly*, 19 June 2014

3. *Las Vegas Weekly*, ibid.

4. Michaelangelo Matos, *The Underground is Massive*, Dey Street Books, New York, 2015

5. *Mixmag*, July 1997

6. *The New York Times*, 6 July 1997

7. *Washington Post*, 29 March 1998

8. *Washington Post*, ibid.

9. The American Presidency Project website
10. *Guardian*, 17 April 2014
11. *Pitchfork*, 28 March 2012
12. *Mixmag*, 6 March 2014
13. Deadmau5 website, 14 December 2015
14. *Mixmag*, 29 June 2015
15. FMS, 12 June 2015
16. Tim Dressen, *The Outsider's Guide to Las Vegas*, Otington Press, Roseville, 2015
17. EDMBiz panel, Las Vegas, 16 June 2016
18. *Las Vegas Weekly*, 13 December 2012
19. *The Daily Beast*, 26 July 2015
20. *New Yorker*, 30 September 2013
21. *The Daily Beast*, 8 August 2014
22. *Thump*, 20 May 2014
23. *The Daily Beast*, ibid.
24. *Thump*, 11 December 2015
25. *Magnetic Magazine*, 29 April 2016
26. *Pitchfork*, ibid.
27. *The Underground is Massive*, ibid.
28. *Mixmag*, August 1997
29. Deadmau5 website, June 2012
30. *Vibe*, February / March 2013
31. *Mixmag*, 22 November 2012
32. *GQ*, 29 March 2013
33. EDMBiz panel, Las Vegas, 16 June 2016
34. *The Verge*, 1 July 2014
35. *The Verge*, ibid.
36. *New York Post*, 30 August 2014

Chapter Five

1. *Future Sound of Mzansi*, directors: Nthato Mokgata, Lebo Rasethaba, 2014
2. *Future Sound of Mzansi*, ibid.
3. MTV Iggy website, 11 October 2011
4. Alec Russell, *After Mandela*, Windmill Books, London, 2010
5. Cape Town Electronic Music Festival lecture, 4 February 2015
6. *Thump*, 20 September 2013
7. Cape Town Electronic Music Festival panel, 4 February 2015
8. Under the Label, Issue One, 2015
9. Gavin Steingo, *Kwaito's Promise: Music and the Aesthetics of Freedom in South Africa*, University of Chicago Press, Chicago, 2016

10. *Guardian*, 24 August 2016

11. *Boiler Room x G-Star RAW: Johannesburg*, director: Chris Kets, 2015

12. *Woza Taxi: Secret Stash Out of the Locations*, director: Tommaso Cassinis, 2016

13. *Mail and Guardian*, 4 July 2014

14. *Mail and Guardian*, ibid.

15. *Woza Taxi: Secret Stash Out of the Locations*, ibid.

16. African National Congress website

17. *Mahala*, 7 July 2015

18. Bridges for Music panel, Sonar Festival, Barcelona, 14 June 2013

19. *After Mandela*, ibid.

20. *Guardian*, 8 June 2009

Interlude

1. *Resident Advisor*, 28 August 2012

2. Facebook, 15 May 2014

3. AllCrimea website, 31 July 2014

4. Interview for Al Jazeera English by Robin Forestier-Walker, August 2014

5. Democracy & Freedom Watch, 16 September 2014

6. *Argumenti i Fakti*, 4 March 2016

7. 1News, 18 July 2016

Chapter Six

1. *Le Monde*, 29 April 2016

2. *La Nouvelle Republique*, 2 May 2016

3. Facebook, 25 February 2016

4. Hakim Bey, *T.A.Z.: The Temporary Autonomous Zone, Ontological Anarchy, Poetic Terrorism*, Autonomedia, New York, 1991

5. Steve Beard, *Aftershocks: The End of Style Culture*, Wallflower Press, London, 2002

6. *Ex-TAZ*, director: Xanaé Bove, 2015

7. Communiqué de Presse, Manifestives Nationales des Collectifs Techno, Facebook, 17 January 2017

8. *Le Monde*, 2 May 2011

9. AFP, 16 August 2016

Chapter Seven

1. Goa Hippy Tribe page, Facebook, 15 March 2010

2. Bleep43 website, 14 April 2010

3. Erik Davis, *Hedonic Tantra of Goa*, in *Rave Culture and Religion*, ed. Graham St John, Routledge, New York, 2004

4. Tom Rom and Pascal Querner, *Goa: 20 Years of Psychedelic Trance*, Nachtschatten Verlag, Solothurn, 2011
5. *Option*, March–April 1995
6. *Revolve*, 2005
7. *Option*, ibid.
8. *Goa: 20 Years of Psychedelic Trance*, ibid.
9. Isratrance website, 2009
10. *Catalyst*, 30 November 2011
11. *i-D*, August 1992
12. Trip website, 2 December 2003
13. *Hedonic Tantra of Goa*, ibid.
14. Graham St John, *Global Tribe*, Equinox Publishing, Sheffield, 2012
15. *Goa: 20 Years of Psychedelic Trance*, ibid.
16. Robin Sylvan, *Trance Formation*, Routledge, New York, 2005
17. *Revival*, 24 June 2015
18. Red Bull Music Academy website, 25 August 2015
19. *Goa: 20 Years of Psychedelic Trance*, ibid.
20. *Trancentral*, 2 March 2016
21. *Psychedelic Zion*, director: Isri Halpern, 2000
22. *Ha'ir*, 5 June 1998
23. *Psychedelic Zion*, ibid.
24. *Psychedelic Zion*, ibid.
25. *Mushroom Magazine*, February 2003
26. *Mushroom Magazine*, ibid.
27. *Flipping Out: Israel's Drug Generation*, director: Yoav Shamir, BBC, 30 September 2007

Chapter Eight
1. J.G. Ballard, *Empire of the Sun*, Granada, London, 1985
2. Daniel Brook, *Head of the Dragon: The Rise of New Shanghai*, *Places Journal*, February 2013
3. *Time*, 27 September 1999
4. *The Globalist*, 24 December 2014
5. Facebook, 4 October 2016
6. *City Weekend*, 24 September 2015
7. *City Weekend*, ibid.
8. China Music Radar website, 23 July 2014
9. BBC News website, 7 March 2005
10. *Shanghaiist*, 20 March 2015
11. *Time*, 20 January 2003

12. Jonathan Campbell, *Red Rock: The Long, Strange March of Chinese Rock'n'Roll*, Earnshaw Books, Hong Kong, 2011
13. Jeroen de Kloet, *Popular Music and Youth in Urban China: The Dakou Generation*, The China Quarterly, 2005
14. *Global Times*, 22 April 2014
15. Reuters, 9 November 2015
16. Embassy of the People's Republic of China in the United States of America website, 20 June 2002
17. Reddit, 21 February 2016
18. Evan Osnos, *Age of Ambition: Chasing Fortune, Truth and Faith in the New China*, Vintage, London, 2014
19. *Age of Ambition*, ibid.

Chapter Nine
1. *Infusion*, 23 February 2015
2. *Guardian*, 22 January 2015
3. BBC World Service, 30 September 2014
4. Reuters, 10 October 2013
5. Jim Krane, *Dubai: The Story of the World's Fastest City*, Atlantic Books, London, 2009
6. *Dubai: The Story of the World's Fastest City*, ibid.
7. *Dubai: The Story of the World's Fastest City*, ibid.

Chapter Ten
1. *Details*, October 1988
2. *Kiki*, director: Sara Jordenö, 2016
3. *Paris is Burning*, director: Jennie Livingston, 1990
4. *The New York Times*, 18 April 1993
5. NPR, 30 April 2012
6. *Vibe*, November 1993
7. DJ History website
8. *Next*, 24 June 2005
9. *A&U*, July 2006
10. *Next*, ibid.
11. *Resident Advisor*, 7 March 2016
12. *Resident Advisor*, ibid.

Index